Italy and the Enlightenment

Studies in a Cosmopolitan Century

ITALY AND THE

Franco Venturi
Professor of History, Turin University

ENLIGHTENMENT

Studies in a Cosmopolitan Century

Edited with an introduction
by Stuart Woolf

Translated by Susan Corsi

New York University Press
1972

First published 1972

This collection © Longman Group Limited 1972

Library of Congress Catalogue Card Number: 72–77153

SBN: 8147–8752–5

Manufactured in Great Britain

Contents

10525

Introduction

FRANCO VENTURI'S researches into the history of the European Enlightenment began over thirty years ago with his *Jeunesse de Diderot*, published in Paris in 1939. Since then he has written a notable series of articles and books on most major aspects of the Enlightenment. His position as an outstanding scholar of this period was acknowledged in 1960 when he was invited to deliver the general *rapport* on the Enlightenment in eighteenth-century Europe at the XIth International Congress of Historical Sciences at Stockholm. But in English-speaking countries until very recent years his reputation in this field remained limited to the select few, scholars of the Enlightenment; perhaps this was because so much of his work (including the Stockholm *rapport*) has been published in Italian, perhaps also because intellectual history has long been unfashionable in England. Indeed, Venturi became known in England and America rather as a scholar of nineteenth-century Russia because of the translation of his large and impressive study of Russian populism (*The Roots of revolution*, 1964). It was only in 1969 that he was invited to give the George Macaulay Trevelyan lectures at Cambridge University on his major field of interest. These lectures, which have now been published under the title *Utopia and reform in the Enlightenment* (1971), have revealed the range and breadth of his researches and confirmed his reputation to an English audience. If any justification were needed, this would be sufficient for the present translation of a selection of his essays on the Enlightenment.

The historiography of the eighteenth century in Italy, in the years when Venturi began his studies, had suffered grievously from nationalistic and fascist interpretations. The dominating concern, in the 1920s and 1930s, was to prove the autochthonous character of Italian history, ignoring the close relationships between Italy and Europe. The eighteenth century was seen as the prelude to the Risorgimento and those native elements which seemed to point to the future struggle for independence and unity were magnified out of all proportion, often in a wholly unhistorical manner. The influence on Italian development of the French *philosophes*, as of the French Revolution, was belittled. It is enough to glance at the works of (for example) Cian, Rota or Calcaterra, even leaving aside the absurd propositions of the fascist minister De Vecchi, to gain a clear impression of the provincial and distorted interpretations of the Italian eighteenth century prevalent in these years.

The political environment in which Franco Venturi grew up undoubtedly influenced his resistance to and reaction against this vision of the Enlightenment. Son and grandson of leading art historians, he followed his father Lionello Venturi into exile in France, after the latter—one of a small group of liberal academics —had refused to swear loyalty to the fascist régime in 1931. Franco Venturi was then seventeen and completed his education at the Sorbonne, under the guidance of Daniel Mornet and Henri Bédarida, both well known scholars of the Enlightenment in France and Italy. These were the years of Carlo Rosselli's courageous endeav-ours to create a new and effective anti-fascist movement. Franco Venturi was close to Rosselli and shared his ideals; to his memory is dedicated the book on Diderot. During the Second World War Venturi was imprisoned in Spain, handed over to the Italian fascists and sent to live under surveillance in the Basilicata. Released after the fall of Mussolini, he returned to Piedmont where he took an active part in the Resistance, in the radical *Partito d'Azione*, which derived directly from Rosselli's *Giustizia e Libertà* movement. Living in Nazi-occupied Italy, Venturi not only fought as a partisan, but was almost solely responsible in Piedmont for producing the party's propaganda.

His experiences in exile and in the Resistance have left a deep imprint on his writings. Like so many members of *Giustizia e Libertà* and the *Partito d'Azione*, Venturi looked back to the historical intuitions and heroic self-sacrifice of the young anti-fascist Piero Gobetti, who died after a fascist attack in 1926. It was Gobetti's brief sketches of two eighteenth-century Piedmontese rebels, Alberto Radicati di Passerano and Dalmazzo Francesco Vasco, who suffered exile and imprisonment for their heterodoxy, that were to lead Venturi to trace their ideas and experiences in impressive biographies. The *Partito d'Azione*, in its short but memorable life, was characterised by the moral intransigence of its mostly intellectual leaders, who saw the Resistance as leading to a renovation of Italian life (and not a mere return to pre-fascist Italy), in which socialist reforms were to be accompanied by respect for the liberties of the individual. Venturi's works display alongside his constant concern for historical objectivity, his own political commitment and what could almost be described as his sense of affinity with the political determination of the *lumières*. His reformers of the eighteenth century, in their arduous attempts to work on and transform the political realities confronting them, call to mind the hopes and plans of the members of the *Partito d'Azione*. In an early essay on Jean Jaurès as a historian, published in 1948 and now in French translation (*Historiens du XXᵉ siècle*, Geneva, 1966), there are constant indications of Venturi's own contemporary experiences, more visible here than in his later writings : Venturi is particularly interested in how Jaurès arrived at socialism through democracy and in Jaurès's concern about how to bring together the state and the working masses; he takes care to note the reactionary implications of a demagogic leader like Boulanger.

Gobetti's intuitions may also have played their part in stimulating Venturi's interest in the Russian revolutionaries. Once more it is the pre-revolutionary moment, the intellectual formation and determination of small educated minorities to fight against the deep-rooted injustices and conformity of Russian society, their readiness to face exile, imprisonment or death in their attempts to achieve their vision of greater human happiness, that has attracted Venturi's attention. He had learnt Russian during his enforced residence in the Basilicata and used the years he spent soon after the war as cultural attaché to the Italian embassy in the Soviet Union to carry out massive researches in the libraries of Moscow and Leningrad. The major result of this research, which established his reputation in the field, emerged in his two impressive volumes on *Il populismo russo* (1952), later translated into English.

In subsequent years, Venturi has continued and extended his researches into Russian history, displaying his characteristic concern for the circulation of ideas throughout Europe, his acute awareness of the interaction between currents of thought of a historical period and the political, social and traditional realities of an individual state. His short book on the Decabrists (*Il moto decabrista e i fratelli Poggio*, 1956) is conceived in the context of the wave of liberal revolutions which had commenced in Spain in 1820, and accurately traces the penetration of Enlightenment ideas in a Russia which had passed from the age of Catherine II, without the ruptures of a revolution or the romanticism of a restoration, to the post-Napoleonic era. The faith of the Decabrists in a constitution, typical of late Enlightenment writers as Venturi points out, is directly linked to the preoccupation of so many European conspirators about how to carry out a revolution without allowing it to degenerate into Jacobin terrorism or Napoleonic tyranny. In a later work on Herzen and other Russian exiles in Piedmont (*Esuli russi in Piemonte dopo il '48*, 1959) Venturi is attracted by the freedom and rapidity of the circulation of ideas which emerged with sudden impetus during the 1848 revolutions and by the unexpected contacts which developed in their aftermath, such as those between Herzen and the Piedmontese democrats.

Venturi's particular interests in Enlightenment ideas in France and Italy were reflected in his earliest books on Diderot (1939), Dalmazzo Francesco Vasco (1940) and the origins of the *Encyclopédie* (1946). But his constant concern, whether in the study of individual personalities or of broader movements, has been with the cosmopolitan world of the Enlightenment. In his own words, 'the Enlightenment must be studied and understood as a phenomenon of all Europe, understanding by Europe what was understood in the eighteenth century, that is a civilisation that extended from Moscow to Philadelphia, from Stockholm to Rio della Plata. This is the Europe of the eighteenth century, a Europe which is not geographical, but that of the Enlightenment.' This interpretation has led Venturi to stress the free interplay of ideas among all the intellectual reformers of the Enlightenment, their sense of participating in the common task of criticising and attacking established traditions, attitudes and structures, of striving towards the creation of a better, more just world, in a mutual endeavour which surpassed national boundaries. There is little need to stress the implications of this broad perspective for the study of Enlightenment ideas in any one country. The Italian Enlightenment has emerged, under Venturi's pen, in all its richness and variety, learning from the experiences of French, Spanish, German, Scottish writers and reformers and making its own original contribution to the cosmopolitan debate.

At the basis of this interpretation rests Venturi's fundamental interest in the personality and contribution of each individual writer or group of men. Only thus can the full variety of the world of the Enlightenment emerge, in all its modulations and contradictions. The reader of the present volume cannot but remark Venturi's scholarly reconstruction of the biographies of obscure minor figures, his passion for the individual detail, his sensitivity towards the nuances of the specific situation, his constant preoccupation with the changing significance of words and slogans, such as 'socialism' or *'sapere aude!*' Out of this sparkling portrait gallery of the small educated minorities who made up the Enlightenment are re-created the intense discussions and struggles, the hopes and disillusions of the *lumières*. Nowhere can this be seen better than in his masterly biographical introductions to the large anthologies he edited of the Italian Enlightenment writers (*Illuministi italiani. Riformatori lombardi piemontesi e toscani*, 1958; *Riformatori napoletani*, 1962; *Riformatori delle antiche repubbliche, dei ducati, dello Stato pontificio e delle isole*, 1965) and in his contributions to the *Dizionario biografico degli italiani* (1960–).

The search for the practical realities behind words, concepts, myths has formed a constant motif of Venturi's works. It is not surprising that Venturi should have such admiration for the work of Sir Lewis Namier. Despite the English historian's hostility towards ideologies, Venturi saw in Namier (as he wrote in an interesting essay, now republished in his *Historiens du XXe siècle*) his determination to reveal the concrete realities behind the superficial polemics or abstract generalisations about eighteenth-century English society : 'A desire to find a meeting point between biography, or the knowledge of the individual, and the understanding of a political group. As Namier liked to repeat, five hundred men placed together do not make a centipede, but remain five hundred men and to understand them one must, if possible, begin to know them one by one.'

This concern of Venturi's has led him to distinguish his own approach to the study of the Enlightenment from that of others with increasing clarity. Too often the study of the Enlightenment has been directed into literary or philosophical history. For Venturi the major pitfall of such history lies in its abstraction. The search for the origins of ideas can lead too easily to an intellectual history remote from the realities of the period. Reacting against the Crocean tradition, Venturi has criticised Carl Becker and, more recently, Peter Gay, precisely because of their tendency to turn back to philosophical origins, in the tradition of Cassirer's interpretation of the German *Aufklärung*. The philosophical systems which derive from similar interpretations cannot, for Venturi, explain the effective workings of the Enlightenment. 'We must go back not to the origins of the ideas, but to their function in the history of the eighteenth century.' Even where humanistic myths of the classical age survived, their sense of importance had been transformed and reduced to minor or superficial significance in the *philosophes'* vision of the world.

But Venturi has reacted with equal vigour against Marxist interpretations of the Enlightenment as the expression of a rising bourgeoisie. His criticisms, particularly in recent years, have been turned against structuralist attempts to explain the Enlightenment in terms of a social situation or any single internal mechanism. He wholly rejects 'the claims of a total history, of a vision of society as a global structure whose internal logic, the law of whose existence, can be revealed if subjected to a suitable interpretative instrument, whether it be the class struggle, quantification or structuralism'. The constant danger of such interpretations, for Venturi, lies in a distortion of historical judgment.

For Venturi, in fact, the history of the Enlightenment is to be discovered by examining the rhythm of development of the ideas, criticisms and proposals of the individual *philosophes* and reformers and the practical reasons which explain their attitudes and choices when confronted by a political and social reality they were endeavouring to transform. As predominant a characteristic as his concern for the individual and the group, in fact, is Venturi's preoccupation with the political, social and economic framework within which the new ideas developed. It is the 'creative and active moment' of ideas which he sees as important, rather than the philosophical origins. His concern is with the affirmation and organisation of these ideas because of their practical renovating influence on society. The movement of the Enlightenment is seen predominantly as a movement of reform and the new ideas of the *lumières* are viewed as 'intellectual weapons' created to influence, modify and transform the religious, political and social situation. Eighteenth-century society, with its inherited traditions, its rigid structures, its inequities, its own internal developments, is viewed through the eyes of these reformers and their constant struggle to break through the obstacles to change and create a more just world. Anticlericalism and the questioning of religion, the critical approach towards all accepted beliefs, the attack on torture and the death penalty, the search for the 'natural laws' of political economy, the later critiques of feudalism, or the hopes placed in constitutions, the myth of republicanism, are all facets of this same reforming drive, at different moments and in different places, dependent upon the specific situations and personalities. The study of the individual reformer or intellectual, of the works he read and the situations surrounding him, of the diffusion of his own writings, constantly referred to the wider world of the cosmopolitan reforming movement, gains in perspective, while enriching by its variety and detail the more general picture. Venturi's Enlightenment is the history of a movement and its programmes, struggling to assert itself against the obscurantism, deadweight and contradictions of the society from which it emerges and which it is trying to reform. Not by chance he has entitled his new history of eighteenth-century Italy *Settecento riformatore* (1969).

Any attempt to summarise Venturi's interpretation of the Enlightenment cannot but do injustice. The reader of the essays in this volume will see how the basic themes re-emerge, each time viewed in a different perspective. The origins of the Enlightenment are to be found in the *crise de conscience* of the beginning of the century, in the criticism of revealed religion and the search for tolerance of the English and Dutch deists and free-thinkers. But then, in the 1740s, the focal point moves decisively to the France of Diderot, Rousseau, d'Holbach, d'Alembert, Condillac and the other young intellectuals who were to write the *Encyclopédie*. For one moment, in Montesquieu's *Esprit des lois* (1748), Venturi sees all the different strands of the Enlightenment drawn together. With the great collaborative effort of the *Encyclopédie* in the 1750s, the French *philosophes* decisively shifted attention away from religious, moral and legal problems to political, social and economic concerns. The impulse of the *encyclopédistes* drove outwards (in Venturi's words) in concentric circles, reaching as far afield as the English colonies in America and St Petersburg in the 1760s. These are the years the reformers attempt to collaborate with the rulers and administrators throughout Europe, from Russia to Spain, Milan to Naples, Austria to Corsica.

But in these same years the French movement of the *Encyclopédie* breaks up, weakened by the contradictions between the practical desire for reforms and utopian visions of the just society; as the different currents draw apart, the individual writers and groups each follow their own path, while rivalry and diffidence often develops towards the others. To some extent, the Seven Years War marks the moment of crisis, as the *philosophes* are brought face to face with the difficulties of change. The new concern for the economy is crystallised in dogmatic form by the 'sect' of the physiocrats. But Quesnay's ideas only penetrate slowly and with difficulty by the 1770s, and arouse the sceptical reaction of such reformers as Galiani at Naples, about the dubious effects of the physiocratic proposals on more backward, agriculturally-based countries, without strong manufacturing industries. By the mid–1770s the differences between the party of the physiocrats and the *encyclopédistes*, now divided among themselves, weakens the reforming movement. Opposition to the 'abstractions' of the physiocrats leads to a more general and increasingly bitter attack on the entire Enlightenment. In southern Europe, in Italy and Spain, the reformers—Verri, Beccaria, Olavide, Jovellanos—have entered the administration. In France—despite, perhaps because of, Turgot— the *philosophes* remain in opposition, more critical, but more impotent. In the later phases, as the vigour of absolutism revives and the strength of the traditional oppositions, the weakness of the state structures emerge ever more visibly, more radical solutions begin to be proposed, from atheism and the belief in a wholly human world to the faith in constitutional liberty and the revival of the republican tradition. This world of the Enlightenment was to end with the French Revolution, with its ardent patriotism, its concept of the active role of the state and its abandonment of the physiocratic faith in a free economy. The age of cosmopolitanism had ended; that of national patriotism had begun.

The essays in this volume have been selected with a view to presenting to an English audience as wide a range as possible of Franco Venturi's researches, which would at the same time offer a broad and comprehensive picture of the Enlightenment. Over the past twenty years Venturi has concentrated his attention on reinterpreting the Enlightenment in Italy. It is for this reason that no essays have been included from his earlier works on the French *philosophes*. The present volume is concerned more specifically with the progress of the Enlightenment in Italy. Nevertheless, Venturi's interpretation of the cosmopolitan character of the Enlightenment in Europe, outlined in the first general survey, emerges vividly from all the other essays dedicated to more specific aspects or personalities. Each essay illustrates the close connections and reciprocal influences between the Italian and other European reformers and intellectuals. The progress of the movement of the French *philosophes* emerges as a constant point of reference, while particular attention is paid to the common problems facing the Spanish and southern Italian reformers. The present work, in fact, is less a history of the Enlightenment in Italy than a history of the European Enlightenment seen from the viewpoint of Italy.

Stuart J. Woolf

Editor's Note

The essays have been drawn from a variety of sources, some of a more specialised character than others. I decided, reluctantly, to omit footnotes where they appeared in the original essays because of stringencies of space. In consequence, the dates of works cited by Venturi, formerly in his footnotes, have been inserted into the text. Where the contingent occasion of an article was the recent publication of works by other authors, reference to these works has been limited. Apart from one quotation which has been omitted from the final essay, because it appears in an earlier essay in this volume, the texts appear in full form.

I wish to thank Franco Venturi for his extremely helpful and generous collaboration in the preparation of this volume.

The original titles and details of publication of the essays are listed below:

The European Enlightenment: 'L'illuminismo nel Settecento europeo', *XIᵉ Congrès International des Sciences Historiques, Stockholm, 21–28 Août 1960. Rapports. IV. Histoire Moderne,* Uppsala, 1960, 106–35.

Was ist Aufklärung? Sapere aude!: 'Contributi ad un dizionario storico. Was ist Aufklärung? Sapere aude!, *Rivista Storica Italiana,* lxxi, 1959, 119–28.

Oriental Despotism: 'Contributi ad un dizionario storico. Despotismo orientale', *Rivista Storica Italiana,* lxii, 1960, 117–26, translated by Lotte F. Jacoby and Ian M. Taylor in *Journal of the History of Ideas,* xxiv, 1963, 133–42.

Socialism: 'Contributi ad un dizionario storico. "Socialista" e "socialismo" nell'Italia del Settecento', *Rivista Storica Italiana*, lxxv, 1963, 129–40.

Radicati's Exile in England and Holland: *Saggi sull'Europa illuminista I. Alberto Radicati di Passerano*, Turin: Einaudi, 1954, 200–44; 'La conversione e la morte del conte Radicati', *Rivista Storica Italiana*, lxxv, 1963, 365–73.

Enlightenment Versus the Powers of Darkness: *Settecento riformatore. Da Muratori a Beccaria*, Turin: Einaudi, 1969, 355–89.

Pasquale Paoli: 'Nota introduttiva', *Illuministi italiani*. vii. *Riformatori delle Antiche Repubbliche, dei Ducati, dello Stato Pontificio e delle Isole*, edited by G. Giarrizzo, G. F. Torcellan and F. Venturi, Milan, Naples: Ricciardi, 1965, 721–41.

Cesare Beccaria and Legal Reform: 'Cesare Beccaria e le riforme giuridiche', *La Cultura illuministica in Italia*, edited by M. Fubini, Turin: Edizioni Radio Italiana, 1957, 120–9.

Pietro Verri in Germany and Russia: 'Riflessi in Germania di alcune opere di Pietro Verri', in Università di Torino, Facoltà di Lettere e di Filosofia *Arte e storia. Studi in onore di Lionello Vincenti*, Turin: Giappichelli, 1965, 429–47; 'Pietro Verri in Russia': *Miscellanea per Nozze Castelnuovo-Frigessi, 24 Ottobre 1962*, Turin, Einaudi, 1962, 11–13.

The Position of Galiani Between the Encyclopaedists and the Physiocrats: 'Galiani tra enciclopedisti e fisiocrati', *Rivista Storica Italiana*, lxii, 1960, 45–64.

The Enlightenment in Southern Italy: 'Il movimento riformatore degli illuministi meridionali', *Rivista Storica Italiana*, lxxiv, 1962, 5–26.

Spanish and Italian Economists and Reformers in the Eighteenth Century: 'Economisti e riformatori spagnoli e italiani del '700', *Rivista Storica Italiana*, lxxiv, 1962, 532–61.

The Enlightenment in the Papal States: 'Elementi e tentativi di riforme nello Stato Pontificio del Settecento', *Rivista Storica Italiana*, lxxv, 1963, 778–817.

S.J.W.

Acknowledgements

We are grateful for permission to reproduce copyright material to the *Rivista Storica Italiana* for the following essays: *Was ist Aufklärung?*, Socialism, The Position of Galiani, The Enlightenment in Southern Italy, Spanish and Italian Economists and Reformers, The Enlightenment in the Papal States and the last part of the essay on Radicati; to Giulio Einaudi editore s.p.a., Torino for the essays on Radicati's Exile and on Enlightenment Versus the Powers of Darkness; to the *Journal of the History of Ideas* for the translation of Oriental Despotism by Lotte F. Jacoby and Ian M. Taylor; to Riccardo Ricciardi Editore Milano—Napoli for the essay on Pasquale Paoli; to Edizioni Radio Italiana, Turin for the essay on Cesare Beccaria; to Giappichelli, Torino for the essay on Pietro Verri in Germany.

Preface

I F, at the beginning of the eighteenth century, one had asked an 'honnête homme', or 'gentleman', or 'signore' what the word *cosmopolite* meant, he would probably have reacted in one of two ways. One group would have had recourse to classical, humanistic culture, recalling the stoic tradition of the citizens of the world. Others, more than one might suppose, would have thought of the disturbing, mysterious world of the alchemists, the followers of Alexander Seton, Michel Sendivogius, Eireneus Philathetes and the other baroque magicians listed by John Ferguson in his *Bibliotheca chemica*—where one can gather how widespread was the use of the pseudonym *cosmopolite* among such men at the time. This, at any rate, is the meaning which a writer like Fontenelle, without too much deliberation, attributed to this word in 1722 when speaking at the Parisian Académie des sciences in praise of Jeffroy, who had revealed 'les principaux tours de passe-passe qui pratiquent les prétendus adeptes, enfants de l'art, philosophes hermétiques, *cosmopolites*, rosecroix etc., gens d'un langage mistérieux, d'une conduite fanatique, de promesses exhorbitantes'.

If half a century later, in 1775, one had asked Pietro Verri—one of the greatest economists and reformers of the Italian Enlightenment—the meaning of the word *cosmopolite*, he would probably have replied, if he too had not gone back to the classical origins of the word, that the term was synonymous with *patriot*. In the spring of that year, when writing to his brother, Alessandro, about a mutual friend, Count Sormani, he called him in the same breath both 'true cosmopolite' and 'most loyal patriot'. There was no contradiction. On the contrary there was a connection between feeling oneself to be a citizen of the world and desiring to transform and enlighten that little corner of the world where one had been born or brought by destiny to work.

After only a few more years had passed, the word *patriot* was to become charged with all the hatred and all the love of nascent modern nationalism, while the word *cosmopolite* became the symbol of an ideal political unity, sought after yet always unattainable. Kant might still look at the history of the world *in weltbürgerlicher Absicht*, but in many ways his was the last voice of a disappearing age. With the French Revolution the cosmopolitan century came to an end and there began the age of the nations and the internationals.

And yet, to write the history of the eighteenth century, it is necessary to return to this cosmopolitan vision, enriched as it is with the classical and Renaissance past (though perhaps filtered through the hidden channels of the baroque age), charged with all the hopes, the daring and revolts of Enlightenment thought, sustained by the desire to work in a practical way among people, without ever losing sight of humanity as a whole.

One day it will certainly be necessary to write the history of eighteenth-century cosmopolitanism. The fortunes of this word will show how complicated and unpredictable, how relentless yet tortuous the progress of ideas can be. Between what Fontenelle understood by *cosmopolite* and, let us say, Kant or Robespierre, two or three generations had passed, during which traditional, classical interpretations remained, new meanings rapidly emerged, modern ones were transformed and died, in a process which contains the historical secret of that century.

In the essays which follow I have attempted to reconstruct this extraordinary life of some words in the cosmopolitan age. *Socialism* was born at that time. *Oriental despotism* had its roots in a new vision of the relationship between Europe and the world. It is from the classical past that Kant derived his definition of the Enlightenment: *Sapere aude*, filtered and profoundly transformed through the seventeenth-century experience of Gassendi and the reforming urge of Poles and Austrians, Italians and Germans. The new Enlightenment faith, born in the mind of Alberto Radicati di Passerano from the religious, political and social conflicts of the age of Victor Amadeus II, finds its cosmopolitan dimension once more, this time tragically, in the death in exile of this Piedmontese nobleman, in the anguished comparison which he continued to make, up to the last hours of his life, between the ideas of deism and atheism and the religious traditions of Catholicism and Protestantism. The shadows of the past, against which Radicati had rebelled so energetically at the beginning of the century, seemed to fade like morning mist in the noonday of Enlightenment, halfway through the eighteenth century, when magicians and witches seemed to disappear for ever beneath the ironic, humane criticism of the Venetians, the forceful decrees of Maria Theresa and the scientific drive of the German *Aufklärung*. Cosmopolitanism had nothing to do with magic for any of these. But then we see in the far-off island of Corsica, in the person of Pasquale Paoli, another new and different relationship between *patriotism* and *cosmopolitanism*. Here too the classical tradition had considerable importance but the problems faced by the Corsican leader are of a completely unexpected kind and seem to anticipate more modern struggles against colonialism.

These are so many attempts to reach the reality of the eighteenth century from the most diverse starting-points. But the broader aim, which can be deduced to a certain extent from the pages devoted to Pasquale Paoli but is reflected particularly in the closing essays of this volume, is that of observing *in weltbürgerlicher Absicht* the reform movement of the Enlightenment in Italy. The negative proof —of the impossibility of understanding this period of Italian history if one moves from nationalistic ideas or simply if one sees in it merely the origins of the Risorgimento—has been repeatedly supplied in the years between the two world wars. The need for a cosmopolitan perspective, on the other hand, has been proved, I feel, in the studies of the last thirty years, and not only on themes of obvious universal relevance, like that proposed so forcefully by Cesare Beccaria in his book *Of crimes and punishments*. Even problems apparently more distant, somewhat esoteric, like that of the importance of Pietro Verri's thought in Germany and Russia or the connections between Spanish and Italian reformers, can show how tenuous and at the same time resilient are the threads which link the different experiences of the Enlightenment in Europe. It may seem paradoxical to speak, in conclusion, about the age of Enlightenment in the Papal States—without doubt one of the worst governed, most divided and backward states not only in Europe but even in Italy at the time. But perhaps even paradoxes can help to show how penetrating and widespread were the ideas of the Enlightenment, even in the most unexpected corners of the eighteenth-century world.

The essays which follow have been chosen by the editor of this volume (whom I should like to take the opportunity of thanking here). If they help to draw attention to the Italian eighteenth century and promote the understanding of it *in weltbürgerlicher Absicht*, the author will consider himself more than satisfied.

Turin, January 1971   FRANCO VENTURI

1 The European Enlightenment

THESE pages do not represent a new attempt to define or describe the Enlightenment. Neither, of course, do we mean to give here an outline of the history of Europe in the eighteenth century. Our interest is in the relationship between one and the other, between the Enlightenment and political, social and economic life in the eighteenth century.

This is a relationship, as has often been said, between men and things, between the individual actions of those who draw up formulae and create ideals, new instruments, and that reality which appears dominated by a collective, objective law of development in the eyes of those who are determined to influence it. Or else, as we would prefer to say, it is a relationship between a movement—the Enlightenment—and the political, social and economic forces which were in the course of development in the various countries of Europe in the eighteenth century. It is the story of a movement which had its origins and roots, development, internal struggles, stages of crisis, renewal and dissolution. It was the work of men who were aware that they had elements in common, who sought and created new forms of organisation and action, who thought and worked in terms of these and who, on each occasion, created an awareness of their own activity in the world which surrounded them and a consciousness of the place which they occupied in society and history.

An important part of modern historical research on the eighteenth century sets out to study and define the various aspects and stages of such a relationship between the Enlightenment and the European eighteenth century.

This direction is followed by research in the history of ideas—which can be satisfied less and less with the apparent logic of intellectual forms and increasingly seeks to understand what the terms, words, concepts and myths really meant. It is sufficient to re-read Cassirer's work on the Enlightenment to have an idea of the kind of progress which has been made.

To this same point turn, though perhaps unwillingly, the historians of social structures, interests, groups and classes. When they really study structures they come face to face with the limits of the realities which they have investigated. Delving among the accumulation of traditions and social stratifications, they discover the traces, the fossils of those ideas and myths which once left their imprints there. In this sense Namier's work is exemplary, with its continual insistence on the relationship between classes, states and intellectuals, perhaps with the aim of discrediting a few legends and depriving of their weight and influence ideas which formerly had been considered of fundamental importance. His studies and those of his disciples and the men who continued his work and of still others, like Butterfield and Pares, on structures in eighteenth-century England by now constitute a prerequisite for posing anew the problem of the relationship between the European Enlightenment and the reality of Great Britain and her colonies. Social history encourages the history of ideas, if only by contrast.

In other European countries, France in particular, even the school of 'total history', open and attentive as it is to the study and even the commemoration of climates of opinion of the past, the relationships between the sciences, skills, conceptions of the world and the artistic, social and administrative life of Europe under the *ancien régime*, even this school is turning towards such problems. The danger of this school arises at the moment when the ideas it studies risk becoming structures in themselves, when, in the history of ideas too, there is no grasp of the moment of birth, affirmation, organisation, but only a description of the solidification and stratification of new mental forms. As the English school is useful for the polemical distinction it makes between ideas and facts, so the French school holds subtle dangers on account of its temptation to equate the two.

What we must search for, then, is a relationship, making a clear distinction both in the method of investigation and in the work of historical comprehension, between the movement and the political, social and economic reality. What is important above all is not to establish this relationship beforehand and petrify it in a vision of superstructure and substructure, ideology and facts, thus determining it from the beginning, deciding in advance whether one element or another is the essential, original one. The historian's task would risk being over before it began. Research and only research can tell us what, at any given moment, was an idea and the movement in which it was being put into practice, what it counted for and what it meant.

Apart from the theoretical systems which tend specifically to define the relationship between the movement and the reality even before they have studied and investigated them, there are many others who see in the Enlightenment above all the reflection, the consequence of specific political and social conditions and situations. Echoes of a tired positivism chime in alongside Marxist interpretations.

It is sufficient to think of the problem of the origin, the first roots and ideas of the Enlightenment in Europe, to recall the facile repetitions of the theory that they derived above all from weariness caused by the endless religious wars, from disgust with and detachment from the world of the Counter-reformation. Thus it is precisely the moment of action, the newest and most fertile element, which is lost in the general crisis of the closing years of the seventeenth century and the beginning of the eighteenth which Paul Hazard has called the European *crise de conscience*. Our concern is to establish clearly which were the groups who in the midst of wars—the harsh, ferocious wars which followed one another in quick succession from the revocation of the Edict of Nantes to the Peace of Utrecht, 1685 to 1713—really maintained a policy of tolerance, desired a new contact between men of culture and the ruling classes of the great European states, and succeeded finally in imposing even a fraction of their programme on a Europe which was emerging from its struggle against Louis XIV.

It is not weariness with the religious wars but the desire for tolerance which is of historical importance. It is the latter which, in the last analysis, eventually gave a new meaning to a series of conflicts which had begun as dynastic or religious disputes and which became transformed and widened until they drew together and involved all the elements of European life at the beginning of the eighteenth century, including that precious, forward-looking element which was contained in the moral revaluation of tolerance. The great states emerged strengthened from the conflict. Even in France there was no going back, and the Edict of Nantes was not put into force again. Situations crystallised (and they were those which were to remain fundamental throughout the early part of the eighteenth century). It might seem like the triumph of *étatisme*, of the monarchies, mercantilism and autarchies built up in the seventeenth century. Yet a new element intervened. The coalition among the enemies of Louis XIV created a common spirit among men and states of differing creeds and mentalities, between the Empire and England, Holland and the Duchy of Savoy. There was already a group of people inclined not only towards interpreting this new spirit but also towards acting on it and spreading it. Those concerned are especially the group of Huguenots from whom Jurieu and those who remained orthodox had dissociated themselves, a group which had entered into increasingly intimate contact with the England of the Glorious Revolution and Locke, and which already had connections and links with the furthest corners of Europe.

One name sums up this group: it is, of course, that of Pierre Bayle. His dictionary began to appear in the very year of the Peace of Ryswick, as if to give ideological consecration to the compromise which had been reached. His work developed autonomously, not parallel to the policy of any power, and sought to open up for itself a previously untrodden path. Strange to say, Bayle's politics have not yet been studied in depth. They have appeared equivocal, wavering, but this was only the price to be paid by a nascent intellectual force attempting to emerge in the midst of the giants of war, diplomacy and repression. Doubt, irony, chiaroscuro were subtle arms of destruction, intellectual instruments placed in the hands of a man who continually risked being swept away and yet knew how to maintain his fundamental direction in a tempestuous age. He certainly inherited much from the past and associated himself, even in a political sense, with those Dutch noblemen who opposed war to the bitter end and the militarism of the Princes of Orange, linking himself with the Arminians rather than with the orthodox elements. He was also the continuator of the most mature French culture, as he was of that irenic branch of Protestantism which Orcibal has described. The inheritance of the whole of humanism was alive in him. But in Pierre Bayle there was something more than his genius as a scholar, critic and man of culture. He knew how to create new intellectual weapons ranging from his *Dictionary* to his reviews. Even in the most difficult straits, he succeeded in holding firm to his new political line which pointed the way towards that of the men of the Enlightenment. He knew that without the assent and concessions which modern states, perhaps absolute monarchies, would have to make to the Enlightenment, neither tolerance nor a renewed political and economic life would be possible. He was not just an intellectual of the new century; he was already seeking to create a relationship with states which was as profoundly different from that of the learned humanist as from that of the man of letters at the court of the Sun King, or of a professor at one of the European universities, even if it included elements of all three such predecessors. Pierre Bayle was international in his relationships and in his politics, and he already made use of the myth of the republic of men of letters to achieve aims which went beyond those of learned men, scholars and writers.

It is sufficient to take a look at England in those years of the 'European *crise de conscience*' to feel that the situation was already riper than in the world of the exiles gathered in the United Provinces. In England the group, the movement, formed rapidly: it is what we call deism. What deism really is still needs to be discussed in depth. Only too often, from Lechler down to the most modern scholars, its theological formulae have been traced rather than its origin and practical efficacy. Too often historians have left in the dark what was really its most active element—its link with English politics at the transition between the seventeenth and eighteenth centuries. And yet Toland, Collins, Tindal and their numerous colleagues and followers are there to tell us how a movement of intellectuals, champions of ideas, was born. They were not men of letters—the great English writers of the Augustan age despised and misinterpreted them, and a shade of this negative judgment still lingers over their memory. They were not even politicians who, by means of their pen or the periodical press, worked out a way through the intricate maze of Whig and Tory splinter groups, through the complicated struggles between the organised forces of English religion. They were not even a sect, like so many which arose and flourished at that time on British soil. They resembled, one can even say that they camouflaged themselves so as to be confused with, Arminians and Socinians, as with Sabbatarians and Arians. But they were not strictly one of the sects—in spite of the fact that they retained so many aspects of them and seemed to mingle in their midst. They were, however, not infrequently men who lived by the pen. Toland even tried to earn his living from a kind of circulating library of semiclandestine manuscripts, and it is in this way that he began to spread the works of Giordano Bruno in England. They were men who carried an idea amidst the religious and political conflicts of their time, letting themselves be guided, with greater or lesser coherence, by the logic of its development, through the adventurous life they led and the national and international struggles of their time. Toland supported the Protestant succession, exalted the ideological reasons for the War of the Spanish Succession, was linked with Prince Eugene, sought in every way to spread his ideas on the Continent as well, and eventually came to dream of an ideal brotherhood which would unite all those who felt and thought as he did, a brotherhood he describes for us in his *Pantheisticon*. Right at the beginning of the century, in 1700, he published in London the works of Harrington with the inscription: 'I. Tolandus Libertati sacravit. MDCC. Commerciis. Opificiis' and with an engraving depicting Brutus, William II, Moses, Solon, Confucius, Lycurgus and Numa, which expresses better than any programme what his political ideas were. Anthony Collins not only took part in the Whig struggle but launched his pamphlet on free thinking just at the right moment with a calculated political gesture. As A. Boisbeleau de la Chapelle, the French translator of a pamphlet against Collins written by the English critic Richard Bentley, noted: 'Les exemplaires furent distribués au mois de Février. Le Parlement étoit assemblé. Le capitale regorgeoit de monde. Les esprits étoient dans une fermentation terrible. Les Whigs craignoient tout pour les libertés et pour la religion du royaume. Les Tories négligeoient pas le moindre occasion de mettre le pied sur la gorge de leurs adversaires.' Collins had not written with the aim of pleasing either group but precisely so that he could take advantage of this moment of tension to state his own views, to attach himself to 'the symbols and faith of all Christian churches'. The book was attributed to Toland. The real author, Anthony Collins, went off to Holland and there too did what he could to spread this work of his. Boisbeleau de la Chapelle thus told the story of a work which was particularly important among the works of the English deists: it is sufficient to consider the enunciation of free thinking that was already contained in the title and would come to form an integral part of the thought of the Enlightenment. As for Tindal, his story is less important, perhaps, but no less characteristic, with its extremely successful attempt to use theological formulae to affirm his faith in the fixity, immobility and eternity of natural law.

When *Christianity as old as creation* appeared in 1730, the deists' message, fundamental for an understanding of the historical roots of the Enlightenment, had by this time been made clear. First of all they had affirmed, with a formerly unheard-of resolution, the moral value of anticlericalism by demonstrating the negative character of every privilege, law and sanction which consecrates an élite, gives it a permanent form and imprints on it the mark of an apparent and artificial distinction, separating its members from the community and society of men. This was an extremely fruitful germ, a seed of political equality and of the fight against all privilege. It is true that deism was still attacking the clergy in particular and not élites in general, not political and social privilege. But the radical negation of a ruling class, once the idea had been planted, would lose no time in spreading to other fields as well. Later deists, including Morgan, Chubb and Annet, were to demonstrate this, even if the real political and social consequences of deism were one day to be drawn by others, the writers of the Enlightenment in France. But the atmosphere in which they would work could already be discerned in the pages of the first deist book, *Christianity not mysterious*, a title which has misled many people. In reality Toland meant that it was deism which was not mysterious. Christianity had become mysterious, administered as it was by a group of people who reserved the truth for themselves. This book was already a typical history in the manner of the Enlightenment, the history of a religious or political élite's usurpation which had to be overthrown by the controlled use of reason.

But what gave deism, which was apparently so cold and detached, the vigour it was already beginning to display by pointing to the practical consequences to be derived from it? It was certainly a religious myth well suited to the age of Newton, to the age of the great scientific discoveries in mathematics and physics, to the affirmation of natural law in all fields. In its own way it expressed the anxiety and at the same time the sense of fulfilment felt in a period in which science dominated men's minds. It certainly gleaned, at least in part, the heritage of unitarian and antitrinitarian currents, of the late Renaissance in general. Like many other movements of the time, it consciously referred back to the doubts and disputes of the later humanists or the French Epicureans of the seventeenth century, or their contemporaries, the English Platonists. Finally, it crystallised the religious rationalism of so many thinkers in the latter half of the seventeenth century—and in particular of Locke who had written *The Reasonableness of Christianity*. Yet all this does not suffice to explain the acrid ferment of enlightenment there was in deism. To find an explanation we have to think about the editions of Harrington or Algernon Sidney which Toland used; or it is enough to open the catalogue of Collins's well-stocked library to understand what lay at the roots of deism. As Humphrey Prideaux, famous at the time for his oriental studies and his solid conservatism, wrote in 1693: 'I find the Republicarians in these parts openly sedulous to promote atheisme, to which end they spread themselves in coffy houses and talk violently for it . . .'

Prideaux was right: it was the seventeenth-century republican tradition which had found its sublimation, its universal formula in deism. It almost seemed to comprise all the nuances of the two English revolutions, from the extremism of the sects to the Whigs' constitutional equilibrium. Between Toland and Shaftesbury, between Molesworth and Tindal, Gordon, Trenchard and Collins, there were differences, even deep ones, yet the deist myth created by them contained a common element which seems sometimes to be the commemoration, sometimes the revival, or the theorisation, the exaltation or the memory, of the various forms the British revolution had assumed during the seventeenth century. This revolution had not triumphed; it had not crushed its opponents; it had been forced to accept restrictions and compromises. But the spirit which animated it, restrained by this time within the stable, solid, well-tried forms of English legality, lived again in non-mysterious Christianity, in pantheism, in free-thinking, in a whole series of attempts to renew on a different plane the 'Good Old Cause'. It was in this way that the experience of the Puritan and Glorious Revolutions passed into the eighteenth century.

One must note immediately that only in this way could a vital part of the English seventeenth century be transmitted not only to the new century but above all to the Continent, to lands and societies outside the British world. Cromwell and William III had constituted an integral part of seventeenth-century European history, but there had been only a few isolated attempts to imitate them on the other side of the Channel. Deism, on the other hand, was from the beginning destined to become a cosmopolitan creed and a republican ferment passed thus, by means of it, into France, Germany, Italy etc.

The historical process was a slow one: the time-gap necessary for the political effects of these ideas to be made plain was often very different from that for battles, treaties and revolutions, but this does not make it any less important or profound. It is enough to look at France in the twenty years which followed the death of Louis XIV to perceive this. The ideas which permeated from England helped to precipitate the changes which had been slowly maturing in the French situation. It is the period which Paul Hazard has placed at the centre of his description of the European *crise de conscience*. Here too, twenty-five years of research carried out since the appearance of this work have underlined the need to reconsider its conclusions in the light of a more definite awareness of the political conflicts of the age. The dominating factor in this period is the coalition among the most diverse forces in European countries against France's desire for supremacy and, with this, the insurgence, actually during the reign of Louis XIV, of forces which undermined and transformed French absolutism and expansionism. In the end, when the accounts were drawn up on the death of the Sun King, not only were the two principal enemies, France and England, to be reconciled, but they were even to arrive at an awareness that there was already a common cultural atmosphere in the process of formation and an increasingly integrated civilisation. This Franco-English relationship was to remain fundamental, on both the ideological and the political plane, throughout the early part of the eighteenth century, and this was to be the basis from which the Enlightenment would rise.

The processes of transformation inside France, which were only revealed in full at the end of the Spanish Succession war, but which were already well advanced in the last thirty years of Louis XIV's reign, were, originally, just the opposite of what we have seen happening in England. There was not the crystallisation and elaboration of an originally revolutionary element which by that time had become constitutional, fixed in legal forms, which had penetrated to the depth of British society and custom, nor was there the ever-changing mixture of liberal and libertarian elements, of Whig forces and the myth of the Good Old Cause, of constitutional realities and republican ferment. The picture was a very different one: that of a king who seemed to be triumphant both inside his country and abroad, who seemed to have made the dream of universal monarchy and absolute monarchy come true, but who met his limit precisely in the class of nobles, in those state organisms which were, after all, the very bases of his power. They either had no intention of paying taxes or wished to pay very few. They revived the power of the *parlements*, exalted the autonomy of the higher clergy, professed faith in the various, opposing Jansenist and quietist religious trends. They found a voice even in the army, in men like Vauban, just as they did in the consciences of scholars and learned men, of all those who could not adapt completely to the atmosphere of conformism of the Sun King's last years. All these attempts at resistance and containment, these criticisms and rebellions would finally pave the way for that crisis which we call the period of the Regency.

It cannot be stressed enough that that truth about the French Revolution, perceived by a few of the best historians of the nineteenth century and later studied in depth and defined by Mathiez and Lefebvre, the fact, that is, that it was the nobles' rebellion which gave rise to the Revolution proper, is applicable to the whole of the French eighteenth century and to the initial formation of the ideas of the Enlightenment. These ideas did not descend directly from the rational administration, from the scientific technique of waging war or conducting diplomacy, nor did they derive from the idolisation of the monarch, for this too was to come later, a few decades later, for Louis XIV as for Peter the Great. They were formed instead out of the new interpretations of the forces set in motion by the reviving *parlements*, by the religious currents which acquired new vigour and the increasingly lucid criticism of the heirs of the free-thinkers, in short by all the elements which eroded the monarch's desire for uniformity. Franklin L. Ford's recent studies of the magistracy and nobility, the constantly renewed problem of the political significance of Fénelon, on the one hand, and the *appellants* on the other, new research on Fontenelle and the erudites of the seventeenth century reconfirm, by closer analysis, the importance of the renewed consciousness of their own rights, privileges and origins to be found among the different strata of the French ruling class at the transition from the seventeenth to the eighteenth century. As always happens, this revolt of the nobles was not straightforward, prompt defence of specific fiscal and formal privileges. Dazzled by Saint-Simon's powers of description, we continue to hold before our eyes the spectacle of a myriad of characters and figures and fail to see the ideological importance of the whole picture. The ferment in France in the last decades of the Sun King's reign gave rise to that liberal element favouring legal processes which was one of the essential ingredients of the Enlightenment in France. At that moment began that dialogue which was to continue within the bounds of the movement even during the French Revolution and beyond, the dialogue between the vindication of the right of freedom, on the one hand, and, on the other, the desire for rational, egalitarian transformations. Even before Louis XIV's death, this dialogue had already found expression in two outstanding men, the Abbé Dubos and Boulainvilliers. It is not by chance that the figure of the latter and not the former has recently been the subject of investigation and comment. It is, in fact, difficult to find a more characteristic example of a paradoxical, contradictory but fertile urge towards an aristocratic revolt, a return to the ideas of the late Renaissance, towards scientific but at the same time astrological forms, of Spinoza-like love of reason, with at the same time so libertarian a passion for independence as to see the camel-drivers of Mohammed's time as ideals. The person of Boulainvilliers ties together all the contradictions of the France which fought the War of the Spanish Succession and underwent the consequences. The conclusions of so many of his attitudes, already savouring of enlightenment, have the sharp taste of discovery, of an improvised solution. Dubos's considerations on the development of the French bourgeoisie, though far more rational, are pale in comparison. In him too we see the birth of some aspects of the Enlightenment, but without those passions, those contrasts, that determination which were one of the reasons for its strength and effectiveness.

By 1721 Montesquieu's *Lettres persanes* had already brought this first phase of the French Enlightenment to an end. This masterpiece, by sheer power, achieved a harmony among those ideas which had begun to appear in France ever since the revocation of the Edict of Nantes. Montesquieu displayed his remarkable capacity, which was to emerge most fully in *L'Esprit des lois*, of holding together different ideas and ideals within a construction which still kept them alive, which did not limit or overshadow them in any way, preserving them in that superior form of eclecticism which he knew well was a precondition of freedom in a multiform 'civil' world. Thus the virtue of troglodytes, love in the East, religious satire and a new cosmopolitan humanity eager for reforms and a thousand other themes are successfully brought together and made to exist side by side in that book which was the first great work of the French Enlightenment. With Montesquieu, France assumed again its role of intellectual leadership which it had been obliged to relinquish to the Protestant exiles, the free Dutch and the English who had emerged great and victorious from revolutions and wars. Not only did the period which we call the Regency—which would perhaps be better described as the postwar crisis following Louis XIV's reign—create expressions of a refined artistic, scientific and intellectual civilisation, but it showed that it was capable of assimilating those ideas which had been formulated outside France during the great struggle for supremacy. This cultural revival which contained all the germs of the century which had just begun corresponded to the European political compromise based on London and Versailles.

The young Voltaire and the young Montesquieu, *Oedipe* and the *Lettres persanes*, already possess the strength of a programme and the maturity of intellectual products where liberal ideas and deism, the desire for knowledge and desire for reform meet and are assessed, and in which we already discern vigorous answers to the religious, political and economic conflicts of their time.

Why then did this intellectual movement, which began so strongly, seem to dry up and lose its impetus in the following years, let us say between 1725 and 1740? International conflicts continued in those years but they did not have the significance that the Spanish Succession war had assumed. Internal disputes seemed to fade and die out. It was a period of economic stagnation or recession. That freedom which had asserted itself during the Regency was limited or suppressed. Voltaire's life shows us this and the development of that 'clandestine organisation' of scholars that Wade described confirms it. Ideas continued to make progress but kept underground so that there was almost a return to the erudite and non-erudite libertinism of the previous century. Abbé Meslier's tragic and grandiose testament was copied and circulated, but no other country priest could express his revolt in Meslier's manner. Fréret, Dumarsais and Fontenelle thought and wrote but their works seem sometimes to go back to academic forms, with less connections with the political and religious reality of the era. Groups, academies, masonic lodges followed on from one another but did not create a movement—neither Abbé Alary's *Entresol* nor the Count of Clermont's Academy of Arts and Sciences.

The general situation in Europe, even outside the borders of France and England, certainly influenced this situation and helps explain it, beyond the contingent reasons of the static governments of Cardinal de Fleury and Walpole. Spain, Germany, Italy, Russia etc. were preparing the raw materials and elements of what would be the general movement of the Enlightenment in the second half of the century. For the moment it was merely a question of isolated elements, none of which was in a position to create a genuine intellectual movement. Eighteenth-century Europe had already broadened its intellectual frontiers and was to broaden them still more, even in this period. But so far it was only preparing that real intellectual unification, that cosmopolis of the Enlightenment which would be achieved in the following decades.

Spain offers, above all, the spectacle of the slow conclusion of the period which began with Charles V. The change of dynasty was important and, in this case, did actually mark the beginning of a different era. The age of Philip V was to be that of the Feijóos, of Uztáriz and other scholars, thinkers and economists whom we cannot consider as belonging to the Enlightenment but who, nevertheless, affirmed the need for rationalisation within the system of ideas that they found dominant in their country, whether Catholic dogmatism or Spanish mercantilism or colonialism. One of the most difficult problems anywhere, for those who consider Europe in the early eighteenth century, is to understand how far this rationalisation was merely technical—acting completely within the mental structures which provide its framework and context—and how far, instead, a new mentality corroded and dissolved the framework which still kept it bound and restricted. Spain is one of the countries where this problem is more difficult to solve, not least because scholars who have considered the question most recently have concentrated—in the Iberian peninsula as in Italy—on the second half of the century and neglected the preparatory phase of the Enlightenment.

Something similar may be said for the German-speaking part of Europe, where the *Frühaufklärung* stage, if one can so call it, was much more varied and complex. When studying a man like Wolff and the problem of the efficacy of his action on the reality of the German states, the principal difficulty is precisely that rigid limit at which the spirit of reason, that urged on Wolff and his followers and other rationalists of their time, stopped suddenly in front of clear political and religious barriers, refusing to demolish them, even respecting them, with an attitude we cannot but call sincere, although it is clearly contradictory. Wolff had a completely eighteenth-century sense of cosmopolitanism which was nevertheless tempered and limited by German particularism and regionalism. He felt a desire, which he inherited from Leibniz, for reconciliation among the various religious sects and this was nourished by his wish to manœuvre among the various confessions. However, he retreated from the only formula which gave an emotive and expansive charge to the irenism he inherited from the past—deism. He was dignified, intelligent and determined in his resistance to abuses of power and to the militaristic and pietistic obscurantism of his adversaries, enemies and rulers. More than this, by his position he created the first typical conflict between the new intellectuals and state and ecclesiastical powers to be seen in eighteenth-century Germany. But his limitation, his desire never to go beyond certain definite barriers finally elicited from the man who set himself up as the protector of philosophers, Frederick II, a statement which defined with the utmost clarity that detachment, that division of labour between men of culture and statesmen which was only to be overcome with very great difficulty later in Germany and is precisely the limitation of the greater part of the *Aufklärung* as opposed to the *lumières*. The latter arose specifically from the desire to transform religion and politics. On the other hand, in 1740 Frederick II could write to Wolff in such flattering terms as these: 'C'est aux philosophes d'être précepteurs de l'univers et les maîtres des princes', only to add immediately something much more concrete and precise: 'Ils doivent penser conséquemment et c'est à nous de faire des actions conséquentes. Ils doivent instruire le monde par le raisonnement et nous par l'exemple. Ils doivent découvrir et nous pratiquer ... .' It was a division of labour which also meant putting the philosophers in their place, a definition of enlightened absolutism *a parte regis*, while the most fertile definitions were still to come *a parte philosophi*. And yet in the myriad of German states too a new ferment was born, even from so controlled and respectful a brand of rationalism. Even if we leave aside the Edelmann episode (which merits further study), we can see the seeds of freemasonry, *confréries*, academies, Alethophiles and sectarians who formed not only religious but cultural groups, that ferment of organisations which would transform enlightened ideas, sciences, new techniques into an organised force capable of bringing pressure to bear, if not actually of imposing themselves on the powers, the Churches and the universities. Meanwhile that extraordinary accumulation of learning and knowledge continued, that historical research which made the early eighteenth century in Germany an exceptional age of learned men and historians, from Mosheim to Baumgarten, from the jurists to the Leipzig reviewers. The *Frühaufklärung* is, then, a world which should be examined as a whole, once its various branches have been explored. Then it will be possible to define what exactly was its influence in German political life.

This is what scholars are doing for early eighteenth-century Italy, which presents some important similar elements to the German situation. Nevertheless, the essential element in Italy was the search for a new relationship with the Church. From a renewed ghibellinism, a continuation and revival of a legal sense and spirit, from a nascent historical vision of the Italian Middle Ages, a concept of juridical rights arose which gave a new dignity to states and writers who defended their rights before the Roman Curia. Giannone, Muratori and the new élite which gathered in Piedmont under Victor Amadeus II were only the most outstanding examples of this phenomenon. In only one marginal and abnormal case did this jurisdictionalism come anywhere near English deism, the mentality of the young Voltaire or of the Montesquieu of the *Lettres persanes*, even reaching the borders of utopia. This is the case of the Piedmontese nobleman, Adalberto Radicati di Passerano. But it is an exception. In general, Italian jurisdictionalism too meant to remain and did remain firmly within the framework of the past and Catholic orthodoxy and did not emerge except through the brilliant and profound intuition of Giannone's *Triregno*. The path which led to the European culture of the various Burnets, Tolands, Tindals, Middletons, Frérets and Montesquieus was difficult and rough, and it is precisely these isolated attempts which explain how long it was. In the rearguard, so far as his culture is concerned, dominant in his capacity to anticipate problems and solutions, stands Giambattista Vico, a man who stood outside his time because he was both too backward and too advanced, a thinker who still needs to be reappraised specifically from the point of view of the consciousness and reality of his position in relation to the early life of the Enlightenment in the eighteenth century.

If historical, religious and juridical elements were present and active in Spain, Germany and Italy in the early eighteenth century, in Sweden, Poland and Russia the questions were mainly political, often elementarily and brutally political. Nevertheless, the conflicts which took place in the countries of eastern and northern Europe, though so different, had something in common with what was happening on the rest of the Continent. It was precisely for this reason that they soon aroused the curiosity of Europeans who began to look to Charles XII, Peter the Great, or to Poland, which was at the time at the centre of a succession war. In Stockholm, Warsaw and Petersburg the struggle between absolutism and aristocracy was not a conflict coloured, as in France, with the light cadences of Fénelon, with the utopistic accents of the Abbé de Saint-Pierre's polysynod, or the treacheries of the Regency, nor, of course, with the British experiences and compromises. There 'the time of liberty', the *liberum veto*, and the revolts of the nobles when Anna Ivanovna ascended the throne, meant the undisguised, unmitigated self-assertion of the noble classes. Absolutism, too, meant something much more precise, incarnate in gigantic form in the person of Peter the Great. And there too, in the most diverse forms, it is from the dialectic of these two forces, and not from the victory of the one over the other, that a situation arose into which fitted *les lumières*, the desire which gave to the claims of the privileged classes the form and meaning of freedom and constitution and to absolutism the value of technical, administrative, organisational progress. Thus the germs of the forces of enlightenment, whether they came from France or Germany, whether they were of English origin or belonged to the humanist tradition, existed and spread increasingly in those countries which contemporaries called the countries of the north, in the Russia of Kantemir and Feofan Prokopovich, in the Sweden of Linnaeus and in the Poland of Stanislav Konarski, the Zaluskis and so many others. In those countries of Europe the new intellectual class still did not exist. It was still the priests and bishops, the diplomats and professors, the cultured and enlightened noblemen who performed the function that the intelligentsia would later have and who prepared the ideas, the paths and the basis for it. The constitutional struggles, the assertion of absolutism, the defence of the Swedish and Polish constitutions, found apologists and moralists but as yet no true political theorists. Even in Poland it was to be Montesquieu who would give a modern outlook to the traditions of the nobles, as the French philosophers would provide a justification for the *coups d'état* of Catherine II and Gustav III. It was from France that enlightenment, the new intellectual and political force was to come.

It came equally from the major representatives of the generation which had been formed in the first half of the century as from
a group of new men who had emerged in the mid-eighteenth century—to give examples, Voltaire, Montesquieu and the *Encyclopédie*
group.

The first, Voltaire, politically speaking, seemed the most anxious,
sensitive and intelligent searcher for a path which would lead
enlightenment to an accord with absolutism. There were others
with him, for example d'Argenson, to mention only one Frenchman. But no one possessed that energy and ability which would
make, for instance, the correspondence between Voltaire and
Frederick II one of the masterpieces of the century. No one knew
as well as he how to search and search again, with the King of
Prussia as with Machault, just as no one was capable of bringing
into these attempts such a profound sense of tolerance and freedom, which had been nourished in England, reconfirmed in the
solitude of the Bastille and Cirey, rediscovered in the history of
Henry IV as in his scientific research and in that deistic religion of
his of which Pomeau has now given us more intimate knowledge.

In 1748 Montesquieu produced the masterpiece of eighteenth-
century equilibrium, the brilliant proof that a superior accord
could and should be reached between the freedom of the cultured
and privileged and the desire for justice contained in natural law
and the classical tradition. To consider *L'Esprit des lois* a reactionary book, as Albert Mathiez has done, is to misunderstand the
whole intellectual history of the eighteenth century. The recent
studies of R. Shackleton have once more brought us face to face
with the inexhaustible richness of Montesquieu's thought. His
concept of despotism and of virtue, his demand for a balance of
established social forces which would bring the existing disputes
and conflicts of a given society onto a plane of freedom and not
iron them out into apparent uniformity, his new sense of the
history of single communities of human beings, linked to a serenely
cosmopolitan vision—these and so many other themes were to be
found in this book which brought together elements and currents
which the second half of the century would then take upon itself
to divide, analyse and develop separately. *L'Esprit des lois* is the
great watershed of eighteenth-century political ideas.

The group of young men, Diderot and Rousseau, but also La
Mettrie, Condillac and d'Holbach, brought a new energy into a
Europe which was emerging from the Austrian Succession war. It
brought revolt and rebellion, a nascent, immature force and energy,
which expressed itself in paradoxical forms and filled with new
meaning forms inherited from the past; they were often lost in

digressions but these possessed all the characteristics of an intellectual and moral thrust destined to last and echo far and wide. There was Jean-Jacques's revolt against civilisation and inequality, Diderot's enthusiastic and vital atheism, Condillac's break with every concept of a system and the materialism of La Mettrie and d'Holbach; between 1745 and 1754 all the elements which differentiate the French Enlightenment from the *Aufklärung*, from English deism and from rationalism in other countries had already appeared.

This ferment—the word appeared then—found its organisational form in the *Encyclopédie* thanks to the genius of Diderot. It was a wise and constantly renewed compromise of the already firm tradition of enlightenment and the libertarian and atheistic revolt, between science and the sense of the social utility of all human knowledge: the *Encyclopédie* gathered around it and developed the forces of two generations, thanks to Diderot's energy, d'Alembert's prudence and the variety and excellence of those who contributed to it. Through it and around it was born the philosophers' 'party', which from that moment would never cease to be an autonomous force. It was born of a crisis following a war, in a France which was in the process of changing its foreign policy and carrying out perhaps its most serious attempt to arrive at some internal, particularly financial, reforms. Disappointment caused by Louis XV's repeated incapacity to move along the path towards enlightened absolutism favoured its cause, as did the conflicts between the different religious currents of French Catholicism. The tolerant and enlightened spirit among a section of the ruling class saved its life at certain decisive moments. But what counts most is the fact that a group of intellectuals was now dominated, more or less profoundly, as is natural, by the belief, deeply rooted in the young Diderot, that it would be better to remain silent rather than not talk about religion and government.

No pre-existing organisation dictated the form of the philosophers' party: neither the masons (whatever has been written) nor the academies, nor journalism, nor the salons. It was a new undertaking. Even the details of its origins and development are important and revealing: its original link with England, the importance it attributed to economics, industry and to human work in general, its progressive widening to absorb men from different backgrounds. No less interesting are the echoes which this group of philosophers immediately aroused and which continued to reverberate later even in England, in Switzerland, beyond the Rhine and the Alps and eventually in eastern Europe.

The crisis was to come with the advent of the Seven Years War.

It was a crisis which reflected more than the internal disputes and difficulties of the philosophers' party or the internal conflicts of a France warring against England and Frederick II. By now it was a crisis of the whole of Europe. The *encyclopédistes* were considered, and in fact often were, cosmopolitan, pro-English and particularly pro-Prussian, at the very time when the war was going badly for their own country. These intellectuals had won an indepedence of judgment and action which dissociated them not only from their country's internal politics but also from her international policy. It was precisely the abstractness, the universal validity of their principles and passions, the element of negation in their revolt—with which they and the whole of the Enlightenment were endlessly reproached from then on by the conservatives —which made them autonomous and led them to the conclusions they derived from their experience in the great decade of the *Encyclopédie*. For Rousseau it would be the *Social contract*; for D'Alembert the need to organise with increasing knowledge, patience and even prudence the diffusion and defence of the Enlightenment in France and Europe; for Turgot and the physiocrats the need to shift the bulk of their efforts towards economic reforms, social transformation, agriculture; for d'Holbach and the *côterie holbachique* the desire to stake everything upon the struggle against religion, seeking arms and instruments in the English deist tradition, in the original theories of Nicolas-Antoine Boulanger or in the tenacious will to systematise of d'Holbach himself; for Voltaire it would be the beginning of the great campaign of *écrasez l'infâme* and tolerance; and finally for Diderot it meant the attempt to hold together those various elements which had been united in the *Encyclopédie*, revolt and equality, utopia and economics, atheism and philosophy. Diderot is thus truly the *philosophe*, who more than any other individual personified the ideal of the philosophers of the Enlightenment.

The extraordinary intensity of this experience in France in the age of the *Encyclopédie* resounded throughout Europe. This was not only on account of the exceptional diffusive capacity of the thought of the men who had participated in it, but because everywhere the Seven Years War had precipitated situations and thought and provoked different movements, sometimes very different in both nature and appearance, yet which were concentric in respect of the Paris movement and which found their focal point more or less rapidly in the *encyclopédistes*.

The conflict between cosmopolitanism and patriotism which, as we have seen, was one of the reasons for the crisis of the *Encyclopédie* in 1759, could be seen too, in this and the following years, wherever the war had aroused passions which were no longer merely territorial, dynastic or traditional. Frederick II was looked on then, not only as the model enlightened sovereign, but as something more and different, as a ruler who inspired passions which already found expression in the *vieux mot de patrie*. Even in Russia the *coup d'état* which brought Catherine II to the throne was accompanied by patriotic passion—which amazed the Empress, as she wrote in a letter to Poniatowski. The polemic against cosmopolitanism was kindled then, more or less everywhere, by a more intense participation in the local past, by the revival of old forgotten images or the birth of new ones, from Swiss patriotism, for example, to a kind of patriotism which recalled the Burghers of Calais, from primitive Germanism to the nascent myth of Geneva. It was the world of what has been called pre-Romanticism, which has been studied more from the literary than the political point of view and which emerges more and more, as we explore the works and writings of the time, as a multicoloured reflection of the contradictions and debates which were at the very heart of the Enlightenment, at the moment of its greatest affirmation and expansion, torn between nation and cosmopolis, revolt and reason, liberty and equality.

These echoes and feelings, however, did not form the essential element in the evolution of Spain, Italy and the countries of central and eastern Europe. In these countries the period of the Seven Years War, in some places more rapidly, in others more slowly, represented a decisive thrust towards enlightened absolutism and reform. Charles III's Spain prepared the way with its struggle against the Jesuits, with the modernisation of the instruments of administration and education, with the appearance in embryo of that ruling class, that enlightened élite which Jean Sarrailh has recently described so well. Campomanes, Floridablanca, Olavide, the birth of the 'Economic Societies', a renewed awareness of Spain's past—the whole process culminated in those two geniuses produced by the Iberian peninsula in the eighteenth century, Goya and Jovellanos. In Portugal the Marquis of Pombal boldly embarked on a swift, violent attempt at change, destined to remain exemplary in eighteenth-century Europe, but which failed to destroy the contradictions inherent in enlightened Catholicism and finally assumed on occasions the dark tones of a tyrannical withdrawal. In Naples (which had so many connections with the Iberian peninsula, from the bond which linked Genovesi to the Spanish Verney, to the common anticlerical policy), the seed sown and tended by Genovesi himself began to ripen and a class of intellectuals asserted itself which was really, as has been written, a new nation, so much did it tend to broaden its activities and leave its mark upon all the country's essential problems. With the accession of Peter Leopold in Tuscany those reforms began which were to make this tiny country an example admired far and wide for its free trade and physiocratic policies. In Milan the initial vigorous independence of the new enlightened ruling class met in a particularly significant manner the reforms imposed from above. Lombardy and the kingdom of Naples became the two focal points of the Italian Enlightenment. *Il Caffè*, Alessandro and Pietro Verri and Cesare Beccaria responded to the determination of Kaunitz and Firmian and collaborated in reorganising and modifying schools, university chairs, the administration, customs duties, censorship and the Inquisition. They accomplished all this while still maintaining that intellectual freedom which distinguishes them from the technical advisers of the modern state, which made them men halfway between the *grands commis* of absolutism and the *philosophes* of the Enlightenment. In Italy the decisive period for enlightenment thus stretched from 1763 to 1773, the decade which began with the first issue of *Il Caffè* and ended with the suppression of the Society of Jesus and which saw some of the most daring proposals for a 'reform of Italy', to adopt the formula of one of the writers of the time, Carlantonio Pilati of Trent.

There were many reasons why this was such a flourishing period. Not least of these was the direction events were taking in Vienna. It was in Vienna that there developed what was to be, in the final analysis, the enlightened absolutism that left the most durable fruits on European soil. The foundations of that policy which was to take its name from Joseph II were already being laid in the last two decades of the reign of his mother, Maria Theresa, as the studies of Winter and Maas have clearly indicated. It was a long time before those outside the Habsburg Empire realised what was happening. Voltaire still had many doubts at a time when reason had already made great progress on the Danube. The sons of the *lumières* only met at a late stage, and perhaps without fully recognising them, those who had been educated by the teachings of Wolff or Muratori, all those who had left their mark on the culture of Austria, Hungary and Bohemia. And yet in their proposals they were moving closer together and influencing one another, and this applies even to the mentality of men like Voltaire and Joseph II (in spite of the fact that, as is well known, they were careful to avoid a personal meeting). Even the most enlightened officials, the reformers of Austria, men like Sonnenfels or Justi, tended to utilise the ideas of the *lumières*, to apply them and transform them into institutions which could be fitted into the monarchical structure.

The relationship between sovereigns and intellectuals came close to that between employer and technician, king and minister, even though by this time both had assimilated to a considerable degree a culture, the ideas and even the ideals of which came from countries like France and England where the intellectuals constituted an autonomous political force, even a 'party'. Hence the 'fashionable' appearance which the *lumières* tended to assume in those countries, of which Austria is only one example. It is enough to think of Russia to see the importance of this attitude. It was a fashion precisely because the ideas did not correspond to the way of life and social function. This does not mean that they were not important or that they did not exert an increasing influence on the civilisation of these countries.

In Germany, particularly in Prussia, enlightenment which came from above eventually produced a rapidly deepening split between political power and men of culture who began to dream about, if not yet put into practice, those protests and revolts which showed their desire not to be instruments and means of civilising, but an active part of a free civilisation. Their revolt was two-sided: they rebelled in the name of the past but also because they could not control the machine of state and of the *Aufklärung*. German *Sturm und Drang* led to the coincidence and confusion of particularist, retrograde elements with libertarian accents, the latter generally of French or English origin. The bandit took over the function and heritage of the solitary man, Rousseau's savage. In general, the terms used by the Enlightenment in Paris and London were translated into artistic, religious and historical forms, in this way escaping from political, economic and legal problems.

In Russia the decade 1762–73 marked the period of the greatest enthusiasm for reform and receptiveness towards the ideas of the Enlightenment and witnessed the greatest diffusion in society of the formulae of the *encyclopédistes*. It was also the moment when the field had been cleared of other elements—above all the influence of the Church—so presenting Russia's threefold yet single problem with greater clarity: autocracy, nobility, peasantry. Within ten years of Catherine's assumption of the throne the opposition of the nobles had begun to assume organised legal forms with constitutional tendencies. The peasant opposition took on the appearance of a revolt which challenged the validity of all the structures of society and the state. Pugachev pointed to the terrain on which reforms were needed in Russia. After his defeat the relationship between autocrat, nobles and serfs tended to become more stable, even static. For this situation to change the slow, difficult emergence of the 'third estate' was needed, the transforma-

tion of a noble-based economy, the modification of autocracy towards forms of monarchy, the spread of culture among the ruling
class and, last but not least, the emergence of a new force, the
intelligentsia. It makes its earliest appearance in this period, as an
isolated and closed group (even forced to take refuge in masonic
sects), as important as it was numerically small and soon destined
to be persecuted. The intelligentsia was of vital importance precisely because from the very beginning it took upon itself enormous
tasks, out of all proportion to its very limited powers, tending to
make up for all that was lacking in Russian society. The ideals
which inspired Novikov and later Radishev, to name but two, were
the ideals of the Enlightenment, selected and imported from France,
Italy and Germany with a strong eclecticism which corresponded
to Russia's immediate needs, to the moral and political problems
which loomed large before the minds of cultured men in Russia
and began to dominate their sensitive souls. When Radishev linked
these ideas to the problem of freedom for the peasants, he found
the formula which was to dominate the intelligentsia for a century
and more.

On the other side of Europe, in England—to conclude this rapid survey of the world of the Enlightenment at the moment of its greatest
expansion—it is interesting to note how there too the years which
followed the Treaty of Paris marked the beginning of radical
agitation, of movements which became increasingly complex and
numerous in the British Isles and the English colonies. However,
in spite of the links which did exist, as is natural, between agitations
and ideologies on both sides of the Channel and both sides of the
Atlantic, we cannot say that a single current including both England and the Continent was always present. Wilkes was more a
friend of d'Holbach than of the English intellectuals. The latter did
not constitute a party, one particular trend, but represented all the
nuances of a free and diversified public opinion. Only in Scotland,
where the unified action of scholars, erudites and intellectuals
sharing common ideas proved more necessary, was a movement
born which had a strong resemblance to the French movement.
We can see very similar religious and ethical concerns and parallel
economic and political problems arising in the two countries. We
witness the development of societies which gathered together the
most active forces and acquired considerable weight in Scottish
society, such as the Select Society and the Edinburgh Society.
Scotland in those years was no longer a poor, abandoned, despised
and rebellious country but was experiencing rapid economic development, at the same time as it became one of the brightest centres
of the European Enlightenment. Thus Scotland was one of the

points towards which Europeans turned their eyes. Men like Hume, Smith, Ferguson, Millar and Monboddo found their starting-point and the basis of their development there, forming a pleiad of writers such as only Paris possessed. The contrast, the difference between Scottish and English culture in the eighteenth century, even in their reciprocal influence, offers a highly characteristic example of the development of the ideas of the Enlightenment in two different situations.

By 1774, when Louis XV died, we can say that all the essential elements of the Enlightenment had already found expression. This time too the most daring formulations had come from France. It took Paris to draw the deepest and conclusive consequences of the whole movement of the century. Often these most mature formulations of the *philosophie* have been considered extremist elements, foreign to the real nature of the Enlightenment. But this is only a posthumous judgment, interpreted by the historians of philosophy (not excluding Cassirer), of the *Aufklärung* on the *lumières*. When faced with the ideas asserted in Paris around 1770, not to see that these were the highest expression of the thought of the *philosophes* is to misunderstand the internal logic of the whole of the eighteenth-century movement. It is true that the power of the Churches had diminished throughout Europe. It is true that tolerance was accepted a little everywhere, despite continuous disputes. But it was the *philosophes* who at that moment went beyond ecclesiastical decadence, beyond tolerance, to assert the value of liberty. It is true that the aspiration towards legal equality was spreading everywhere but it was in Paris that the first affirmations of real equality occurred. All Europe had experienced a long period of economic improvement, expansion and development of trade, manufactures and agriculture, a movement which, as Labrousse has rightly noted, stretched from 1750 to 1770. But only the Parisian writers saw beyond these improvements and set their sights on a world of equally shared wealth and riches. Everywhere old systems of repression, the old ecclesiastical and civil legislations, from the Inquisition to torture, were breaking up. But the idea, born in the mind of Beccaria, of a total abolition of the death penalty and of all forms of torture was accepted only at the very centre of the Enlightenment, as was the belief in the need for a complete distinction between guilt and sin, using exclusively as its basis, even in penal law, the criterion of social utility. A sense of progress and development was present wherever cultured men lived in eighteenth-century Europe. But the theory of progress, of perfectibility, of the infinite space ahead of man through the increase of his possessions and values was only asserted in the world of the

French *lumières*. The belief in and desire for utopia, and for an egalitarian, atheistic, technical utopia was expressed in a thousand ways, and revealed once more the most hidden and vigorous springs of the Enlightenment. It is impossible to give comprehensive examples. It is, however, essential to underline certain fundamental conclusions which were arrived at in France between the 'sixties and 'seventies and which were passed on as achievements to future decades.

Above all there was atheism, expression of the desire for a completely human world. The *Système de la nature* appeared in 1770. This book marked the final break, not only with all forms of a more or less sentimental attachment to tradition. It represented a difference of generation, of mentality, which also implied a different attitude towards intellectual and metaphysical problems, as well as towards political and practical ones. This had been seen clearly a few years previously in the dissensions over whether to publish the posthumous work of Boulanger and *Le Christianisme dévoilé* by d'Holbach himself. It was a question of knowing whether it was advisable to preach irreligion ever more widely and radically or to continue keeping such ideas within a small circle of people; whether it was not socially dangerous to proclaim the non-existence of God, whether this truth ought to remain a secret for a chosen few. In his discussions with Voltaire, d'Holbach had said that laws and the magistracy were no longer just harmful but useless. A completely human world was not only desirable but possible.

However, would this entirely human world be also a just world? This was the great torment of the *philosophes*. Helvétius looked to education for the solution. Diderot saw it in a radical shift of the limit and relationship between what was traditionally called morality and nature, life. But for him, nevertheless, the world remained partly the possession of the Devil and partly of God, which was the criticism brought against him by Dom Deschamps, the thinker who made most conscious progress on the road towards the abolition of this distinction. Deschamps, together with a considerable number of others, went so far as to seek in the abolition of property and the sharing of possessions the radical instrument for abolishing social evil on earth. Morelly had been the greatest theoriser of this idea and his *Code de la nature* became widely known when it was included in an edition of Diderot's works. Morelly, Dom Deschamps, Mably etc. thus created one of the most lasting and enduring formulae which were to transmit the problems and solutions of the Enlightenment to the nineteenth century.

On the political plane, the idea of democracy was asserted in this period. The *Social contract* provides its broadest and most lucid formulation. It undoubtedly owed much to the theoreticians of natural law, as Derathé's study of Rousseau and his predecessors has accurately shown. But here too what counts is the new element. And this too was to remain basically unchanged until the great experience of the French Revolution.

The reforming spirit, opposed yet linked to this desire for total solutions—whether democratic, on the political plane, or communistic, on the social plane—not only expressed itself with extraordinary vigour in the years immediately before and after 1770 but at that time found what were politically its most active and important formulae. We need to remember that it was in this period that the *lumières* became specifically antifeudal. A polemic developed, which it would be interesting to follow in detail from Coyer to Boncerf. It is not true that the whole of the Enlightenment, from its outset, aimed to attack feudal privileges. This was a development of the *lumières* which acquired ever-increasing importance in the last decades of the century.

Even more striking, at least at the beginning, is the polemic against cruelty and intolerance, particularly with regard to penal law. Alongside this there was the development of the campaign against begging and pauperism, in favour of the transformation of the family, in short, that multitude of plans, proposals and utopias which looked at all aspects of social life and which constituted the fragmentation of the Enlightenment and at the same time its penetration into all the interstices of the society of the *ancien régime*.

By this time the spirit of reform was enlightened and guided by a general vision of human society and its development, a vision which had been formulated in various parts of Europe, particularly in Paris after the *Encyclopédie*, in Edinburgh at the high point of the Scottish Enlightenment, in Italy in the most diverse places, in Lessing's Germany, Iselin's Switzerland etc. Civil society was studied and analysed in all these various attempts, taken to pieces in its ranks, orders and classes, in the superimposing of one upon another, in the causes of their formation, development and decadence, in the comparison and connection of the different forms of men's work, from agriculture to manufacturing. This was the beginning of 'l'histoire de l'homme en société' (Boulanger), 'the history of men' (Hume), 'the history of civil society' (Ferguson), the 'Geschichte der Menscheit' (Iselin) etc. A science of society and the idea of progress expressed two complementary aspects of a single concept and the relationship between them altered and varied according to the different visions of civilisation—a word which began to be used at that time and which became endowed with increasingly rich meanings.

There were two important practical results : a new historiography prepared by Voltaire and brought into being by Gibbon, Robertson and Hume and a new political economy based specifically on an integral vision of economic processes in human society, created by the physiocrats and brought to fulfilment by Adam Smith. Social history and political economy were born simultaneously and, perhaps more than aesthetics and economics, were, to use Benedetto Croce's definition, the two worldly sciences *par excellence*. Whereas, in the case of the first, the link with the political problems of the day was clear, the desire of the second for scientific abstraction often tended to obscure those multiple ties which appear increasingly clear to all the scholars of today who investigate the relationship between eighteenth-century political economy and the society of that century. The physiocrats' demand for evidence, repeated *ad nauseam*, was indicative of the desire for absolute truth possessed by the fathers of modern economics. Their attempts at organisation, their banding together—which made them appear in the eyes of contemporaries as though they belonged to a 'sect' rather than to a free current of ideas—their theorisation of legal despotism, showed the new difficulties which arose in the path of intellectuals, *philosophes* of a new and different kind who were looking for ways in which to impose their economic concepts. These new intellectuals were technicians at the same time; as reformers they trusted public opinion and state power in a different way from the *encyclopédistes*. The birth of political economy thus transformed the relationship between *philosophes* and states. The extraordinary diffusion which the physiocrats were able to secure for their ideas in the most diverse countries of Europe shows the efficiency, not only of their principles, but also of the instruments they had created to spread them.

One man represents the synthesis of the dramatic transition from *philosophes* to *économistes*. Turgot had been among the very first to move in the direction of the philosophy of history, of a general vision of the development of human society. On the other hand, he was the person who had theorised about the force and value of *evidence*. There is no need to add that he was a brilliant economist and administrator. Destiny willed that the decisive experiment of the French *ancien régime* should be his. Before he rose to power, his friends were becoming ever more convinced that nothing more could be done to push the monarchy onto the path of reform and that only a revolution would emerge from that increasingly evident impotence. This was how d'Holbach felt and he said so to David Hume, adding that if a revolution did not break out in France, it was on account of the cowardice of the nobles. (As we can see, it was from that quarter that he too expected a first affirmation of liberty.) By 1773 Helvétius had come to the conclusion that the destiny of France had already been decided: 'Nulle crise salutaire ne lui rendra la liberté, c'est par la consumption qu'elle périra, la conquête est le seul remède à ses malheurs et c'est le hazard et les circonstances qui décideront de l'efficacité d'un tel remède.' Diderot, in 1771, was convinced that 'nous touchons à une crise qui aboutira à l'esclavage ou à la liberté' and he said one day that the only way to bring about the regeneration of France was to follow the example of Medea who 'rendit la jeunesse à son père en le dépeçant et le faisant bouillir'. And yet he too hoped that the change of king would open up great new possibilities. Turgot, in 1774, caused these hopes to rise again; he aroused enthusiasm and succeeded in carrying out certain measures of great significance for a transformation from within, only to be stopped very soon and removed. From that moment enlightened absolutism foundered on the rocks.

As in a body which wastes away, so the progressive weakening of state power in France brought to the surface the bones, structures and established organisms which attempted to take the place of the central authority by gradually assuming the role of political guidance which the latter was no longer in a position to fulfil. The *parlements*, privileged classes, regional assemblies etc. became organs of freedom and gave the illusion of a struggle for the rights of citizens and social groups. France had entered the crisis which led to the Revolution. It was both a political and an economic crisis. The former aspect has long been studied and analysed. The latter has been investigated in exemplary manner in the last four decades by Ernest Labrousse. The Enlightenment too was in crisis during the fifteen years which preceded the Revolution. It is possible even to trace a parallel between this crisis and that of the *ancien régime*: the party of the *philosophes* was not united or firm enough to lead public opinion. Its political force remained but it consisted in clarifying and deepening the rifts which were opening up in French society, in giving a common mental basis to the various currents, which ranged from pro-English to pro-American feeling, from the return to old and the creation of new models of freedom, to the republican and libertarian hopes which were appearing on the horizon, from Brissot to Marat and from Lafayette to Condorcet. The party of the *philosophes* was by this time merging with and strengthening the new forces which were entering the field. It was the beginning of what would be accomplished in the Revolution, the outcome, but also the dissolution of the Enlightenment. The physiocrats had a more precise programme, a more lucid vision, but their economic reasoning did not take into account those demands for equality, those libertarian revolts which were to be of such importance in the years of the revolutionary conflict. In this too physiocracy showed that it was a branch, a very important one, but still only one branch of the movement known as the Enlightenment.

In the rest of Europe outside Paris there was a parallel evolution after 1774. It is a date of significance, not only for France, but for Europe and the world, as it marks a coincidence of events in East and West. A book which came out then 'pour servir de supplément à l'Histoire philosophique et politique et des établissements et du commerce européens dans les deux Indes' offers a true picture of the world of the time. It was intended as a supplement and conclusion to Abbé Raynal's book, the work which contained the fullest collection of the agitations and utopias of the political feeling of those years in the world of the *philosophes*. The supplement was entitled *Tableau de l'Europe* and it was the work of an intimate friend of Diderot, Rousseau and Condillac. It presented a description of the waning of the Enlightenment, just before its decline and crisis; it showed clearly the relationship between men and things which led to the Enlightenment's cosmopolis ('le peuple entraîne les philosophes et les philosophes mènent le peuple'). Shadows were already beginning to appear in the author's doubts about customs and the practical possibility of really changing society. It marked out clearly the borders of the world which he still calls Europe but which was in reality the world of European civilisation, between Philadelphia and Moscow, Sweden and Spain. It offered a varied and critical picture, still dominated by faith in the Enlightenment's capacity for expansion. It was a static picture, at the very moment when the European world was entering into its phase of revolutions, of violent and irrevocable conflicts.

Corsica had already made men dream of an open conflict between poor and rich, corrupt and pure. The figure of Pugachev had already provided a distant flash of the threats of peasant revolt. The internal conflicts which had accompanied the beginning of the Polish crisis had already posed anew the whole range of problems from that of the freedom of the nobles to the question of religious tolerance and reform from above. The *coup d'état* of Gustav III had already reopened similar questions. But the events of the South, East and North had not been sufficient to launch the era of revolutions. This was achieved by the American colonists, the War of Independence, its international repercussions, the appeal to public opinion, Franklin, Jefferson and above all by the emergence of a new federal solution which the states beyond the Atlantic had found for the eighteenth-century problem of authority and freedom, of the intermediary organisms and central power, together with a vision, which was full of suggestion for an extremely wide range of individuals in eighteenth-century Europe, of a republic of philosopher farmers, ruled by scientists with a philosophical tolerance, by liberal generals and republican aristocrats, by men cosmopolitan by origin and conviction, patriotic by passion and sentiment. The *esprit révolutionnaire* had been born.

For this to pass from the outer edge of the European world to the centre and become rooted there, for this revolutionary spirit to become an integral part of European life—for it had nothing specifically American about it but was only the Enlightenment coming to grips with the problems of a world in a state of crisis and in the process of economic and political transformation—it was necessary to follow paths on the Continent which were very different from those followed by the United States of America but were also more natural and suited to a more complex and stratified society. The paths had been marked out once more by the experience of enlightened despotism, both where it had succeeded and where it had failed.

One of the most exciting studies is to observe the reactions of the various Habsburg territories to Joseph II in the decade preceding the Revolution. Here too, as in Prussia, enlightenment had come from above but bringing with it a capacity for change unequalled in continental Europe. As everywhere where a ruling class inspired with a spirit of reform was arising, in the Empire too at least part of this class found enough energy to try to continue to walk alone when international events and finally the French Revolution led the monarchs away from reform and towards reaction. In Naples (considerably influenced by Austrian experiences), in Milan, in the German territories and in Spain we witness the way in which a fraction of the new enlightened ruling class moved straight to 'Jacobinism'. The men who were in possession of the new techniques, the new sciences, finally began to think about a state in which they would govern without ever needing monarchs any more. The political importance in Germany of men like Schlözer, or of the others who have been studied with such acuteness by Valjavec, give us an idea of the potential for development in these new-style rationalists, these jurists and politicians who in so many ways already resemble those who were to rise to power at the time of the Revolution or in the days of Napoleon. But they were unable to assert themselves without the support of the French armies. The figure of Georg Forster symbolises the tragedy of those men who passed from enlightenment to 'Jacobinism'. Their fate was similar in Italy, the Rhineland, Hungary, Germany and in Spain too. Nor were they to succeed in their other attempt, which was not 'Jacobin' but 'constitutional'. This was the other form of reaction which can be seen in the Habsburg states, in Pietro Verri's Milan or among the Hungarian noblemen, as the recent studies of K. Benda have clearly shown. This was the great illusion of the wisest and most moderate men of the late eighteenth century, the belief that it was possible to crown the edifice of reform with a constitution. Perhaps even more interesting is the reaction of another territory of Joseph II, Belgium, where the reactionary and liberal spirits were together successful in setting in motion a process which, even though it did not find its own outlet and was eventually incorporated into the mainstream of the great French Revolution, nevertheless possessed its own logic and vitality. In Belgium the struggle for the preservation of traditional privileges against enlightened absolutism broadened and deepened in the direction of democracy. There was also that element which can be found in other Habsburg dominions—the love of one's country, its past and traditions which, combined with more modern tendencies, gave rise to patriotism. *Pro aris et focis*, as Jean-François Vonck used to say. In more recent times Valjavec and Markov have rightly stressed the importance of this late *Aufklärung* for an understanding of the origin of national movements, particularly in central Europe and the Balkans, but also in the lands between Germany and France. The Serbia of Dositei Obradovich, Slovenia, to a certain extent Bulgaria and Bohemia as well as the Rhine territories studied by Jacques Droz, and Belgium and Holland, extracted from the culture of the century the elements to vindicate their existence and give a tentative beginning to their national revivals. They were soon to find in various, much more virulent, thoughts and ideas, as they had already found in the eighteenth century in Herder's philosophy of history, formulations and hopes which were more active and more in harmony with the nascent national feeling. But the fact that they continued to feel part of the Europe of the Enlightenment, that love, that veritable cult of culture which was to play such an important role in their revivals, originated in these minor countries in the atmosphere of the last decades of the eighteenth century.

In sharp contrast, in this same period, to the impatience and reforming improvisations of the Habsburg sovereign, who in ten years succeeded in carrying out extremely important changes in central Europe, stood the passivity, the complete incapacity for reform of the oligarchic states, the lands dominated by the patriciates, countries which had been born as free countries, which in a certain sense still were so, but which by this time had witnessed the final estrangement from their structures, constitutions and customs of the ideals of freedom of the century which was nearing its close. From the largest to the smallest of these states, there was Poland, the United Provinces, Venice, Geneva, Genoa, Lucca, Ragusa. Their problem has fascinated historians in the last few years and it is quite understandable how similar crises in institutions can fascinate men who have witnessed other, more tragic crises for free countries in the times in which they lived. Jean Fabre, the best Polish historians, Cobban, Berengo and many others have given a new interpretation of the dissolution of the old republics. One fact is quite clear: it was not the 'Russian mirage' which blinded the *philosophes* about the relationship between Russia and Poland. It was not propaganda, or only propaganda, which made Voltaire, Diderot and the other men of the Enlightenment believe that reforms could not be born in the land of the *liberum veto*. This was the practical truth. The revolts of the nobles would unleash revolution at the end of the century in France, but it would be effective precisely because it would take place on ground already prepared through the centuries by absolute monarchies. The reaction of the nobles in the old patrician republics, whether Poland or Venice, whether of the aristocratic class or the poorest nobility, constituted an element of political dissolution, not of revival and renewal. Nevertheless, Warsaw and Amsterdam, Venice and Genoa had been penetrated by the Enlightenment and new intellectual forms, new mentalities were ripening. It is of immense interest to see the transplanting, the partial and difficult transformation of old ideas of freedom into eighteenth-century constitutional concepts and humanistic spirits blossoming again on old stock. These were processes which were ideal rather than relevant to immediate politics, even if they were to achieve a considerable degree of effectiveness in Poland, the United Provinces and Geneva.

Even the greatest, richest, most vigorous of the countries governed constitutionally by a noble ruling class, England, proved incapable of reform through the means and instruments of the eighteenth century. Reform could not come from above, in so far as it was attempted by George III and the 'King's friends'—and this is not the place to discuss with Namier, Butterfield and Pares the extent to which the royal prerogative and pressure could be exerted from above. It could not come from the most typically aristocratic opposition which was then forming and which possessed so much in common with the parallel phenomena we have seen on the Continent (it is no chance that Edmund Burke, the theoriser of these aristocratic concepts, was soon to become known on the other side of the Channel). Nor could it come from the radical elements who tried every means, from uprisings to the organisation of clubs, from adherence to the most jealous traditions of the Whigs—for example, on the centenary of the 1688 Revolution—to the return, with developments and modifications, to social utilitarianism, to the economic calculus of the *philosophes*, to Helvétius and Beccaria. It was to be this last attempt, that of philosophical radicalism, which would produce the most important results from these experiences. Fifty years later, in changed conditions, the path which had been noted was to open the way to reform.

Bentham, Price, Paine, Godwin, the whole band of English thinkers who appeared at the end of the century, represented the delayed but vigorous and deep Enlightenment in England. At last there had been born in England too a current which would have its own experiences, its internal struggles, its polarisations between utilitarianism and communism, atheism and sentimentalism. England, which had not led the intellectual movement when it was at its peak halfway through the century, would very soon acquire its historical role in the struggle against the French Revolution and Napoleon, while maintaining, saving and developing both constitutionalism and radicalism, the two great products of the Enlightenment in Britain.

But the initiative in the great European upheaval at the end of the eighteenth century was not to come from that direction. The French Revolution had begun in Paris. That circle, that relationship between France and Europe which we saw at each of the crucial moments of the eighteenth century would have to emerge again, to spread once more in increasingly grandiose proportions.

2 Towards an Historical Dictionary

Was ist Aufklärung? Sapere aude!

HERE appeared in the issue of the *Berlinische Monatts-chrift* of December 1783 an article by Zöllner entitled: 'Would it perhaps be a good thing to do away with religious solemnisation of marriages?' It was an attack against the secular mentality of the Enlightenment, against 'those who devote themselves to undermining the bases of morality, denying the value of religion and leading astray the heads and hearts of men under the pretext of enlightenment', '. . . unter dem Namen der Aufklärung'. The author then stopped for a moment as if surprised at what he had written and added in a note: 'Was ist Aufklärung?'. 'This question, although it is almost as important as the question: what is truth, still ought to be answered before the work of enlightenment is begun. However, I have not been able to find an answer to it anywhere!'

During the following year, 1784, by no means the least interesting part of the Berlin review was devoted precisely to answering this question. In September Moses Mendelsohn published his article 'Ueber die Frage: was heisst aufklären?' (*On the question: What is Enlightenment?*) Anyone seeking to go back to the origins of the term and concept of Enlightenment will find in these pages, rather than original ideas and considerations, some statements about the newness, the immaturity, so to speak, of the words *Aufklärung, Kultur, Bildung*, which, as Moses Mendelsohn wrote, 'are still new-comers in our language. For the moment they still belong exclusively to the language of books. Ordinary people do not understand them.' Was this perhaps a sign that enlightenment itself and culture were new and recent things in Germany? To this question he gave a negative reply, showing us in this way too that a mature and thriving intellectual need and reality was crystallising at that moment into a term like *Aufklärung*.

In December 1784 Kant's famous article *'Beantwortung der Frage: Was ist Aufklärung?'* (*Reply to the question: What is Enlightenment?*) appeared in the *Berlinische Monattschrift*. We shall not linger over the content of this article, which has been much studied and commented on, but we shall concentrate instead upon the formula which seems to capture so vividly the spirit which stood out from the very first page of Kant's essay: *Sapere aude*. 'This is the motto of the Enlightenment'.

This motto had come a long way since the day when it was created by Horace for inclusion in the second epistle of *Ad Lollium*, Book I, line 40: *Dimidium facti, qui coepit, habet: sapere aude, Incipe* . . . ('He who begins is half way to his goal: dare to know, Begin . . .')

In the Horatian context, of course, the meaning of *Sapere aude* was far from the one which Kant had attributed to it. If we take a look at the eighteenth-century translation by Dacier (1727, 1733), we shall find a version which restores faithfully, if somewhat diffusely, the Horatian savour of the motto: '. . . ayez le courage d'être vertueux.' And in a note Dacier explained further: 'Pour aspirer à la sagesse, il faut du courage, et ne pas se rebuter par les difficultés. C'est pourquoi Horace dit *aude*, ose.' It is true that other translators did seem to come closer to the meaning that the word eventually took on. Giovanni Fabbrini da Figline, in his translation published in 1570, had written: 'Have the courage to know', and Aurelio Bertola, in his edition of Horace which appeared almost simultaneously with Kant's article, an edition which belongs completely to the Enlightenment, even down to the portrait of Peter Leopold with which it so appropriately opened, accepted the version: '. . . be courageous that you may become wise'.

But it is not an investigation of the interpretations of Horace which we are attempting to carry out here, even if that could evidently lead to a fuller account of the prehistory of the motto under examination. Without going further back than the eighteenth century, it will, we believe, be worth following the fortunes of *Sapere aude* in that world of the Enlightenment in the process of formation which was to find its conclusion and crystallisation in Kant's article.

In 1736 a medal was coined in Berlin which, about a century later, the historian Heinrich Wuttke could consider, not without some justification, as a kind of symbolic starting-point of the philosophical fortunes of the Prussian capital. He said that in

Berlin, 'which from that time remained the capital of philosophers', a medal was envisaged, discussed and finally created which bore the bust of an armed Minerva (with undoubtedly Teutonic features we might add). On the helmet, adorned with crowns and feathers, were the heads of the two philosophers Leibniz and Wolff, in the manner of a two-headed Janus. Around the medal was written: *Sapere aude*, and the reverse side bore the inscription: 'Societas Alethophilorum ab Ern. Christophoro S.R.I. co. De Manteuffel instituta. Berol. 1736'.

The Society of Alethophiles had been founded in that very year to gather together all those who were not only convinced followers of Wolff but also disposed towards positive action in defence of their master's philosophy. At the court of Frederick William I, at a decisive moment in the history of the diffusion of Wolff's ideas, the formation of this circle had appeared indispensable. Although a heavy atmosphere of mistrust and militaristic disdain surrounded philosophy, the sympathy which Wolff had managed to win among the Prussian ruling class, ecclesiastics, administrators, bureaucrats and jurists was nevertheless firm and lasting. The founder of the Society of Alethophiles was Count Ernst Christoph von Manteuffel, a man of great culture and great ambitions, a characteristic figure of the first half of the eighteenth century, halfway between adventurer, politician and learned cosmopolite. The nickname by which he was known was undoubtedly significant. His close associates called him *le diable*. The Society had begun at the same time as, and probably as a parallel group or branch of, a *confrairie de francmaçons* founded by him (with trowel, set-square and feasts) but ostensibly it was no more than a little academy. Its main distinguishing feature was the spirit of proselytism which obviously inspired it. Its members did not confine themselves to proclaiming their faith in Wolff's philosophy and maintaining the need for it to be divulged everywhere but also asserted that it was the precise duty of all those who were in possession of the truth in general to make it known to their fellow men.

They summarised their maxims in six points and called this statute of theirs the *Hexalogus Alethophilorum*, without doubt a most interesting and important document of the nascent mentality of the Enlightenment.

I—Let truth be the only aim, the only object of your mind and will. II—Do not hold anything to be true, do not hold anything to be false until the moment when you have been convinced of it by sufficient reason. III—Do not be satisfied with loving and recognising truth, but seek also to divulge it and make it known to and loved by your fellow citizens. The man who buries his own awareness of truth, buries that which was given to him for the greater glory of God and deprives human society of the benefit which it might have derived from it. IV—Do not deprive of your love and aid those who strive in all sincerity to know truth, to seek it and defend it. It would be shameful and contrary to the true qualities of an Alethophile to refuse any manner of protection and help to the man whose aim coincides with yours. V—Do not contradict the truth if you feel yourself being convinced by another whose idea is more correct than your own. An Alethophile would make himself unworthy of the name if he allowed himself to contradict the truth through pride, stubbornness or other irrational causes. VI—Have compassion for those who do not know the truth or have a mistaken concept of it. Instruct them without bitterness and strive to lead them to the right path by the force of your reasoning alone. You will dishonour the truth and render it suspect if you arm it or defend it with weapons other than those which reason places in your hands.

The Society of Alethophiles continued in Berlin for a few years: Count von Manteuffel, the well-known theologian Johann Gustav Reinbeck, the bookseller Ambrosius Haude would meet together in the evenings amid pipe smoke. Later it spread and widened its membership until it included the famous writer Gottsched and his wife, Formey and Deschamps, 'Aléthophiles français', and attracted into its circle even Madame du Châtelet. The Society survived even the personal fortunes of its founder. Writing to Wolff from Leipzig on 10 February 1741, Count von Manteuffel announced joyfully:

Il s'est formé icy depuis peu une espèce de société de 8 ou 9 savans qui se piquent tous d'être partisans de votre philosophie. Ces messieurs m'ayant fait l'honneur de me demander la permission de prendre le nom d'*Aléthophiles*, et prié de regarder leur Société comme une fille de celle que nous nous sommes avizéz, M. R.[einbeck] et moi (par badinerie plutôt que dans une intention sérieuse) de former à Berlin. J'ai non seulement fort approuvé leur dessein, les aiant même regaléz chacun d'une de mes médailles, mais je suis même venu icy pour leur assurer la protection du Duc contre le clergé orthodoxe de cette Résidence qui commençoit à la persécuter . . . Ces nouveaux Aléthophiles tinrent hier leur première assemblée solemnelle . . . Je ne sais si je me trompe, mais il me semble que de telles compagnies, quand elles sont un peu protégées, et qu'elles se conduissent avec quelque prudence et sagesse, sont très propres à avancer la verité, surtout dans un pays, comme la Saxe, où les ortodoxes tiennent encore le haut bout.

Groups of Alethophiles formed in Stettin also and in other German cities.

A germ, as we can see, of the German *Aufklärung*, which yet retained something of the spirit of secret society or even sect out of which it was growing and developing. Interpreted in the light of the *Hexalogus Alethophilorum* and the letters of von Manteuffel, the motto which the society had chosen, *Sapere aude*, acquired in effect a new meaning and was already becoming the motto of a definite urge towards the spreading of enlightenment. The coin bearing this inscription was now circulating in Saxony and other German provinces, was illustrated in the numismatic review published in Nuremberg by J. D. Köhler and, even more, was beginning to arouse some discussion and conflict.

One of the most famous engravers in Europe at that time, the medallist of the Republic of Geneva, Jean Dassier, published under the pseudonym 'Alethophilus' a series of articles of art criticism and other topics in the *Historische Münz-Belustigung*. He felt that the information given on the leaflet distributed with Count von Manteuffel's medal was a piece of boasting. He had read there that the Berlin society had taken as a model an ancient coin which depicted Socrates and Plato joined together as Leibniz and Wolff were on the modern one. But Dassier maintained that he had never heard of such a coin. He then added: 'I am amazed that the man who devised this medal should have taken as an inscription to place above his Minerva: *Sapere aude*. This could be taken very badly by anyone wishing to attack him and is capable of being interpreted in quite a different sense from that which was probably meant.' He would have done better to use another quotation from Horace: *Sapiens uno minor est Jove*.

It seems probable, indeed very likely, given the curiosity that Horace's words were arousing, that one would be able to find them here and there in documents of the years immediately following 1740, when the words just quoted were published, but we do not come across any such references before 1767, when a book entitled *De cultibus magicis* by Konstantin Franz de Cauz was published in Vienna by Trattner. After a lengthy preface numbered separately, at the top of page one we see an engraving of a medal: no longer a bust but the whole figure of Minerva, seated, with a lance resting on her right arm and a book in her left hand. With her are the shield, other books and the owl, and she is wearing a helmet where we search in vain for the image of the two German philosophers. The goddess is considerably more attractive than before. We are no longer in the age of Frederick William I but of Maria Theresa. The motto is still the same: *Sapere aude*.

The author, de Cauz (which we also find written de Kauz, de Khauz), scholar, historian and jurist, had originally concerned himself with biographies of learned men, from the fourteenth century to the seventeenth, collected in 1755 in a work to which he gave the title *Attempt at a history of Austrian scholars*. A year later, under the influence of Martini and other Viennese jurists, he published *De scriptura sacra tamquam prima juris ecclesiastici fonte*, then to go on to a career as professor and high official of the *Bücherhof-commission*. He was a member of some distinction of a society of learned men in Vienna which arose around 1760 and to which the greatest of the Austrian reformers of the period, Sonnenfels, also belonged.

The book is one of the most interesting pieces of writing to come out of the polemic against superstition in the latter half of the eighteenth century, at a time when enlightened absolutism was at its height. De Cauz takes up previous discussions of demonologists and summarises them broadly, making particular reference to those, like F. Spee and Ch. Thomasius, who had attempted to cancel out or at least diminish the harmful effects of ancestral prejudices and superstitions and recalling the discussion which, from 1748 onwards, had flared up among G. Tartarotti, S. Maffei, G. R. Carli and other Italian and foreign scholars, on the subject of witches and magicians. In some ways the book represents the conclusion of the dispute which had had as its origin the work of Tartarotti and the academy of Rovereto (de Cauz himself was a member and bore the name Quirinus), but the practical aim behind it was by this time increasingly obvious. With the mentality of a jurist and the spirit of a reformer, the author's intention was to support, publicise and justify the measures which the Empress was putting into force to combat the most dangerous and fearful superstitions: the vampires of Bohemia and the demons, witches and ghosts in other lands of her dominions. The second part of the work was thus composed of two chapters, one *De noxiis effectibus opinionis artis magicae in processu criminali* and the other *De adplicatione doctrinae hactenus traditae ad jurisprudentiae legislatoriae illustrationem*. In spite of the weight of the juridical and erudite apparatus in the midst of which von Cauz moved, it can certainly be said that his book was worthy of the motto *Sapere aude*.

To find further words inspired by this motto, still in the same period, we have to look at Poland under Stanislas Augustus, at his attempts at reform and that atmosphere of a very special kind of enlightenment to be found in his monarchical republic, which Jean Fabre described so effectively in his *Stanislas-Auguste Poniatowski et l'Europe des lumières*. In 1765 the King had a medal coined, as a sign of gratitude and homage, in honour of Stanislas Konarski, who was perhaps the greatest of the Polish reformers in the middle of the century. On this medal, next to the image of the learned ecclesiastic, was written: *Sapere auso*. The Florentine review, *Novelle letterarie*, publishing Konarski's obituary on 3 September 1773, admirably illustrated this fact:

> Even warlike Poland was able to savour the pleasure of good studies and useful science as a result of the untiring devotion to his task of a famous priest of the 'Scuole Pie' who died last August at the age of seventy-three. We are referring to the well-known Stanislas Konarski, who was the first to introduce into his country the study of geometry, of pure Latin, criticism, languages and good scientific methods. We know that having to oppose the tyranny of ingrained barbarity and blindness in that enormous kingdom, in which a few, perhaps to further their own evil ends, kept the vast majority of intellects ensnared, caused him much toil and tribulation . . . The present King of Poland, Stanislas Augustus, justly had a gold medal made bearing the image of such a worthy servant of God and of the works composed by him for the public good, with the characteristic inscription *Sapere auso*.

'C'est l'audace', commented Jean Fabre, 'qui va donner à Konarski sa grandeur, lui permettre de vivre cette geste intellectuelle au bout de laquelle il rejoindra son siècle et permettra à ses compatriotes d'y accéder de plain-pied'.

Konarski's life and work were indeed of great interest: educated in his youth in the Paris of Fontenelle and Rollin, a pilgrim to Rome, Dresden and Vienna, a pamphleteer in his own country during a particularly difficult period for Poland in the eighteenth century, he became a diplomat in Paris and Luneville and finally found his own path when he became the reformer of his country's educational system. Amid the political factions and power struggles he always showed strength and determination, but, to quote further what Jean Fabre wrote about him:

> 'Cet homme vraiment vertueux' n'avait eu à sa disposition qu'un génie trop pauvre pour faire la synthèse de tant d'antimonies. Il lui restait la gloire d'avoir essayé. *Sapere auso*: pour Stanislas-Auguste, le drame de Konarski était surtout d'ordre intellectuel, le drame d'un homme dépassé par son rôle, d'un esprit embarassé par ses propres conquêtes. Avec Konarski, la vieille Pologne humaniste est partie à la poursuite du xviiie siècle et a tenté de rattraper en une génération plus d'un siècle perdu. Si d'autres y réussirent mieux, ce fut, peut-être, en sacrifiant trop délibérément au modernisme un passé qui avait

marqué d'une si profonde empreinte la physionomie intellectuelle de Konarski.

The allusion to Horace's expression had thus once more seemed obvious and natural to express a moment in the fight to affirm the spirit of enlightenment.

When, a decade later, Kant declared that *Sapere aude* was the motto of the *Aufklärung* itself, the words of the Latin poet had reached the zenith of their fortune in the eighteenth century. Having come into common use they can be found, for example, on the frontispiece of a book which appeared anonymously with the place names Frankfurt and Leipzig in 1788. Entitled *History of the papal nuncios* in Germany, it was one of the very numerous works of Friedrich Karl von Moser, the writer who, following the example of his father, had begun to treat somewhat esoteric topics of public law and cameralism, as for example, *Treatise on court etiquette, or those rules of polite behaviour of high society which do not have their origin in the ceremonial founded upon agreements or tradition,* or *Thoughts on the correct procedure of chancelleries,* or *Documented history of forms of address of court functionaries and the disputes which have arisen in this connection* (more than 400 pages long). Later, however, after being caught up in the conflicts between the German princelings and the Empire, persecuted and forced to wander from place to place, he ended up by advancing a line of political thought which, though by no means original, was at least characteristic of the revival of imperial ideology in Germany in the latter half of the eighteenth century. His work *The Master and the servant* (1759), like that *On the German national spirit* (1765), though devoid of originality and acumen, are nevertheless the expression of two significant moments in the political discussion in Germany. With the passing of the decades, Moser had allowed his Enlightenment polemic to become increasingly open and explicit, particularly after 1784, when he founded and directed periodicals which made a considerable impression, such as *Das patriotische Archiv für Deutschland* and, later, the *Allgemeine Literatur-Zeitung*. To this period belonged the book which bore the motto *Sapere aude*. A weighty accumulation of facts on the history of the papal nuncios in Germany, this work contained the documentation and the essence of an age-old polemic to which Moser gave a slant no longer explicable in terms of Protestantism but quite clearly attributable to the Enlightenment. It was no mere chance that he took as his other motto the words of Lessing: 'Not all those who deride their own chains are really free.' His preface began with an attack on Rome, both in style and spirit deliberately reminiscent of Voltaire. 'In the last two centuries Italy has sent us atheists and Machiavellis, Latin depravities and Jesuits; the good and the bad which we have received from that direction are lemons, oranges, macaroni, relics, the Genoese lottery, castrati and papal nuncios.' Protestantism did not suffice as a means of combating all these, especially the last. Only 'love of the patria' could supply the remedy. Only to patriots was it not a matter of indifference 'whether in Germany it were day or night. Patriotism has no religion as history has none . . .'

Thus Horace's motto had come to designate the world of feelings and ideas in a Europe which was moving towards the French Revolution. It had come a long way since the days of the Society of Alethophiles. We do not claim to have mentioned here more than a few of the stages on that journey. Others will certainly come to fill in the gaps, to increase the number of stages and bring them closer together. But to have trodden this path, however haltingly, will perhaps be of some use in providing an answer to the ever pertinent question : *Was ist Aufklärung?*

Oriental Despotism*

THE history of the terms *despot* and *despotism* up until the beginning of the eighteenth century has been the subject of a recent study by R. Koebner. The conclusions of his ample and painstaking research are both fascinating and important. From the very beginning, Plato and Aristotle, these terms are associated, on the one hand, with the relationship between master and slave and, on the other, with the forms of Oriental political organisation. The medieval translators of Aristotle attempted to communicate the original sense of the terms by using such words as *despoticum, monarchia despotica*, and *despotizare*. At the beginning of the fifteenth century, a Dominican preacher, one Frate Giordano, spoke of 'Herod, who ruled in manner despotical,' and Nicolas Oresme, echoing Lucan (*Pharsalia*, vii, 442–5) in his commentary on Aristotle, spoke of the peoples of the East who are accustomed to slavery and in consequence submit to a 'prince despotique'. 'Et per aventure nont pas memoire que leur pays feust oncques en liberte.' The humanists, however, were unable to accept

* Translated by Lotte F. Jacoby and Ian M. Taylor.

terms so far removed from the purity of classical Latin as *despotes*, *despoticus*, and *despotizare*. Leonardo Bruni, for example, used *dominator* and *dominatio* in their place, and these terms became widely accepted. French writers, like Loys le Roy, and later Bodin, attempted to translate the classical concept in terms of medieval experience, which was that of *seignorial* rule based on the relationship between the seigneur and the serf. And so Bodin spoke of *monarchie seigneuriale*:

Il y a encores en l'Asie et en l'Ethiopie, et mesmes en Europe les Princes de Tartarie et de Moschovie, desquels les subjects s'apellent Chopes, c'est à dire Esclaves, ainsi que nous lisons en l'histoire de Moschovie et pour ceste cause le Roy des Turcs est appellé le grand Seigneur, non pas tant pour l'estendue de pais, car le Roy Catholique en a dix fois autant, que pour estre aucunement seigneur des personnes et des biens. (*Six livres de la République* [Lyon, 1579], 189–191).

It remained for Hobbes to go back to the original terms and speak once more of 'bodies politic *patrimonial* and *despotical*', of a '*kingdom despotical*', using the concept as part of the foundation for his doctrine. As R. Koebner says: 'To him [Hobbes] despotic monarchy is neither "barbarian" nor "oriental"; it originates in quite a normal, "natural" way . . .' *Despotic*, for Hobbes, defined a government established by conquest. From Hobbes and the discussion touched off by his work, the term returned to France, where we have it, for example, from the pen of Sorbière and of La Bruyère, and where in the second half of the seventeenth century it was to become charged with the incipient polemics against the absolutism of Louis XIV. The famous pamphlet *Les Soupirs de la France esclave* (1689–90) sets out, in fact, to describe 'les tristes effets de la puissance arbitraire et despotique de la cour de France'. The comparison of French absolutism with the 'tyrannie du Turc' and with the 'puissance du Grand Seigneur' becomes commonplace and is often to be found as a motif in polemics. Here again we find two essential elements characterising the despotic régime which had apparently laid hold of France: 'que les sujets du royaume sont dans la servitude, qu'ils n'ont rien à eux.' It is then, and only then, at the very end of the seventeenth century that the term *despotisme* comes into being as if to sum up the hostility of all those opposed to the policy of the Roi Soleil. Chapters lxiv and lxv of the *Réponse aux questions d'un provincial* by Pierre Bayle (1704) are entitled 'Du Despotisme', and pass in review all the problems raised by Hobbes, Sorbière, and the other seventeenth-century writers in general. Of the two central themes which we have seen emerge from the very beginning of the concept of despotism—the absence of political liberty and a distribution of property which reduces the subjects to serfdom—it is the former which prevails here. We may therefore assume that tyranny rather than servitude was what counted for the polemicists of the end of the seventeenth century. Indeed, Bayle concludes his chapters by remarking: 'Après tout, soyez assuré, Monsieur, qu'il n'y a rien de plus doux que la liberté. On n'en peut pas dire comme on l'a dit de la guerre, qu'elle n'a des agrémens que pour ceux qui ne la connoissent pas. *Dulce bellum inexpertis.* Plus on la goûte, plus la veut-on goûter. Elle a principalement des charmes pour ceux qui ont éprouvé le joug de la servitude.' The concept of *despotism*, as opposed to that of liberty, had finally come into being; its content was essentially political rather than social.

Amplified by this new word the concept of despotic rule entered its continuous political career in the last years of Louis XIV's reign. The deficiencies of the régime manifested by the War of the Spanish Succession had caused the malcontents of the foregoing decade to become a secret opposition group which prepared for the accession of a new king. To members of this group —Fénelon, St Simon, Boulainvillers—'despotisme' was the name of a system which ought to be mended . . . (R. Koebner).

It is enough to look forward fifty years, to 1748, the year in which the *Esprit des lois* first appeared, and to open it at the passage which deals so insistently with the concept of despotism, to realise what a long way we have come. Liberty is still the essential antithesis to despotic fear. 'Il faut de la crainte dans un gouvernement despotique . . . On ne peut parler sans frémir de ce gouvernement monstrueux.' Montesquieu, however, in his great work synthesising the political wisdom of past ages, seems also to have taken into consideration the second of the elements, which from earliest times was implicit in the term *despotism*, or in those which substituted for it. It is not only governments which are despotic; society may be so too. It is not only disregard for or negation of the law of the land which characterises this type of rule, but it is also the violation of the laws of society and the transformation of men into instruments of the will of the despot. 'Dans les pays despotiques, où l'on est déjà sous l'esclavage politique, l'esclavage civil est plus tolérable qu'ailleurs. Chacun y doit être assez content d'y avoir sa subsistence et la vie. Ainsi, la condition de l'esclave n'y est guère plus à charge que la condition du sujet.'

Montesquieu had elaborated his concept of despotism out of all previous discussions on freedom, overlordship, sovereignty, civil bondage, serfdom, oriental practices. If these elements are considered together—and we may refer now to the analysis of them by Robert Shackleton, today's greatest expert on Montesquieu—the *Esprit des lois* may once again take its place as the turning-point of eighteenth-century political ideas. Indeed, after its appearance, the elements synthesised there were to break up and become dispersed once more.

It was Voltaire who anatomised dryly the purely gratuitous and imaginary attributes which had come to be associated with the idea of despotic absolutism. 'Nous attachons à ce titre l'idée d'un fou féroce, qui n'écoute que son caprice; d'un barbare qui fait ranger devant lui ses courtisans prosternés, et qui, pour se divertir, ordonne à ses satellites d'étrangler à droite et d'empaler à gauche.' Absolutism, 'enlightened despotism', as we call it nowadays, was much too serious and important a matter to be confused with the whims of Oriental potentates. And, in fact, the true nature of Chinese, Turkish, and Indian rulers was very different from that which Montesquieu and his followers had claimed. What really interested Voltaire was the relationship between absolutism and liberty, and he was eager to disencumber the discussion of all superfluous matter.

In so doing Voltaire opened a road which most of the physiocrats were to tread. For them despotism meant a particularly conscious and energetic form of absolutism which was in conflict with the constitutional assemblies, the magistrates, the corporations, or the cities which had usurped the powers of the monarch. In this conflict despotism was merely attempting to re-establish and enforce the natural legal code, the laws of nature which rightfully should regulate economic and social existence. This was the 'legal despotism' talked about so much during the period which was decisive for the political activity of the physiocrats; in other words, during the last ten years of the reign of Louis XV, from the end of the Seven Years War until 1774. Thanks to Quesnay and to several of his followers this 'legal despotism' assumed the exotic colouring peculiar to the Chinese empire. The absolutism of the Far East was now extolled as the type of legal despotism, in direct contradiction to the traditional concept of Oriental tyranny. We have here, in fact, the complete reversal of a concept which had slowly matured from the time of Aristotle to that of Montesquieu. While this traditional concept had fundamentally been a mixture and a confusion of political intent with social structure, the physiocrats used it to mean, quite precisely, the idea of a total disengagement of government from economic laws; and the absolute respect on the part of the ruler for the objective validity of such laws as naturally govern society. The use of the term by the *économistes* was so paradoxical that it gave rise to all manner of polemics and violent discussions, while men like Turgot, very close to the physiocrats in their philosophy, refused to accept it and even condemned it. The result was that it never became current in politics—also because of the political defeat suffered by the physiocrats—but remained the symbol of a lost cause and a vain attempt. Gorani, in his book *Il vero dispotismo* (1770), tried, for his part, to evolve a theory concerning the new workings of absolute monarchy in central and eastern European states, where, in fact, this type of institution was of greater importance than in France. But from the point of view of terminology at least, this attempt must also count as a failure. 'Enlightened despotism' is an expression derived from the vocabulary of the historian and not from that of the men of politics and *philosophes* of the second half of the eighteenth century. Nor, in and about the year 1770, were other paradoxes wanting to be grafted onto that first propounded by the physiocrats. The apologies for despotism, penned by Linguet, were a curious symptom of discussion and crisis but were not, for this reason, any the less destined to wither quickly and to disappear without leaving any lasting trace.

The main direction of the development of the term *despotism* was the one which came from Montesquieu. It is explicitly to Montesquieu if but to contradict him, that Nicolas-Antoine Boulanger referred in his *Recherches sur les origines du despotisme oriental* (1761), a work in which, with great energy of thought, he examined the historical and religious origins of the initial confusion of subject with serf.

Montesquieu's ideas concerning despotism were taken up again shortly after by another writer, this time to examine, not the early origins, but the present reality and to put it to the test by comparing it with actual conditions in the East. And so it was Anquetil-Duperron, an explorer and traveller of remarkable character, who initiated the concluding phase of eighteenth-century discussion concerning the term *despotism*. From the very beginning, as we have seen, this term had been associated with the East. But was it really true that, east of Europe, monarchies existed which were founded upon political abuse and upon a total lack of any guarantee for the property of the subject? Was there any basis, in fact, for this notion of Oriental despotism which had become so widespread and deeply rooted with the centuries?

Abraham-Hyacinte Anquetil-Duperron had the advantage of having been in Asia for many years and was one of the pioneers

in the discovery of the ancient civilisations of Iran and India. A
enormous thirst for knowledge had led him to leave Paris and li
in India from 1755 to 1761. His first task on returning to Euro
was to publish the fruit of his discovery, the *Zend-Avesta*, preface
by an account of his travels in India. But immediately afterwar
he seems to have been troubled by another consideration. H
countrymen, and generally speaking all the men of the West, ente
tained incorrect notions concerning both the religious ideolog
and the early history of the Asiatic peoples. They were also m
taken in their views on the social and political régimes of Indi
Turkey, Persia, and Asia in general. And so Anquetil-Duperro
filled a fat notebook with polemics, notes, observations and quot
tions which he then called: *Le despotisme consideré dans les tr*
états ou il passe pour être le plus absolu, la Turquie, la Perse
l'Indoustan. Ouvrage dans lequel on prouve: (1) Que la maniè
dont jusqu'içi on a représenté le gouvernement despotique ne pe
qu'en donner une idée absolument fausse, (2) Que dans les tr
états qui viennent d'être nommés il y a un code de loix écrites q
obligent le prince aussi que les sujets, (3) Que dans ces trois éta
les particuliers ont des propriétés, ou biens meubles et immeubl
dont ils jouissent librement.

He was evidently convinced of the great importance of h
claims, and from the outset seems to have been persuaded that h
observations could be of particular importance for the coloni
policy not only of France but of the other European countries to
The term, Oriental despotism, he maintained, was not merely
symbol to be used by Westerners, versed in the literature of trave
in the Orient, in their attempts to oppose, reform, or even justi
the absolute monarchs of their own countries. Chardin, Tavernie
and others who had supplied Montesquieu with his basic inform
tion, could not have been simply instruments in the argumentatio
of the Roi Soleil and his successors on freedom in Europe or c
the need for monarchs to use their power in order to establi
even better and more natural economic laws. Colonial expeditio
rivalries, and wars made it important to know whether Orient
despotism, this two-faced monster made up of political oppressi
and social serfdom, really existed. Anquetil-Duperron knew the
countries at first hand and felt himself to be in a position to pr
vide adequate answers to these new and diverse questions. He se
his manuscript to the famous Comte de Vergennes, Louis XV
foreign Minister, that he might meditate thereupon.

Montesquieu was the principal, we might say and the onl
object of his polemic. Anquetil went back to the sources up
which the author of the *Esprit des lois* had drawn.

Mon étonnement a été extrême à la vue du portrait que les voyageurs font des peuples de l'Asie, portrait tantôt de fantaisie, tantôt d'intérêt ou de prévention . . . Sur le rapport de ces voyageurs . . . on a fait une espèce particulière de gouvernement existant sous le nom de despotique : point de loix fixes, point de propriétés dans ce gouvernement.

Montesquieu had edited these impressions and accounts to suit his own purposes. He was the very type and model of all those publicists who 'sur le rapport mal compris de ces voyageurs' had formulated 'un système de despotisme qui n'existe réellement nulle part'. In Asia there were slaves, it was true, but not everybody was one. The laws were violated in Asia, but so they were in other places; and this was no reason for supposing that they did not exist. The system of taxation was different in the East (and not necessarily worse : 'En Perse, ci l'on en croit Chardin, il n'y a ni taxes sur les personnes, ni taille'). This did not mean that there did not exist a fundamental distinction between the property of the subject and that of the sovereign. While with regard to natural law, in the case of prisoners of war, for example, only shortly before, as Anquetil-Duperron pointed out, during the troubles in India, 'les Marates en 1775, donnoient aux Européens des leçons bien cruelles de droit des gens'. And, finally, the capacity for conducting a foreign policy worthy of the name was certainly not lacking in the annals of Asian history, no matter what Montesquieu might have written to the contrary. Economically speaking, agriculture and trade flourished in India, and contracts were as safe in Asia as anywhere else.

The truth of the matter, as Anquetil-Duperron pointed out in the introductory part of his manuscript, was that the concept of despotism had simply been made to serve as the instrument of justification for the oppression practised by the Europeans in Asia. He dedicated his book : 'Aux peuples de l'Indoustan,' and concluded :

Falloit-il que le bruit de vos richesses pénétrât dans un climat où les besoins factices n'ont point de bornes ! Bientôt de nouveaux étrangers abordent à vos côtes. Hôtes incommodes, tout ce qu'ils touchent leur appartient . . . La voix de l'équité ne peut se faire entendre. Au moins, malheureux Indiens, peut être apprendrez vous qu'en deux cents ans un Européen qui vous a vus, qui à vécu avec vous, à osé réclamer en votre faveur, et présenter au Tribunal de l'Univers vos droits blessés, ceux de l'Humanité flétris par un vil intérêt.

Quite clearly the indignation of Anquetil-Duperron was not intended to remain shut in a drawer or to be read by the Comte de Vergennes alone. In 1778 Marc-Michel Rey of Amsterdam, publisher of the *Philosophes*, published a quarto edition of the work, enlarged, corrected and revised. The title was no longer concerned with despotism in particular, but modified to *Législation orientale*, as the author thought that so it might 'présenter avec plus de dignité et d'intérêt l'objet qu'il s'étoit proposé'. And in this edition he extended his wrath beyond Montesquieu, to other French writers who had dealt with despotism during that period.

In the work of Nicolas-Antoine Boulanger whose *Recherches sur l'origine du despotisme oriental* had been published posthumously in 1761, he found a concept of the very type against which his efforts had been directed. Despotism for Boulanger was a classification, a moment in human history, and not an actual social system. 'Si l'on y prend bien garde, son ouvrage est plus théologique que politique', as Anquetil points out, and goes on to say: 'Quoiqu'il fasse mention des différentes sortes de gouvernements, qu'il insiste sur le despotisme, on voit que l'origine des religions qui dominent sur la surface du globe est proprement l'objet qu'il se propose d'éclaircir.' Up to a point this was true, for Boulanger did, in fact, tend to go after the historical and religious bases of despotism and so provide a better authenticated justification for it, than Montesquieu had done.

Not only Boulanger but other of his contemporaries had attempted to find—not without success nor without a considerable degree of insight—some peculiarly significant revelation of the religious spirit in general, and of primitive religions in particular in the forms of Oriental despotism. Amongst these was Guerin du Rocher. But Anquetil-Duperron was not in a mood to comprehend this fertile amalgamation of the history of religion with that of political systems: his task was to compare all this theorising with the facts, and particularly with the facts of political and social history. In consequence, much of his book was concerned with showing that, although there was certainly no lack of tyrannical spirit in the East, one could not with justice designate these governments as despotic in the true sense of the word; that is, without laws and without property rights. In this he drew on his own experience and that of others, such as Niebuhr, Dow, Rhoe, Ricaut, de Chinon, and a host of travellers and missionaries to the East.

It is typical that it was this second aspect of Anquetil-Duperron's work, the structure of society, which received the most attention. In disproof of Boulainvillers, who had maintained that 'la barbare loi de l'Orient anéantit la propriété des biens', of the many writers who had asserted that property in Turkey was nothing but 'des propriétés précaires', of the travellers who had related that in

India 'toutes les terres dans l'Empire du Mogol appartiennent au prince', or of those who, as Bernier, still insisted that 'la Turquie, la Perse et l'Indoustan ont ôté *le mien et le tien* a l'égard des fonds de terre', Anquetil-Duperron quoted laws, provisions, and contracts, and described customs and habits in order to demonstrate the actual existence of property rights. He went further in fact, pointing out that just as the idea of despotism had served to justify the violent intervention of Europeans in the East, so the conviction that no private property existed there had proved of considerable use in supporting the claims of those who favoured the confiscation of all native territory. He found what he considered an excellent example of just such a pretext in the writings of the Englishman, Alexander Dow. 'Ce procédé seroit juste dans le 18ᵉ siècle? Toutes les terres d'un pays conquis appartiennent-elles *en propre* au conquérant? . . . C'est ainsi que les droits les plus sacrés disparoissent aux jeux d'un vil intérêt. Ne nous faisons pas d'illusion, François, Anglois! je plaide içi la cause de l'homme . . .' The conquerors' line of reasoning was by now quite clear : 'Le despotisme est le gouvernement de ces contrées. Le Souverain se dit propriétaire de tous les biens de ces sujets. Devenons ce souverain, et nous voilà maîtres de toutes les terres de l'Indoustan. Ainsi raisonne la passion avide. Mais elle se cache sous des dehors qu'il lui faut arracher.'

The energy and ardour with which Anquetil-Duperron attempted to redefine the true nature of despotism explain why later on he was often to reopen the discussion and promulgate his viewpoint. In his *Recherches historique et géographique sur l'Inde* he extended his attacks even to such authors—and in particular John Dalrymple —as had maintained that in many parts of India the 'terres sont la propriété de la *communauté*' and that in no case was there 'la propriété individuelle des terres, la culture de celles qui appartiennent à chaque village se faisant par la communauté du village et le produit étant (ensuite) partagé en certaines portions'. For Anquetil-Duperron such statements were simple 'assertions sans preuves'. 'Cette propriété de communauté n'existe pas dans l'Inde.'

A great many years later, after the Revolution, he was to come back to the problem once again. In 1802, the by now seventy-year-old Anquetil-Duperron had accepted the invitation to edit a French translation of the *Viaggio alle Indie Orientali umiliato alla Santità di N. S. Papa Pio Sesto da Fra Paolino da San Bartolomeo carmelitano scalzo*, already published in Rome in 1796. The French edition had hardly gone to press when, in 1805, he died. But in the Appendix to the Third Volume, from page 509 on, one might read once more his *Observations tendantes: (1) à confirmer ce qu'il a été dit dans la législation orientale et dans les recherches historiques et géographiques sur l'Inde pour prouver l'existance de la propriété individuelle, foncière et mobilière dans ce pays, (2) pour établir le même point pour l'Egypte, régie par les lois de l'Empire Ottoman.*

Anquetil-Duperron here answers the criticisms which Father Paolino da S. Bartolomeo had directed against him in several of his works. According to the missionary, the French orientalist 'claims that private property is to be encountered among the heathen Indians. We, however, would say that M. Anquetil du Perron too often allows himself to be carried away by his spite against the English, and that he sometimes denies the truth of things too certain to admit of denial.' In his *India Christiana* too, he had pointed out that 'contra communem sensum et quotidianam exsperientiam Indis hominibus, etiam privatis, jus absolutum et proprietatem agrorum mendaciter adscrivere conatur'. Anquetil answers him with a long disquisition concerning the concept of property and the application thereof in Eastern countries. It was not strictly true that in India, Persia, Tartary, Turkey, or Egypt, the people were 'vendus physiquement et pour toujours' to their sovereigns, 'supposition impossible en soi, et contredite par l'histoire de toutes les nations.'

> J'ai toujours assez bien présumé de l'homme pour croire que nulle part il ne se dépouilloit jamais absolument de son droit de propriété réelle : et je puis dire que la lecture de l'histoire et des voyages faits dans les quatres parties du monde n'a fait que confirmer à mes yeux une vérité que je crois essentielle au repos du genre humain.

But what was most interesting to Anquetil-Duperron was the discussion which arose with the English, whose colonial policy made it indispensable to understand the true nature of Oriental despotism. A few years after having published the *Législation orientale* he had received a letter from Charles William Boughton Rouse, who had also sent him a copy of his *Dissertation concerning the landed property of Bengal*, published in London in 1791. It was a problem which could not fail to interest 'a person who has already discussed the general question of property under the Asiatic governments with the greatest ability : so that, if you had been possessed of sufficient materials, I am confident you would have rendered any further demonstration superfluous . . .' He too was convinced that England should give up her 'tyrannic notion of exclusive property in the lands of Bengal'. He had said it clearly in his book, rendering to Anquetil-Duperron the homage which was due to him from 'every friend of justice and humanity for under-

taking to vindicate the great empires of Turkey, Persia, and Indostan from the character of barbarism that has been ascribed to
them, and reprobating as they deserve the despotic projects of those
speculators, who would deny to any part of mankind the blessing
of permanent property'.

After all, concluded Rouse, was not this dominion of the prince
over the property of his subjects, held to be characteristic of
Oriental despotism, very similar perhaps to that right of demesne,
that feudal overlordship which the law allowed the medieval rulers
of old? The comparison might even be taken further, when one
noted how property rights in general had first appeared in Germany, the very stronghold of imperial practice. 'In drawing a
parallel out of Germany for the execrable doctrines of despotism,
I discover with great satisfaction a parallel in the same empire for
the rise of hereditary possessions and honours.' Rouse then went on
to quote Montesquieu, Robertson, and Victor Riqueti de Mirabeau
in support of his views on the evolution of property rights. He
was convinced that such evolution held both for the East and the
West. And so the concepts of despotism, after having served as a
weapon (and a two-edged one at that, as we have seen in the case
of the colonial powers) in the hands of those who opposed absolutism, or attempted to reduce it to a theory, now tended to
become absorbed, at least partially, into the ever-increasing flow
of anti-feudal polemics—particularly as regards its social content.

Nor did Rouse's work pass without comment in England itself.
James Grant discussed the legal aspects of the question in his *An
Inquiry into the nature of zemindary tenures* (London, 1791) and
it persisted in all debates on Indian policy of the time. But what
mattered to Rouse was, to quote from another letter of his to
Anquetil-Duperron, the reaffirmation of 'the existence of land-
property in the Asiatic nations as a *radical principle*, which had
been denied by Mr Grant'.

And so the problem passed into the nineteenth century, where it
was to continue to enjoy no little importance. Here would be
another fascinating subject for close attention. From the English
Radicals to Marx and Engels, from Mill to Plekhanov, the term
Oriental despotism was to remain big with political and ideological
implications. Certain elements of this later development appear in
the pages of the latest writer to have tackled the problem: Karl
A. Wittfogel, *Oriental despotism. A comparative study of total
power* (New Haven, 1957). It is to him and to his bibliography that
we would refer the reader at this point, even if, rather than a piece
of historical research, it is yet another attempt to crystallise into
a theory the concept of Oriental despotism.

Socialism

IT is by no means unknown that the term 'socialist' was already
in use in Italy in the eighteenth century. It is to be found, for
example, in the *Italian etymological dictionary* of C. Battisti and
G. Alessio. But it is worth the trouble to make a closer examination of the setting in which this word came to be used, the meaning which it had and the way in which it began to circulate in
eighteenth-century Italy.

It occurs for the first time, so far as we know, in 1765, in the
*Notes and observations on the book entitled Of crimes and punish-
ments* by Ferdinando Facchinei. What a strange character was
this friar from Vallombrosa. Following his trail and seeing him
appear and disappear amongst the most diverse intellectual attitudes
makes one want to ask at times with Father Bolgeni : 'What kind of
madman is he anyway?' But there is a thread, at least a psychological one, which seems to link these disparate attitudes and can
lead us into some corners of the Age of Enlightenment which are
the most inaccessible and remote, but not for this the least curious.

Facchinei's family probably came from Corfù, but he was born
in Forlì in the Romagna somewhere around 1725. In 1750 we find
him in Vallombrosa, a young rebellious monk with a thirst for
knowledge, his heart full of sarcasm and scorn for the ignorance
and oppression which surrounded him, eager only to learn foreign
languages, to study science and mathematics and read books which
he knew were anything but orthodox. His greatest friend was
Gabriel Cramer, the mathematician from Geneva. When barely
twenty-five, Facchinei had annotated 'especially the works of
Melanchthon, Beza and Erasmus . . . and I would make them known
if I did not fear that this is the last which would be heard of me',
as he wrote in an ardent and desperate plea for help and assistance
from Giovanni Lami. 'I have always had to study in secret here',
he said, 'because otherwise they would have stoned me.' Sickly all
his life, he had devoted himself feverishly to the composition of a
work which he was sure would bring him glory and freedom, a
Life of Newton, written with all the enthusiasm of a novice and
with an outstanding knowledge of English language and literature.
In a letter of dedication, dated 10 November 1749, he told of his
attempts to translate and make known the works of Newton. In-
voking their authority, his superiors had raised this objection :
'Do you not know that it is not even permissible to read the works

of English and Dutch philosophers, let alone praise them?' He, like so many others in those years, had by this time been branded with 'the infamous and disgraceful title of heretic and deist'. Very soon disaster struck. Imprisoned and treated in such a way that 'the pains of the world could pass for delights in comparison with what [he had] suffered in the dungeon' where they had thrown him, he was eventually tried and acquitted 'at the price of a confession completely unworthy of me', as he wrote to Lami on 20 September 1751. He had walked out of his monastery without saying goodbye and taken refuge with some other monks in the hope of being able to begin his life again. 'A plague on whoever invented monks. I, born free and by nature quite opposed to all these works of the devil . . .', he said a few days later. But Lami, the learned Florentine journalist to whom these words were addressed, did not reply. He had no respect for him. His *Life of Newton* seemed to him an 'abortion'. He was obviously horrified by the rebelliousness and violence of the young friar.

For eight years Facchinei disappears from view. Then at the end of 1759, we find a letter from him to Lami, written in Novara. His words still have a sarcastic ring but by this time they have become more gentle and his irony is no longer directed against the world in which he lives. On the contrary, he has joined the ranks of the satisfied and the prudent. He smiles, or rather grins, at the shocked reaction which his Florentine correspondent could not fail to have on seeing him in the orthodox camp, among the friars. His rebellion had turned into realistic cynicism. On 14 November, in the last letter which he sent to Lami, he wrote: 'You will see that when I was in a position to be able to write real things, I was dreaming, and now that I am good for nothing but dreaming, I am really publishing something . . .' His ardent wish for literary fame had at last begun to come true. But it was not his *Life of Newton* nor his commentaries on Erasmus which had become known, but a *Letter concerning the physical cause of dreams*. And even this was not without numerous obstacles and difficulties on account of the 'incredible strictness' of the Piedmontese censorship.

The *Letter* showed a pronounced taste for German culture, Leibniz, Wolff, Formey, Haller. This was something which was to remain with him. 'At the moment Germany is the country where the best methods of scientific study are employed', he was to state in his *Essay on a new method of teaching science to children*. There is nothing original to be found in this *Letter* which, on the contrary, displays a predominantly provincial, academic, mundane tone.

Much the same could be said of his contributions to Abbé Jacopo

Rebellini's *La Minerva*. These are articles which often translate into oratorical terms, thereby stifling them, themes which were the burning questions of the Enlightenment in those years, as for example the *Discourse whereby it is proved where happiness is to be found* (1765). Nevertheless his culture is always broad and well-informed. In this *Discourse* there appear 'the great president Montesquiù' and the 'famous Mr d'Allambert'. And he was not insensitive to the society which surrounded him. In 1764 he delivered a speech 'On the opening of a new Agricultural Society which was being instituted in Brescia', He well knew that Italy was passing through 'times of extreme shortage', of terrible famine. He looked to England as a model of agrarian policy and similarly stressed all that had been done in France by Mirabeau and the Agrarian Societies etc. In other regions of Italy, Tuscany and the South, he pointed to the example of Montelatici, Intieri and Genovesi. Locally, in Brescia, there had been much 'opposition' and many 'difficulties' standing in the way of 'your nascent Society'. But with warm words Facchinei attempted to overcome them. He seemed to become a good propagandist of slow progress and of a slow, moderate introduction of enlightenment.

On reading the works of Verri and Beccaria, his spirit was troubled again and his impulse towards hatred and revenge was aroused once more. Even many, many years later, when the situation had changed profoundly and he had every reason to tone down his violent polemic against the men of the Enlightenment, he still could not manage to forgive them. His adversaries continued to appear to him as persons who did not know how to coordinate mind and heart, reason and will. He noted in particular the influence of Milanese thought on Venice. He looked around him and a profound rage drove him to attack those who declared themselves to be reformers and yet who seemed to him to be incapable of understanding the practical consequences of the ideas which they professed.

> There were in Venice [he wrote in 1797] three or four thousand scientists, and at least as many in the provinces, who knew almost by heart the works of Montesquieu, Rousseau and the book *Of crimes and punishments*, read by all with real enthusiasm and reprinted several times in the presses of your capital, although it contained more than forty propositions which declared indirectly that your government was ridiculous, wicked and tyrannical. Why then, after more than thirty years of enthusiastic reading of such works, have you not taken the trouble to reform your law-courts, and straighten out in some way your antiquated, bizarre form of government, while instead you have done all

you can to speed the process of disorganising it and making it every day more oppressive and hateful?

This was not just hindsight. Already in 1765 his polemic against the reformers had aimed at being realistic, had attempted to confront men with the practical consequences of their actions, by demonstrating to them not only that they were defeating their own ends, but also that they were speeding towards certain ruin along with all the society which admired and supported them. Facchinei's dispirited and unsuccessful revolt had found an outlet in a desperate and extreme defence of the traditional world.

He began to attack everyone and everything. Baretti had written a favourable review of his *Letter on the cause of dreams*. He had even put him on his guard against a 'very wicked race of writers' called 'twisted-necks because those who belong to it have for the most part the most unfortunate habit of keeping the neck just slightly inclined towards the left shoulder'. In 1764 Facchinei published a violent attack against Baretti in the September and November issues (nos. 31 and 33) of *La Minerva* and a year later he prepared, with Gianfrancesco Scottoni, a new edition of Appiano Buonafede's *Pedagogical Ox*. Facchinei wrote a whole book against Beccaria, which marked the apex of the reaction against the Milanese philosopher in Italy and elsewhere. The *Notes and observations on the book entitled Of crimes and punishments* appeared, with no indication of place or publisher, in Venice, printed by Zatta in 1765. The violence of the attack was such as to suggest a political intrigue. Beccaria himself thought so. Writing to Morellet on 26 January 1766, he said: 'I shall send you the book by the friar called Vincenzo Facchinei of Corfù, a monk from Vallombrosa who thinks he can win the favour of the Republic of Venice, which has strictly banned my book, believing it to be the creation of one of its subjects who belonged to the party which opposed the State Inquisitors in the latest disturbances.' Three decades later Facchinei still had to defend himself against the accusation that he had been—as in fact he was—the tool of the State Inquisitors. But it seems that his own psychology or, as he called it, 'terrible destiny', provides a more plausible explanation of his violent yet lucid attack than any outside intervention.

In Beccaria and the other *philosophes* he was attacking three ideas in particular which he considered basically wrong: (1) It was not true that republics and kingdoms had been formed 'by the free choice of all men who lived in a particular province'. In human societies the law of the strongest or the will of providence had always prevailed. (2) It was not generally true to say that men were free beings. 'A sovereignty where every subject is sovereign, a subject who thinks he has the right to create sovereignty—these will never make a perfect society.' (3) It was not true that all men were equal since there existed distinctions among them on the grounds of age, sex, circumstances and opinions. 'What? would Beccaria by any chance wish to suggest that we should mete out the same punishment to a man who punches some rough labourer as to one who committed the same offence against a general?'

In his book Facchinei coins and repeatedly employs a new word to indicate and define those who believe in the contractual origin of a society of free and equal men. This word is *socialist*. Thus we find on page 9 : 'It is absolutely certain that on this earth there never has been a perfect society created by the express will and choice of free men, as our author imagines, and I challenge the socialists and anyone else to find me a single example in all the histories and annals of the world of societies created in that way . . .' On page 23 he concludes the attack against the idea of sovereignty based on general consent by saying that it would, of necessity, mean permanent revision and reform of the laws. 'And this is where the reasoning and systems of nearly all the present-day propagandists of certain sects, and especially the socialists, rashly lead.' In short, they had a radically mistaken idea of society. 'Although man is a social animal, as can be deduced from his needs and inclinations and their effect, and also belongs to a species which multiplies greatly, he is, nevertheless, by nature so proud and inclined towards freedom and independence that it is not conceivable that he should willingly subject himself to obeying other men.' Only force, human and divine, created societies. 'Fear preserves kingdoms', with the consequence that all traditional methods (from torture to capital punishment) were permissible and it was right to retain and preserve them intact. The polemic against the death penalty conducted by the *socialists* seemed to him particularly absurd : 'I would ask the most prejudiced socialists whether a man, in his primitive, natural state of freedom, before becoming a member of any society, whether a free man, then, has the right to kill another man who might attempt to deprive him of his life in any way. I am sure that all socialists, for once, will say yes.' From this argument, of course, he deduced the legitimacy of the death penalty. Forced labour was certainly not sufficient to curb crime and precisely for reasons which the *socialists* did not suspect. 'We have before our eyes the example of very many who of their own free will lead lives which are harsher than the harshest form of slavery, but you will find only a few madmen who do away with themselves.' If we add to this the accusation of being enemies of Christianity, which Facchinei was wont to hurl at his adversaries, we will have done the round of the ideas and attitudes which he had come to sum up and crystallise in the term *socialist*.

Pietro and Alessandro Verri retaliated: 1765 saw the publication of their *Reply to a document entitled Notes and observations on the book Of crimes and punishments*. All the most violent, insulting epithets which Facchinei had hurled at Beccaria were gathered together, listed and underlined, including 'raving lunatic', 'stupid impostor', 'unruly satirist', 'brazen', 'contemptible', and so on. But the word *socialist*—probably because it was unfamiliar—was not considered worthy of mention.

When Facchinei read Pietro Verri's *Meditations on happiness*, he thought it was by Beccaria and annotated it with accusations and attacks, creating for himself the image of a composite writer in whom he seemed to find all the ideas against which he was fighting. He thought he could see the 'Italian Rousseau' and in a preface he also stressed the differences which he thought he saw between this man and Jean-Jacques: 'Rousseau is fanatical by nature or else he became so through writing to free others from fanaticism. The author of the *Meditations*, however, is perfectly sane but would like to see the world full of Rousseau's fanaticism. One is a French sceptic, the other an Italian politician' (1765). But for neither of these did Facchinei have any further occasion to use the word *socialist*.

In 1797 Facchinei was to say that his work of persistent accusation against the men of the Lombard Enlightenment had had the effect of generating 'hatred and detestation', and reducing him to 'silence under the weight of the slanderous charges' brought against him. This was true up to a point—if we consider his contributions to the *Corrier letterario* in 1767, '68, '69, that is to the review which was particularly open to the ideas of the philosophers of the Enlightenment in Venice in those years and which had in fact begun in 1765 as an actual reprint of *Il Caffè*, the *Estratto della letteratura europea* and several articles of the *Encyclopédie*. Facchinei had obviously returned to his more peaceful activity as a publicist, introducing into his dispute with the writers of the century tones of rigorism, pro-Jansenism and anti-probabilism. This evoked two sharp replies from the defender of probabilism, Father Gian Vincenzo Bolgeni, who reprimanded him even for having favoured with his rigorist, critical attitudes 'the ironic pleasantries of the author' of Pilati's book *On the reform of Italy*. Bolgeni took pleasure in underlining all the contradictions of his adversary: 'Admit that you have, if one can so express oneself, a head which is both amphibious and hermaphrodite.' But was this not the man who had had the courage to include even Parini in his attacks and then to take up the defence of Voltaire himself?

The pro-Jansenist attitude was certainly the most striking element in the last stormy period of his life. In 1780 he carried on a correspondence with Giuseppe Maria Pujati. In 1791 he published in Lugano, a well-known centre for Jansenist-orientated publications, his *Essay on a new method of teaching science to children*, where he mentioned Giovanni Lami's struggles against the Jesuits and his own fight against 'probabilism, Molinism, obsequiousness, both sacred and profane', without ever forgetting, it is true, to attack 'that fanatical, blind, most pernicious system called naturalism'. A few years later, in the *Catalogue* of his books, he was to say: 'This little work which has cost me so many years of meditation has, until now, been read (as far as I know) only by a few of my acquaintances and then only on account of what was contained in the last note of the same work.' There indeed is to be found an open tribute to the reforming Bishop de' Ricci's Synod of Pistoia, 'a masterpiece of dogma, morality and discipline', 'synod and code which deserves to be called the triumph of the doctrine of grace . . . and at the same time of the Augustinian-Port Royal group'. He hoped that there would be born from the ruins 'of the most absolute and transcendent despotic government', that of the Pope, the unity of all Christians, Protestants included.

Facchinei had by then been living in the monastery of San Sepolcro d'Astino, near Bergamo, 'for more than twenty years'. He was making great pedagogical plans and sometimes these led him to be reconciled with Rousseau himself. But he did not seem even to spare a thought for the *socialists* against whom he had fought in his youth. When the Revolution came to Italy in 1796, he was quick to cry: 'Long live the Republic of Bergamo', once more giving vent to his uneasiness and dissatisfaction with the monastery in which he had had to live for so many years ('I can't live there any longer', he wrote) and once more attempting desperately to give order and meaning to his contradictions and a line to his writings, both published and unpublished, which he obligingly listed in a special *Catalogue*. He revealed himself politically in the declaration: 'I approve of the French Constitution of 1793 [he probably meant 1795] provided that nobody tries to tell me that it is perfect.' He meant to be the champion of religion and tolerance, freedom and democracy. He signed his *Miscellany*; 'Citizen Ferdinando Facchinei, monk from Vallombrosa'. Above all, he gave vent to his desire to say everything bad he could think of about the fallen Venetian government, the 'Republic of the lion-fox'. Apparently he lived until 1812 and died in Forlì.

We have seen Ferdinando Facchinei in contact with Appiano Buonafede in their common polemic against Baretti. It is in the works of Buonafede that we find once more the term *socialist*. This is not, it is true, in the earliest of his very numerous works, published under various pseudonyms, of which the most famous remained Agatopisto Cromaziano. We find nothing in fact among his youthful literary output, nor in the *Critical and philosophical history of reasoned suicide* (1761), nor in the work *On famous conquests examined in the light of the natural law of peoples* (1763), and not even in the volumes *On the history and nature of every philosophy* (1766). Only when he set about writing, in his own way, the history of modern thought, giving it the title: *On the restoration of all philosophy in the sixteenth, seventeenth and eighteenth centuries* (1785), did he encounter those writers whom he saw fit to term *socialists*.

Chapter xxxvi, in volume III, bore the title: *On the moral restoration attempted by Hugo Grotius*. He had perceived at the heart of this man's thought a fundamental concept: '*Sociality* or the *custody of society* is the beginning of every law of nature and peoples.' The school of natural law had subsequently abandoned 'that one general principle of *sociality*', replacing it with numerous others. A *single social principle* returned with Pufendorf (examined in chapter xxxvii) and this he expressed with the term *sociability*. 'From this same *sociability* derived the absolute rights and duties among men, not to do evil to anyone . . .', that is, all natural law. Cumberland had subsequently come to modify and complete this idea of *sociability*, arguing with Hobbes in the name of the 'greatest goodwill' of each man towards others. Barbeyrac, translating, annotating and placing side by side these three classic writers on natural law (Grotius, Pufendorf and Cumberland), 'set up', said Buonafede, 'the philosophical triumvirate of the laws'. Quite naturally, without any apparent claim to provide a new definition, this historian was led to class these men in a single category as *socialists*. Discussing the value of Cumberland's ideas, he added: 'It is thought, however, that the Englishman may be discredited in this company and the most common view is that many of the accusations brought against him are true and that many others already brought against the systems of the *socialists* could also be brought against his.'

Buonafede went on to talk about the most diverse re-elaborators and adversaries of these socialists. Next to Montesquieu we find Linguet, who saw the origin of society not in a principle but in the fact of hunters who banded together to fight wild animals and feed themselves. 'The romances of the *socialists* and Montesquieu are opposed to this *new romance*.' Perhaps the most famous system of all was the one which bore the 'proud' name of *Code of Nature*, the well-known work of Morelly and the most important communist book of the eighteenth century. In his case Buonafede did not use the word 'socialist'. He was content to expound Morelly's thought polemically at great length and to stress the fact that, according to this writer, 'the first and greatest work of nature is *human sociability* based on the unity of substances and the common use of products'. It was useless for those who held such views to attempt to imitate *'primitive Christianity'*. Summing up his thoughts on the *Code of Nature* in the index, he concluded: 'It is founded on the *abolition of ownership* and this alone is sufficient to refute it.' It did not occur to Buonafede to use the term *socialist* for another 'friend of equality' either, Jean-Jacques Rousseau himself—on the contrary, he 'displayed a spirit which was adverse to society', to the extent that his ideas could be termed *salvatichezze*—meaning the opposite of sociability. Even in the part where he summarised and refuted the *Social contract*, what struck him most was again the element of revolt innate in the work. All modern political thought, the 'new, much-vaunted prodigy of natural law' appeared to him as 'Hippogryph' and 'Titan'. Rousseau's work in particular he imagined 'cast haphazardly among packs of haughty peasants who read and understand nothing except that they are completely free to create and destroy all governments and to crown or strangle sultans and potentates at will'.

The book ended with praise of Vico and Genovesi, who were contrasted with the tumultuous, rebellious and chaotic development of thought from 'over the mountains and beyond the sea'. On the last page this thought was presented in all its moral, philosophical and legalistic contradictions, forming 'the heterodox vortex', 'breeding ground of discordant, fantastic, abortive and godless systems'. There, in the first place, were to be found 'the contradictions between *socialism* and *savagery (salvatichezze)*'.

For the first time, if we are not mistaken, the word 'socialism' was used together with the word 'socialist' in an attempt to summarise those ideas on natural law which, in Buonafede's confused presentation, had become enriched after the classic works of Grotius, Pufendorf and Cumberland, through the contradictory and rebellious thought of the eighteenth century.

The term 'socialism', meaning exactly the opposite of *salvatichezza*, seems to have remained in use, at least in some scholastic and academic circles. In 1803 Bartolomeo Paroni published in Vicenza a *Refutation of anti-socialism: a philosophical work by Giacomo Giuliani, monk from Vicenza.*

This professor of penal law at the University of Padua had written his book in order to combat the spirit of rebellion which had exploded first in the thought of the Enlightenment and then in the Revolution. 'The new system envisaged in the policy of the *philosophes* is one in which society itself is made hateful.' They had attempted to prove that 'civilised society was the work of violence, force and self-interest, that it was a vortex of contradictions and conflicts, of wretchedness, injustice and oppression'. It was not true that the *philosophes* in doing this had in mind that men should return to the woods, 'but they did it to efface in them all former habits of subjection to and respect for the laws and their natural ruler and thus to prepare them for a social metamorphosis'. In order to combat such ideas it was necessary to return to the conception of man as a being destined by nature herself for society, a 'social being' by definition, to go back, in short, to the assertions of those whom Buonafede first called 'socialists'. Giuliani attacked Rousseau and Raynal, all those who preached 'the chimaera' of 'complete equality of fortunes', and those who imagined happy, perfect savages, quoting Vico on the origin of human societies, defending '*original* ownership' in every way and thus arriving at his moderate, rather weak conclusions. 'In comparison with all the ideas which we have so far put forward, analysed and developed, the system of anti-socialism falls into ruins. Everything points to its being precarious and insubstantial, a ridiculous, hare-brained romance produced by the exalted imagination of a spirit sick of civilised society.' Here, we could conclude, the idea of *sociality*, *sociability* and *socialism* seems to have become exclusively the instrument of benevolent, enlightened conservatism.

Having examined the beginnings of the term 'socialist', we should pause for a moment to consider the changes undergone by this word in Italy during the eighteenth century. I think that what we have quoted from Appiano Buonafede proves that it arose from the reflections of the exponents of natural law upon *socialitas*. The inspiration might have come to him too from the renewed interest in the Latin term that he found, for example, in Naples when he became part of that university world which was dominated by the figure of Antonio Genovesi, who halfway through the century dedicated an important part of the fourth volume of his *Metaphysics* (1752) to *socialitas*. In the final analysis, a 'socialist' was one who placed social instinct, benevolence and potential progress at the beginning of society and not one who looked towards the beastly origin, the struggles and conflicts of primitive humanity.

Facchinei too may have been influenced in a similar way by this same terminology, but in his case, as we have seen, it was the idea of social contract, equality and liberty which eventually prevailed. 'Socialist' meant a follower of Rousseau, it meant Beccaria or Verri, not Grotius, Pufendorf and Cumberland. In both writers, however, though beginning with two different meanings, the word tended to take on the ideas of the century, to express a more radical desire for equality, to end in utopia and plans for the abolition and transformation of society which were so common and so important in the eighteenth century.

Why did the word not catch on and spread outside the circles of those who preached and those who refuted the ideas of the Enlightenment? The story of some of Facchinei's writings seems to suggest an answer. It was a polemical term, almost an insult, which was not taken up by Beccaria, Pietro and Alessandro Verri, that is by those against whom it was directed, and so it fell, a strange, premature attempt to give them a common stamp and definition. As a scholastic term which had only just begun to acquire the tones of new concerns, to reflect new rebellions, *socialist* or *socialism* lost all its incisiveness after the Revolution and came to be merely a definition of the anti-Hobbesian trend in natural law and the most traditional and conservative element of it.

3 Radicati's Exile in England and Holland

ALBERTO RADICATI DI PASSERANO is the most surprising and significant political and intellectual product of the age of Victor Amadeus II. In the last decades of the seventeenth century the duchy of Savoy had been in danger of becoming swallowed up and assimilated into Louis XIV's 'universal monarchy'. A poor country, difficult to hold together, after long struggles it nevertheless retained its independence through the will of its duke, its noblemen, its peasants, mountain people and soldiers. Piedmont was the first Italian state to establish in any lasting way a modicum of religious tolerance towards Protestants. This tolerance was of a very narrow, mean nature, but it was still very different from the intolerance and inhumanity of the other states of the peninsula, where the great oppression of the Counter-reformation held sway.

This situation provided the new starting point for a Piedmontese nobleman, scion of a family which had settled in the hills between Asti and Turin in the middle ages and for centuries controlled one of the most important routes between Genoa, Turin and France. Alberto Radicati di Passerano, in conflict with his family and environment from an early age, embarked, through a series of rebellions and discoveries, on a laborious course towards Protestantism, and from there towards criticism of all positive religion, an increasingly broad and all-embracing tolerance, a deism inspired by British models. At the beginning of the 1720s he sought to persuade the duke, Victor Amadeus II, who in the meantime had become king, first of Sicily and then of Sardinia, of the need to imitate the great models of a new kind of politics—Henry VIII, Louis XIV, Peter the Great. What he was asking was that the government of his country should carry to its logical conclusion the conflict which had recently broken out with the Papal Curia, expropriate the Church, abolish the Inquisition and thus establish ever more firmly the control of political over ecclesiastical power. But these proposals were too daring and too obviously heretical for Victor Amadeus II. Radicati was forced to go into exile and left for England. In London he wrote his main work, the *Discours moraux, historiques et politiques*, which he once more vainly attempted to bring to the attention of his sovereign.

Having lost all hope of being able to publish his *Discours moraux, historiques et politiques* in Piedmont, Alberto Radicati di Passerano decided to publish them in England. It seems, moreover, that this very soon became his predominant concern, once he became convinced that he had lost his chance in Piedmont and that he would have to go permanently into exile.

His repeated attempts to give a worthy form to his *Discours*, the numerous editions which he prepared and his obvious desire to provoke discussion of his ideas, all give an indication of the importance he attached to his work : the product and, in a sense, the summary of all his past experience.

In the early months of 1730 an extract from it was published in the form of a pamphlet, one of the many pamphlets to appear in London during that year which marked the zenith of the deist polemic. The title itself, *Christianity set in a true light*, was in accord with the prevailing atmosphere. It said on the cover *XII Discourses, political and historical* but it contained, in fact, only a general index and the first of the discourses, the one concerned with 'the precepts and actions of Jesus Christ'. This was a preview of a book, as if his impatience to make known even a part of it, or, more probably, his inability to meet the expenses of publication of the whole work, had induced him to issue this fragment immediately. The last page bore the title *Discourse II* at the bottom, indicating that this was only part of a volume, as if in proof form. However, it was duly registered at the Lincoln's Inn Stamp Office for a fee of nine shillings and offered for sale at one shilling a copy. A Dutch review, in a note on the pamphlet, stated that the publisher, John Peele, intended to issue 'tous les mois un volume'. This system was not likely to guarantee that Radicati would see his work published very quickly and, in fact, that pamphlet proved to be the end of the first edition.

Nevertheless it had attracted the attention of the Dutch reviews. The *'Lettres sérieuses et badines'* just said in their English news section :

Il n'est pas que vous n'aiez entendu parler du Comte Adalbert de Passerano. Où n'est-il point connu par ses entreprises contre le clergé, et par la vengeance que ce redoutable corps en a tirée, en le réduisant à s'enfuir de sa Patrie et en le faisant brûler en effigie? Ce fameux fugitif, dépouillé de ses biens, est à présent à Londres, et il y fait imprimer en anglois un livre qu'il avait dédié en italien à S.M. le Roi de Sardaigne.

The *Bibliothèque raisonnée* confined itself to a mention of the pamphlet, adding that: 'Cet ouvrage est attribué à M. le Comte de Passeran.'

Radicati had chosen as a motto some words of Cicero which were a clear reflection of his proud, rather arrogant state of mind and his overriding determination to say what he had to say at all costs: *Pericula, labores, dolorem etiam, optimus quisque pro veritate et pro patria suscipit* ('Every excellent man bears danger, toil and pain for the sake of truth and for his native land'). And, inspired by this knowledge, he had written a long preface to his book where he used the transparent allegory of pretending that his *Christianity set in a true light* had been written by a 'pagan philosopher newly converted', that is a Catholic who had only recently opened his eyes to the true light. It was preceded by an autobiographical 'particular Account of his Conversion'.

He must have become convinced, while writing his story, of how successful he was with this type of allegorical and satirical pamphlet, which, for present-day readers, inevitably calls to mind the name of Voltaire. The practical obstacles encountered over the publication of his *Discours* must also have encouraged him to write shorter, livelier pieces. Two years after *Christianity set in a true light* he published a short pamphlet entitled *A Parallel between Muhamed and Sosem*, the meaning of which was already alluded to in the title, if we note that 'Sosem' was an anagram of 'Moses'. It was dated 'London, 23 of the Moon Maharrem, in the Year of Hegira 1108 and of Christ 1731' and was as good as signed: a note referred to the *Discourses political and historical* by the 'Count of Passerano', adding that 'this work will speedily be publish'd'.

These parallel lives of Mohammed and Moses take the form of a rapid sketch of these two impostors and prophets, drawn with such 'impartiality' as to bring the author and possibly the reader to the conclusion that 'it would be better . . . to be an atheist than to worship a Being chargeable with such enormous crimes and iniquities'.

There is no lack of erudition here. Radicati had obviously read with great enthusiasm books on Mohammed, histories of religion and biblical and theological controversies. As already in the preface to his *Christianity set in a true light* and later in his other writings, we can see proof in this pamphlet too of the way in which he devoured books and the keen curiosity he showed in investigating everything concerned with ceremonies, superstition, idolatry and religious mania. He has the free-thinker's erudition together with the rationalistic detachment of the deist, who has an already clearly defined standpoint from which to judge all religions and to recognise in them a constant phenomenon. Radicati played with his learning in a masterly manner. There was nothing pedantic about him, even if he did enjoy quoting Arab chronicles. He even managed to use for his own ironic purposes the philological scruples of those who were struggling to restore the text of the Bible to its original primitive form. He expressed, for example, his proposal to follow in the footsteps of the 'great and learned Dr B-t-y' (Bentley), who had edited Milton's works and been scrupulous in unearthing mistakes which his predecessors had missed. In the same way he would correct the text of the Bible where it talks about the plagues of Egypt and the rain of frogs, correcting this to a rain of toads. It was in fact very likely, he said, that the Egyptians had the same tastes as the French, Italians and Spanish, who were great eaters of frogs 'in their politest entertainments' and would doubtless consider a shower of such creatures 'a blessing from Heaven'. 'After a Shower of Frogs [they] would have feasted most elegantly.' Therefore the word *frog* must have been mistakenly substituted for *toad* by Hebrew interpreters.

This example will suffice to indicate what value Radicati attached to scholarship and in what frame of mind he read the many books on Mohammed and Islam quoted here and there in this and other works of his. Besides, there was a very lively interest in these things in England at the time. A whole generation of Arabic scholars, from Prideaux to George Sale, had provided Radicati with a wealth of material. This interest had also spread outside university and scholarly circles. Radicati was able to witness a very good example of this in the person of Joseph Morgan, whom he came to know about this time and who very soon, as we shall see, became involved in the reaction provoked among the authorities by the publication of Radicati's books. Joseph Morgan had already published, almost ten years previously, two volumes which purported to be a complete picture of Arab cosmogony and mythology, taken from an ancient manuscript. This strange text, Morgan's note and the fascinating illustrations which he added give us a clear idea of the atmosphere into which Radicati was entering with his satire and his polemic. On the other hand, it might be worth mentioning that those years, 1730 and 1731, saw the publication of the two editions of Boulainvilliers's *Vie de Mahomet*. What readers sought in this was exactly what induced Radicati to present his own ideas in Arab guise. As a reviewer of the first edition said: 'Ce qui nous paroit plus admirable dans cette histoire, c'est de voir qu'un homme ose se donner pour prophète et réussit à se faire un nombre considérable de sectateurs, sans alléguer d'autre preuve de sa mission que la force de ses raisons et l'éclat de l'éloquence.'

The part relating to Moses was the most original. The religious polemic became more direct. Perhaps inspired by what John Toland had written in his *Origines judaicae sive Strabonis de Moyse et religione judaica historia breviter illustrata* (1709), Radicati compared classical texts concerning the history of the Jews with the Bible. He did this not only to point out the greater verisimilitude of the former as against the contradictions of the latter but especially to establish the validity of the interpretation of Moses as a great political leader who would even have recourse to deception in order to save his people. What seemed to him profoundly immoral, on the other hand, was to attribute these human expedients and even acts of cruelty to a supreme being. According to him, the account given in the Bible was as 'extravagant as impious'.

Very shortly after the *Parallel between Muhamed and Sosem* came the publication of his account of the abdication of Victor Amadeus II, king of Sardinia. The protection afforded by the English laws on this occasion gave Radicati confidence and made him bolder, so that by the end of the same year, 1732, he had published the most daring of his works, *A Philosophical dissertation upon death*.

This too had strong autobiographical roots. That desire for 'peace' which had tormented him ever since his youth, the changes of fortune he had had to endure, the wretched life he led in London, all the stages of his past life made him approach the problem of death with a desire to free himself 'philosophically' even from this 'dreadful and most horrible idea'.

Radicati took Locke's thought to its furthest conclusions. It had obviously impressed him when he first became acquainted with it, probably as soon as he arrived in England. Now he wanted to prove that even the idea of death was 'really acquired, as all other ideas are acquired'. But his plan really took shape through contact with a conception of nature where Epicurean elements were mingled with a cosmic vision of a totally dynamic material, composed as he saw it, 'of a diversity of contraries' and which therefore 'cannot in any wise be in repose'. The cosmos was explainable in terms of matter and movement, but these mechanical elements were dominated by the qualities and attributes inherent in nature itself, 'power, wisdom and perfection'. 'Nature, being herself superlatively perfect, ever was and ever will be active; nor can she once cease from operating, even for the shortest instant, or in the smallest part of the whole universe, because inaction is the very summit of imperfection'. What are life and death in comparison with this perfection? Nothing other than the dissolution of certain particles which then take on new forms. Stones, metals and plants had their cycle of existence just like the human body.

Terror of dissolution could not therefore be a natural factor. What kind of experience could men possibly have of the dangers and evils inherent in death? This fear too, like all other fears, was the result of deception and trickery. 'In all countries, and at all times, there have been found ambitious men, who, not contenting themselves with the state of equality which Nature had given them, took it into their heads to thirst for dominion over others; and because they could not, by open compulsion, bring about their designs, they employed cunning and artifice'. They used comets, eclipses and other natural phenomena to create the idea of an angry deity whom it was necessary to placate if one wished to avoid being punished not in this, but in another life. Only when human beings believed in the claims of these impostors did they begin to be afraid of dying. They had to free themselves from these fears. Then they would understand death 'to be what delivers us from the persecutions of our adversaries, from the tyranny of the mighty, from the disquiets which molest us, from the anxieties which cruelly torment us, from the infirmities which tyrannise over us, and, in a word, from all misery'.

Likewise, men ought also to see how all ethical concepts were acquired and derived from social habits and customs. Every people had its own ideas about murder, adultery, theft, tyranny and revolt. Everywhere religion moulded these ideas of morality into different forms. 'Who then must instruct us how to discern, which are the good and which are the bad morals? An oracle? A prophet? These certainly may unveil to us the great mystery. But the difficulty is to know which of them all we are to credit, since all of them are different in opinion.' Conscience was not a reliable guide since it too was dominated by religious conceptions. It was sufficient to think of the idea of virginity which existed in Catholic countries in order to see this. Habit and custom held sway over mankind. In order to find ourselves on firm ground again, we had to go back to the idea of physical harm and good and follow that concept of nature which alone was beyond prejudice. 'Provident nature has ever formed all things which were necessary for the maintenance of her creatures, and has always given to each individual a full liberty of making use of everything requisite and convenient for it, and never failed to endow it with a knowledge to discern the good from the bad, that it might enjoy the one and abstain from the other.' Nature is jealous of her laws. Men have been tempted into violating them by superstition, avarice and ambition, with the sole result of making themselves into 'accursed children of education'.

Happiness is their ultimate aim, like that of every animal. Freedom is an inalienable right which could and should be defended even by suicide. Human creatures were foolish enough to think that they were like God. The wise man had to re-establish this rational, natural relationship even with himself and his own life by showing that, if necessary, he was capable even of killing himself. 'A man weary or satiated with living may die when he pleases, without offending nature: since in dying he makes use of the remedy which she kindly has put into his hands, wherewithal he may cure himself of the evils of this life.'

This was what the 'friend to truth' wanted to say 'for the consolation of the unhappy', as he wrote on the title-page of his pamphlet.

The 'friend to truth' and the 'unhappy' were, of course, both Radicati himself. The life which he was leading in London, as described to us by the diplomatic representative of the King of Sardinia, was such a constant reflection of this dual role as to make him appear mad to the ironic, knowing gaze of the ambassador. 'J'ai lieu de croire sa tête toujours bien dérangée, par les discours qu'il tient sur les moines et sur la religion', he said in May 1728 and a month later he repeated: 'Sa tête est bien dérangée, par les discours qu'il ne cesse de tenir contre les moines, et les abus qu'il prétend qu'il y a parmi les ecclésiastiques, quoique j'aie tâché de lui persuader qu'il faut laisser à Dieu le soin de les reformer.' 'Si mon indisposition augmente, comme il y a toute apparence', wrote Radicati himself to the ambassador, Marquis d'Aix, in July of the same year, 'je serai bientôt à la fin de tous mes malheurs, et j'aurai la satisfaction de quitter une vie qui m'est à charge dans un pays de liberté, hors de la puissance de mes ennemis.' In December, after the break with Victor Amadeus, Marquis d'Aix had already mentioned Radicati's 'wretched' circumstances, adding that: 'L'homme chez qui il loge a dit il y a quelques jours qu'il craignoit qu'il se cassa la tête d'un coup de pistolet.' Two years later the new ambassador, Cavaliere Ossorio, described him as a person 'dans la dernière misère et dans état à se désespérer'. At the very time when he was publishing his *Philosophical dissertation*

upon death he was almost dying of hunger and leading a lif
which was 'celle d'un bandit'. 'Il n'est jamais deux jours dans l
même maison, il porte continuellement du poison sur lui.'

Radicati wrote his pamphlet on death in Italian and gave it t
Joseph Morgan to be translated into English. It was published b
William Mears at the end of 1732 and immediately caused
considerable scandal.

The Bishop of London, Edmund Gibson, into whose hands i
fell shortly afterwards, described it as widely read and immediatel
proceeded to express his own indignation at the work. On 4 Nov
ember he sent a copy to the Duke of Newcastle, one of th
secretaries of state, accompanied by a letter which reflects th
relationship existing at the time between the ecclesiastical an
civil authorities in England. After stating that the author of th
pamphlet 'is one Passeran' and adding that 'the publisher has fairl
set his name to it', he hastened to write:

> I would not be understood to complain of it as a book highl
> *irreligious*, because it seems now to be an establish'd maxi
> among us, that everyone is at full liberty to say and write wh
> he pleases against religion. But teaching the people that the
> are under no restraint from committing all manner of wicke
> ness but the danger of a discovery, and that they need not valu
> harrying if they be discover'd, seem to me doctrines very terribl
> to *civil government*.
>
> I know not what law there is against such a book, or whethe
> any; nor, if there be, how far it will be judg'd advisable to tak
> notice of it in a judicial way, but I think the mischievous i
> fluence it has upon civil government deserves the consideratio
> of our superiors in the State.

The Duke of Newcastle passed this accusation on to one of h
assistants, Delafaye, and two days later the latter received anothe
letter from the Bishop of London, whose indignation had move
him to gather together every scrap of evidence which might pe
suade the government to take action against Passerano. On glancin
again at the pamphlet on death, he had noted that the autho
quoted from another of his works, namely the *Historical an
political discourses*. On opening the issue for the previous Saturda
4 November, of *The Craftsman*, one of the most important review
to appear in London at the time, he had seen an advertisemen
of the coming publication of this work, one of Radicati's man
attempts to give a worthy form to his greatest book. In particula
this confirmed that the bishop's attribution of the work to 'Alb
Count de Passeran' was correct. But did this announcement n

also prove the audacity of this unbeliever? He thus passed the information on to Delafaye, including the cutting from the review, in the hope that he would finally persuade him to take action. A few days later he insisted on repeating his accusations in person and refused to be satisfied with the answer that there was no law under which Radicati could be charged. After various steps, which it is not possible for us to trace with any accuracy, he eventually wrote a third letter on Saturday 11 November, in which he reiterated his demands and expressed the conclusions which he had reached:

> Since I saw you, I have learnt that Passeran's book was written by him in Italian, and then put into the hands of a common translator in town, to be put into English, as it is now printed. I have also learnt that they are shy of selling it at Mears' shop, because as the word there is, they are apprehensive of being called to account for printing it. There is a strong demand for justice, but if the Attorney and Solicitor can find no law to punish, I think that should be understood, and leave given to speak it freely, in vindication of the Ministry; the facts, as to the author and printer, being clear, and by consequence no impediment in the way, but the want of law.

This time, contrary to what happened when the pamphlet on the abdication of Victor Amadeus appeared, the same magistrate who had previously deemed that there were no legal grounds for prosecuting Radicati, was so shocked by the content of the *Dissertation upon death* that he ended up by agreeing with the Bishop of London. Delafaye had sent him the pamphlet and he returned it to him on 15 November saying: 'I really think it the most impious and immoral book I ever read.' It contained 'a general attack' against all religion and morality. 'For which reason', wrote the Attorney General, 'I conceive the author and publisher are punishable for it by law.' He said that as he had gone through the pamphlet he had already made a note in the margin of the most typical passages and that therefore half the work was already done if it came to preparing a charge. In his view the matter had taken on a much more serious complexion than Delafaye realised. 'It seems worth while to endeavour to find out the real author for I can't help thinking that there must be some very ill design at the bottom of it, and can scarce believe that it proceeds merely from the foreigner who is suspected.' And he closed with a suggestion of the procedure that might be adopted in order to punish the printer too.

In spite of all this, the Duke of Newcastle did not seem convinced and he let ten days or so go by without taking any action. The Bishop of London resumed his campaign. 'There seems to be a good deal of uneasiness among serious people' on account of the fact that, as yet, nothing had happened to Radicati and his publisher. 'I think,' he concluded sharply, 'it will be much for the service of the Government not only to do it, but to do it as speedily as may be.'

On the following Monday, 27 November, the bookseller, William Mears, was arrested. Radicati and his translator, Joseph Morgan, were 'taken into Custody of a Messenger'. Radicati returned the same evening from his 'examination before Mr Delafaye' and was 'ordered to Bail'. Delafaye once more consulted the Attorney General with regard to the amount of the bail and on 29 November he received a reply recommending moderation. The Bill of Rights clearly stated that the sum demanded should not be excessive. In this particular case, he said, it was possible to work on the basis of a precedent, the deist Woolston, 'which was something of the like nature'.

Passerano should be made to pay £400 and each of his guarantors £200. 'As to Morgan, if he is so poor as is represented, low bail should be taken.' We know nothing of further measures concerning the bail and we have not been able to trace the names of the guarantors of Radicati and Morgan. However, the sums must have been paid because neither of the men was imprisoned.

But William Mears, the printer, did go to prison, for an unspecified period which was probably fairly long since he eventually addressed a 'humble petition' to the Duke of Newcastle, pointing out that he had carried on his profession for twenty years, that he had a wife and three children to support and apologising for having published the *Philosophical dissertation upon death*. He did not know Italian, he said, and, as he trusted the translator, he had not even read the pamphlet and was thus unaware, or so he claimed, that it was something 'immoral, repugnant to Christianity, impious or Athiestical [*sic*]'. He added that he still had in his shop the original manuscript which had been given to him by Count Passerano and that he had never made any secret of the identity of the author or translator when he was arrested. It would have been more than just to punish the man who had 'premeditatedly contrived the indignity' against religion, rather than himself 'who fell into the offence' while pursuing his normal method of earning his living and had never been suspected of 'entertaining such principles'.

Radicati had displayed great dignity and nobility at the time of his arrest. The letter which he wrote to the Duke of Newcastle on 27 November 1732 was a clear statement of the reasons which had induced him to write the *Dissertation* :

My Lord,

I am a man, whose misfortunes are sufficiently known to the English world; but few only are acquainted with the real sense of them. Some people not well informed or prejudiced against me have given out on this present occasion, that I was forced to fly my country for the wickedness of my writings, which is absolutely false. For the truth is, that I fled merely to escape the rage and fury of the Papish clergy, for having with too much zeal and integrity endeavoured to propagate the Protestant interest in Piemont, as some performances of mine (which I wrote to serve and obey the late King Victor and which will be published in English very shortly) do well testify.

And had I, My Lord, not been so unhappy as to have met with so cool a reception here in England since my refuge, now of seven years, I should not have exposed to publick view my Philosophical Dissertation upon Death, nor have consequently put my original Italian in any one's power to translate and publish it in English.

But two reasons, My Lord, and strong reasons, have compelled me to do it : First, down right want obliged me to sell the Italian manuscript, to prevent my starving. Secondly, as the subject of my pamphlet is of the greatest consequence and importance to all mankind, I was really willing to publish my opinions in this country (wherein the people, enjoying the liberty of expressing all matters of faith, are more learned than in those regions, where men are injustly deprived of such a right) that I might know by the objections or approbation of persons of erudition and candour, if my notions are just or erroneous, good or bad; and from thence, either persist in such my sentiments, or abjure them accordingly; which I shall always be ready to do, whenever I shall be convinced by solid reasons, that I am in the wrong, not having any farther scope in my said philosophical inquiries than truth, and the benefit of mankind.

But I humbly trust, that your Grace will have the goodness to consider, that the method of converting hereticks by violence, and not by argument, as it is the detestable practice of the Inquisition, is no truly Christian method, nor proper to convince any one of his errors.

I am with the greater respect, My Lord,
Your Grace's
Most obedient and most humble servant
ALBERT DE PASSERAN

If we look at this conflict with the English authorities as a whole, we can conclude that Radicati was one of the few writers of that period who actually became entangled with the law. Freedom of the press was already operative in England at the time and the conflict arose out of the extreme nature of his convictions, which surprised and shocked not only the Bishop of London, but also the Attorney General, Yorke, otherwise well known for being particularly open-minded. The authorities were more or less compelled to take action on account of the scandal which had been provoked, but even so they were not severe and chose a course which enabled Radicati to remain free and even, as we shall see, to go on publishing other works no less 'impious and atheistical' than this one. Had he someone to protect him? It is possible that this was so, especially if we think of the need to find guarantors and to produce large sums of money, which Radicati certainly did not possess. But we know nothing about this and there is no evidence of it to be found among the papers of the Secretary of State.

He certainly did not receive any assistance from the Sardinian embassy. On the contrary, Cavaliere Ossorio seemed to delight in the difficulties in which Radicati found himself, since this seemed to him to confirm, if nothing else, what he had always maintained —that Passerano was devoid of any sense of balance and discretion. On 15 December he wrote to Marquis d'Ormea: "Le Comte de Passeran qui s'est sauvé du Piémont pour se dérober aux poursuites de l'inquisition a été assez habile pour faire naître une inquisition exprès pour lui en Angleterre.' After summarising in his own way the pamphlet where Passerano had said 'd'une manière si grossière et si infâme que les hommes ne sont que des machines', he talked about the arrest of Radicati and his translator and added that the English authorities intended that he should be judged 'à la rigueur des lois'. 'Ce qui a porté plusieurs gazettiers ici d'imprimer sur son compte dans leurs papiers que voilà une belle occasion au Comte Passeran de confirmer la doctrine par la pratique, et que s'il ne fait point, le monde le regardera comme un fripon et un imposteur.'

Setting aside this invitation to commit suicide which Cavaliere Ossorio seemed to find so appropriate, we can note that the London periodicals did indeed give wide coverage to the affairs of Passerano and his ideas in the remaining weeks of 1732. The *London Journal*, perhaps the most widely read weekly paper in the early part of the eighteenth century, mounted a real campaign against him. In 1729 it had already run a series of articles attacking Woolston, the most scandalous deist of the period, and Radicati's pamphlet provided a good opportunity to revive this polemic. The issue which appeared on 25 November 1732, no. 700, carried a leading article entitled 'A Discours on the Principles of some modern Infidels, occasioned by several late Books and Pamphlets'. The accurately reflected the attitude of those who had no intention of accepting the extreme consequences to which the spirit of enlightenment might lead and who felt quite content with the liberal balance which had been reached in Walpole's England. It was precisely this attitude of mind which was to limit and restrict the progress of the deist movement in England, although it contained in embryo so much of what was to come to fruition twenty years later in the Paris of Rousseau and the *Encyclopédie*. And it is this fact which bestows a general interest on the discussion aroused by Radicati—an eloquent example of English reaction in the face of the more virulent strains of 'philosophy'. We cannot rule out the possibility that behind the campaign of the *London Journal* were those same persons who were then seeking the most suitable means of using the law to attack Passerano. In any case, the articles in this paper give a very good idea of the motives and feelings which prompted their action.

The writer of the article, who signed himself 'Socrates', began by stating that: 'We have oppos'd superstition . . . because it is a most terrible enemy to all that's great and good among men.' But he hastened to add that 'superstition is not the only enemy to virtue'. There existed in fact a group of persons who 'under a pretence of rescuing mankind from the power of superstition, have dug up the very foundations of common honesty'. There was a great increase in the number of atheists and 'Socrates' felt unable to refrain from relating a few of the most characteristic stories about some of them. 'There was an old atheistical Gentleman, well known in town', who, in the time of Queen Anne, died of a broken heart on the day when Parliament passed a law which provided for the building of fifty new churches. 'There is another now living of these Anti-Enthusiastical Enthusiasts' who always crossed the road to avoid meeting a priest. So great had been the spread of 'the schemes of Hobbes and Spinoza', which tended to destroy virtue and divinity, that even on the editorial staff of newspapers reporting parliamentary sessions there were some of these 'fashionable Free-Thinkers'. 'And we have just now seen a pamphlet call'd, *A Philosophical dissertation upon death*, wherein murder, adultery, sodomy, treachery and all kind of villainies are justified and affirmed to be no crimes.' If this were so, we should have done ourselves a very doubtful service in getting rid of superstition. 'Who had not rather live with the ecclesiastical savages in Spain and Italy, than with these unnatural savages?'

A week later, the leading article in this periodical was devoted entirely to Radicati. 'The author has thrown together the worst things that ever were said by the most infamous men, concerning deity, the universe, human nature and human actions.' In order to persuade people to kill themselves 'when they are out of humour', he had asserted that there was no right and wrong but that everything happened according to custom and fashion. 'He has not indeed attempted to reason about morality; but has brought together a vast number of what he calls facts, to shew, that different nations had different and contrary notions about every instance of moral good and evil.' And as proof of all this he quoted what Radicati had written on adultery, sodomy, private property and human sacrifice. Passerano had attributed everything to nature and attempted to justify everything with this name. However, 'most of the barbarous customs among the heathens, flow'd not from nature, but superstition; and many of them which we count savage, were not absolutely so, but had a mixture of goodness in them.'

This in fact was the thesis that 'Socrates' was to develop in an article which appeared the following week, entitled 'A Vindication of the Law of Nature against the Philosophical Dissertation upon Death'. Radicati had merely drawn the ultimate conclusion from the ideas of all those before him who had either denied morality completely or who had reduced it to a simple concept of happiness. According to him, nature invited men to follow her and any resistance could only make them unhappy. 'Our author says, nature bids him, when desire is warm, lie with any woman he can come at; and when he wants money, nature bids him rob, plunder, or murder, as most suits his convenience and safety.' According to the writer of the article, it was precisely these practical considerations which he dwelt upon at length with the obvious intention of shocking his readers, that proved that Radicati's idea of nature was a false one.

> Our passions are only a part of our nature, and the inferior part too . . . And we must live single and solitary (like our fellow beasts of prey) within our dens or caves, our little fortresses or entrenchments, sword in hand, as long as others stronger than ourselves will permit us to live. This would be the deplorable case, if we liv'd according to nature in our author's sense.

The only conclusion to be drawn, said 'Socrates', was that 'nothing has been made so bad an use of as the word nature'.

He was anxious to save this concept from being completely ruined by Passerano and others who thought as he did. Religion was not superstition and nature could not be equated with the passions. He wrote another article for the following issue where he explained that liberty and freedom of thought were also something different from what this 'friend to truth' would have us believe. As the word itself suggested, 'Free-thinking [is] the only effectual guard against superstition and immorality.' Superstition, he said, had usurped and betrayed the cause of virtue, the enthusiasts had exalted themselves above it and the followers of Hobbes had openly declared that there was no such thing as vice or virtue. There was only one remedy for these different but related evils: 'What but the full exercise of our reason on all subjects, or free-thinking, is able to preserve us against this torrent of superstition and immorality?' Freedom alone enabled us to prove the existence of a being who was infinitely powerful, wise and good at the head 'of the affairs of the universe', only thus was it possible to discover real differences in the things of nature, 'to see the natural standards of all actions'.

'Socrates' was, in short, setting down theoretically what the authorities were at the same time putting into practice by letting Radicati and Morgan go free. There had been a great scandal, they had had to submit to the processes of justice and the bookseller still remained in prison for some time, but, in spite of everything 'freedom of thought' was proving effective.

Passerano was, however, still on bail and this probably made it more difficult for him to carry out the plan which continued to be his prime concern, to publish a complete edition of his *Discourses*. At the beginning of 1732, when he published his pamphlet on Mohammed and Moses, he had referred to it in a note as about to be published. At the end of the year, just when his *Dissertation* was beginning to be talked about and to arouse suspicion, he put an announcement in the *Craftsman* (4 November) about a de luxe edition of *Discourses historical and political inscrib'd to all lovers of truth and liberty*. He opened a subscription at a guinea a copy, half to be paid at once and the other half on publication of the book. 'The book will be finished by Lady-Day next', and he promised that anyone who requested it should have his subscription returned. Then he gave the addresses of the booksellers from whom the book could be ordered. This list gives us a full picture of the publishing world in which Radicati was struggling to find enough money, first of all to survive and then to publish his work.

But the idea of a subscription failed, both through lack of subscribers and through the ensuing conflict with the authorities. He still had more than a year to wait to see it published, but in February 1734 J. Martin, who had a shop in Warwick Court, Holborn, at the sign of Lycurgus, at last made his dream a reality. Instead of his name, the *Discourses concerning religion and government, inscrib'd to all lovers of truth and liberty* bore the initials

A.C.-s. Was it the danger—a very real one, as we shall see—th
further legal action would be taken against him which persuad
him not to sign his book? This remains a possibility, even thoug
many years later, a German review put a very different int
pretation on the matter and suggested that Radicati was prompt
by the desire to make the work pass for a posthumous work
Anthony Collins.

Not many months had gone by before Radicati was able to iss
a reprint of his work, 'printed for the author' and on sale at boo
sellers and pamphlet shops in London and Westminster. Its public
tion was advertised by the *London Journal* and the *London Eveni.
Post* on 25 May 1734 and it was also mentioned by the *Daily Po
on 28 May. These announcements contained a brief editorial no
on how the author had written this book on the orders of t
King of Sardinia and how he had subsequently been forced to lea
the country and had been burnt in effigy 'at the prevailing instig
tion of the codexes of that kingdom, whose injust power he h
proposed to be restrain'd in the Twelve Regulations offer'd to th
Prince, which may be seen at large in the twelfth and last D
course'.

These announcements also informed the public that J. Mart
had in his shop another work by Radicati which was even mo
stimulating than the *Discourses* written for Victor Amadeus. T
work in question was a reprint, with a few modifications a
additions made by Radicati himself, of that autobiographical pie
which in 1730 he had used as an introduction to his *Christiani
set in a true Light.*

It bore a title which sums up Passerano's whole spirit at t
time: *A comical and true account of the modern canibal's religio
by Osmin true believer. To which is added a select piece, call'd t
Story of stories. Taken from the canibal's chronicle.* The ca
nibals were, of course, the Catholics. The *Story of stories* was
satirical transcription of the Old and New Testaments and t
history of the Church. It told how six or seven thousand yea
ago there lived in an unknown land a powerful prince who rul
a desert kingdom. So great was his bounty and wisdom that
decided to fill it with plants and animals. Thus his splendid pala
became surrounded by a great garden inhabited by all kinds
living creatures. Everything obeyed his will until the day wh
the bees alighted on some flowers which he had forbidden them
touch, not because they were harmful but simply because
wished to test their obedience. The prince was furious and w
ready to destroy them all, but his daughter, 'a most beautiful a
most virtuous virgin', interceded on their behalf and sacrific

herself to suffer in their place. She became a bee and went to live in a hive, where she preached greater obedience to the laws of the lord, but the bees would not listen and eventually stung her to death. 'As soon as this virgin was dead, she return'd to her father, and fell to interceding for the poor bees, whose debt she had paid, and for whose crimes she had suffer'd, which mediation she still continues.' Thus the hives were given a chance to reform and many of them tried to follow the prince's laws. The hornets in time even persuaded the bees that they were immortal and if their bodies perished, the 'buzzing part' in them would survive for the purpose of obtaining either punishment or reward in the after-life. And this was only one of the many 'chimeras' with which these 'crafty hornets are continually filling the heads of the silly bees'. For this service the hornets were rewarded with a larger share of honey and exemption from all work. 'All they have to do is to invent some thing to terrify the bees.' Any bee who rebelled against them was killed, whole hives were massacred because they followed other hornets and they went as far as to forbid the bees to suck flowers or make honey on certain days of the year. The hornets justified all this by saying that they were the guardians of an ancient tradition which went back to the prince himself, whose sayings were 'transmitted . . . down to them, partly impress'd upon wax'.

We have given a summary of this fable because it is very characteristic of the atmosphere surrounding Passerano in London. The tale, however, is not his own. He took it from an English book which appeared the year before, *The Travels and adventures of James Massey* (London, 1733). The 'Fable of the Bees' can be found on page 292 and Radicati was content with making some changes at the beginning and the end and transforming the son of the prince into a daughter. The English book itself, as could be seen even from the title, was a translation from the French, the *Voyages et aventures de Jacques Massé* (Bordeaux, 1710), one of the most famous and important accounts of imaginary journeys to be written at the beginning of the eighteenth century. The author, whom Sylvain Maréchal was the first to identify as Tyssot de Patot, was born in London of a Norman family. Shortly after his birth they had returned to France, only to be forced to flee at the time of the persecution of the Huguenots. He lived in Holland but kept in constant touch with England and wrote various free-thinking and deist pamphlets and books. Marquis d'Argenson was one day to say that the 'Fable of the Bees' was the main reason for the renown enjoyed by the *Voyages et aventures de Jacques Massé*. Voltaire put a modified version of the tale into verse form. And, as we have seen, as soon as it appeared in English, it attracted the attention of Radicati too.

When the Bishop of London, Edmund Gibson, heard about Radicati's new enterprises, he was naturally very surprised and was quick to protest. He made notes in the margins of a book which was probably the first edition of the *Discourses* and sent it to Delafaye with a request that he should glance at it so as 'to judge what a height of licentiousness is come to when a person actually under prosecution for one blasphemous book, thinks he may with impunity publish another of the same kind'. He deplored the fact that all his efforts to have something done about Passerano had been in vain. 'I have often spoken to Mr Paxton about Passeran's affair depending in the K.'s Bench, but I do not know that any judgment has been yet given or demanded.'

When he read the announcement about the second edition of the *Discourses* and the *Account* of the cannibals, his indignation knew no bounds. 'It is not credible that such an open insult upon religion and its abettors should be ventur'd on without encouragement and assurance of impunity from one quarter or another. He is certainly a very wicked man, but I do not take him to be mad.'

Nevertheless Gibson was wrong in believing that Radicati had found some powerful protectors. He was obviously 'mad' enough to push ahead blindly and risk everything provided that he could publish his writings. In the author's 'Declaration' which preceded the *Discourses*, he stated that he had expressed his own ideas, even though 'I know myself to be wholly destituted of friends' but he hoped that 'Almighty God, whose power is above all human artifice and malice, will protect me against those that will certainly promote my destitution for having openly espoused the cause of truth and equity'.

However, this time too, the Bishop of London probably received a polite request from the offices of the Secretary of State to remain calm. Indeed, in his reply a few days later to a letter which has not come down to us, Edmund Gibson said: 'When I sent you Passeran's advertisement, I did not mean that any thing should be done upon it, but only to show you the insolence of the man in advertising with such an air while he is under prosecution, and the incredibleness of his doing so, if he thought he had anything to fear. Mr Paxton can best tell why nothing is yet done upon the first book.'

This is the last piece of evidence we have concerning Radicati's stay in England. Almost a year later we find him in The Hague in circumstances which were becoming increasingly difficult. In a letter to Marquis d'Ormea he attempted to re-establish contact with the court in Turin 'après dix ans de souffrances'. Whatever legal proceedings were begun against him and although it is unlikely that these ever resulted in a sentence being passed, Radicati realised that it was becoming more and more difficult for him to stay in England and he decided to take refuge in Holland in the latter half of 1734 or early 1735.

The atmosphere in which Radicati found himself in Holland during the two or three years which he spent there was not very different from that which he had left in London. For several decades the French 'refugees' had formed a permanent link between the world of pamphlets and newspapers in England and its counterpart in Amsterdam, Rotterdam and The Hague. Literary reviews were sometimes compiled together by writers from both countries, the London correspondents had an important place in the papers of the United Provinces and we have seen how carefully they followed what Passerano had already written. Ideas circulated rapidly between what were the two strongholds of freedom of the press in Europe at the time.

We do not have very much information about Radicati's stay in Holland either. We can just catch a glimpse of him, getting poorer and poorer, in that world of writers and journalists who were shocking half Europe with the boldness of their writings and way of life, yet who were also providing the newspapers, reviews and translations which were most eagerly sought after and read all over Europe. As Voltaire put it, with their writings they even went to 'réjouir les cours d'Allemagne et de Russie'.

One of these writers, La Barre de Beaumarchais, an unfrocked priest from Paris, had already mentioned *Christianity set in a true light* in 1730, in his *Lettres sérieuses et badines*. Ten years later he wrote about Radicati again in his *Amusements littéraires*. His tone was insulting and the accusations of impiety were violent and also somewhat hypocritical. The familiarity with which he talked about Radicati would suggest either that he knew him or at least that he had heard a lot about him in the circles in which he moved. In describing various types of wanderers and adventurers, he compared Radicati with Baron Ripperda, who had ended up by becoming a Muslim and taking the name of Osman Pasha and who had just died at Tetuan. La Barre de Beaumarchais felt that his life was 'encore moins odieuse que celle de certain écrivain, qui a mis depuis peu au jour un parallèle impie entre le mahométisme et le paganisme. Osman du moins n'avait abjuré le christianisme que pour mettre sa vie et sa fortune en sûreté, et de plus il conservoit dans un égarement les apparences du respect pour

Jésus-Christ.' Passerano, on the other hand, 'de gaîté de coeur sans intérêt . . ., attaque Dieu, Moïse, la Bible avec l'insolence plus effrénée qui fut jamais'. As we can see, La Barre de Beau marchais was quick to praise apostasy when there was somethin to be gained from it, but condemned it violently when it w disinterested.

From what we can gather, a similar view must have been he by another writer and adventurer whom we also meet, more less casually, on Passerano's path in Holland. La Mothe, also know as La Hode, had studied in France and had been a Jesuit. He le the priesthood and eventually went to Constantinople where stayed with Pasha Bonneval, the well-known French count who ha become converted to Islam. He too had temporarily embraced th Muslim faith but, to use the words of Marquis d'Argens, 'comm la vie de musulman vous ennuya, vous quittâtes l'Asie pour r tourner en Europe avec un prépuce de moins. Votre aventure aya fait trop de bruit en France pour que vous osassiez y revenir, vo débarquâtes en Hollande.' Once in Holland he had set about becom ing a writer and published the apocryphal memoirs of Cou Bonneval, a history of Louis XIV, a *Histoire des révolutions* France and, of course, two volumes of *Anecdotes historique galantes et littéraires du temps présent, en forme de lettres*. It not difficult to discern in this and other of his writings frequen signs of an irreligious, free-thinking spirit. Thus, for example, his *Vie de Philippe d'Orléans, petit-fils de France, régent royaume pendant la minorité de Louis XV*, he said that he ha made the 'tribunal de la pénitence un tribunal de terreur et vengeance' and that the blame for this could be attributed direct to the idea that men had formed of God :

> On ne parle que de charité, que d'amour de Dieu, en mêm temps qu'on le représente comme un maître dur et impérieu qui veut moissoner ce qu'il n'a pas semé, qui punit parce qu'c n'a pas reçu ce qu'il n'a pas jugé à propos de donner, ce qu'il refusé, ce qu'il a même ôté, et l'on veut persuader que le pl grand effort et la perfection de l'amour est d'aimer celui s l'amour duquel on ne peut compter.

Likewise, as he told in his own way the story of Bonneval's lif he said that the reader would certainly be interested in a man wh 'a si étranges aventures, qui, semblable au Danube, finit par n'êt pas même chrétien'.

This critical spirit did not prevent La Hode from re-establishin contact with the Jesuits and putting himself at their service whe he saw that this was the most beneficial course for him to tak

'Il faut rendre justice à la Société, elle ne fût jamais ingrate envers les personnes qui se consacrent à son service', said a journalist talking about his adventures.

Who but La Hode should be chosen by one of the best-known writers then publishing his works in Holland, Marquis d'Argens, as Radicati's opponent in a dialogue between dead men. In this *Dialogue entre les avventuriers Passerano et La Hode* each criticises the other for his way of life and both were deliberately chosen by the author to prove that common sense is needed even in attacking churches and that it was priests who should be taken to task, not religion itself. When Radicati recalls some of the spicier episodes of La Hode's life, the latter finally replies in this way:

Quelque débauché et libertin que j'aie été, mes crimes et mes folies sont bien au dessous des vôtres. Je n'ai pas, ainsi que vous, horriblement maltraité deux femmes, encore toutes deux vivantes, après leur avoir mangé tout leur bien. J'ai vendu en bénéfice, il est vrai, et je me suis fait circoncire, mais vous, non content de renoncer au christianisme, vous avez fait ce que vous avez pu pour le détruire dans votre patrie : et votre Prince, voulant prévenir les maux que vos opinions dangereuses pouvoient causer, a été obligé de vous faire condamner à la mort. La sentence qu'on rendit contre vous a été exécutée par défaut, et si vous n'eussiez pris la fuite, vous auriez péri sur un échafaud. Je sais que, pour vous excuser, vous alléguez la haine des prêtres et des ecclésiastiques. Vous trouveriez bien de juges indulgents, si c'était-là la seule cause de votre malheur; car depuis longtemps, dans toutes les différentes communions du christianisme, les gens sensés reconnaissent que l'ambition, l'envie de dominer et la passion de nuire à ses ennemis sont des vices nés dans l'âme des trois quarts des ecclésiastiques. Mais quant à vous, vous avez donné aux prêtres un juste sujet de vous persécuter; vous attaquiez la religion avec l'audace la plus effrontée.

The idea of Radicati's life which emerges from these various accounts is vague and often misleading. Nevertheless, even from these few scattered and rather curious details, we can gain some insight into Radicati's life in Holland in the midst of the men of letters who were gathered there, yet at the same time isolated in his own 'madness' or 'audacity'.

In the few years which remained to him he was able to republish many of his writings which had already appeared in London, making some corrections and adding a few more of his works. In their French form they were more accessible to the educated public in Europe than in English.

In 1736 a book appeared, supposedly published in Rotterdam but more probably in The Hague, entitled *Recueil de pièces curieuses sur les matières les plus intéressantes. Par Albert Radicati, Comte de Passeran* and containing some old and some new pieces.

First of all there were the *Discours* that he had written for Victor Amadeus II. Whole chapters had been changed and many details modified. They were no longer dedicated to the King of Sardinia but to Charles of Bourbon, King of Naples. Up to about a year before this, he had hoped to establish the kind of working relationship with Charles Emmanuel III of Sardinia which for a time had seemed possible with his father. But by now this course, which at various stages he had attempted to follow, was permanently closed to him. Once more he described in detail the events which ten years previously had led him to conceive of the possibility of becoming the king's trusted adviser in a work of fundamental political and religious reform. He was setting down these facts both to justify himself and that they might be handed down to prosperity, but also in order to vindicate once more the part which he had played in the conflicts between Church and State in Piedmont. But he wrote with the detachment of a man who is talking of a hope which has vanished and a chapter which is closed. By this time he was turning his attention elsewhere, not to Charles Emmanuel in Piedmont but to Charles of Bourbon in Naples and urging him to accomplish what had not been possible in Turin. He declared that he was a subject of the King of the Two Sicilies, not by birth but because he foresaw that one day the king would reign over the whole of Italy and he alone would be capable of freeing her from papal oppression.

Quoique je n'aie pas eu le bonheur d'être né votre sujet, l'Italie n'ayant pas celui d'etre gouvernée par un seul monarque, je me regarde néanmoins comme tel, dans l'espérance où je suis que Votre Majesté en sera un jour l'unique et paisible possesseur; et par conséquent je me crois obligé et en droit de pouvoir me présenter aujourd'hui devant Votre Majesté pour lui recommander les veritables interêts de ma chère patrie, qui gémit depuis plusieurs siècles sous le plus accablant et le plus cruel joug qu'il y ait jamais eu au monde.

Without stopping to see how Charles of Bourbon's policy could have aroused such great hope in Radicati's mind, it is sufficient to point out that this is the first and one of the clearest statements to be made in the eighteenth century of the idea of Italian unity.

The *Discours* were followed by an *Histoire abrégée de la profession sacerdotale ancienne et moderne: dédiée à la très illustre et très célèbre secte des esprits-forts, par un free thinker chrétien*. A German reviewer wrote of this pamphlet that 'the author had only repeated what had already been asserted more than one hundred years previously by Edward Herbert, Baron Cherbury, in the fourteenth chapter of his *De religione gentilium* and the reasons for which Anthony Collins had frequently criticised the clergy'. But it was precisely this which made Radicati's pamphlet so interesting. He was attempting to condense a very lengthy debate into a few pages, to summarise the discussions on the role of the priest which had taken place in England 'depuis la glorieuse révolution'. He felt that the time had come to draw some conclusions, to look at the problem as a whole, as a constant struggle down through the centuries between 'les partisans de la raison humaine et les fauteurs de la profession sacerdotale'. There was no 'impartiale et régulière' account of this conflict which lay at the heart of all human affairs, and it was this, even if a shortened version, which Radicati set out to provide. This was the path which would later be followed by Voltaire and the numerous other 'historians of reason' in the eighteenth century.

From the very first pages, Passerano emphasised his position in a paradoxical way by saying that the first of the 'esprits forts' was Eve on the day when 'à la permission du serpent, elle mangea la pomme'. 'Ainsi Eve qui, suivant Moïse, était la mère de toute chair, a aussi été la mère des esprits forts.' Instead of saying, like Tindal, that Christianity was as old as creation, it was more correct to say that 'la liberté de penser' was born when the world began. From here Radicati set out to examine the history of the East, of Jews and Christians, and everywhere found evidence of the havoc wrought by the priesthood. His style was naturally ironic and cutting and incorporated those apparent concessions to orthodoxy which later, in the hands of Voltaire, were to become one of the most effective weapons in arguments of this kind. As a finishing touch and without any apparent bitterness, he even wished a brilliant career to the Bishop of London, Edmund Gibson, who had been the instigator of the difficulties which he had encountered in England.

There followed one of his most characteristic works, *Nazarénus et Lycurgus mis en parallèle*, in which, developing a theme which had already appeared in his *Discours*, Jesus and the Spartan lawgiver are presented as propounding the same ideas. Indeed both proposed to 'délivrer les hommes de toute tyrannie' by establishing perfect equality and democracy. In his summing-up, Radicati leaned towards Jesus, because he had taken as the object of his reform 'tout le genre humain' and not only Sparta, and especially because he had shown greater political skill. Poor and without aid he had succeeded in gaining the attention of the crowd by preaching against wealth and ambition, threatening the wealthy and the ambitious with eternal punishment and promising a reward to the poor and humble. Thus he was able to win 'la populace' over to his side by instilling into it a doctrine which 'tendoit à établir la communion des biens et l'égalité parmi les hommes'. This had, of course, provoked a reaction among the rich and powerful and the Jewish priests, who in the end had him killed. Nevertheless he had succeeded, amidst countless difficulties, at least in revealing the truth which lay at the heart of his preaching, that is his determination to restore men to that blessed state in which they were before they fell into sin, to bring them back to their natural condition 'où il n'y a ni *mien* ni *tien*, ni supériorité d'aucune sorte'.

We shall not be surprised to discover that this pamphlet of the *Recueil* very soon became the object of particularly keen discussions and attacks. The *Bibliothèque française* began the discussion of the egalitarian conclusions that Radicati was attempting to draw from the Gospel. 'Le Sauveur, quoique dans un état de bassesse et de pauvreté dans ce monde, n'a jamais condamné les richesses et les dignités en elles mêmes, mais le mauvais usage qu'on en pourroit faire. Les apôtres, non plus que le Sauveur, n'ont jamais enseigné que la pauvreté fut un caractère essentiel du chrétien.' It continued thus at length to defend an interpretation of Christianity which had a strongly Protestant flavour and ended up by quoting a classic passage from the *Epistle to the Corinthians*: 'Que chacun—dit Saint-Paul—se conduise selon le don qu'il a reçu de Dieu, chacun selon que le Seigneur l'a appelé.' 'L'apôtre établit ici que le christianisme ne porte aucun changement à nos relations et aux vocations humaines, en sorte que ceux qui embrassoient la religion chrétienne pouvoient et devoient quelque fois demeurer dans la vocation et profession qu'ils exerçoient auparavant.' As we can see, the opposition of the 'calling' to an egalitarian vision of society emerges clearly from this polemic against Radicati.

Radicati had proposed an exegetic criterion upon which he based his own interpretation of the Gospel. He had maintained that Christian precepts concerning poverty, charity etc., should be interpreted literally and not metaphorically, particularly since Jesus himself had lived and acted in accordance with them. The *Bibliothèque française* replied thus:

Les moeurs de Jésus-Christ sont certainement conformes à sa doctrine, mais il ne s'ensuit nullement que les préceptes qu'il donne doivent absolument et entièrement s'entendre dans le sens littéral, ni que tous les hommes doivent prendre pour raison de leur vocation celle du Sauveur : il faut envisager Jésus-Christ sous la qualité d'envoyé de Dieu pour instruire les hommes et pour les sauver.

Or si les moeurs de Jésus-Christ . . . doivent servir de règle à l'interprétation de ses préceptes par rapport aux autres hommes, il faut donc nécessairement supposer qu'ils doivent se trouver dans les mêmes circonstances. Jésus-Christ a prêché l'obéissance aux souverains; si ses actions doivent en tout servir d'explication à ses préceptes, il s'ensuit que lorsque des juges iniques cherchent à faire mourir un innocent, il doit se livrer entre leurs mains, quelques moyens qu'il ait d'éviter leur fureur et cela parce que Jésus-Christ s'est livré volontairement à ses persécuteurs et qu'il eût pu éviter la mort, s'il eût fait usage de ce pouvoir qu'il avoit en main et suivi les loix de la prudence, ce qui en tout autre cas que dans la vue particulière de sa venue au monde, auroit dû avoir lieu.

'L'exemple du Sauveur', therefore, 'est un modèle que nous devons imiter selon . . . les circonstances de convenance que nous avons avec lui.' So far as community of property was concerned, Radicati was likewise confusing the aspects of Christ's 'conduite morale' which should be 'nécessairement l'objet de notre imitation' with what belonged more specifically to his role as Messiah.

The reviewer reacted even more violently to Radicati's comparison of the Kingdom of God to the state of nature and the life of savages, whose existence was free from domination by other humans and founded on the community of property.

Nous laisserons à démêler aux lecteurs par quels motifs personnels M. le Comte de Passeran donne la préférence aux sauvages sur les chrétiens. Nous ne nous arrêterons pas à réfuter ce qu'il avance; nous le prierons seulement de nous donner une docte dissertation, par laquelle il nous prouve clairement que les sauvages ont tout en commun parmi eux. Notre charité nous porte à lui souhaiter parmi les chrétiens de ces bienfaisans sauvages, qui suppléent à la confiscation de ces biens. Et si les chrétiens parmi lesquels il vit ne se trouvent pas dans cette favorable disposition pour lui, nous lui conseillons d'aller habiter parmi les sauvages pour lesquels il a tant de considération, et d'abandoner ces chrétiens qui ne sont pas assurément dignes d'avoir parmi eux un aussi grand homme qu'un Comte de Passeran, si distingué par ses lumières et son savoir.

The man who realised that Radicati's ideas on the state of nature, as related to savages on the one hand and the doctrine of Christ on the other, raised certain vital issues which needed to be seriously discussed and refuted, was the great German ecclesiastical historian, Johann Lorenz Mosheim. In 1722 he had already written a pamphlet against John Toland's *Nazarenus*, which maintained that because the Ebionites and Nazarenes had observed the true Mosaic laws and believed in the humanity of Christ, they had been the real, genuine Christians. The problem of the new, political law which Christ had come to establish on earth had scarcely been touched on in Toland's work, but it must have contained some hint capable of arousing Radicati's interest and of suggesting to him, if nothing else, the name Nazarenus which he gave to his interpretation of Christ. Mosheim had devoted particular attention to a philosophical and historical discussion of Toland's theses.

Two years later, however, in his dissertation *De vera natura communitatis bonorum inter primos christianos cogitationes* (*Reflections on the true nature of the community of property among the early Christians*) (1725), Mosheim had approached a problem which was much more closely concerned with the ideas which he was to come across in Passerano's *Recueil*. With a degree of erudition and historical certainty which are certainly not surprising in a man such as Mosheim, he spoke about the ancients and then about the communities of Moravians and Bohemians and the way in which they had been defended by the Socinian Daniel Zwicker. Then—something which is particularly interesting from our point of view—he went on to link these conceptions to the beliefs of those who maintained that the Christian religion originally 'nihil aliud fuisse, quam essenismi species'. Thus his battle with Toland was extended to include all those who were inclined to see at the heart of all Christian doctrine the 'communitas bonorum'.

On taking up the *Recueil* Mosheim soon saw that it was precisely this idea which formed the basis of all Radicati's conceptions and that he had expressed the idea in a particularly effective way. In order to argue against the Jesuits, he devoted a long section of his discourse on morality to examining whether or not it was true that the Chinese had preserved deeper traces of 'true wisdom and doctrine' than all other people apart from Christians. The same claim had also been made for the Spartans. But these comparisons, which are already so characteristic of the birth of the Enlightenment, had, Mosheim declared, recently found someone who had taken them to their extreme consequences. 'One of the boldest and, at the same time, most inept detractors of religion ever to appear has recently dared, in a work unequalled in vulgarity and stupidity, to compare our blessed Saviour to Lycurgus, the Spartan legislator.' The author of this work, on his own admission, had been condemned to death in Italy. 'If what he says is true', Mosheim went on to say, 'this sentence, which is otherwise so unjust, was never so justly pronounced as in his case, nor did the King of Sardinia ever act more wisely or honourably than when he refused him his protection.' Radicati had in fact said to Victor Amadeus that 'a prince who rules over Christians may take away from them all that they possess and earn without their having the slightest right to protest'. This was because he was convinced that 'the first quality which Christ demanded from his disciples was total poverty'. It was certain that

the Count and his friends had nothing to fear from such a political maxim. They are not Christians and have no intention of becoming Christians. According to their faith, wealth is the supreme good since possessions allow wicked, lascivious men to give themselves up entirely to their evil desires. And if the prince behaves towards his subjects in accordance with their ideas, it is obvious that he will eventually cast their way a good proportion of those possessions of which he has deprived the Christians.

How can a man who has looked, even in a superficial way, at the New Testament, dream in such an absurd fashion? Would Jesus have wished to wipe from the face of the earth all authority and position, abolish all rank and cancel out the difference between rich and poor? Is this the same Jesus who taught that we must render unto Caesar those things that are Caesar's and to God those things that are God's, who ordered the rich to help the poor in their need and who promised to recognise and reward on the day of his return all charity and acts of kindness done towards the needy as if they had been done to him?

Mosheim was so shocked by this central nucleus of Radicati's ideas that he had to set aside 'even the respect due to this man's class and nobility' and was compelled to 'speak the truth'. In short, not even the title of 'Count' which Passerano bore could prevent Mosheim from protesting against the idea of attributing to Jesus the intention of 'introducing complete equality among all men and of destroying all authority and hierarchy along with all idea of *mine* and *thine*'.

He ended up by examining the laws of Lycurgus in order to prove his thesis of a radical difference between this *Staatstugend* and Christian doctrine.

Mosheim's polemic, which, as we have seen, is not without

interest, was widely read and discussed in German theologica
circles in the eighteenth century. We see Radicati's name appear
again even where we should least expect to find it, as an author to
be refuted along the lines of the writings of the famous historian
Thus, for example, in 1742 M. Johann Pregitzer, 'Preacher to th
garrison at Hohen-Asperg' in the duchy of Württemberg, felt duty
bound to write a 'defence of holy scripture and divine revelation
against the attacks of two 'shameless blasphemers of our age', 'th
Italian Count Passerano' and 'the German Edelmann'. This preache
did not have very much that was new to offer in his reflection
except this comparison of Radicati and Edelmann, meaningfu
from a historical point of view. After attacking Toland who 'ha
tried to imagine a Christianity without mysteries', taking Moshein
as a guide, he went on to talk about Passerano, who had dare
to compare Lycurgus and Jesus.

> Since the Christian religion prescribes and defines exactly among
> its duties the justice which every man owes to others as a mean
> by which order and peace may be maintained in the state, in th
> relationship between rulers and subjects, to the satisfactio
> of both sides, it is obvious that Radicati's wild opinion ca
> have no validity and that his wicked falsification of the word
> of Christ has been arbitrarily deduced from the poverty of th
> apostles.

Again, some twenty years later, a doctor of theology and vice
chancellor of the University of Copenhagen, E. Pontoppidan, in hi
book entitled *The Power of the truth to convince atheists and
deists* (1758), quoted what Mosheim had written 'about the Coun
of Passerani'.

Thus we can see that of the pamphlets collected in the *Recueil*
the one which attracted the most attention was *Nazarénus e
Lycurgus mis en parallèle*. It did, in fact, make explicit the idea
contained in the *Discours*. The more autobiographical aspect, how
ever, was represented by the *Récit fidèle et comique de la religion
des canibales modernes, par Zelim Moslem*, which was a Frencl
version with numerous variants of *A comical and true account o,
the modern canibal's religion*, published in London, as we have
seen, in 1734. It did not contain the *Story of stories* which had
appeared as an appendix to the English edition. In place of this
Radicati added a declaration from the 'Imprimeur au lecteur judi
cieux' which outlined his political ideas or rather his whole con
ception of the nature of politics. It was no accident that he should
place this declaration in the mouth of Machiavelli, in a lively
allegory concerning the fate of the author of the *Prince* in the

sixteenth and seventeenth centuries. Condemned at first by the powerful of the earth for exposing the dark side of politics, Machiavelli had finally found a haven in the Kingdom of Spain and amongst the Jesuits—in both cases among men skilled in using the weapons which the cynical Florentine secretary had forged. However, Machiavelli was not the kind of man to bow beneath an ecclesiastical yoke, even a Jesuit one. His ideas on politics possessed an intrinsic vitality which prevented them from becoming mere instruments of a religious order's desire for domination. 'C'est pourquoi je pris la résolution de les quitter et de m'en aller avant qu'ils m'eussent entièrement épuisé.' So here we have Machiavelli reduced to poverty, despoiled by the Jesuits and forced to act as adviser to Roman prelates or to the college of *Propaganda fide*. And yet he seemed to be reborn with a new and different political motivation, the kind which Radicati felt in himself, first when he was advising a king on a great reform and later when he was convinced to his cost that the maxim to follow was 'Vis loin des tyrans si tu peux et tu vivra heureux', but always able to express openly his ideas on religion and human society. Although this preface does not seem to have made much impression on the eighteenth-century readers of the *Recueil*, it contained, albeit in a fragmentary form, a vision of Machiavelli which was highly significant: seventeenth-century Machiavellianism was dead by this time and, after offering support to free-thinkers, now took on a new life in the form of an Enlightenment revolt. Radicati added an ironic note in the Latin licence which he placed at the beginning of his *Récit fidèle et comique*, attributing it to Benedict XIII, most liberal with indulgences and celestial gifts to all who read this pamphlet. He even went so far as to say that 'Insuper plenariam in articulo mortis concedimus [indulgentiam] morituris omnibus, qui dictum opus super lecto collocaverit'.

He ended the *Recueil* with a translation of one of Swift's most bitterly scathing pamphlets, *A Modest proposal for preventing the children of poor people from being a burthen to their parents, or the country, and for making them beneficial to the publick*, thus bringing it to a close in a way which clearly recalls the English atmosphere of the book and seems to sum up not only Radicati's experience in Piedmont but also all that happened to him in London.

The year following the publication of the *Recueil* two small volumes bound together and bearing the false imprint London appeared in Holland. These contained what Passerano had not been willing or able to include in his book, as if he wished to round it off and thus conclude his life as a writer.

La religion muhammédane comparée à la païenne de l'Indostan par Ali-Ebn-Omar, Moslem, épître à Cinkniu, bramin de Visapour was a new version of *A parallel between Muhamed and Sosem*. At first glance the comparison this time would seem to be between the religions of Mohammed and Vishnu. But the latter is really only an ironical, satirical transcription of the religion of the Old Testament. The part concerning Islam has been shortened, whereas everything concerning the Hebrews has been thoroughly revised and extended. The aim behind it was very clear to a learned German theologian, Michael Lilienthal, who read the work at Königsberg in 1740. Radicati's intention was to convince the reader 'either that God (called here Kiotua), in performing the acts described in the Bible, had been wicked, ignorant and cruel, or that Moses (rechristened Vishnu for the occasion) had been a great charlatan, or else finally that the Old Testament (the *Veda*) was a pack of fairytales'.

The second pamphlet, published at the same time, was called *Sermon prêché dans la grande assemblée des Quakers, par le fameux frère E. Elwall, dit l'inspiré* and contained the French version of the third of the *Discourses* as it appeared in the English edition of 1734. The main change which it had undergone in this new version can be seen in the title—in the fact that Radicati should attribute his own, very personal ideas on the state of nature, the community of property and the real meaning of the message of Christ to E. Elwall, one of the most characteristic of English dissenters in the first half of the eighteenth century.

Elwall was not a Quaker but rather a sabbatarian, for he held the view that the day of rest established by Moses was still valid for Christians and therefore ought to be respected by them. This idea, far from corresponding with Passerano's way of thinking, was basically opposed to it. For him, it was not in the Old Testament but in the New that it was possible to find the true law; in order to restore the law of nature upon earth, it was not to the Bible that man had to turn but to the message implicit in the teaching of Christ. And, needless to say, Radicati was certainly not interested in or impressed by ceremonies and rites. Hence it could not have been on account of his initial sabbatarianism that Elwall was chosen as a pseudonym by Radicati, but rather for his rebellious, rationalistic attitude which, after numerous stages of religious evolution, had eventually turned him into an orthodox Quaker, or as a contemporary put it, a 'Socinian Quaker'. Elwall had adopted more or less consciously the ideas of the Ebionites and, among other things, at one time wore a blue mantle in the form of 'a Turkish habit, out of respect to the unitarian faith of the

Mahometans'. In 1724 he had published a pamphlet entitled *A True testimony for God . . . against all Trinitarians under Heaven*. In 1726 he was in London where he stood trial for his religious views. The title of one of his last pamphlets sums them up exactly: *A Declaration against all the kings and temporal powers under Heaven, shewing that they have no authority over their subjects in spiritual things; but that Jesus alone is King in his Church, God having made him both Lord and Christ: And that neither popes, prelates nor priests have anything to do to prescribe creeds, or make demands upon mankind; but that all religion ought to be free, and neither forced nor hindered* (1741). At the very beginning he challenged George II to a duel, calling him out into St James's Park and allowing him the choice of the day, the hour and the exact spot. However, the weapons would not be swords but only the Bible and reason. 'I believe every wise and good man will agree with me, that the Voice of Reason is the Voice of God.' This pamphlet, like his many other writings, did not contain anything corresponding exactly to Radicati's particular ideas on perfect democracy and religion. It was a bold defence of freedom against all ecclesiastical and political authority. This must have been precisely what attracted Radicati to Elwall's writings and he probably came across many of them when he was in England. There is, however, no evidence to prove that he knew the author, although Elwall was in London during Passerano's stay there.

Certain passages in Elwall seem to have been written deliberately to attract his attention. 'That murtherer Cain was the first that taught the hellish trade, by hating and killing his innocent brother, merely on a religious account'; or 'our Protestant Papists (of which we have not a few, but indeed almost all)'. It would be easy to find similar sentences in a pamphlet of 1742 which was often attributed to Radicati himself, even though he was certainly not the author and which was entitled *The Supernatural incarnation of Jesus Christ proved to be false; having no foundation in the prophets, nor in all the Old Testament; and utterly inconsistent with his being the Son of David. But the main prop and support of all the absurd doctrines, both of Papists and of Protestants; to the great scandal and reproach of the Christian religion. And that our Lord Jesus Christ was the real Son of Joseph and Mary*.

Thus once more Radicati was able to make use of Elwall's name to say what was in his mind. As was written in La Barre de Beaumarchais's *Amusements littéraires* in 1740, in Radicati's pamphlet

on prétend faire voir que le but de l'Évangile est de rétablir les hommes dans cet heureux et innocent état, où Adam se trouve au sortir des mains de Dieu. Mais comment croyez-vous, Monsieur, qu'on s'y prenne pour démontrer cette thèse? On établit que l'ambition et l'avarice ont éteint la démocratie parfaite parmi les nations qu'on appelle policées, que cette démocratie consiste à rendre tout commun entre les hommes et à ne laisser entre eux aucune sorte d'inégalité, ni de partage; que par conséquent les femmes et les enfants ne doivent avoir d'autres maris et d'autres pères que la république même, que l'usufruit de tout appartient au premier occupant, que c'est là ce que Jésus-Christ exige de nous, que c'est dans cette vue qu'il s'est incarné et est mort.

About a year after the publication of his *Recueil de pièces curieuses* and a few months after the appearance of the two pamphlets *La religion muhammédane comparée à la païenne de l'Indostan* and the *Sermon prêché par le fameux frère E. Elwall*, when he was still in a period of intense intellectual activity, Radicati fell seriously ill. It was 4 October 1737. After three weeks his weary frame, racked by tuberculosis and worn out by the circumstances of his exile, by poverty and ever-increasing anxiety, could fight no longer and Alberto Barin (as he was calling himself by this time) died on 24 October 1737.

What happened during those three weeks attracted the attention of his contemporaries. The rumour spread that on his deathbed this man, who had been expelled from England for his unorthodox views on death and religion and who had come to Holland to spread his strange, personal interpretation of natural law and religion, had been converted and had repudiated his rebellious and blasphemous thoughts. In the decades following his death, as attacks against the philosophers of the Enlightenment gradually increased, the story was frequently told in Germany and Holland of the conversion and death of Count Radicati as a permanent warning for those who by this time had already been responsible for the success in Paris, London and all over Europe of many of the ideas that had been his. Eventually, in 1781, Frantz Georg Christoph Rütz, who was a minister of the Lutheran community in The Hague, had the idea of beginning a series of writings against deists with a large volume on Radicati, giving a detailed account of his life and especially of his death. He sought out all the documents pertaining to his conversion, read books and other written evidence by contemporaries, interviewed eye-witnesses who were still living and thus was able to put together the largest, most detailed and well-informed book ever written on this rebel from Piedmont.

The French-speaking pastors in Dutch cities had felt impelled to take action on the publication of Radicati's writings. On opening the *Recueil* and reading what must be considered Radicati's most important work, *Nazarénus et Lycurgus mis en parallèle*, Jean Royer, the preacher from The Hague, had been particularly shocked. His staid, very orthodox outlook obviously made it impossible for him to tolerate the publication of such things in his city. At the Synod of Naerden in 1736 he was entrusted with the task of asking the Grand Pensionary of Holland, van der Heym, 'de vouloir s'employer à arrêter le cours de certains livres empies et scandaleux qui se débitoient en Hollande'. He brought up the subject again the following year at the Synod of Breda and finally, at the Synod of Ziericksee in 1738, Jean Royer was able to give an account of what he, together with the minister from The Hague, Superville, had done to prevent the spread of books by Radicati and to bring about the repentance and conversion of their author.

There could not be a better representative of the second generation of Protestants who emigrated from France in order to escape the persecutions of Louis XIV than Daniel de Superville. His father, who was also called Daniel, had been one of the most active fighters for the cause of reform in the late seventeenth and early eighteenth centuries. The younger Daniel was born in Rotterdam in 1700 and 'sa vie a été en général assez unie et peu chargée d'événements', as we are informed by an *Éloge historique* attached to his collected sermons. He studied at Leyden and became a minister in 1723. He was called to Rotterdam in 1725 and ever afterwards refused to move from there. He spent his time preaching and contributing every so often to the *Journal littéraire de la Haye* and the *Nouvelle bibliothèque germanique* (where he attacked *L'Esprit des lois*). He also translated a few theological and philosophical works from English and eventually died in 1762. 'M. de Superville étoit maigre, d'une grande taille, l'air du visage grave et sérieux, mais d'un abord doux et gracieux.' He was an educated and charitable man, well-liked by his church, 'l'assemblage de ces qualités a fait de M. de Superville un homme heureux'.

Yet even the most fortunate of men have their moments of crisis and when fate brought him into contact with the very unfortunate Radicati, he was just recovering from the only real period of depression in his whole life. In 1736 he had been struck down by a 'maladie dangereuse'. 'Un épuisement de tête et des insomnies continuelles lui interdisoient toute application suivie. On attribua cet état à un excès de travail et peu s'en faut qu'on ne desespérât du rétablissement.' He was treated by the most famous doctor of the period, Boerhaave, sent to rest in the country and became well again. At thirty-seven, having recovered his calm and his regular pastoral manner, he was ready to perform his duty and attempt to save the soul of Count Radicati.

Daniel de Superville had very definite ideas about what was happening in the country from which the Piedmontese count came. A few years previously, on 22 November 1733, he had had occasion to give a sermon at Ysselmonde 'devant les Vaudois' on the subject of *Les Promesses faites aux fidèles persécutés*. And, of course, he had often preached against the modern unbelievers and their 'obstination dans le mal'. Once he had even neatly divided a sermon of this kind into three parts: 'les *juifs*, les *incrédules*, et *vous mêmes*' (that is his listeners). The most difficult to handle were precisely the *incrédules* because they moved continually between two opposite poles: pyrrhonism and absolute faith in reason. 'Tantôt on déprime la raison humaine, ou plutôt on la décrie à un point que si ces déclamations étoient fondées, rien ne seroit desormais certain ni prouvé et que tout deviendroit équivoque et problématique . . . Tantôt on érige la raison en souveraine, ou plutôt en juge infaillible.' But the goal of the unbelievers was always the same. 'En décréditant la raison on espère d'envelopper la révélation même sous ses ruines. Et en faisant de la raison une espèce de Dieu on compte bien que ses oracles l'emporteront sur ceux des livres sacrés.' It was useless to hold up before them 'les monumens historiques qui se trouvent dans l'Ecriture . . .', miracles, prophecies, the Resurrection. So often this was just wasted effort. 'Car, mes frères', as Daniel de Superville said in another sermon, 'ne nous y trompons pas, la conversion est beaucoup plus difficile qu'on ne pense . . .' 'Que faut-il dans la conversion, telle que la révélation nous la décrit? *Nouvelles idées* dans le coeur.'

It was with these thoughts in his mind that Daniel de Superville was to meet Radicati, who had been seriously ill since 4 October and was eager, in Rütz's words, 'to reflect seriously and attentively upon the course of his past life' and to obtain 'aid and assistance in a task of such gravity and importance'. He gave an account of their first meeting to his friend Royer in a letter which has not come down to us but which was summarised by Rütz. Radicati had confessed to being the author 'of various naturalistic writings'. He had shown that he was repentant and beseeched Superville to write a letter for him soliciting the friendship of Pastor Royer in The Hague.

In the report which the latter presented to the Synod of Zierick-see it was also said that

'intérrogé sur ce qui l'avoit fait changer d'idées, [Radicati] répondit que l'état de langueur et de souffrance où le tenoit depuis longtemps une phtysie lui avoit fait sentir le ridicule du système à peu pres spinosite qu'il avoit embrassé depuis quelques années; qu'il avoit vu l'absurdité qu'il y auroit de prétendre qu'un être accablé de maux comme il l'étoit put faire partie d'une substance qu'il avoit toujours reconnu souverainement heureuse; qu'ensuite il avoit beaucoup réfléchi sur les difficultés de son système, aussi grandes pour le moins que celles qui l'avoient choqué dans la révélation; sur la prodigieuse diversité de sentimens qui regnoit parmi les incrédules, jusques là qu'il n'en avoit pas trouvé deux qui eussent les mêmes principes; sur les motifs de vaine gloire qui l'avoient fait agir et qu'il avoit reconnu qui entroient pour beaucoup aussi dans la conduite des patrons de l'incrédulité; enfin sur les preuves directes de la vérité de la religion chrétienne protestante, lesquelles lui avoient été continues dès l'Italie.

The report added that

il souhaitoit extrèmement de vivre assez pour composer un ouvrage où il retracteroit ses erreurs; mais, se sentant affoiblir, il voulut au moins dresser une déclaration qui fit foy de ses sentimens présens. N'ayant pas eu la force même de composer cette pièce, et prêt à partir pour la Haye où il avoit souhaité d'etre transporté, Mr de Superville dressa sous ses yeux la déclaration suivante, où il s'attacha à n'exprimer que ce que le comte lui avoit dit plusieurs fois et qu'il ne signa aussi qu'après l'avoir lu à diverses reprises et en avoir pesé tous les termes.

And this was Radicati's declaration:

Comme depuis le temps que j'avois ouvert les yeux sur les erreurs de l'Eglise romaine dans laquelle je suis né, j'ai eu le malheur de tomber dans l'irréligion et de semer mes mauvais principes dans des ouvrages qui ont vu le jour et que Dieu m'a fait la grâce depuis quelque mois de faire des reflexions qui m'ont convaincu du tort que j'avois et qui m'ont persuadé de la vérité de la religion chrétienne telle qu'on la professe dans les communions protestantes, j'ai cru devoir reparer le scandale que j'ai donné en retractant publiquement mes erreurs, en déclarant que je les déteste et en protestant, comme je le fais ici, que je ne souhaite la vie que pour l'employer à défendre ces memes vérités que j'ai méconnues et que j'ai eu le malheur de combattre. Si je ne donne pas dès à présent les raisons de mon retour au pur christianisme, c'est que l'état de foiblesse où ma maladie de poumon me reduit ne me permet pas d'entrer dans ce détail; quoiqu'en m'ôtant les forces du corps, ella me laisse toute la liberté de mon esprit. Aussi ai-je voulu en faire au moins cet usage, c'est de donner la présente déclaration, en attendant mieux.

Je la signe dans toute la sincerité de mon coeur et prie ceux que mes ouvrages ou ma conversation auroient pu engager dans l'erreur et en général tous ceux qui rejettent la religion, faute de la bien connoître, de l'étudier mieux et de profiter de mon exemple pour lui rendre plus de justice. Fait à Rotterdam, le 14 octobre 1737.

The signature at the bottom of the document was in his own hand: Albert Radicati comte de Passeran.

Even through the prism of Daniel de Superville's personality Radicati himself is still recognisable: the return to his youth, to Turin, when his rebellion against Catholicism, his discovery of Protestantism and then his atheistic, free-thinking conclusions had followed one another in quick succession. We can see him thirsting after a 'pure Christianity' so that he was led to identify the law proclaimed by Christ with the communistic law of Lycurgus. Then there is that bold materialism which made him formulate his own very personal interpretation of Spinoza. And at this point, when he was ill and exhausted, we see him retreating into the bosom of the Reformed Churches, which he had come to know through his own violent religious polemic in England and Holland.

On 15 October 1737, the day after signing this declaration, Radicati arrived in The Hague. He went to live in Bagynestraat and very soon received a visit from Pastor Royer, who, as Rütz assures us, went to see him 'with no idea at all of making converts'. But this was really the beginning of a long, painful series of demands and concessions which ended only with his death. 'Radicati admitted freely and openly, to his great shame and sorrow and with hearty repentance, that, many years ago in Italy, he had been unfortunate enough, having been shocked by the behaviour of many Roman Catholic priests, to feel hatred and even repugnance for the Church itself.' Afterwards in England, 'having become acquainted with Collins and Tindal', he had begun his campaign against religion and Christianity. 'He mentioned that he had first incurred the hatred of the Jesuits in Italy when he advised King Victor Amadeus to prevent them from teaching in the schools.' Besides Collins and Tindal in England 'it seems that he met other naturalists'. He now begged Pastor Royer to publicise the recantation which he had authorised in The Hague, in the hope of obtaining the forgiveness of those whom he had offended.

But, to Radicati's amazement, Royer replied that this recantation was not enough and that he had to write it in his own hand and mention 'all the papers, pamphlets and other writings which you, Count, have spread abroad, giving their full titles and a description of them, disowning and condemning them'. 'Alas' replied the

Count, 'this I cannot do, since my illness has deprived me of the necessary strength and it is as if my hand were already dying.' 'It is indeed a great pity', said the philanthropic minister, 'and a great misfortune for you. For without having such a recantation from you I cannot in all honesty send it to press as you so fondly desire.' Mustering all the strength that he had left, Radicati wrote this new recantation in the space of three or four days. It 'took up six pages of quarto when he had mentioned all the things that he had written under their full titles'. He hoped that this would be sufficient. But when he handed it over to Royer 'the Count was once more surprised to hear that this would still not do'. In addition, Radicati would have to send for all those whom he had offended by his writings, explain to them what he now thought about his works and about religion and show them his confession in the presence of a notary and witnesses. 'The Count replied that unfortunately in The Hague he knew only a certain du Clos, a scholar who lived in the same house.' Du Clos was duly summoned and he came willingly and made a written statement that the Count was truly penitent for all his works and, furthermore, that in a moment when he believed that he was alone 'he had sighed and cried out in Italian in a clear voice: "Oh God! be merciful to a poor sinner, for the love of Jesus!" '

The notary and witnesses had been called for 24 October and they were to meet in Radicati's house to draw up the document as soon as Royer had finished preaching in the French church.

But it pleased God to put down and call the Count unto himself at the very moment when Mr Royer was before God in the temple offering prayers and supplications on behalf of his sick brother: so that it was impossible to sign the document owing to the death of the Count.

All that remained for the pastor to do was to make arrangements for the funeral.

Radicati was buried in the new cemetery . . . His papers (among which was also a codex of a notorious tract *De tribus impostoribus* . . .) together with his few articles of clothing were placed in a case and sealed up. What happened to them nobody knows.

The list of his works which Radicati was supposed to have written in his own hand has been lost. Already we find Rütz expressing his disappointment at not being able to see it (though it seems strange that Pastor Royer could not enlighten him on this matter since it was obviously from him that he obtained the information quoted above). But there is in existence a recantation written by Radicati on 19 October, which was attached to Royer's report. It is in his own hand and the shaky, erratic lines of writing make a very striking impression. It is Radicati's deathbed confession. The overwhelming weight of his situation, of all the expressions which he heard constantly repeated, the tremendous effort he was having to make, can all be felt bearing down tragically upon his hand as it wrote these last words, reproduced here with all the errors:

Ayant depu mentes années, recherchés et reconnu les erreurs du Papisme, ou j'ete eleve, je voulus passer outre pour examiner les autres Religions, mais j'eus le malheur de me plonger dans dans des grands embaras et de tomber a force de vouloir paroitre trop savant; de la j'ai fait pire, car j'ai composés plusieurs ouvrages qui contiennent de tres execrables principe, impies, et ils sont parsemés dans la plus part des mes livres, imprimés maintenant, et comme ces principes, sortant de moi même, sont tot a fait contre les principaux dogmes ou verites contenus dans les Livres sacres qui étoient regardes de moi commes des erreurs et fables, par conséquent me livres sont très pernicieux, il y a longtems que je avois resolu de me declarer en public de mes erreurs et fautes passes, se la est en moi depuis maintes années, quoique fort negligé, et c'est de quoi je me repans de tout mon ame et de mon coeur, faché de me trouver dans un état à ne pouvoir retracte et detester que comme je fais en presence de ce Dieu, le demandant à témoin de la sincerit de ce que je dis ici, faché, dis je, que mes maux m'apechent de remplir mon devoir à s teur, ce que je promet en ca presence du Pere, de Fils et du Saint Esprit que j'adore en Dieu seul dont l'attends le pardon de mes fautes, etant sur que sans le pardon de Dieu, en sa misericorde infinie et le sang de Jesus Christ mon Divin sauveur je suis perdu eternement.

J'indique ici les endroits principaux de mes livres, infectes de mes très horribles erreurs, afin qu'on puisse sans garder peu dans les Discours, beaucoup dans une tres mauvaise Piece intit Nazarenus, dans le recit des Canibales, dan un livre Anglois sur la mort, dans deux livres qui viennent de paraitre, epitre à un Quaker et un recit Hist. ente deux legislateurs, que je deteste et comme les autres, et à present je ne dis pas d'avantages que Die m'accord un peu de force.

En foi d qui ce 19 october 1737 j'ai signé
ALBERT RADICATI DE PASSERAN

He had only five days left to live. As we can see he was by this time incapable of remembering the exact titles of books, still less of writing correctly even the simplest words. He was merely repeating the expressions offered by those around him. But the reference to the *Discours* by means of which he had sought to convince Victor Amadeus II is all his own and there is a deep sincerity in that very human ending: 'Que Dieu m'accorde un peu de force.'

Royer and Superville reported the conversion and death of Radicati in the *Bibliothèque françoise*. The Grand Pensionary van der Heym, who was worried about the harm that Passerano's works might still be able to cause, sent for Pastor Royer and together they decided to confiscate 'as quietly as possible', all the copies still to be found in the bookshops. For reasons that are not clear they also decided not to publish the documents concerning the conversion. With the report which was presented to the Synod of Ziericksee in 1738 the Radicati affair was closed and the papers concerning his death were locked away in the 'chest' of the Walloon church in The Hague 'where they remain to this day'.

F. G. Ch. Rütz, who concluded his narrative thus (and almost two hundred years later we can only repeat his assertion), also left us some hope of one day finding something else written by Radicati—by Radicati the atheist and free-thinker. As we have seen, his biographer writing in 1781 already did not know what had happened to the papers which were found in Passerano's room when he died. However, Rütz himself, at the very beginning of his book, informed the reader that he had in his possession a manuscript collection containing some unpublished writings by Radicati. Furthermore, it was this—he said—which had originally given him the idea of discovering more about the circumstances of the Count's life and writing an account of his death, naturally with apologetic intent. In the third chapter of his work he stopped to list Radicati's published and unpublished works and thus came back to the subject of the contents of his precious manuscript. Meanwhile he informed us that he had seen published versions of *La Religion muhammédane* and the *Sermon prêché* but that they also existed in manuscript form in the collection which he possessed. Along with these there were some unknown works, notably a '*Discours sur les miracles de Notre Seigneur*, par Albert Radicati comte de Passeran, 59 pages of quarto written in a very small, neat hand. These 59 sheets, printed in the same way as the *Recueil*, would come to about 80 pages.' What was being offered here, Rütz added, was 'a deist dish, heated and prepared with a bitter sauce, a dish which Tindal, Collins and especially Woolston had already served up before in one form or another'. From this comment and from the lengthy analysis of this work made by Rütz in his book, it seems possible to deduce that it was not just a paraphrase of Woolston's tract of the same name. But it was nevertheless 'eene uitbreiding', that is, it derived from it. 'For when Woolston wrote his tract, Passerano was already under the influence of Tindal and Collins. At least in 1728 he was already in England.'

The other, even more important manuscript in Rütz's possession was entitled '*Discours sur les religions et les gouvernmens* par Albert Radicati comte de Passeran, fugitif des Etats du Roi de Sardaigne et réfugié à Londres, 1728'.

> In these discourses [said Rütz] he attempted to prove that the best kind of religion is founded and established by *legislators* with the intention of consolidating their political power and assuring their authority. The conclusion he drew from this was that power and authority, both in ecclesiastical and civil matters, belonged by right to the *sovereign*. This text consists of 122 pages, written in the same manner as the one previously mentioned. Its subject matter is closely related to the *Recueil*, on p. 87, *sub lit.* B

that is the *Histoire abrègée de la profession sacerdotale ancienne et moderne, dediée à la très illustre et très célèbre secte des Esprits-Forts par un Free Thinker chrétien*, to be found on pp. 239 ff. of the *Recueil de pièces curieuses*.

We shall not follow Rütz in his lengthy deliberations—which take up the greater part of the remaining pages of the book—on the moral and religious value of the conversions of deists, the deaths of believers and of Radicati's death in particular. Instead we shall conclude with the hope that the manuscript which belonged to the zealous Dutch Lutheran minister may one day come to light.

4 Enlightenment versus the Powers of Darkness

IT was the Republic of St Mark, not Venice but Rovereto and Verona, which was the scene of the most important attempt carried out in the 1740s to test the power and limits of human reason by matching it against tradition, superstition and prejudice. The Cartesian tradition, critical methods and the nascent modern scientific spirit clashed with a dark, oppressive world of popular belief and theology and sought to penetrate and destroy it. The dispute over witches and magicians, begun by Tartarotti and continued by Carli, Muratori, Maffei and their followers and opponents marked the transition in the middle of the century from rationalism to enlightenment, from Cartesian logic to a determination to use reason as a means of control over religion and human society. It corresponded to the debate on certainty and miracles which took place in France following the appearance of the first two volumes of the *Encyclopédie* and which involved d'Alembert and Diderot, de Prades and Yvon, the party of the *philosophes* and the Sorbonne. The Italian dispute was confined within much narrower limits, as if to test the force and power of reason, which by this time had come into its own, on a single point rather than over the whole field of human belief. Whereas the language used in the discussion in Paris was free and open and marked the birth of modern atheism, in Italy both sides were still confined within the armour of erudition and doctrine. Blows were dealt with much greater caution. But in Italy too, reason was able to give a good account of itself as it revealed festering sores and old, deep-seated fears, broadened its field of conquest and measured more exactly the limits of its own domain.

The first signs of the discussion which was to come had already appeared during the War of the Austrian Succession. A book by Marquis Giuseppe Gorini Corio was published in Milan in 1742; it was far from being unorthodox but nevertheless it did arouse suspicion and opposition on the grounds, among other things, that it completely denied the existence of all magic arts. Because the authorities so wished, and because it appeared at a time ill-suited to the airing of such problems, this first spark soon died out.

When Girolamo Tartarotti turned to these matters in 1744, he gave his attention not to magicians but to witches. This was a significant choice and one which he defended ever afterwards, even against adversaries like Scipione Maffei. He clung to his original inspiration, even when rapid changes in the cultural environment seemed to make his decision incomprehensible, if not absurd. But Tartarotti knew that it was connected with his whole personality as a scholar and writer.

When he had begun writing, at the beginning of the 'thirties, the time had already passed for armed confrontations between different philosophical systems. Cartesianism was heading for defeat, crushed by the weight of the theological battles which had been waged over it, and lived on only as an early source of critical methods and as an incentive to use them to test scientific and historical traditions. Tartarotti's personality suited the situation well. As Clementino Vanetti said: 'Abbé Girolamo had more intelligence than imagination and more judgment than either.'

He came from Rovereto, from a modest provincial patrician family and began his literary career with a vigorous attack on scholasticism. He felt that it contained something sinister and unhealthy, something which was capable of divorcing man from his own nature and making him the slave of dreams and illusions. For him scholasticism represented an enchantment which reason had both the power and duty to break: 'When I see the yoke which burdens the most glorious, noble talents and the monsters created in their hundreds by this wicked Circe with her enchantments. . . . But yet a great desire has arisen in me to reveal the truth so ill-defended against the barbarous, filthy, hideous hordes.'

As he said to a friend who was trying to persuade him to take things more easily, it was still necessary to keep up the fight: 'It may be that eventually the enchantment will disappear.'

He was determined not to 'rest at night' until he had dealt at least a few blows against 'these troubled and corrupt minds'. This was why he wrote his verses and a satirical poem attacking the theological disputes among the monks and why he published in

1731 his *Idea of logic, scholastic and modern*. It was an impassioned defence of modern philosophy against all the deep corruption and distortion of morality and logic which were still being disseminated by traditional philosophy, thus cutting off at the source that passionate love of truth which was the only means of defence against the powerful 'enchantments of scholasticism'. Modern logic—Arnauld, Mabillon, Bernard Lamy, Jean Le Clerc and Gravina—was alone able to reach the level of the recent scientific, anatomical and other discoveries. But was logic alone, because it was still chained to outdated forms, 'destined to be excluded from the benefits which all the other arts enjoy'? If it were reformed it could have great potential as an educational tool —real education as opposed to the overweening pride instilled in the minds of young people by the aimless meanderings of traditional logic. Thus it would be possible to re-establish a genuine relationship between thought and language and to return to a simple and truthful style of thought, by keeping faithfully to the 'positive method, which means giving a clear, unadorned explanation of precepts without quibbling and without rhetoric'. This was an essential procedure, not only in philosophical and religious matters, but especially on the civil plane. Those who emerged from the traditional schools with their heads full of empty formulae and complicated games of logic and had to pass 'from philosophy to the forum, to public office', would inevitably take with them 'little love for truth'. This was the most serious consequence of the ways of reasoning which they had been taught. The worst thing of all was that they 'became accustomed to maxims which are completely opposed to the light of reason and, in short, lost the feeling which is common to all other men', and became dominated instead by a spirit which is 'hostile and harmful to practicable things'. The only possible outcome of this was the 'ruin of all good arts'. 'In this way the garden of natural science which is extremely beautiful and abounding in delights has been sown by them with thorns and nettles.' In the case of astronomy and physics, a situation had been reached where peasants and artisans knew more than the pseudo-scholars turned out by the schools. 'In matters concerning the heavens the workers in the fields are, without a doubt, much better informed than they are and butchers and craftsmen are much better qualified to talk about the composition and properties of bodies.'

Thus Tartarotti's work contained an appeal for a stricter and more modest conception of the role of logic in the world of truth, a rejection of all logic divorced from the arts, civil life and religion, a deepening, but at the same time a limitation of the function of reason in philosophical research. Logic was 'the study of man' and it was time that it returned to its original Socratic inspiration. Like the good scholar he was, Tartarotti was careful to explain in detail where such an impulse came from. He referred in particular to the humanists of the fifteenth century, Ermolao Barbaro, Pico della Mirandola and Lorenzo Valla, explaining how a modern philosophy had developed in the sixteenth and seventeenth centuries as a method of scientific enquiry and erudition.

As he explained in the following year, 1732, when he was discussing a work by Giuseppe Valletta which he had just had reprinted, it was no longer a question of going back to the past and taking up the Renaissance polemic against Aristotle, nor even of continuing to preach the philosophy of Descartes. The moderns recognised two other great masters, Bacon and Galileo, and they were not prepared to become 'faithful followers of any one particular philosopher'. 'It is true', he added, 'that you cannot be Cartesian without also being modern, but it is not true that you cannot be modern without being Cartesian'. Modern philosophy knew only one principle, 'the pure search for truth in whatever place it may be found'. He took his principles from Valla, Pico, Vives, Telesio and Patrizi, but at the same time he was conscious of the fact that 'a free method of philosophising' had in fact been established, thanks chiefly to two men, 'Galileo Galilei in Italy and Francis Bacon in England'.

There were obviously two names missing in this genealogy of the modern spirit: Newton and Locke. It was still too soon in 1731–32, even for a man as receptive and sensitive as Tartarotti. But not even later on did he choose to follow the direction of his century, remaining faithful, even in the years that followed, to his original inspiration—critical and modern, erudite and eclectic. In 1734 he dedicated to Muratori his first piece of historical research on Rovereto and in 1740 he published a *Dissertation on critical methods*.

In 1741 he went with Foscarini on a diplomatic mission to Turin and there too he was more interested in books and ancient codices than in the political disputes of his age. By 1744 he had made his decision: he would devote all his energies to fighting the myths connected with witchcraft, that most sinister form of hallucination which had induced the theologians to prescribe such harsh measures. He read extensively and wrote long chapters which he circulated to fellow scholars in manuscript form. Finally, in 1749, Giambattista Pasquali published in Venice, with the imprint Rovereto, *On the nocturnal gatherings of witches, three volumes by Girolamo Tartarotti, with the addition of two dissertations in the form of letters on the art of magic. To His Lordship Ottolino Ottolini, nobleman of Verona, count of Custoza etc.*

It was a long journey into a world of horror and in order to penetrate it there was an initial opaque diaphragm which had to be broken: the rationalisations and justifications which the theologians had built around it for centuries. Tartarotti possessed the right instruments to carry out this essential preliminary operation. The critical method, Muratori, the polemics against the casuists, his whole age had taught him that history was difficult to write precisely because there had been so much reasoning about facts instead of looking at sources, that jurisprudence had been ruined by annotation and commentary which obscured 'equity and reason', and that 'Christian morality' had 'been spoiled and confused by the great throng of casuists with their copious output'. History, jurisprudence and moral theology had become aware of the need to free themselves from the weight of the past in order to go back to the beginning and ensure a rational approach. Tartarotti meant to do the same in the darker, more mysterious and less clearly defined field of superstition.

He felt compelled to do this by a feeling of compassion towards the victims of that cruel, fossilised form of reasoning. Here too it was necessary to return to the most basic human feelings and to allow oneself to experience the repugnance which could not fail to be aroused by the thought of the 'terrible slaughter' and 'pitiful tragedies' which everywhere, for centuries, had repeatedly been the outcome of witch hunts. No longer was he moved, as in his youthful verses, by a feeling of pity for 'every glorious, noble talent', weighed down beneath the yoke of scholasticism. Now he was concerned with a much more wretched situation, the plight of poor, ignorant, sick women.

Patiently, with the aid of simple logic, Tartarotti gathered together the theories which had been advanced over the years and subjected witchcraft to a test of plausibility. How could witches fly so fast and so far? How could the devil have such power over bodies? How was it that witches could lie with the devil without ever becoming pregnant? How could they really eat at the devil's feasts and never be satisfied? Why did the devil not free them from prison, why did he not help them? It was not in fact very difficult for Tartarotti to show that witchcraft did not square with the physics of his age nor with the conception men of his time had of good and evil. His was a typical rationalistic examination of a reality stripped bare of the theological cloak in which it had been enveloped for centuries.

What then remained of witchcraft? If it was definitely removed from the sphere of religion by excluding the possibility of the devil's intervention, if it was considered in terms of logic and morality, what was it? In spite of the caution with which he proceeded, Tartarotti's originality lay in his attempt to provide an explanation which was not medical or psychological but rather historical and social. He attempted to 'investigate the true source of this popular belief which so far has not been clearly or adequately explored' and to trace it back to the 'remains of idolatry in the European dark ages'. He came to the conclusion that it was derived from the cult of Diana and was convinced that he could prove the 'association between the cult of Diana and modern witchcraft'.

His scholarly research was able to take him this far. He tried to go one step further by viewing with unprejudiced eyes a fact that was repeated with monotonous regularity in the frightful chronicles of the Inquisition: that the witches were poor women living in wretched conditions in isolated villages. Tartarotti was particularly struck by the social character of the phenomenon which he was studying. It always involved 'poor persons in the countryside, not the rich in towns'. Here lay the key to witchcraft. 'These poor country women live almost entirely on milk, herbs, chestnuts, pulse vegetables and other such foods which make thick, sluggish blood and produce horrible, frightening dreams.' Geographically too, the phenomenon seemed restricted to the poorer, more dismal countries: 'the cold, primitive lands where the people have nothing to do and no means of amusing themselves, where they drink beer and milk, also play a large part in producing this effect.' It was difficult to say exactly how this came about. 'The fact is that, in spite of the substantial amount written on the subject by various authors, we still do not have a complete history of the powers of the imagination.' Meanwhile it was necessary to establish not only the social but also the geographical nature of these occurrences, as well as of vampirism which was widespread particularly in 'Hungary and Serbia'.

His investigations into witchcraft revealed to Tartarotti a whole wretched, gloomy world, so far removed from civilised society that it remained isolated and alone even in its dreams and fantasies. One could not even imagine a witch as a wealthy, educated person.

It is likely that a nobleman, or a noblewoman, for the sake of example, who is young, cheerful and good-humoured, married to a gentleman who is also young and wealthy, should seek pleasure in the companionship of others in a civilised country with an agreeable climate like France or Italy. However, I consider it impossible that such a person should become a witch, that is agree to take part in a nocturnal gathering of witches and demons, and I am ready to admit defeat if my opponents can quote me a single example.

What he found even more horrible was the persecution carried out by educated, civilised people on poor, ignorant wretches. This happened everywhere, especially in Germany where there was 'incredible slaughter' of witches; nor was it completely absent even in Italy (Tartarotti mentioned, among others, the case of Domenica Pedrotti, a witch beheaded not far from his native Rovereto). He was very pleased to discover that Muratori, in a treatise on the powers of the imagination which appeared just when he was writing the last part of his book, had also denied the reality of witchcraft. However, he felt obliged to correct his master on one point, on his assertion that no one believed in witchcraft any more. 'Truly this would be very desirable, but not even Europe has yet reached this happy state, let alone other, less civilised parts of the world.' The psychological explanation provided by Muratori, which Tartarotti finally seemed to accept, did not take away the obligation to view the matter calmly and critically. A phenomenon like that of witches was not dismissed so easily and did not yield entirely in the face of goodwill and commonsense.

Magic seemed to him to be of a very different nature. This, he said, was a phenomenon of men who belonged to the cultured, learned, civilised world. Here the critical method did not seem to him an adequate instrument to rule out a genuine religious character, a real desire to violate divine law by appealing to diabolical forces. The reality of witchcraft could be denied without touching upon the theological problem of the devil, but the same could not be said about magic. The historian was bound to recognise that magicians had existed, that there had been much discussion about magic among philosophers and men like Pomponazzi, for example, who, perhaps mistakenly, had been accused of similar offences. Just as when he was studying witches Tartarotti had come upon a world full of poverty and hunger, so when he spoke of magic he discovered a whole current of thought which, with the curiosity of the scholar, he felt obliged to study and investigate—the world of Ficino, Paracelsus, Cardano. How could its existence be denied? In similar manner to the rediscovery of humanism, which was taking place in Florence around Lami and other Tuscan scholars, and the voyages of discovery into the age of the Renaissance which Marco Foscarini and Angelo Querini were engaged upon at that time, Tartarotti too found himself face to face with a fascinating, half-forgotten world. Those old ideas and discussions seemed far too interesting to be dismissed with a sceptical shake of the head and a knowing smile. Tartarotti believed that the problem of the relationship between these philosopher-magicians and religious tradition really existed and was very different from the case of the poor witches in the villages.

But the logic of rationalism could not be halted to accommodate the scruples of this scholar, historian and Catholic who wanted to remain within the fold. The step which Tartarotti refused to take was very soon to be taken by others. Gianrinaldo Carli, a young professor of navigation at Padua, who also came from a Venetian province, Capodistria, and who was younger and bolder than Tartarotti, told him plainly after he had read the manuscript of the *Nocturnal gatherings* that one could not stop halfway. Tartarotti had done very well to fight superstition and to make a clear distinction between the devil and madness, between the provinces of religion and medicine. It was true, he said, that belief in witchcraft was much more widespread than was generally admitted:

I know that in Slavonia, Istria, Dalmatia, Albania, the Levant, Venice itself, in Friuli and elsewhere among simple women and slow-witted men the most common and firmest beliefs are those concerning witches, enchantments, spells and nocturnal gatherings, although some claim that this is not so . . . but when (if you will permit me to say so) we come to the question of magic your ably constructed work collapses.

What distinction could possibly be made between witches and magicians? In both cases it was a question of charlatanism. It was precisely for this reason, he added, that they deserved punishment, 'not because of their power, but because of their awareness of error, their conscious and depraved sins'. Both were deceivers and as such could and should be punished.

Tartarotti was amazed to be attacked in this way from the quarter 'from which he least expected'. He had been afraid of having 'denied too much', not too little. It was obvious what was worrying him. Christian Thomasius, the famous German jurist, 'at the beginning of the present century' had alienated even his Protestant public by upholding such ideas as those now expounded by Gianrinaldo Carli. It was a path which led straight to loss of belief. He well understood the mentality of scientists (and, we might add, in particular of scientists with Cartesian roots like himself):

Truly it seems that natural philosophers are very reluctant to believe in what they cannot see and touch. Their constant contemplation of the tangible world in which they can observe an amazing order, rule and measure, has the effect, so to speak, of immersing them in matter, and with its various forms, movements and combinations they imagine that they can explain all the phenomena which appear in the great theatre of the universe, including even the most wonderful and surprising of all, human thought.

We can almost see the appearance at this stage of the discussion on witches and magicians of a character who just at that time, in 1748, had come upon the scene in European philosophy, de la Mettrie's *l'homme machine*, also of Cartesian origin.

Tartarotti was aware of this temptation in the logic of his thought, but he rejected it. The world, and in particular the human world, was too mysterious and complex to be explained in mechanical terms. It was sufficient to think of men like Democritus and Paracelsus. Natural magic could be found in Bacon and as for black magic, 'Holy Scripture, ecclesiastical and civil history, the monuments and traditions of every people and every nation' gave patent proof of its existence. How could a historian and scientist deny a fact which was so universally accepted? 'If we deny this fact, shall we not by the same reasoning and just as easily be able to deny all other facts? And will not the denial of all these amount to the destruction of the link which binds together and preserves our civil society?' Beyond reason existed the facts and it was on these and not on reason itself that certainty and human society were based. The task of the thinker was not to deny facts but to understand them. 'It is the philosopher's duty to extract the truth even from fables . . .' The limits of historical criticism here became very obvious: its task was to understand, not to destroy its subject.

In order to guard against taking that further step along the path of reason which Gianrinaldo Carli was asking him to take (but where could one stop?), Tartarotti eventually came to cling to magic (and even to such things as sprites and elves) as to a reality which he was not prepared to relinquish. It made no difference to him that in Germany Eberhard David Hauber had produced 'thirty-six little volumes and perhaps more' with the aim of fighting against magic. He took no notice at all of what Bekker had written. 'I do not have in my possession nor have I ever read any book by this writer.' He was obviously concerned to show that he kept even his library within the bounds of Catholic orthodoxy. He even went as far as to offer the trials and sentences inflicted upon magicians as proof of the existence of magic. But he returned time and again to his favourite argument. Carli had maintained that magic was a bastard child of Pythagoras. How then could it be compared to witchcraft? 'One is an abortion of philosophy and the other of imagination. One is a form of ignorance or deception on the part of priests, doctors and others who cultivate the sciences, while the other is a form of illusion or fanaticism which affects for the most part poor, simple women and other unfortunate individuals of base extraction.' He concluded by saying to Carli and all who thought as he did (for example Dr Antonio Rossi, who had written to him to say that 'If we admit the existence of magicians I do not see why we should not also admit the existence of witches') that they were trying to stretch the limits of human reason too far 'by demanding from human intellect what human intellect is not permitted to know'.

Tartarotti had obviously been unwise in his choice of battle-field. It was useless for him to repeat that what concerned him was to 'recognise real witches' and 'real magicians', both historically determined and yet very different from one another, and his attempts to oppose fact to reason were in vain. The ground would very quickly begin to crumble beneath his feet. Historical reason applied to the devil could not be upheld in critical, historical terms. If he had been talking about anything else his statements concerning the limits of human knowledge might possibly have appeared convincing, but in talking about the devil he was standing over an abyss. In dealing with diabolical forces it was fatal to invoke the absolute authority of proof, reason and logic.

Before the end of 1749 the decisive step had been taken with *Magic arts dismissed. A letter from Marquis Maffei to Father Vincent Ansaldi of the Order of Preachers*, published in Verona by Agostino Carattoni. With great assurance, Scipione Maffei, who boasted that in all his seventy-four years he had never seen a sprite, declared not only that magicians were impostors but that no general consensus on magic existed at all (Hippocrates and Pliny laughed at it), and that 'magic art today is non-existent'. As he had already done when arguing the case for usury, here too he covered himself by means of a historical distinction. In the Old Testament the incidence of magic practices was too frequent to be denied, but with the New Testament all this had changed. In the modern world such phenomena did not exist except in the form of prejudice and superstition: the kind of prejudice which had caused even Maffei to be accused of being a magician when he had carried out some electrical experiments in France with his friend Séguier and the kind of superstition which ought to be allowed to sink gradually 'into silence and oblivion'. 'If in a place where there have been no evil spirits from time immemorial a rumour spreads that a holy man has arrived who is able to cast them out, you immediately see hysterical women and hypochondriacs rushing to the place, children being brought . . .' If then it were really necessary to combat superstition openly, it would be better to begin with magic which was much more widespread, rather than with witchcraft. 'In Italy at least' witchcraft was laughed at 'even by ordinary folk who were not dull half-wits'. Hauber had done well to publish his *Magic library* and Tartarotti too should have followed a similar course.

We shall often find the term 'non-existent' used in the eighteenth century on both sides of the Alps. The problem itself was dismissed and reason triumphed. However, judges, preachers and archbishops did not seem prepared to give in so easily. In the same year that Maffei's book was published, on 21 June 1749 a nun called Maria Renata Singerin was beheaded at Würzburg. She was convicted of having had relations with the devil from the time she was a child and having succeeded in concealing such wickedness up to the age of seventy-three. Her body was burnt. During the ceremony the Jesuit father Georg Gaar had made a speech in which he stated that if 'thieves, murderers, adulterers and the like are, according to the laws, to be punished by death, who would dare to exclude magicians?' 'Charles V is especially worthy of everlasting praise inasmuch as according to his constitution, article 109, magicians are to be burnt alive and this will now be put into practice.' The spectacle which Father Gaar took part in with so much conviction was in his eyes a beneficial one from many points of view, not least that of giving a warning to 'unbelievers, for there are such people in our time who do not believe in witches or magicians, nor in the devil, nor even in God himself'.

When a friend provided Tartarotti with an Italian translation of the text, he found in it the confirmation of all his ideas and hastened to publish it in Verona, 'convinced that he was doing a great service to Italians who for a long time had not been accustomed to such spectacles'. He immediately added that 'in order to avoid the prejudicial effect which the woeful example of this death might have on weaker persons or less enlightened courts, I have thought it advisable to balance this by adding some *Annotations* in the most important places'. Tartarotti took advantage of this opportunity to draw some grave conclusions about the state of German culture. He felt that it should also be noted that the people of Würzburg had received the speech with enthusiasm and approval. The very culture of priests like Father Gaar could only have been a product of 'those German gymnasiums in which Emmanuele Tesauro's *Aristotelian telescope* is still held in great

esteem'. As for the unbelievers, their opinion on witchcraft, th
conviction that it was merely a 'trick of an unhealthy, disorde
imagination' had to be shared by the 'best and most learn
Catholics'. 'No amount of sorcery can disprove this hypothesis a
what is more, in spite of thousands of witches having been bu
in Europe the Epicureans have never yielded, nor are they lik
to do so on this account.'

In Würzburg cathedral on St Mary Magdalene's day, Fatl
Gaar gave another great sermon confirming his theses. When
received news from Verona about what had been published c
cerning him, he replied with some *Responsa ad annotatio
criticas Dr F.A.T.* He too could not fail to notice the inher
contradiction in the thought of his opponent: how could
believe in magicians and not in witches? He was particula
shocked by the absence in Tartarotti of a due sense of submissi
to constituted authority. Who gave him the right to criticise
magistrates of Würzburg? 'Quis te constituit judicem su
judices?' Johann Baptist Graser answered Father Gaar in a pam
let published in Venice, which was later translated into Gern
and published in Bayreuth. Graser, a Franciscan, was to rem
ever afterwards a faithful follower of Tartarotti and when
latter died, he delivered an enthusiastic funeral oration. He brou
to the chair of moral philosophy in Innsbruck, to which he v
appointed in 1761, a spirit of tolerance and enlightenment wh
had first manifested itself when he took part in this debate. H
we have reached the point where the significance of Tartarot
polemic changes as it is transmitted to the new generation. Gra
was already a freemason, a friend of Gregorio Fontana, and
had a part in that complicated sectarian movement which v
so important in the Trentino at the end of the eighteenth cent
and the beginning of the nineteenth. He was one of the links
that area between Tartarotti's critical approach and the enlighte
attitude of Carlantonio Pilati.

Meanwhile, halfway through the eighteenth century the pole
was increasing in range and depth. The most formidable adversa
proved to be those nearest home. The Venetian *Novelle della
pubblica letteraria* had already warned Tartarotti that he
'embarked in a sea full of sizeable rocks'. Still in Venice, Fran
cantonio Zaccaria, in his *Storia letteraria d'Italia*, defended
Jesuit Del Rio, the most famous and fanatical persecutor of witc
among the theologians of the past, with the implication that neit
Tartarotti nor Carli had considered the consequence 'to which th
opinions might lead'. Of greater interest, and this time favoura
to Tartarotti, even though of an almost exclusively legal charac

was a dissertation by Bartolomeo Melchiori published in 1750. In Florence, Giovanni Lami's *Novelle letterarie* did not dare to take a firm stand on the matter and sheltered behind the opinion of Muratori. They published a letter written by him on 18 June in which he expressed wholehearted enthusiastic support for Tartarotti:

> I am accustomed to assess the value of books according to the contribution which they are capable of making to the common good . . . I cannot overstress the benefits to be derived from this book over such a wide area of Europe. I would never have imagined that such a deadly, malignant form of superstition could still persist in so many places, have had so many defenders and have caused so much harm . . . This book ought to be translated into German, Hungarian and the various other languages of the lands where such insane opinions still abide . . .

Maffei too came in for his share of discussions and replies, even if in his case the accusations and threats were less explicit. There was too much respect for the great scholar and writer and then, basically, Tartarotti was correct in saying that the polemic against witches touched on a more sensitive, vital point than that against magicians. Besides, Maffei was a better, more able polemicist than Tartarotti. He had no hesitation in employing a curious device— he set about writing his own defence (though it is difficult to say how much it could really have been expected to deceive anyone). It contained some generous compliments to himself and was written in a language which was more German than Italian, heavy and involved, with extremely ungainly sentences and all the verbs at the end. He published this pamphlet under the title *Magic arts annihilated. The reply of Don Antonio Fiorio, Dean of Tignale and Valvestino, Vicar Forane*, with the imprint Trent 1750. Shortly afterwards, in 1751, he received proof of the fact that some minds were still completely impervious to his reasoning and debating skills. At that time a pamphlet was published entitled *Magic arts proved* by Bartolommeo Preati. The author had a very high opinion of the 'devil's science', his 'power and his malice' and was certainly not prepared to see all the devil's attributes dismissed so easily. 'By allowing the use of charms and spells God makes his power appear all the greater, not only to the good but also to the wicked, and in particular to those who claim that there is nothing in the world except what can be seen by mortal eyes and who deny the existence of spirits, demons, angels and God himself.' The Oratorian Andrea Lugiato had something similar to say in his *Observations on the pamphlet entitled Magic arts dismissed*. The discussion was in danger of being buried in arguments which had been repeated for centuries without making any progress along the path of greater understanding.

Still in 1751, the publisher Simone Occhi issued a small anonymous volume entitled *Critical observations on the nocturnal gatherings of witches in the form of letters addressed to a scholar*. Its author was the most authoritative and most reactionary of Trentino scholars, Benedetto Bonelli. It was dedicated to Marco Foscarini, whom a scholarly dispute had estranged from Tartarotti, once his friend and secretary. Bonelli appealed to the famous Procurator of St Mark to put a stop to these dangerous disputes concerning witches and magicians as soon as possible. Was it not perhaps better to keep to the wise old Venetian practice of not disputing their existence or nature, but being satisfied with a 'fair examination' and 'precise criterion' by which to 'remove all the nonsense surrounding them' and 'separate the true from the false'? One had to 'admit that the devil is able to do more than we can imagine with those who have lost all conscience and faith, although it is not often that God allows him to use such power to harm men'. This was, in short, a refined, moderate theology, aimed above all at masking the new problems which had arisen in the discussion sparked off by Tartarotti. It was better to go back to Sarpi and the Venetian practice which admitted lay magistrates into the courts which judged witches. But did not the very fact that the republic had acted in this way prove the existence of witches? 'Likewise the laws against simony, usury etc, presuppose the truth of the fact.' Moderation yes, denial no—while the great achievement of Tartarotti and Maffei had been to put an end to a long series of appeals to caution and understanding in order to arrive at a radical denial. This was just what Bonelli feared. 'Does not the denial of the existence of devils facilitate or even lead to a denial of the existence of God also?'

In an appendix to his work Bonelli reproduced the texts of the dispute with Father Gaar 'in order to introduce and publicise them in Italy where so far they are known to very few'. They would serve to put a check on those who were aiming to 'enlighten secular and ecclesiastical tribunals . . . and reform the whole world with new doctrines'. It was fortunate that in the meantime there was no lack of authoritative statements in favour of traditional doctrine and practice.

And here I feel compelled to mention the death sentence carried out upon a witch in Salzburg, following the one in Würzburg and the other one at Landshüt. She was convicted on her own confession and executed after an extremely lengthy debate and a very thorough examination and trial. There was a careful scrutiny of the books of the *Nocturnal gatherings* and there were various undertakings on the part of those who would like to dismiss witchcraft and magic and, by order, there was a second hearing after the original trial—in short, all imaginable measures were taken in order to discover the truth.

It was true. Tartarotti had undertaken the attempt to save the life of the youthful witch of Salzburg. He himself described what happened in his reply to Scipione Maffei in the summer of 1751 and this is one of the best things he ever wrote. At almost exactly the same time as the execution in Würzburg of Renata Maria Singerin, he said :

At Landhut [*sic*], a Bavarian fortress, a laundress was also beheaded for the same crime. There is at the moment in Salzburg one of her assistants, an unfortunate girl of sixteen who is in grave danger of meeting the same fate as her mistress. A knowledgeable and able person is doing all that is humanly possible to help her, making the judges read Father Spee and the *Nocturnal gatherings* (I say this through love of the truth and not because I wish to boast).

He was not optimistic but he was doing all he could. Surely it was not wise in these circumstances to distract or perhaps even shock the judges by talking about magic too. Did not Maffei's ideas risk confirming the magistrates of Salzburg in their prejudices?

I should certainly have been afraid that by demanding too much I should not achieve anything or, by denying the devil's magic with so little proof, make it possible for the evils of witchcraft to gain strength and eventually triumph. We ought to weep hot tears over and wonder at the awful consequences produced by certain books, the work of enthusiastic sophists who, fanatically clinging to their own views through thick and thin, have not noticed that they were waging war on the human race and kindling the flames that would consume so many innocent victims because they upset and anger less intelligent and experienced judges with their fallacies, quibbling and lies.

Witchcraft was, in short, a question of conscience for Tartarotti but magic was not. How could Maffei not understand the difference? 'The life of a human being is not a trivial thing.' When you were attempting to snatch the victim out of the hands of the judges, any wrong word or move became a crime. The facts seemed to prove Tartarotti right. The young witch was executed.

But even before this happened, how could anyone maintain that it was not worth fighting against the trial of witches?

> It is easy enough to say that it is all tales and nonsense, but it is not so easy to prove this to everyone. If scholars no longer believe in them, courts and judges do . . . However ridiculous, unlikely, shocking these tales may be, though they might seem fit only for the heathen, they have, nevertheless, found learned, scholarly men, of great authority and intellect, willing to publish large volumes protecting and defending them and they are still defended by many renowned theologians.

What then was to be done? 'Is it any good standing with our arms folded and saying that they are popular superstitions and that wise men laugh at them? Are our responsibilities only towards wise men or towards everyone?' How was it possible to accept the argument, so often put forward in this discussion, according to which, in Italy at least, these prejudices had ceased to have such tragic consequences. 'Is the man who writes books writing only for his own nation or for all nations?' Thus Tartarotti opposed Maffei's local scepticism with a vigorous cosmopolitanism. 'As far as I am concerned, I should be just as pleased if my book saved the life of a German or an Arab as I would if it saved the life of an Italian from my own town since they are all equally members of the human race . . . Are only those who speak our own language to be called our brothers or all those possessing a body and a mind?' Besides, it was not true that in Italy prejudices concerning witchcraft had completely disappeared. In 1741 a book had appeared, written by a judge—he was talking about Giovanni Sebastiano De Vespignanis—who approved of the death sentence passed on a witch and of life imprisonment for her daughter 'for having been seduced'. 'This gentleman, who also possessed very fine and rare gifts and was the author of various other books, died a few years ago in Genoa where he was an ecclesiastical judge.' The theologians were even worse. A typical example was Father Daniele Concina who had devoted several pages of his *Theologia christiana dogmatico-moralis* to a discussion *De Lammis, sagis et strigibus* (*On witches, magicians and screech-owls*), showing that he believed that witches really existed, 'rara utique haec sunt' (although these things are rare). 'Even in Italy', then, it was not 'only dull half-wits' who believed in witches. 'It is not only beyond the Alps and in barbarous regions that you hear of, death sentences carried out upon them.'

These judges and theologians were persecuting an obscure, popular world while magicians, as Tartarotti, with the aid of a wealth of quotations, attempted to prove to Maffei, had links not only with the classical world but especially with the humanistic world of the fifteenth and sixteenth centuries. There was, for example, 'that phoenix of intellects, Giovanni Pico della Mirandola' who had most certainly been attracted by it in his youth. Tartarotti was unwilling to tear himself away from this world and renounce it completely. Right to the end he upheld his thesis according to which magic ought to be considered a phenomenon related to philosophy and religion. He continued to lay stress on the general consensus which proved the existence of real magicians, even if there had also been many false ones. There was no point in quoting Pliny, who was 'an atheist', nor Hippocrates, who in reality had never entirely denied these facts. And so he went deeper and deeper into a thick forest of quotations, proofs and verifications where Marquis Maffei could just as well leave him to lose himself completely.

Tartarotti thus defended an important position against everything and everyone, on one point alone and in a somewhat paradoxical way. Facts ought not to be denied, or it would be a 'strange rule for the new art of history', 'and if it became established, the Pyrrhonists would have won the day'. 'Human faith' was certainly fallible and subject to error. 'Nevertheless, there are certain facts, in both ancient and modern times, which have been confirmed by so large a number of witnesses of various nationalities, religions and ways of life, that without doing a grave injustice to reason they could not be doubted.'

Thus historical faith and reason fought over the devil himself and carried the contrast between criticism and logic to the point of absurdity. Tartarotti was aware of the price to be paid for this dispute. 'Meanwhile human society continues inasmuch as men believe one another. And nature seems to have grafted a mysterious inclination to believe one another onto men's minds simply because, without it, human society would be just like that of animals.' Or else, we could add, as was already being said around him, it would be a society completely based on reason, social contracts and equality and not on faith, belief and trust. We can see how Tartarotti was stopping just at the edge of the Enlightenment but refusing to take that final step which would lead to a completely practical and rational conception of human society.

When Maffei set out, in 1754 with *Magic arts annihilated*, to say his own last word on the subject, the dispute had become somewhat broader. By this time he could count fourteen combatants lined up in the lists and these certainly presented a very variegated picture. They included Clemente Baroni of the marquises of Cavalcabò who a year previously had decided to resolve the question by appealing to pure reasoning. Why continue to appeal to authority? What had to be done was to prove logically that it was impossible for the devil to work magic. Until this was accomplished, those who 'toil with worthy writings to root out ancient prejudices from the minds of others' would never succeed in their intent. Therefore 'the controversial issues involved here are for the most part still in the balance and it is uncertain which way victory will go'. Men did not have enough faith in the 'powers of philosophy'. He would prove 'the fundamental impossibility and consequently the falsity of just one of the many claims that were made for the devil's power'. He chose 'one of the most vaunted and widely credited, something which really forms the basis of belief about witchcraft, that is the power to transport human bodies from one place to another'. The devil could not carry out this operation 'by means of whirlwinds', nor could he use the 'condensation of the air'. He could not 'raise bodies into the air by taking away their specific gravity', nor was he able to 'teach men to fly'. Therefore it was impossible to fly and witchcraft did not exist and philosophy had resolved the whole question.

In the front line of the opposing ranks stood Father Tommaso Maria Mamachi who, at the beginning of his long career as persecutor of free-thinkers and philosophers, had limbered up by attacking *magiae oppugnatores* (opponents of magic) in the third volume of his *Christian antiquities*, published in Rome in 1751. Somewhere between these two positions lurked the shade of one of the most important representatives of Neapolitan Cartesianism and anticlerical thought, Costantino Grimaldi, who had died shortly before, on 16 October 1750. At this time his work was appearing posthumously, edited by Ginesio Grimaldi. Maffei suspected that it had been tampered with in Rome, perhaps by Mamachi himself, in order to make it more favourable to tradition. It was, however, a violent attack against all who had dared to deny the power of enchantments. He wrote among other things that 'with unprecedented boldness, Marquis Maffei, himself a very learned man, has dared, in the heart of Italy, at Verona, to come out against pacts with the devil and other magic practices by dismissing them all as daydreams'. Here Grimaldi undertook a long winding journey into the world of superstitions, often cautiously rejecting them but never fighting them openly. He wrote in conclusion that it had been his intention 'to make men cautious in judging phenomena which have the appearance of being produced by supernatural causes'. 'I wish to prove that there are no definite, infallible rules for distinguishing the effects of natural or artificial magic from real or black magic.' This was the only contribution, and a rather slight and ambiguous one, which was made to this dispute by the South.

The theses expounded by Paolo Frisi, a young scientist who came to Milan in 1754, went much deeper. In his last lesson of meta-physics at the schools of Sant'Alessandro he had made a clear statement of his conviction, not only that the nocturnal meeting of witches with devils '*commentitus est et phantasticus*' (is invented and fantastic), but that the existence of magicians '*nec solido argumento aliquo probari potest, nec rectae rationi videtur satis esse consentaneum*' (cannot be proved by any substantial argument, nor does it seem at all reasonable to the thinking mind), except, of course, he hastened to add, with regard to the Bible, in pre-Christian times. This was the first stand made by a man who was destined to become the friend of the Verri brothers and Beccaria and one of the most typical representatives of enlightenment in the scientific field in eighteenth-century Italy.

In the midst of all these adversaries stood the triumphant figure of the old but still very active Marquis Scipione Maffei. When he finished writing on 1 June 1754, 'he was fortunate enough, by the grace of God' to be entering 'the eightieth year of his age', which he proudly announced to his readers with the presentation of his work *Magic arts annihilated*. The title of the work explained better than anything what Maffei meant. His first rapid attack had caused magic arts to retreat and now, beneath the weight of his tremendous final onslaught, they were completely annihilated. He would admit no obstacles to his desire to do away with all this nonsense once and for all. Tartarotti's distinctions did not hold, either in theological, philosophical or even moral terms. Was it really necessary, in order not to condemn a poor woman, to prove that she was practising magic and not witchcraft? And how could Tartarotti be sure that the harm done by witchcraft was less than that done by magic? No amount of reticence or scruples could change the basic, indisputable fact that it was impossible to find 'anywhere on earth a genuine, practising magician'. Authority and reason united in denying the existence of such a being. With the consummate skill of the his-torian and antiquarian, Maffei showed how magic had arisen, how the idea had been developed not by great thinkers and philosophers, nor by historians 'enlightened by wisdom and gravity', but by imaginative poets beginning with Homer and some 'latter-day Platonists' and, along with these, various theologians of paganism. Through them had been created the great fable of an inexistent 'oriental wisdom', while all the greatest writers among the Greeks and Romans had laughed at such tales. It was true that legends about magic had been handed down through the ages and had perpetuated themselves. 'Romances in *ottava rima* are full of them.' But by this time all that remained of the old magicians and witches was confined to works of literature—Tasso and particularly Ariosto and the fairies and sprites that appeared in theatrical productions. Magic arts faded away in the light of Maffei's reason just like the gods, superstitions and traditions in the sky of Olympus in the marvellous fresco which Tiepolo was painting precisely in those years in the elector's palace at Würzburg.

Many years later Gianrinaldo Carli who, as will be remembered, was the first to discuss Tartarotti's ideas, was to remark that in this way the 'diabolical amphitheatre' was closed once and for all after so many contests. As far back as 1752, Francescantonio Zaccaria had written that by that time magic had become 'the Helen fiercely contested among our men of letters. I do not think that sorcerers could ever have hoped to have the honour of being the subject of so many disputes on the part of learned men.' When the polemic had long since ended, Ippolito Pindemonte, from afar, expressed his amazement at the fact that it could arouse so much passion. 'I am tempted to believe in magic since there seems to be something supernatural or magical in all the excitement generated by this controversy.' Andrea Rubbi, who was collecting Maffei's works in 1790, wondered whether 'that flood of writings supporting the existence of nocturnal meetings with witches, incubuses and succubuses had not been the product of a sick imagination. We cannot forgive our century for so much upheaval except by saying that it was still a child.' He noted how 'the magic affair' had rapidly and unexpectedly become a real 'colossus'. 'Its shadow alone covered almost all the domains of literature.' It was to Maffei's credit that he had driven away these shadows. 'When his new book [*Magic arts annihilated*] was published, this threat gradually began to disappear.'

Crisis of the emerging age of reason and enlightenment, this dispute was also reflected on the other side of the Alps. A translation of Maffei's first contribution, *Magic arts dismissed*, was published in Paris in the same volume as a reprint of the *Traité sur les apparitions et sur les vampires ou les revenans de Hongrie, de Moravie etc.* by the well-known Benedictine, Augustin Calmet. The work was first published in 1706 and like so many writings of this author had represented a step towards the critical spirit already in the first decades of the eighteenth century. By now his caution and circumspection seemed outdated in the eyes of many contemporaries, but it still seemed fitting that his work should appear again in Paris accompanied by a much more radical denial of the world of magic such as Maffei was able to provide. It was a confirmation of the ideas being expounded at that time, in opposition to Dom Calmet, by Lenglet de Fresnoy, a well-known Pyrrhonist and free-thinker; 1751 saw the appearance of his *Traité historique et dogmatique sur les apparitions, les visions et les révélations particulières* and the *Recueil de dissertations anciennes et nouvelles sur les apparitions*. At the end of the latter work Lenglet de Fresnoy gave a very full bibliography where he mentioned Maffei's works in both their Italian and French versions, but he did not seem to know Muratori or Tartarotti or the other participants in the dispute.

In Spain we do not find any tangible influence of the dispute about magic which took place in Italy, but the problems it raised were very much alive in the Iberian peninsula too. Father Benito Geronymo Feyjóo, the most typical representative of early eighteenth-century critical thought in that part of the world, devoted a considerable amount of attention to magicians and witches. However, he could never bring himself to declare that they did not exist. They were few and their influence was 'almost non-existent'. But there was no doubt that God had created them also. It was left to the Italians to bridge the gap between 'almost non-existent' and 'non-existent' in the middle of the century.

The effects of the polemic were felt much more strongly in Austria and Germany. The 'diabolical amphitheatre' had scarcely become silent when very disturbing news began to arrive in Rovereto from beyond the Alps. It was no longer a question of witches and magicians who at least were 'living things' or, at any rate, claimed to be so. 'Heavens above! Here we have a crowd of rascally dead magicians, drinking and becoming intoxicated with the blood of the living.' A new wave of vampirism had been passing through lands famed for it: Moravia, Bohemia and Hungary. As Gerhard Van Switen said: 'On 30 January 1755, to the amazement of the population, news arrived in Vienna of a strange trial which had taken place in a town in Moravia near the border with Hungary and Silesia. Certain clerics who were not only unenlightened but downright wicked had permitted the trial of a number of dead men and sentence to be carried out against them.' A group of bodies had been exhumed in order to have their hearts pierced, their heads cut off and their ashes scattered, so as to prevent them from visiting the living in the night, sucking their blood and causing them to die a frightful death. This was the usual procedure which had been employed against vampires for a very long time. But this time the Empress Maria Theresa, 'our most wise sovereign lady', was very shocked and 'immediately' sent 'two of the most eminent physicians in Vienna to ascertain the exact nature of the occurrences. After careful experiment, thorough examination of witnesses and scrupulous sifting of all the evidence, they were able, through their experience, to come to the conclusion that it was all the result of vain fears, superstitious beliefs, the dark, disturbed imagination, simplicity and ignorance of the people.' The horror of that 'barbarous trial of poor dead men' and 'the profound indignation' of the sovereign had induced Gerhard Van Switen, one of the most powerful men in Vienna in those years and Maria Theresa's personal physician and adviser on all problems of a cultural nature, to prepare a report in French on the phenomenon of vampirism. He hastened to say that his belief in the existence of the devil was completely orthodox. As for the devil's influence on human affairs, he too was inclined to banish him beyond the reaches of his own world, seeing his works, not among civilised peoples and classes but only among peasants and country folk. In this case the arguments of the Protestants seemed to him excellent.

> No Christian can deny that there have been persons possessed by the devil and consequently that he does have power over human bodies . . . Protestants themselves admit that the heathen in India display all the wickedness of the abominable master whom they serve but that as soon as they have freed themselves from the devil's bondage and become members of the Church through the holy sacrament of baptism, these diabolical illusions come to an end and this has helped to convert many people.

In the case of vampirism too, Van Switen was very willing to listen to those who maintained that it was a phenomenon not originating in Catholic countries but in those under the domination of the Orthodox Church. 'Posthumous magic', the kind which concerned corpses, was to be found 'where ignorance reigned and it is very probable that the Greek schismatics were its principal authors'.

Having said this, the doctor in him took over and he went on to describe these sinister phenomena in detail, showing just how absurd they really were. One of the vampires 'executed' in 1755 was said to have been swollen with blood, 'since the executioner, a completely reliable man, no doubt, in matters concerning his trade, claimed that when he cut up the bodies which were sentenced to be burnt, a great quantity of blood gushed forth . . . Nevertheless he afterwards modestly agreed that this great quantity was about a spoonful. And this is a very different matter.' Van Switen then gave a learned exposition of the different ways in which dead bodies could be preserved underground and concluded that one had to be an 'ignorant quack' to find evidence of the supernatural merely in the presence of facts which were scientifically verifiable and very common. In the case of apparitions and the prejudices and fears of common people, it was necessary to take into consideration the fact that they often affected persons who had 'chest complaints which caused them great distress when they were in bed'. Besides this, everyone knew that 'fear alone can be the cause of terrible suffering'. Instead of taking into account such simple, well-known facts, men had succeeded in concocting the most extraordinary tales and the judges had allowed themselves to become involved in such macabre ceremonies.

Sacrilege was committed, the sanctity of the tombs was violated, the reputation of the dead and their families was sullied . . . the bodies of children who died in innocence were put into the hands of the executioner . . . Not only are their bodies handed over to the executioner to be reduced to ashes, but there is a clause in their sentence stating that if they were alive they would be punished much more severely and that their bodies are to be burnt shamefully in order that this may serve as a lesson to their accomplices. Where are the laws that authorise such anomalies? Everyone has to admit that they do not exist, with the cynical proviso that custom demands it. What a tragedy! This grieves me and makes me so angry that I see that I shall have to end here in order not to become carried away.

This report was the source of the most important legislative measures taken by Maria Theresa to deal with witches and magic, decrees which are among the most curious documents of the struggle against superstition in the age of enlightened absolutism. A decree forbidding the casting of spells had already gone out in July 1753. There was a further one against vampires and so-called 'posthumous magic' in March 1755 and finally, in August 1756, the decree against superstition and magic. All three were intended for the hereditary land of the Empire and it does not appear that any similar provisions were made for Austrian territory on the other side of the Alps.

Giuseppe Valeriano Vannetti, who translated Van Switen, felt that he had to mention all that had been written on these matters 'by that wise philosopher . . . our own illustrious Girolamo Tartarotti'. He said that he was particularly impressed by the forceful manner in which the Empress had attempted to stamp out these abominable practices.

Since the removal of deep-rooted superstitions requires resolution, determination and a strong hand, Her Majesty wisely ordered that strict edicts should immediately be issued to magis-

trates, police chiefs and governors throughout all the provinces
These edicts are meant to ensure not only that superstition:
should be prohibited, punished and eventually removed alto
gether but also, if there were some occurrence not readily ex
plainable in natural terms, that no one in the future should
interfere without first informing Her Majesty. Having ordered
that she should immediately be apprised of the situation, under
threat of severe punishment for those who disobey, she will then
be in a position to order what she considers most fitting and
expedient.

This was in fact the crux of the edict of March 1755: it removed
from the parish priests, inquisitors and local authorities all power
to deal with the world of magic, while the state, at the centre
assumed all responsibility for the struggle against it.

Not very many years later the kind of attitude which had
produced these measures served to protect the tomb and memory
of Tartarotti. He died on 16 May 1761 and the town of Rovereto
decided to give him a burial in the church of San Marco and to
erect a monument to him. Graser gave the funeral oration, which
was later published in an elegant edition together with a group
of sonnets in memory of the deceased. However, when it came
to putting up the monument bearing his image in April 1762, the
bishop's representative protested and a typical jurisdictional battle
between municipal and ecclesiastical authorities arose. This led
to the passing of an interdict on the church of San Marco, the
intervention of the civil authorities in Innsbruck and eventually
to a communication from Maria Theresa on 22 May 1762, request
ing the bishop to remove the interdict under threat of confiscation
of all his property in the territory of Rovereto. The ecclesiastical
authorities would not yield. The Empress repeated the injunction
but ended up by asking the inhabitants of Rovereto to remove
the monument to Tartarotti, 'not because you have no right to
erect it, but on account of the unfortunate consequences it has
produced'. There followed a series of protests, plots and threat:
from Vienna to arrest three of the town councillors. The church
was ultimately reopened but the monument was gone. It had
been removed to the town hall and by order of Maria Theresa a
new, different inscription was placed on Tartarotti's tomb.

The witches were at least partly responsible for this conflict
which went on for almost nine months, but the real cause of the
bishop's stubborn hostility on this occasion lay elsewhere—in the
rapid despatch of the historical personage of the much venerated
Saint Adalpreto carried out by Tartarotti, one of the most success
ful of the numerous eliminations of saints which many learned

Italians specialised in in those years. Subjected to the test of Tartarotti's critical methods, Saint Adalpreto had proved to be neither saint nor martyr and the inscriptions which mentioned him in Trent had proved to be false.

It is indeed a delicate question because it involves interfering with long-established opinions, which, although they may be false, still have a large following and there are many who disapprove of any attempt to discredit them. Nevertheless, since truth must be preferred to all else . . . I shall undertake the task willingly, secure in the knowledge that, if not the majority, at least the most enlightened persons will approve my resolution to purge our country's ecclesiastical history of fairytales, for this certainly needs to be done.

Tartarotti obviously enjoyed his task and carried it out to perfection. In spite of a long tussle which dragged on for many years, right into the twentieth century, Saint Adalpreto never fully recovered and today is no longer recognised as a saint.

The campaign against the vampires was less decisive and generally less successful. Towards the middle of the 'seventies another wave of these horrors spread through Hungary and the Slav lands. Its effects were felt in Italy too. Only then, in 1774, as a result of hearing this news from beyond the Alps, did the young Domenico Forges Davanzati, the future biographer of Andrea Serrao, decide to publish for the first time a manuscript produced several decades previously by his uncle, Giuseppe Davanzati, Archbishop of Trani, concerning the whole problem of vampires.

Here too we are definitely at the borderline between the early and the later eighteenth century. Domenico Forges Davanzati was to become the friend of Antonio Genovesi and the editor of his *Personal letters*, before becoming a Jacobin and exile in France at the end of the century. His uncle, Giuseppe Davanzati, had been one of the lesser figures but also among the most lively and characteristic of the age of Muratori, Maffei and Prospero Lambertini (Benedict XIV), the friend with whom he corresponded. Born in 1665, he travelled all over Europe in his youth and met Pierre Bayle in Rotterdam, Leibniz in Vienna, Leclerc in Geneva and Tournefort in Paris. When he was nominated Archbishop of Trani in 1718, he began a campaign against superstition which was to continue throughout his long life. This prelate from an ancient Florentine patrician family which for centuries had had links with the South, devoted all his energies to fighting popular beliefs in the power of sacred images, effigies, comets, tarantulas and vampires. He did all this in a cheerful, Pyrrhonistic spirit which was mixed with insatiable curiosity about these strange manifestations of that dark world of popular mentality. He had not long been in Trani when he began to go about 'armed with hooks and hammers' in order to destroy the 'old images' which were the object of 'night-time veneration' and therefore not to his liking. He aroused fierce protests from the 'populace' as well as from monks and 'one of the most important ladies in the realm'. He was called to Rome accused of iconoclasm but succeeded in winning his case. In the 'thirties he wrote some pages on comets which were already lost when his nephew and biographer, Domenico Forges Davanzati, was writing about him. 'However', he added, 'Abbé Galiani, Councillor for Commerce, who enjoys substantial renown, has read them and assures me that they were written with great perception.'

Dynasties changed in Naples, but not the ideas of the Archbishop of Trani. In 1740 Celestino Galiani, his very close friend, who was chaplain to Charles of Bourbon, begged him to do some research into the 'nature of the poison of the tarantula in Apulia and what he could gather about the antidote of music and dancing as a cure for it'. The request was followed by a lengthy correspondence between these two learned and enlightened men. In the previous year, 1739, 'when vampires had begun to appear again in Germany', he had set out to write a dissertation on these phenomena which, as we have seen, was never published during his lifetime. 'Yet it soon began to circulate in manuscript form, not only throughout Italy but also beyond the Alps.' 'Burmann said to one of our fellow-countrymen that he had never read anything better on the subject' (and if this is the great Peter Burmann and not his lesser-known nephew, the work could not have taken very long to become known in Holland, because he died on 31 March 1741). At the beginning of his work, Davanzati was amused to relate how Cardinal Schrattembach, Bishop of Olmutz, whom he had met in Rome many years previously, had been so convinced of the existence of vampires that he had shown great disapproval at Davanzati's ironical smile and his scepticism when they had discussed such phenomena together. Slowly, accurately and cautiously Davanzati penetrated deeper and deeper into the colourful world of the various explanations which had been given down through the centuries for phenomena of magic and witchcraft, from metempsychosis and Cardano to Campanella and the Pyrrhonists. It was obvious that his sympathies lay with that imaginary semi-Pyrrhonist philosopher whose views on vampires he expounded at length and who had come to the conclusion that it was brought about by 'human, natural agents' and was most probably 'a contagious disease'.

One of the reasons which induced him to exclude the possibility of the intervention of God or the devil in these phenomena lay in their very local character. Why Moravia and Upper Hungary in particular 'and not elsewhere, Spain, France, our own Italy?' And why was this kind of demon 'so partial to base-born plebeian persons . . . and has so far never been known to assume the form of a man of quality, a scholar, a philosopher, a theologian, a magnate or a bishop?' Why was it always 'peasants, carters, shoemakers and innkeepers?' 'I will tell you the reason and it is that learned men and men of quality are not so easily taken in and deceived as idiots and those of low birth and therefore do not so easily allow themselves to be deceived by appearances.' It was necessary then to concentrate on the common people and continue the fight against superstitions, 'charms and spells' and all ideas of 'incubuses and succubuses'. It was up to 'educated, enlightened' men to understand these 'powerful effects of the imagination' and to attempt to free from their fears 'these half-witted, ignorant people . . . much given to drinking wine . . . encouraged in these beliefs and superstitions by their parish priests who are equally credulous and ignorant'. What by this time was a long experience in Trani had taught him what the material circumstances and psychology of the peasants were really like. He was well aware of the hardships they had to endure and he had attempted to improve their lot by his enlightened kind of charity and by reducing the number of holy days of obligation. He had done what he could and his reactions and barely suppressed smile reflect the healthy, ironic attitude which he derived from the Pyrrhonism of his age. 'Every night he tried to go to bed with cheerful thoughts in his mind and therefore he liked to hear or tell others about happy, amusing things because he said that sombre, melancholy thoughts either prevent us from sleeping or disturb our rest with sinister, frightening dreams.' Vampires were to have no chance of getting into his house.

But it is time to return to the darker scene in Germany. The 'distinguished friend from Vienna' who had sent the French text of Van Switen's work to Giuseppe Valeriano Vannetti, and whom we can most probably identify with the then twenty-year-old Konstantin Franz de Cauz, had become a member of the Academy of the *Agiati* in Rovereto in 1755 and then continued to be interested in questions of magic in the years that followed. In 1767 he published in Vienna a substantial work in Latin entitled *De cultibus magicis* which was a more or less comprehensive account of the efforts which had been made in the previous twenty years by

writers and administrators in the lands of the Empire to comb.
popular superstitions. 'The finest and most exhaustive treatise c
the subject ever to appear,' as Gianrinaldo Carli was to say i
1782. His motto was *sapere aude*. He had a well-founded cultu
and a strong determination to use all possible weapons in tl
struggle against all forms of magic. He was the first to recogni
that it was to the great credit of Tartarotti, of Carli and Maff
to have begun this campaign and that Italy was still the mo
active country in the field. '*Hodie nullibi magis quam a perspica*
bus Italorum ingeniis de rei magicae vanitate persuadetur' (tod.
there is none more convinced of the falsity of magic arts than tl
intelligent Italian mind). He said that there was a much mo
difficult situation in Germany, even though by this time a certa
amount of progress had already been achieved even there.
Franconia, where the attitude of the people had been *fanatic.*
simus, and in Würzburg, which had witnessed the terrible episo
of the execution of Renata Maria Singerin, they were beginni
to reason differently and to think that it was the duty of tl
state, the secular authorities to take 'such a disgrace' into its ow
hands. In Austria the decrees against vampires had marked a tur
ing point; however, it was now necessary to create a whole ne
legislation and it was to further this purpose that Cauz had writt
his work.

He knew that the year before his work was published a gre
debate had begun in Bavaria which took up once again the them
of the Italian discussion and was its most notable reflection
the other side of the Alps. It had been sparked off in 1761 by a bo
called *Das Weltbetrügende Nichts*—the empty fiction which
ceives the world—written by an educated, restless Augustinia
The title of the book could not have been better chosen to reve
its direct derivation from Maffei. The author's pseudonym, /
doino Ubbidiente dell'Osa, was also a kind of quasi-Italian mott
His real name was Jordan Simon. He was born in 1719 and studi
at Constance. He had subsequently been seized by a mania f
travel and discovery and had left his monastery without authori
tion to visit Italy, France, Spain, Germany and part of Russ
After this he did penance and became professor of theology
Erfurt and then Würzburg, but he had to flee from there aft
being accused of a crime. In 1771 he went to Rome, where he fou
it very difficult to establish himself, and from there to Bohen
where at last he found recognition. He died in August 1776.
was the author of an Italian grammar, he translated Murator
Moral philosophy and other Italian books and from the days
his early wanderings had had connections with Italian cultu

In the opening section of his book on magic he explained that his original intention had been to translate *Magic arts dismissed* and *Magic arts annihilated* by the 'immortal' Maffei. But on consideration he had decided that, since these writings formed part of a polemic, he would have to translate Tartarotti also. This did not seem very practical, so he had taken the ideas and facts expounded by Maffei and reshaped them in a work of his own. He had systematically gone through the whole of the debate in Italy and elsewhere, including the contributions of Preati, Concina, Calmet etc., in order to prove that witchcraft and magic were impossible, absurd and simply did not exist. 'Die heutige Zauber-kunst und Hexerey ist ein grosses Welt-betrügendes Nichts' (Today magic and witchcraft are a great empty fiction which deceives the world).

In a speech given in Munich on 13 October 1766, at a solemn session of the Bavarian Academy of Sciences, another monk, the Theatine Ferdinand Sterzinger, had expressed the same ideas, declaring immediately that 'in our enlightened times', when science was reaching the greatest heights, prejudices such as sorcery could no longer be tolerated. He had studied in Italy, at Rome and Bologna. In 1750, at the age of twenty-nine, he returned and then felt the influence of Maffei's polemic. His speech was both flattering and dignified and had the triple purpose of convincing the Elector Maximilian Joseph that witchcraft was absurd, of drawing attention to the merits of Tartarotti and above all of showing his appreciation of the great Maffei. He concluded by saying that any idea of a pact with the devil could only be an illusion or a case of mere invention. Baroni had given satisfactory proof of the fact that the devil had no power to make men fly and all the other prejudices were of the same order. Muratori was right in saying that all such things are a product of the human imagination. Reason was triumphing. There was now no longer even the same interest in the world of superstition and poverty among the people shown by the predecessors of Ferdinand Sterzinger. And in Bavaria it was not, as in Vienna, a question of making the state and the state alone responsible for the struggle against these prejudices. The ideas themselves and the enlightenment should come from the ruler and it was in him that they found their *raison d'être*. Indeed he concluded his speech by saying that 'these doctrines will probably be universally accepted and when this happens it will only be because the noble mind of our most serene founder Maximilian Joseph lives and rules for the enlightenment of his people'.

This speech of Father Sterzinger aroused a long, complicated

'Hexenkrieg' in Bavaria. Animated discussions about witches took place in mansions and inns, classrooms and houses in the city of Munich. There were many pamphlets published for and against magic. The principal supporters of the existence of witches were the Augustinian Agnellus März and the Benedictine Scheyern Angelus März. Their faith in these phenomena was as strong as that of their Jesuit predecessor Del Rio. On the opposing side, just to give a few examples, we find Andreas Ulrich Mayer, whom we already know for his work on vampires, and a half brother of Ferdinand Sterzinger, also a Theatine and destined to become a librarian at Palermo at the end of the century and die there in 1821. The total number of pamphlets written on that occasion and listed by Ludwig Rapp came to about ten and others could be added to it. In all those that we have been able to see, the example of Italy is often mentioned and discussed. Andreas Ulrich Mayer referred, for example, to the atmosphere of tolerance in which Benedict XIV had permitted the discussion to take place in Italy. Maffei, Tartarotti, Grimaldi and Baroni, he said, had all written in Italian, 'in full view of the Pope', but had not been put on the Index. He also made frequent mention of dell'Osa, that is Father Simon, as the man who had introduced Maffei's ideas into Germany. And since he was persistently being asked to talk about Italian writers and theologians (*Wälsche Schrifteller wollen sie haben*) he gave a long list of them. Ferdinand Sterzinger, in his reply to his adversaries and especially to Agnellus März, whom he accused of putting himself *an die Spitze des Hexenarmee*, at the head of the witches' army, defended himself against the charge of having plagiarised the writings of Tartarotti, Carli, Baroni and dell'Osa. He admitted that the thoughts and texts quoted were often the same but denied that this was any reason to speak of plagiarism. He also replied to his adversary who had criticised him for writing in German. 'Such an important objection to make! Did Italian scholars not write in Italian and Frenchmen in French? It was right that they should do so. Why should Germans too not write in their own language? Should a German and in particular a Bavarian always remain in a state of holy innocence?' It was up to him rather to accuse Agnellus März of not understanding enough Italian.

The discussion in these pamphlets often tended to centre around theology and the Scriptures and lacked instead the social and psychological curiosity and doubts which had made the original discussion in Italy so lively. But at least there was in Ferdinand Sterzinger an obvious determination to see reason triumph over the devil's partisans, as they were known at the time. In the following years and decades he steadfastly continued his campaign, arming himself with the pseudonym, which was Italian, like so many things connected with this polemic, of Francone dell'Amavero. As late as 1786 he was fighting against ghosts. He died in the same year: 'a true, even if misunderstood, observer of our religion', said Ludwig Rapp, who gave his funeral oration. The discussion had reached its furthest limits while still attempting to remain within the bounds of tradition.

In 1789 a faint echo of this polemic was once again heard in Berlin in a review called *Italy and Germany* written by two friends of Goethe, K. P. Moritz and A. Hirt. It was noted once again that even among the lowest orders of society in Italy, although they were prey to all kinds of superstitions, there had never been any real belief in ghosts, witches and frightful apparitions. Their songs were proof of this and beneath the clear skies of Italy it was not customary, as it was in Germany, for the peasants to gather together in the evenings to tell one another frightening stories. Once more a problem which had tormented historians, philosophers and politicians seemed to melt into a serene literary observation tinged with Romantic sensibility.

5   Pasquale Paoli

ASQUALE PAOLI was born in Morosaglia di Rostino in Corsic
on 5 April 1725 and grew up in one of the families whic
was most actively involved in the opening stages of th
island's revolt against the Republic of Genoa. His father
Giacinto, wielded considerable power in the villages and arme
bands in Corsica in the mid-'thirties. Then, at the end of tha
decade, the French succeeded in imposing a brief truce. Giacint
Paoli was compelled to leave his native island on 10 July 173
and seek his fortune in the Kingdom of Naples. He left his eldes
son, Clemente, on the island and took the young Pasquale wit
him, secretly hoping to see him grow up far away from the cruelt
and conflicts which characterised life on the island.

A host of legends have grown up around Pasquale Paoli's sta
in Naples, which lasted from 1739 to 1754—legends of the wors
kind, born in the minds of scholars who were prepared to clos
their eyes to the facts in order to curry political favour. It ha
repeatedly been asserted, for instance, that he attended Antoni
Genovesi's lectures on political economy at the University o
Naples, but it is sufficient to glance at the dates to realise that thi
is impossible. When Genovesi took over Intieri's chair in 1754
Pasquale Paoli was already an officer in a far-off garrison, at Port
Longone.

He was resident in Naples only in 1744 and then for a longe
period between 1745 and 1749. He was a soldier and could no
have had much time to study and attend lectures. It is quite pos
sible that he did attend Antonio Genovesi's lectures in this perio
however they were not on political economy but on ethics, as w

are assured by a contemporary, John Symonds, who seems generally very well-informed and whom we wish to quote here in order to evoke the genuine atmosphere of his intellectual training:

> Paoli studied all the usual subjects: grammar, rhetoric and ethics—the last under the direction of Antonio Genovesi . . . But Paoli was not content with this plan of education. Determined to carry his researches further, although he was in the army for a long time, his great ambition was to acquire a thorough knowledge of the ancient states of Greece and Rome. He was stationed for some time in Calabria and Sicily and spent all his free time reading and meditating upon the best authors. And truly anyone who converses with him can easily believe it, for he has an excellent command of Thucydides, Polybius, Livy and Tacitus. Not that he wishes to air his knowledge, but he has the familiarity with these authors which comes from his attempts to make their knowledge his own and to adapt to his new people whatever he finds suitable for them. He himself admits that he hoped to model himself upon such exemplary figures as Cimon and Epaminondas.

His was a classical culture, therefore, the more deeply felt because it had been as if discovered by this young man who came from a poor, faraway island and approached it with the freshness and spontaneity of a self-taught outsider. This classical culture, precisely because of its heroic but generic mould, was able to become the model and example for a new and unexpected experience.

In addition to his youthful experience of the ancient world, we can also see strong links with the most modern and lively elements of the Neapolitan world. The man with whom he seems to have been in closest contact during this period of preparation is Ferdinando De Leon, destined very soon to become, in the manner of Fragianni and Tanucci, one of the most typical representatives of the anticlerical trend in Naples which marks the transition period between the first and second half of the eighteenth century. The 'Neapolitan firecrackers', as they were described by Count Carlo di Firmian, thus had a part to play in the formation of Pasquale Paoli.

With this dual heritage of classical example and modern politics he arrived in Corsica in 1754, when he was not yet thirty, in answer to the summons of his patriotic friends. He had had to overcome violent opposition on the part of his father who wanted to keep him far away from the dangers which threatened anyone who dared to lead the chaotic rebellion in Corsica.

The situation which he found in the island made a deep and disturbing impression on him but did not deter him from his undertaking. Very gradually he succeeded in establishing himself so that for some fifteen years he was able to be the symbol of Corsican patriotism and the personification of the island's aspiration towards nationhood. It was a paradoxical enterprise which ended in disaster and defeat but which was nevertheless able— partly as a result of Paoli's contribution—to become an example in itself and constitute a spur towards freedom in a Europe which was experiencing the noonday of Enlightenment.

The Corsican revolt was, above all, the rebellion of a colonial people against a patrician state, the rich republic of Genoa, the city—'la Dominante'—which had subjugated the island and which, now in a period of decline, was still trying in a grasping, miserly way to exploit it. The resentment of the islanders went very deep. It was blind at first but gradually began to assume an increasingly patriotic character. In rebelling against Genoese domination Corsica was attempting to become a nation.

There had been many attempts in the past to shake off the colonial yoke in the field of economics, commerce and taxes, but the defeats and humiliations had still continued. The Corsicans had sworn undying hatred for the Genoese but at the same time, as often happens with revolts of this kind, there was a vague awareness of how tragic it would be to sever all the links which the centuries had forged. In order to defeat and rid themselves of the Genoese the Corsicans were quite prepared to accept help from anywhere, yet there was still a very strong feeling of belonging to the Italian world and sharing the destiny of the various states of the peninsula. There were other Italian states in the eighteenth century where a similar relationship existed between a ruling city and its subject territories: Turin and Sardinia, for example, and particularly between Naples and Sicily. Even within Liguria, San Remo and the little Riviera ports felt oppressed and tried to rebel, vaguely groping for the way to a new kind of equality. But in Corsica the rebellion was more immediate and violent, more blind and more heroic. So many were indelibly marked by the poverty and the wretchedness, the insults and scorn of the Genoese, the fate which compelled them to serve in foreign armies as if they too were poor mountain folk like the Swiss. To be ignorant and exploited, this was their lot. Seething up inside them was an instinctive rebellion against the contempt with which the primitive, violent customs of the island were treated. With the gradual development of some economic activity in Corsica too, they became increasingly aware of the fact that so long as Corsica remained attached to the ancient, conservative republic of Genoa, she would never succeed in developing her own natural and human resources, neither her mines nor the boundless energy of her menfolk.

As is natural in such cases, the Corsican rebellion was closely connected with the need for internal change. To put it briefly— too briefly—the island had to change in the space of a few short decades from a world of clans, subject to the domination of a few families, finally to become a nation. Pasquale Paoli, better than anyone else, was able to interpret this fundamental need and for this reason he became the undisputed leader of the island. This is the secret of his power and prestige. Our present age—which is familiar with anticolonial rebellions and the sudden crystallisation of nations—is in a better position to understand this than our predecessors, who sought in vain to explain it in the light of the very different brand of patriotism produced by the nineteenth century. It was better understood by contemporaries who paid so much attention to Paoli's social policies, to family and local politics and who took such an interest in backward peoples.

There is need to examine carefully his policy towards vendettas, gangs and the violent rivalries which divided the various sectors of the island, the various parishes, villages, houses and families. He seems to have shown great patience and wisdom. Paoli was able to mediate between the conflicting forces and he was aware that this mediation was possible only in the name of a rapid social and political transformation, by an appeal to a higher entity— the Corsican nation, fighting against everyone else and against the Genoese in particular. Only thus can we really understand the meaning of his 'patriotism', the great weapon which he used in an attempt to balance and settle the island's internal conflicts. And this also explains his failure and defeat when he tried to use the same weapon against France. The force which it was possible to harness to unite the island in the struggle against Genoa and as an instrument for change within the country could not be used against a nation, a culture and a civilisation of a different kind. The weapon of the anticolonial struggle, launched in the context of the old Italian states, proved to be ineffective when employed against a new and different type of intervention in island affairs, against the work of a state which possessed, as France did, a very different capacity for assimilation and progress from the ancient, fossilised, patrician republic of Genoa.

As Paoli gradually discovered and mastered the situation which he found on the island on his arrival, he began to attack it on two fronts, from two different directions. He knew how to make use of the primitive idea of equality, the ancient belief, prevalent in the villages, that everyone has the right to defend himself, to live, fight and have direct access to power by appealing to the leader, speaking to him in an informal manner, without intermediaries.

This was the basis of his democracy, of the General Council upon which his hopes rested and which gathered together the elected representatives of the heads of families all over the island. They were united in their demands, customs and way of life, and the equality that they felt was all the more intense in that it filled everyone's mind and masked—if only temporarily—the distinctions, inequality and injustice that still existed in Corsica as in any such society. On the other hand Paoli attempted to overcome the fragmented family structure of the island by laying the first, elementary foundations of a modern state. He strengthened, or sometimes even improved on his own initiative, the systems of tax collection. There grew up around him in his capital at Corte the first nucleus of a bureaucracy; an army, no longer of volunteers but paid and disciplined; a state prison (imposed despite rebellion and consequent repression); a clergy which was increasingly committed to the emerging nation; a university which was his own creation, almost symbolic of the novelty and multiformity of these state initiatives.

The constitution of Paoli's Corsica, the 'Corsican system of government,' to use the words of a contemporary, found its real *raison d'être* in his dual undertaking. It was something which he inherited but also transformed. By his presence he was able to concentrate around himself—and the new Corsican government— the scattered elements of power which the rebellion against Genoa and the experience of self-government had already created in the island in the generation which had preceded and prepared the way for his own. James Boswell showed great understanding of the complex character of the Corsican constitution and greater insight than anyone else into the social roots of Paoli's policy.

When a proper system of government was formed and some of the most glaring abuses rectified, Paoli proceeded to improve and civilise the manners of the Corsicans. This was a very delicate task. They had been brought up in anarchy, and their constant virtue had been resistance. It therefore required the nicest conduct, to make them discern the difference between salutary restraint and tyrannick oppression. He was no monarch, born to rule, and who received the nation as a patrimonial inheritance. It was, therefore, in vain to think of acting with force, like Czar Peter towards the Russians . . . He was entirely dependent upon the people, elected by them, and answerable to them for his conduct. It was no easy matter to restrain those of whom he held his power. But this Paoli accomplished.

He gradually prepared the Corsicans for the reception of laws, by cultivating their minds . . .

The last step that he took was to induce the Corsicans to apply themselves to agriculture, commerce and other civil occupations. War had entirely ruined industry in the island. It had given the Corsicans a contempt for the arts of peace; . . . Heroes could not submit to sink down into plain peasants . . .

From these causes, the country was in danger of being entirely uncultivated, and the people of becoming a lawless and ungovernable rabble of banditti.

Paoli, therefore, set himself seriously to guard against this; . . .

His administration, in every respect was such, that, far from being rent into factions, the nation became firm and united; . . .

The balance which Paoli was able to maintain between the *terre di comune* and other parts of the island where feudal rule and customs had had much greater influence, the limits which he attempted to impose upon local feudalism, and above all his efforts to channel in the direction of 'patriotism' that fierce antifeudal feeling which was to be found all over the island—these are among the most typical and revealing aspects of Pasquale Paoli's policy. The rebellion against Genoa had originally drawn its strength from the resentment of the local chiefs, the *caporali*. But the struggle. had gradually changed its character. It was no longer a question of asserting customary privileges but of gaining independence and equality. By this time the war against Genoa was being fought above all by men who saw it as a means of freeing themselves from oppression of all kinds, both from inside the country and outside. James Boswell understood this too, or perhaps we should say that he was able to express it extremely well since his account was based on what he heard on the island during his conversations with General Paoli's lieutenants.

Paoli has succeeded wonderfully in settling the claims of the feudal signors. These signors made several applications to the government, praying for the restitution of their ancient rights. This was a very delicate question . . .

The signors had not been foremost in the glorious war. They had much to lose; and hesitated at taking up arms against the republic of Genoa, lest they should forfeit their domains.

The peasants, on the contrary, had plunged at once into danger. These had nothing to lose but their lives; and a life of slavery is not to be prized. If they should be successful, they were fired with the hope of a double deliverance, from the distant tyranny of the republick, and from the more intimate oppression of their feudal lords. This was become so grievous, that a very sensible Corsican owned to me, that supposing the republick had abandoned its pretensions over Corsica, so that the peasants should not have been obliged to rise against Genoese, they would have risen against the signors.

The peasants therefore, would not now consent, to retu under the arbitrary power, from which they had freed the selves, in consequence of their bravery. To propose such measure to them, would have been enough to excite a rev to break the nation anew into parties, and give their enem an opportunity, of again fomenting discord, and hatred, a assassinations; till the Corsicans should themselves do what the stratagem and force of Genoa had attempted in vain.

It would certainly be difficult to find a better, more exact pict of the antifeudal character of the Corsican rebellion and of way in which it influenced all the other social and politi elements which under Paoli were working towards independe for the island.

Just as interesting, if rather different, is Abbé Mably's opin on this problem of the relationship between feudalism and Corsican bid for equality and independence. He was writing a Paoli had already suffered defeat and was attempting to disco how this had come about. Basically, he said in his *De la législat ou principes des lois* which appeared in 1776, the general had been successful because he had not had enough faith in the so basis of the revolt and had not shown enough sympathy a understanding for the egalitarian aspirations of the islanders. republic of Genoa had sought to maintain its position of domina by setting the local notables against one another, preventing a progress and culture in the island. *Felix culpa*, because the re of this had been a general reaction against the 'feudal yoke' a widespread rebellion against that 'barbarous form of gove ment'. The island's independence was a product of the village, maquis. 'The Corsicans, armed with sticks and pitchforks, be the war.' It sprang up out of the 'simple, coarse, modest, fru existence to which they had become accustomed under the Genc yoke'. 'The abolition of all privileges permitted the survival Corsica of only one class of citizens; equality, which politici talk so much about, was established in practice.' But Paoli not been willing or able to draw the full implications from situation. 'How many revolutions which nature has prepared cc to nothing through our own clumsiness.' However, even after defeat, Corsica still remained a symbol of the possibility of equality born of the struggles and conflicts of a still primi world.

Paoli's policy towards the Church is also indicative of an atte to find a point of contact between the instinctive reactions of islanders and a more modern, sophisticated 'patriotic' ideal. It is true that his policy, like his personality, remained tied to a very physical, superstitious kind of religion and that the hold of tradition upon him and his followers was very strong. However, even on the personal plane, there is a remarkable transformation of his primitive Catholicism into a kind of fatalism, of faith in his own destiny, his own work, his own guiding star. This undoubtedly foreshadowed that pagan sense of fate which was to be seen in Napoleon Bonaparte and which Edgar Quinet quite rightly felt to be very far from any religious attitude in eighteenth-century France. It was something much more basic and arose from an unwillingness to break away from the religion of his own people but at the same time a determination not to be influenced and led astray by its more desultory, local superstitious aspects.

It was the move towards a broader vision, towards a kind of religiosity which led Pasquale Paoli, by now an exile, to become involved with the masonic lodges in Britain. But above all it was a way—perhaps somewhat Machiavellian—of overcoming the continuous conflicts between Genoa and Rome, between the Corsican churches and convents and the various authorities, both near and far, and between the patriotism of some of the clergy and monks and the homage paid by a considerable section of the higher clergy in the coastal towns to the Genoese republic. Pasquale Paoli had acquired the elements of his bold jurisdictionalist policy as a very young man in Naples among the young disciples gathered around Tanucci. On 21 February 1765, for example, he could proudly assert that in Corsica it was not necessary to pay heed to ecclesiastical courts 'because our government was born free and without concordats'. And, what is more important, he always tried to use the clergy to further his policy, without accepting any conditions or advice. He ordered the better educated friars to return to their native land to teach the young and did everything he could to encourage the fighting spirit among the lower orders of the clergy. He lived in various convents and churches, rapidly passing from one to another and saw each one as a potential fortress. He was never happier than on the day when, by a complicated manœuvre, he succeeded in putting Genoa into open conflict with Rome. There was something in his words and his actions which almost seemed to foreshadow the conflict of Spain with the Napoleonic empire. In Corsica, too, the revolt had carried with it a large section of the clergy and had temporarily created the atmosphere of a national Church.

Paoli's military tactics were in harmony with the rest of his policy. They have often been considered piecemeal, uncoordinated and inadequate, but in fact the principles he always followed could not have been better suited to the demands of an anti-colonial struggle and partisan war. He needed to take into account the attitude of the people and the amount of support they could be expected to give; he had always to be on the attack, but to be able to retreat with equal rapidity. The leaders had always to be placed in the front line—where they faced the greatest risk but also had the most responsibility—while he constantly sought, by every possible means, to maintain the precarious but essential balance between voluntary service and discipline. One has the impression on reading Paoli's commands and exhortations, his reproaches, his expressions of enthusiasm and disappointment, of hearing a day by day account of the demands of a harsh reality, the inexorable law of guerrilla warfare. In this case too the military instrument shows the limitations of the policy. His war was successful against Genoa but it was impossible to continue the struggle against France. The fact that France was a power on quite a different scale from Genoa was not the only and indeed not the main reason for this. What was significant here was the gradual breakdown of the tenuous relationship between enthusiasm and discipline which had held together the military forces of independent Corsica.

This was the real test in 1769. In spite of all his efforts, Paoli did not succeed in transferring his policy onto an international plane, in finding a place for his Corsican 'patriotism' amidst the conflicts of the great powers in Europe and the Mediterranean. As long as the Seven Years War still raged on the Continent and in the colonies, Paoli hoped that it would spread to Italy, as had happened with every conflict in the first half of the century. This would have been his salvation. It would have allowed a repetition of that foreign support and countersupport which had enabled the Corsican revolt to gain increasing momentum. But Italy remained at peace—once again giving a clear indication of the great powers' general disinterest in Italian problems. One of the longest periods of peace in her history had begun for Italy in 1748. This was a prerequisite for carrying out reforms and continuing the work of enlightenment. But it proved fatal for the Corsican rebellion. In the last analysis Paoli placed his hopes on the conflict between France and England, and here too the wary but hazardous course of his policy was doomed to be checked by a period of calm, a brief truce between the warring nations. England was passing gradually from the triumphs of the Seven Years War to the collapse of her first colonial empire. Canada had been won and the American colonies had not yet been lost.

The rebellion in Corsica aroused enthusiasm, curiosity and solidarity in London. It was hailed by a section of the educated classes
and by the more enlightened and open-minded representatives of
the ruling class, like William, Earl of Shelburne, the friend of
Morellet and the French *philosophes* and one of the pioneers of
reform in Britain. But 1769 was not the right moment for a renewal of the conflict with Louis XV. Paoli went on hoping right
to the end but the English made no move. As he said in a letter
to Antonio Rivarola, written on 8 November 1771, when he was
already in exile, 'truly this British lion loves peace and repose'.
The revolt against Genoa had not turned out to be the initial
spark of a much greater blaze. The Corsican rebellion, out of
phase on the diplomatic level, was destined to fail and be crushed.
But, precisely on account of its unfortunate outcome, it was to
assume the force of a valiant example, an initiative as admirable
as it was ill-starred.

This was very clear to the American colonists who were already
plotting their own rebellion and who formed active societies,
'The Sons of Liberty' and others, ready to support Pasquale Paoli.
As Antonio Pace, the expert on Franklin's relations with Italy has
written:

> By the late 1760s Franklin was following sympathetically the
> struggles of the Corsicans under Pasquale Paoli to free themselves.
> For him, the fierce Corsican revolt against the Genoese was a
> warning to the British that sameness of nation, religion, man-
> ners and language was no guarantee that the American colonies
> would not some day try to break away if irritations became
> acute enough.

Not only the Americans, but a large number of the writers of
the Enlightenment—more than is generally thought—were aware
of the exemplary force of Paoli's rebellion and testified to it in
their works. Though they might all view it in very different ways,
they were together in searching this far-away, unknown island for
a clue, a password which would help them to escape from the
situation of doubt and crisis which they were all passing through
at the end of the 'sixties and the beginning of the 'seventies. All
over Europe in these years of angry clashes and nascent rebellions,
discontent and deep despair grew more insistent, side by side with
the hope for new, previously unimagined freedoms. Thus Corsica
could be admired and praised by both Voltaire and Rousseau
and receive words of acclaim from Raynal and Tissot, Mably and
Deleyre.

Perhaps the reason for this interest was best explained by the

French translator of Boswell's work, Gabriel Seigneux de Correv
who published his translation 'de l'anglais et de l'italien' in 17
under the title *État de la Corse, suivi d'un Journal d'un voy*
dans l'isle de Corse et de Mémoires de Pascal Paoli. The isl
had not only set a great example of virtue and courage but it l
also provided a political stimulus. 'Un peuple qui se forme appr
à un peuple déjà formé à se corriger . . .' He expressed a wish t
the Corsican people might crown their struggle with victory. '
peuples libres, les peuples heureux sous un gouvernement juste
modéré seraient attristés de voir échouer des vues si légitim
un plan si sage et une conduite si digne d'éloges.'

This strange embodiment of enlightened despotism, mixed w
dreams of democracy and attempts at constitutional rule wh
had been Paoli's government in Corsica, made a particularly str
impression in Italy. The 'Corsican system of government' fou
its way into the great debate going on in Italy in the 'sixt
somewhere between the persistent call for reform from ab
and the growing desire for independent participation in the tra
formation of social life.

All enlightened despotism is pervaded with more or less
pressed aspirations towards equality and liberty. The Corsi
revolt helped to reveal these contradictions and embryonic nee
Antonio Genovesi's words are famous, when he wrote of '
Paoli, I don't know whether to call him the Miltiades or Epa
nondas of Corsica' and :

> Corsica, a little island half covered in rocks. It has less t
> half a million inhabitants but this handful of people, inspi
> by ideals of patria and freedom, have shown for forty ye
> where military valour comes from better than the Spartans e
> did. And what proof did they offer? It seemed as if there v
> a certain lack of judgment without which strength leads
> chaos when, behold, Providence showed that the Corsicans l
> an Epaminondas in General Paoli.

Less well-known but no less important is the *Historical essay*
the Kingdom of Corsica from the rising of 1729 up to the mid
of 1768, which tradition, probably correctly, attributes
Domenico Caminer. This is the fullest expression of Venet
sympathies towards Paoli as they were when it appeared in t
small volumes in 1768. He repeated once again the words wh
John Symonds had used to express his admiration for Pasqu
Paoli :

> He found an ardent and fierce people, all on fire in the cause
> freedom but not sufficiently guided by established maxims. 1

Corsicans had been so long accustomed to bearing arms that they hardly knew the meaning of law and justice and were impatient of any restriction. This made Paoli undertake the great work of giving a new form to the government . . . He says that he chose a popular government because he deemed it to be the most suited to human nature, especially when the people are excluded from executive power. Instead of forming a new legal code, he would do it gradually, according to the circumstances, the times and the temper of the people. He was always guided by the nature of the Corsicans and, like Solon, he could say that, if he had not made excellent laws, at least he had made the best that they were capable of receiving.

The outcome was a state which, in spite of its imperfect, provisional nature, could only arouse a deep feeling of admiration.

That a state like Corsica, worn out by thirty years of war, constantly persecuted by the strongest powers in Europe, barbarous and illiterate, should suddenly come to enjoy the freest government in the world, seems to pass all understanding. Furthermore, that this was brought about by a man who had a military training and no other advantages except those which may be attributed to his own personal merit, seems truly miraculous.

It was a government which was deeply rooted in the social reality of the island. 'There are agrarian territorial divisions, not established by law but existing in fact. They live communally but there is hardly anyone who does not have some small plot that he can call his own . . .' If from the political point of view 'the Corsicans today have the kind of heroic role which the English had at the time of their revolution', from the social point of view the island seemed a new model of equality. Alberto Fortis, one of the most lively Venetian writers of those decades, took up these themes in his *Magazzino italico* in a review of Domenico Caminer's *Historical essay*. Corsica was for him 'an untameable nation' which had sought a 'refuge for freedom in its most inaccessible mountains and fearsome caves' and which had then become 'more powerful and enlightened owing to the great ability of one man full of courage and love for his country'. It was Pasquale Paoli who had given the island a government founded on new bases and 'copied almost exactly from the English model'. 'His personal qualities which make him just as competent at handling a siege as a civil reform, his popularity, the interest that he takes in the welfare of others merit all praise.' Paoli was thus a poorer, livelier, more original version of the enlightened legislator. 'If the islanders continue at this rate, and may Heaven preserve for many years that man who alone is the source of their present strength and may be of their future greatness, they will become very famous, even after the war is over, and will repeat on a smaller scale the example of Muscovy under the immortal Tsar Peter.' But it was Paoli himself who was to have the last word concerning his experience, when he was passing through Italy in 1769 on his way to exile in England. He is reputed to have spoken these words to Joseph II whom he met in Mantua (and it does not really matter if this is a legend, for in these cases it is what people believe that counts): 'Where there is freedom there is a patria, where there is no freedom there is no patria.'

The various aspects of the Corsican myth were destined to evoke a considerable response from all over Italy, even later on, as was shown by the voluntary exile and political actions of Filippo Buonarroti at the time of the French Revolution. In Tuscany, where he was born and received his education, the influence of the events in Corsica was felt more strongly than anywhere else. In the 'sixties the bonds between Leghorn and the rebel island were being tightly woven by Italians, Corsicans and Englishmen. Keen sympathy was easily aroused in other cities of the grand duchy too. We can see this, for example, in a letter from Raimondo Cocchi to his wife, Tullia, in which he described with great excitement all that he was doing to help and assist the three hundred exiles, including General Paoli, who had just arrived in Tuscany. We can feel here how political solidarity is accompanied by genuine human warmth. The *Italian letters on Corsica*, published in Leghorn in 1770, which were erroneously attributed to Raimondo Cocchi but were really by Luca Magnanima, provide a particularly good example of the way in which Paoli was able to inspire the men of the Enlightenment in Italy in that period. There were, of course, Francesco Dalmazzo Vasco's Corsican projects which I have discussed elsewhere and let us not forget the famous words with which Alfieri dedicated his *Timoleone* to Pasquale Paoli in 1788:

Writing tragedies about freedom in the language of a people which is not free could perhaps rightly be considered mere foolishness by those who can see things only as they are at present. But whoever can view the future in terms of the constant cycle of past events will not make such a summary judgment.

I therefore dedicate my tragedy to you, to one of those few men who, having a clear knowledge of other times, other peoples and other ways of thinking, would deserve to have been born and to be active in a century far less spineless than our own.

But since it is through no fault of yours that your native land was not set free, as I do not judge men (as the crowd is accustomed to do) by their achievements, but by their deeds, I consider you eminently worthy to hear the accents of *Timoleone*, as one who is fully able to understand and appreciate them.

In these words the specific political significance of the island's experience was already growing blurred as it rose to become the symbol of an impossible and therefore all the more heroic virtue. Paoli was not insensitive to Alfieri's appeal. In a letter written to Giuseppe Ottaviano Nobili Savelli in 1784 he said that, after he had seen the noble Piedmontese wander amidst the amazed admiration of English men of letters who called him 'original in his genre' :

I read his tragedies over and over again and like them more each time, and they don't send me to sleep as always happens If I try to read the complete works of any other modern dramatist all through at a stretch. I feel sorry for those poor creatures [in Italy] because they lack the vitality to be in tune with the great passions which arouse and inspire this writer of tragedies.

On 26 August of the following year, 1785, he added that '*Timoleone* ought to be a *vademecum* for anyone who has to govern a free state'.

But the sublimation of defeat and hope is not what most interests us here. What is more important is that close network which sympathy with the Corsican rebellion and regrets over its eventual outcome created among Italian writers in the eighteenth century, from Verri to Galiani, Vernazza to Parini, Cambiagi to d'Arco, Lampredi to Pignotti, Del Turco to Bettinelli. The effect of the events in Corsica was not sufficient to interfere with or bring about any noticeable modifications in the reform movement which was already under way, but it helped to create a broader, more varied concept of it, at least in the minds of some.

Paoli's exile in England presented him with two alternatives : either to perpetuate his legend and continue to be the hero of liberty, the personality seen by John Symonds and James Boswell and eagerly sought by the Whigs, the admirers of Wilkes and the radicals, or else to continue to be the Corsican 'patriot', who denied nothing of his past yet who considered that the only possible way of returning to his island was with the support of His Britannic Majesty, the English fleet and English power. The logic of a small nation and an unsuccessful rebellion was understandably weighted in favour of this second alternative. Besides, very soon the tragedy of Poland, 'the poor Poles', as Pasquale Paoli called them, was to draw all Europe's attention to them. 'They greatly diminish the compassion which was felt for us', he wrote on 11 June 1772. However, in 1769 Paoli received official pensions and honours and fell in the estimation of many free intellectuals. It is not surprising that he showed little enthusiasm for the revolution of the American colonists. It seemed to him that they were endangering English prestige and power. His admiring interpretation of the British constitution and British society, which he always continued to uphold, bore the mark of that typical attitude —conservative in England and liberal elsewhere—that was to become so popular in the following decades. He became actively involved in English life, while, at the same time, continuing to feel that he was an outsider, an exile and a guest.

He was to spend many years in exile. Through the rare bits of news which arrived from Italy or anywhere else where there were Corsican exiles, he formed a picture of the French monarchy's rule over the island as a considerably worse version of Genoese colonial rule. He always hoped that international circumstances would one day allow him to renew the struggle.

Hence he was all the more surprised and at first unwilling to admit that the spark of revolt and freedom should have come this time not from his island, from the most oppressed and exploited peoples, the victims, but from the conquerors, not from the mountains with their shepherds and guerrillas but from the capital of luxury and riches, Paris, the home of enlightenment. The revolution, which until then had been seen in Europe as a flash on a distant horizon, where the peoples might seem closer to the natural state, had now flared up at the very centre of civilisation.

This time it was the French who wanted freedom. In the beginning he wondered whether they would be capable of restoring it to Corsica too. He was always looking backwards, to twenty years previously. He criticised the island's representative in the Estates General for not having demanded a straightforward restoration of the constitution.

> They had their simple laws and their constitution ready made; why not insist that it should be put into force again? They had seen how, in times which were still difficult, the people had turned away from violence and prosperity had come to the country. The little University of Corte spread more light in three years and trained more students in the sciences than have been seen in twenty years since.

But when he wrote these words from London on 21 July 1789 a great hope had been awakened in his heart.

France deserves her freedom [he declared], and everyone desires that she should obtain it and consolidate it with excellent laws. Corsica enjoyed it once! It cost her so much blood! If the French denied it to her now this would be a sin against the Holy Ghost. It affects their interests, it is a political question, but above all justice must be considered and they should show that this is now their only political idol.

Less than a year later, at the end of March 1790, Pasquale Paoli left England for Paris and on 22 April appeared before the Constituent Assembly where he declared:

Messieurs, ce jour est le plus heureux, le plus beau de ma vie: je l'ai passé rechercher la liberté, et j'en vois ici le noble spectacle. J'avois quitté ma Patrie asservie, je l'ai retrouvée libre, je n'ai plus rien à souhaiter. Je ne sais, depuis une absence de vingt ans, quel changement l'oppression aura fait sur mes compatriotes; mais vous venez d'ôter aux Corses leurs fers; vous leur avez rendu leurs vertus premières. En retournant dans ma Patrie, mes sentimens ne peuvent vous être douteux. Vous avez été généreux pour moi, et jamais je n'ai été esclave . . . J'ose dire que ma vie entière a été un serment à la liberté; c'est déjà l'avoir fait à la Constitution que vous établissez. Mais il me reste à le faire à la nation qui m'a adopté et au souverain que je reconnois; c'est la faveur que je demande à l'auguste Assemblée Nationale.

In Italy too, these words made a deep impression. The *Novelle politiche*, published at Cesena in the Papal States, in their edition for 18 May 1790, no. 40, could not refrain from reporting the news with particular enthusiasm: 'the same General Paoli who, twenty years ago, escaped from his country which was oppressed by a conquering people' and who was abused for having defended 'the cause of freedom', 'is now welcomed, honoured and fêted by that same people in the name of freedom'.

In Corsica, after a triumphal journey through France, he tried to operate a policy which was tortuous, to say the least. On one hand there was an attempt at the difficult, if not impossible, task of harmonising the local bid for freedom, the old rebellion which was beginning to flare up again in the parishes and villages, with the French revolutionary and constitutional movement. On the other, he was faced by the renewed conflicts between families, the sudden and violent reappearance of resentment and the revival of an anticolonial, 'patriotic' mood, suspicious and distrustful, nationalist and insular. It was completely beyond the powers of the old Corsican leader to find a balance between these various forces. And then, by this time, a new generation was beginning to assert itself, one which found expression, for example, in men like Filippo Buonarroti and Napoleon Bonaparte.

To what extent could the memory of the past, the age of Paoli, be useful in welding together such conflicting and disparate forces? Certainly it was just at that time that an image was being formed of Corsica as the forerunner of the European revolutions, of the island which had been able to point the way in a world where the majority of nations had remained insensitive to the appeal of nature and equality. It is a myth which would warrant closer study: it obviously had its origins in the ideals of Paoli's Corsica and at the same time attempts to connect them, more or less artificially, with the ideas which were dominant in France and Europe around 1790. To give only one example, here is a quotation from one of the most successful papers of the time, *Le Compère Matthieu, ouvrage périodique, philosophique et politique,* issue number two:

> Nous sommes à l'époque des grandes révolutions. Il y a vingt-cinq ans que le fameux général Paoli, forcé d'abandonner sa terre natale, fut réduit à mendier un asile chez un peuple étranger. Depuis le triomphe de la liberté ce grand homme est retourné dans sa patrie . . . Ce qui doit nous faire chérir notre constitution, et qui nous comble de gloire c'est de voir que les Corses, ce peuple si fier, si jaloux de ses droits naturels, ce peuple qui a tant répandu de sang pour les conserver, qui naguère gémissait en secret d'être involontairement enchaîné aux destins d'une nation étrangère, c'est de voir, dis-je, ces braves enfants de la nature s'associer d'eux mêmes au peuple français et solliciter de nous, comme une faveur, cette incorporation qu'il regardoient précédément comme une honte. Rien, à mon avis, ne prouve mieux combien notre constitution est conforme aux principes sacrés de l'égalité. Quels hommes seront meilleurs juges en fait de liberté que ceux qui l'ont défendue avec tant d'opiniâtreté et de constance?

At the same time others sought the social roots of Corsica's revolutionary primogeniture. An attempt was made to explain it in the *Register of the deliberations of the 'Comité permanent' of the town of Bastia*, 6 January 1790: 'one of the reasons', it said, 'for the justified grievances of the Corsicans against the Genoese government was always the forcible usurpation of property belonging to the community'. The restoration to the villages of the island of 'communal property', which the French, following the Genoese example, had continued to usurp, remained one of the most powerful incentives towards rebellion and one of the most pressing claims.

Or, as was put more generally by the anonymous *Discours à la Nation Corse assemblée pour l'élection des députés aux États Généraux, par un de ses compatriotes*, published in 1789, the very bases of liberty in Corsica were firmly planted in equality. 'En Corse chaque individu, de toutes conditions, est propriétaire de biensfonds . . . Notre nation fait dépendre toute sa félicité de la justice distributive.' It was constantly repeated in those years (as, for example, in a *Mémoire sur la necessité d'établir trois évêchés en Corse*, a pamphlet dated 2 July 1790) that 'les Corses à l'époque de 1768 étoient le seul peuple de l'univers qui combattit pour sa liberté'. Or again, still in 1790, as Saliceti said in his reply to Buttafoco:

En 1755 . . . sans agriculture, sans arts, sans commerce, nous étions un peuple pasteur, presque sauvage, déchiré au dedans par des discordes civiles, des haines de familles, tourmenté au dehors par un petit état voisin qui prétendant nous avoir acheté, voulait nous traiter en esclaves, et, sous le nom de république, nous gouvernait comme le despote d'Alger . . . M. de Paoli parut, et nous changea dans notre position. Alors, dans la fleur de l'âge . . . il espéra de faire renaître parmi nous les vertus et les beaux jours de Sparte et d'Athène; il nous en enseigna les lois, . . . il nous fit connaître les droits des nations, le dogme de l'égalité naturelle, le charme de la liberté . . . C'était un roman dans la servitude général de l'Europe et alors de telles idées devoient passer pour des rêves.

However, the more this image developed of Paoli as standard-bearer of European freedom, the greater the burden upon him and his friends and supporters of a reality that had little connection with these 'dreams'. Corsica was tending to revert to its former state of a land dominated by the jealousy and rivalry of clans, families and individuals. Paoli was no longer in full possession of the means which had allowed him to control similar socially disruptive forces for a few years in his youth. When the break with revolutionary France came and the rebellion was once more against Paris, it was obvious that Paoli was no longer in a position to re-establish a 'patriotic' unity around himself. Such an appeal had proved its worth in the battle against Genoa, but it had crumbled and fallen away when it had become necessary to fight Louis XV and his generals. It was even less effective against the Convention and the Committee of Public Safety.

The increasingly turbulent relationship with revolutionary France between 1789 and 1793 had released in the island new forces and feelings which had no place in the old kind of 'patriotism'. Anticlericalism, Jacobinism and modern political and social aims could no longer be contained within the framework of the old leader of the people, too much inclined to guile, temporising and threatening silences, as Pasquale Paoli had tended to become with the passing of the years.

Ambrogio Rossi, in his *Historical observations*, which remain the finest record of Corsica in the eighteenth century, noted, quite correctly, how Paoli's attitudes were becoming increasingly irrelevant: 'But this manner, faint echo of a time when he had held the highest position in the land, was becoming "out of date". He fell under suspicion, a way was sought for him to act legally (something which was completely alien to his spirit and, so to speak, unbearable for him) and there he was, guilty before the law and charged as a criminal.'

The Convention accused, attacked and ruined him. In 1794 the Jacobins, Buonarroti and Bonaparte disowned him, fought against him and abused him. Paoli did not yield and handed Corsica over to England. This was a repetition, 'out of date' and in a much lower key, of the manœuvre which he had unsuccessfully attempted a quarter of a century previously, to break away from France and seek refuge in the arms of England. But twenty-five years earlier this move was based on a genuine protest against oppression and tyranny. Now the idea of freedom had aroused the whole of Europe and whole peoples, throughout the Continent, were fighting and dying for liberty and equality. It was hopeless for Paoli to attempt to introduce a tiny national problem into a struggle which had assumed very different proportions and a very different significance. All he succeeded in doing was to make Corsica a dominion of the British Crown and it was the British government which very quickly took steps to remove him since it was unable to tolerate this local leader who did not fit into its plans for more or less indirect colonisation. Paoli was forced to return to his English exile and his island made its last, futile atempt to become a nation.

Corsica went back to being part of the French republic, to which it had been firmly welded by such conflicting events. By this time a new generation had come to maturity, for whom the movement towards equality and freedom but also towards dominion and power could no longer be envisaged outside a great nation.

The relationship between Napoleon Bonaparte and Pasquale Paoli would soon come to offer a typical example of this change of generations in Corsica.

All that was left for the old leader was to turn in upon himself and upon that love for his little country which now, in his old age, assumed the form of a benevolent hope and promise, tranquil and refined, after so many struggles and so much bloodshed. His last thought was for his university in Corte. He no longer saw in it an instrument to help a nation to come into being. It was a peaceful, civilising force in a Europe dominated by Napoleon.

Pasquale Paoli died in London on 5 February 1807.

6 Cesare Beccaria and Legal Reform

THE appearance of the most famous book of the Italian Enlightenment in 1764 at once gave rise to various conflicting rumours, legends and hypotheses which subsequently multiplied at a rapid pace. There seemed to be something miraculous about Marquis Beccaria's work *Of crimes and punishments (Dei delitti e delle pene)*. There were many of his contemporaries who found it difficult to accept the idea that this book, the result of a firm determination to follow a line of thought to its logical conclusion, had been written by a man who seemed hesitant and suspicious and at times apprehensive to the point of ridicule. They were also unwilling to believe that this crystalline synthesis of a century could have come from the pen of a writer of twenty-five, for whom Bacon, Montesquieu, Rousseau and Helvétius were enthusiastic youthful discoveries and not the culmination of a deep, well-founded culture.

As often happens when people fail to understand the causes of a phenomenon, Beccaria's book was severally explained away as a plot or a trick, and as plagiarism.

It was said to have arisen out of the machinations of the Parisian *encyclopédistes*, who had found someone in Milan to serve the interests of their propaganda. It was claimed that Beccaria was not the real author, or at least, as some maintained, that the idea was not really his.

It is interesting to note that another little book belonging to the eighteenth century, Jean Jacques Rousseau's *Discourse on the sciences and the arts*, had aroused heated discussions of the same nature. Had not Diderot perhaps suggested it to him on a hot summer afternoon when still a prisoner at Vincennes? Or was not it too an example of plagiarism or of copying from the hundreds of precursors which were immediately attributed to it?

Jean Jacques and Beccaria, in providing two of the most dazzling examples of intuition in this century of enlightenment, thus astonished their contemporaries into remembering that mysterious motto which adorned the first page of Montesquieu's *L'Esprit des lois*: *Prolem sine matrem creatam*.

And yet, of course, once the empty hypotheses and imaginative ideas about plots have been discarded, it is possible to study the origins of both these books and understand how they came to be written. Both are the product of a small group of philosophers of the Enlightenment who felt the bond which united them as an exemplary kind of friendship, a model for a new free society. The various positions, from one extreme to the other, in the range of thought of the Enlightenment inspired the group as a whole but at the same time tended to be personified in one or other of its individual members. Nature and reason, enthusiasm, discussion, revolt and reform are the constant themes of their life and work. The young men who gathered around the *Encyclopédie* provided Europe with the model for a similar nucleus. The Milanese 'Academy of fists' (*Accademia dei pugni*) relived, in its own way, not without a certain element of pure and simple imitation but with much original passion, the experiences and thoughts of Diderot, Rousseau, d'Holbach, Deleyre, Condillac and so many other writers of the Parisian Enlightenment of the middle of the century.

Beccaria sometimes felt himself to be the Jean Jacques Rousseau of this new group. He saw himself as a wild and solitary man, even misunderstood and persecuted. Like his model, he ended up by breaking with his friends in order to defend his 'freedom and wild independence'. But in the meantime, while he continued to live united with his friends, he enjoyed with them, with all the editorial staff of *Il Caffè* and with the Verri brothers in particular, a new relationship, both on a personal and an ideal level, the symbol of a new equilibrium between nature and reason, between spontaneity and cooperation.

Together with them, Beccaria had relived eighteenth-century thought, from the *Lettres persanes* to the subtle arguments of the mathematician, d'Alembert. And for him too, as for so many young men of his generation, the philosophy of the Enlightenment had seemed like a revelation. He felt the effect of the light of this new thought as a profound shock, a new awakening: 'I arose from the sleepy sea of ignorance where I was vegetating with the rest,

only to see the tempest and storm of passion churning up th
waves, to feel their blows more violently.'

Beccaria lived in perpetual fear of being cast back into th
depths of this sea by his indolent nature, his lack of will-powe
and his rather prickly individuality. To him the group in whic
he lived represented salvation and he saw friendship, the phil
sophical tie, as a true source of help and strength. To give a
example—on 19 July he wrote to Pietro Verri: 'You know th
I am a true friend to you . . . Let us continue to cultivate phil
sophy in our secret hearts, let us do good to men without seekir
any reward, and may we be bound even closer by our friendshi
which is one of the greatest gifts life has to offer.'

Discussion and debate within the group of friends constituted
necessity for him, his most important source of intellectu
stimulation. The atmosphere of enthusiasm among the young me
in Milan was an essential element in his life. He wrote: 'My spir
is in need of continual motion in order to keep it alive; otherwis
I am overcome by boredom and grief at seeing myself humble
and lost among the crowd of common spirits. But what means
there of breaking out of this lethargy which torments me if I ar
not inspired either by ambition or love?' His extraordinary littl
book was the product of a brief period in which Beccaria wa
both ambitious and in love. His ambition was to be one of th
philosophes who were dominating the European intellectual scen
His desire, his love was Rousseau's great myth—virtue. 'Whateve
you are, truth or illusion, come, oh! Virtue, become part of m
substance and make me happy in the brief moments of my exis
ence. Oh! If I could only leave some mark of the great benef
which I have received. This is the only monument that I coul
desire to leave after my insensitiveness.' It reads like a page fro
La Nouvelle Héloise. It was precisely this tension between ration
thought and the myth of virtue, between the ambition and e
thusiasm of the philosopher, which produced the crowning achiev
ment of Beccaria's life. Logical strictness and eighteenth-centur
philanthropy, utilitarianism and sensitivity, combined to give u
Of crimes and punishments.

Later on Beccaria could no longer hold together this two-side
element present in the creative period of his youth. He gradual
slipped back into the dark lifelessness from which the though
of the Enlightenment had helped him to emerge. There is sti
something of Rousseau in him, in his constant refusal to tak
advantage of his glory, to play the game, and in his feeling a
the more persecuted the more he was admired by others. But th
was a passive kind of Rousseau, one who by this time was firml

entrenched behind Epicureanism. Profoundly human in this refusal to act the part of himself, to continue to pretend to feel what he no longer felt, Beccaria was sincere in this too, but it was a sincerity which led to a complete withdrawal. He had foreseen it since his youth: 'I am very far from believing myself to be above other men. I am alongside the rest of humanity rather than superior or inferior.' Beccaria had very soon stepped aside from the mainstream of his time. But his book continued to live for him. In those pages his horror of blood, pain and suffering had been translated into precise, decisive arguments. Beccaria had shown the error of the death penalty, of torture and the confusion between sin and crime, he had been able to say no to the past without setting himself above it but simply through the power of a truth established once and for all.

He took up the two great themes of the century, happiness and equality, and gave them a new political force by showing a fragment, an element of a society in which, as he said, the greatest happiness would be shared among the greatest number. In this society capital punishment and all torture would be abolished and men would see the triumph of a completely new conception of law. But this was only one aspect, one fragment of the whole of society as conceived by Beccaria. His little book left its readers to guess at the rest, or rather, urged the mind to think in the terms he used to solve legal problems and all the other great questions, from economics to forms of government. 'Morality, politics and the arts all derive from a single, primitive science, the science of man, and there is no hope that men will ever make rapid progress in penetrating the depths of all these if they do not take an interest in discovering the primitive principles of this science of man.'

If Beccaria himself was unable to progress further on that path, if the other fragments which he subsequently presented to his readers were no longer on the same level as his first brilliant legal work, his aspiration to remake the whole of society and human life in general was to remain as a constant stimulus, bursting forth from the pages of *Crimes and punishments*.

It is sufficient to open the book at the famous and ever-inspiring pages devoted by Beccaria to refuting the legitimacy of torture, to feel once more how the reasoning which guided it could lead to a completely new conception of equality, while the horror which inspired it could promote an entirely new vision of the relationship of man to man.

A form of cruelty, sanctioned by usage in most countries, is the torturing of accused men . . . This wicked crucible of truth is still in existence as a monument to ancient, savage legislation in the days when trials by fire and boiling water and the uncertain outcome of armed combat were called judgments of God . . . This is a sure means of absolving the hefty scoundrel and condemning the innocent weakling. These are the fatal drawbacks of this supposed criterion of truth, a criterion worthy of cannibals, which the Romans, who were barbarians on more than one count, kept only for slaves, victims of a fierce and overpraised virtue.

At the root of this vision is the problem of social relationships, as Beccaria himself said:

There is no freedom if the laws permit that in certain circumstances a man ceases to be a 'person' and becomes a 'thing': you will then see the efforts of the powerful directed towards eliciting from the mass of legal subterfuges the law which decides in his favour. This discovery is the magic secret which changes citizens into beasts of burden, for in the hands of the powerful it is a chain to bind the actions of the weak and unwary. This is the reason why, in some governments which have all the outward appearances of freedom tyranny lurks unseen or insinuates itself unexpectedly into some corner neglected by the legislator . . . if any distinction, whether of title or wealth, is to be legitimate, it presupposes equality based on law.

Beccaria's thought moved thus in ever-widening circles from the problem of crimes and punishments to touch the whole of human society. In this way it became an active and penetrating force throughout the whole of the Europe of the Enlightenment.

In France, however, it was slow to penetrate. It is true that the men of the Enlightenment were immediately captured by Beccaria's book. Morellet translated it and spread it throughout Europe in its new French guise. The group gathered around Baron d'Holbach adopted the Milanese writer as one of their own. They had nothing but admiration for him, words of praise and encouragement and every kind of consideration. If Diderot had some objection to make he preferred not to declare it to Beccaria for fear of hurting his feelings in some way. The triumph of Beccaria's work could not have been more complete in Parisian intellectual circles. However, *Of crimes and punishments* did not succeed and for a considerable time was not to succeed in breaking down prejudices and demolishing the traditions of the judicial world. To achieve this end, long, harsh struggles were necessary. The *parlements* held out and continued to make use of torture and condemn to death, reasoning according to a legal method which by this time was scandalous in the eyes of the philosophers of the Enlightenment. It was a hard battle because it was linked with political problems, with the conflict between absolute monarchy and the *parlements*, which were defending their own autonomous power. Voltaire led the struggle. But not everyone was always in agreement with his way of seeing things and his course of action.

On the occasion of a particularly shocking case of a death sentence dictated by religious prejudices, the case of the Chevalier de la Barre, the men of the Enlightenment tried to persuade Beccaria to take a personal stand on the matter and to intervene in the discussion and the battle. But he declined to participate and in the following years increasingly avoided involvement. Thus there was no one in France who represented that unusual combination of reason and emotion which had constituted Beccaria's strength. Servan was as humanitarian, the physiocrats just as rigorous in their use of reason, Voltaire was just as eager to make the light shine in the places where tradition weighed most heavily, but Beccaria with his extraordinarily complex personality was absent. He observed from afar, with considerable detachment, how his ideas were caught up in the great tide of the century, went on to break down age-old barriers and finally, just before the Revolution, led to the legal abolition of torture. Later, when the great revolutionary storm had passed and he was already dead, his ideas would be picked up once more in the fifth year of the Republic. It was then that the finest of the French editions of his work was to be published, almost as a return to the origins and principles of the Enlightenment. A review (edited by Roederer, who had produced that edition) called the *Journal d'économie publique, de morale et de politique*, in its issue of 10th Prairial, year 5, recalled the *Caffè* group, the work of Beccaria and his friends and concluded: 'It is interesting to note that all surviving members of the group who were friends of, and who worked with Beccaria—Verri, Lambertenghi and Longo—now occupy the most important posts in the Cisalpine Republic—which is a good omen for its future.'

In England Beccaria's book came into conflict not only with a conservative tendency towards the retention of established legal practices but also with a renewed demand for and more ruthless application of the death penalty, which manifested itself in Britain in the closing decades of the eighteenth century. The lack of a police force organised on Continental lines and a profound revulsion against the very idea of introducing one on English soil, social

conflicts made more acute by the beginnings of the industri⒜
revolution and prejudices of all kinds, together with numerou
other factors, combined to produce this phenomenon. There we⒭
those, however, already in the latter half of the eighteenth centur⒴
who protested against the attitude of the majority of Englishmen
philosophical radicalism from Bentham to Stuart Mill is characte
ised by plans, polemics and campaigns for the reforms uphe⒧
by Beccaria. The Milanese philosopher can be said to be at th
origins and source of this line of thought and action in Britai⒩
Radical utilitarianism constantly looked to him as a model an
the history of this movement begins with Beccaria and Helvétiu

On the other side of the ocean, in the English colonies whic
were in the process of becoming the United States of Americ⒜
Beccaria's work was to have a widespread and lasting effec
Curiously enough, the first work of Voltaire to be published ⒤
America was the commentary which he wrote on Beccaria
treatise. There is historical significance too in the recent discover
that whole pages of Beccaria's work were carefully copied b⒠
Jefferson into his extensive diary of readings, and that it w⒜
precisely *Of crimes and punishments* which persuaded him ⒞
the need to abolish capital punishment and in general seek a ne⒲
relationship between penalty and offence. Eighteenth-centur
humanitarianism and the Quaker tradition vied with each othe
for the honour of welcoming Beccaria's thought on the othe
side of the Atlantic. Already in 1793 a leading American magi
strate noted that 'as soon as Beccaria's principles became know⒩
they found the ground prepared to receive them', and he adde
that this was due above all to the presence of the followers ⒞
William Penn. And indeed, apart from the edition which appeare
in New York in 1773, there were three further editions, betwee
1778 and 1809, in Philadelphia, the headquarters of the Society ⒞
Friends. An important New York Quaker, Thomas Eddy, wh
worked hard to bring about the reform of the penitentiary syster
was repeating at the end of the century what had already becom
indisputable—that Beccaria's ideas 'had the value of axioms ⒤
penal science'.

From the United States of America to Russia. Let us take a loo
at the effect of Beccaria's ideas in the very different political an
social setting of Catherine II's Russia. It is well known that ⒜
one time the Empress thought to summon the Milanese philosophe
to carry out his work as a reformer on the banks of the Neva but h
refused to move, adopting—perhaps more from laziness than fro⒨
conviction—the tactics suggested to him by d'Alembert: reforme⒭
should influence the powerful of this earth while always keepin

at a respectful distance; in this way they in turn will be respected. But Beccaria's work alone was sufficient to produce a considerable effect on Russian minds and hearts and to pose problems and doubts, making a far from insignificant impression in this part of the world too. Catherine II had ascended the throne only a few years previously. She was seeking a new basis for her power and a new relationship with Europe. The whole of Russian society was in a state of ferment. It seemed that at last it would be possible to draw humanitarian, tolerant and enlightened conclusions from the reforms that Peter the Great had carried out fifty years earlier. Catherine II drew up a long series of extracts from *Of crimes and punishments* and, placing them alongside principles taken from Montesquieu and other Enlightenment writers, made up the *Instruction*, which was supposed to act as a guide to the work of the legislative commission which she had summoned. It was Beccaria, therefore, who provided the inspiration for this attempted reform of the codes. The seriousness of the social problems, Pugachev's revolt and Catherine's absolutism very soon set a limit on this tendency towards reform. However, if Beccaria's thought no longer inspired absolutist power, it began to enlighten the minds of the new ruling class which was forming. The sharp contrast between the culture of the Enlightenment and the violence of contemporary reality was soon felt. Beccaria's sensitivity, as much as masonic religion, seemed to offer a new hope for the future. Lopukin, one of the foremost Russian freemasons of the eighteenth century, eventually gave up his position as a judge so as not to be forced to carry out continual violations of his own humanitarian convictions, which were derived from Fénelon and Beccaria. The young Alexei Vasilevich Naryshkin, who belonged to one of the leading families of the Russian aristocracy and who only a few years later accompanied Diderot through Europe to Petersburg, went to Milan to see Beccaria and wrote to him immediately afterwards: 'Of all the benefits which I have derived from my visit to Italy, the one which I consider most precious is the privilege of knowing you . . . If they tell you that a man from the North, from the country where, it has been said, it is necessary to flay a man to make him feel something, if they tell you that he wishes to have your portrait, give it to him, I beg you.' The memory of Beccaria, his book and his humanity would always remain with the young Naryshkin.

The problem of the death penalty and the moral and social justification of the various forms of punishment would continue to occupy the minds of the most sensitive and enlightened Russians and, naturally, the name of Beccaria would remain connected with this anxious search for a solution. The historian Scherbatov started a discussion with him and *Of crimes and punishments* was one of the first books to be translated into Russian by invitation of Alexander I when, with the start of a new century and his accession to the throne, a new era seemed to be beginning. Later, when hopes were dashed, the young *carbonari* officers who were preparing the *pronunciamento* and the liberal revolution of December 1825 once again would turn to Beccaria for inspiration. And again, immediately after 1848, we see the great novelist Saltykov-Schedrin spending the long hours of his exile in Viatka writing a biography of Beccaria and deriving from the latter's thought a meditation upon the 'idea of law'.

Thus in every land Beccaria found men who understood what he was saying and everywhere he set men thinking and aroused aspirations towards reform. According to the local situation, the seed which he had planted grew into utopias or else into modest but concrete attempts at enlightened legislation. Even in Spain, it seemed for a time as though absolutism might find in his treatise an instrument to cast off the weighty heritage of the past. Campomanes, the brilliant writer and reformer, sponsored the translation and distribution of Beccaria's book. Pietro Giusti, an Italian who was in Madrid at the time, hastened to inform the author. On 12 January 1775 he wrote:

Your lordship is by now accustomed to the homage paid by all the most cultured nations to the light of truth as manifest in your book *Of crimes and punishments*, an exceptional work, worthy of a true friend of mankind, which will be a landmark in this century of ours . . . Spain, who has produced many brilliant intellects, just by nature but forced into inactivity not, as some would have it, by the influence of the climate, but by religious and political despotism and bad legislation, came across greater obstacles and difficulties in spreading philosophical ideas. Nevertheless, a translation of your work has just come from the printing presses of Madrid . . . It is published by the Abbé Don Giovanni Antonio de las Casas, a name which has already served the cause of enlightenment in this country when the Bishop of Chiapa revealed to Charles V the atrocities committed by Spanish fanaticism in America . . . It is no mean achievement to have had it published here and this is due to the courage and enlightenment of the procurator Campomanes. Whatever the hypochondriacs who support the theory of a deteriorating world may say, one must admit that the light is gradually spreading all over Europe . . . what is there to prevent us from hoping to see the revolution at a much more advanced stage one day?

Pietro Giusti was too optimistic; everywhere in Europe, and particularly in Spain, the path was bristling with obstacles. As late as 1803, as we can see from an index published recently in Madrid by the historian Paz y Melia, the Spanish Inquisition was examining 'three notebooks without a title, a copy of the treatise on crimes and punishments'.

But what about Italy? We could trace Beccaria's influence through the different states of the peninsula and see reproduced on a smaller scale the pattern of discussion which the book had aroused in the whole of Europe, from the blindest, most stupid conservatism to the most harmonious application of his ideas to legislation. On the one hand the fanatical defence of moral and material poverty, the fierce determination not to change any-thing at any cost, which we can discern for example in certain Venetian polemical writers. On the other hand, for example, Peter Leopold's Tuscany, where not only Beccaria's reasoning but even his spirit seems to live again. Thus, on opening the code of 1786 we read:

> We have observed with horror how easily, in the former legisla-tion, the death penalty was prescribed even for crimes which were not very serious, considering that the object of the punish-ment should be the reparation of the harm done to the in-dividual and society, the correction of the offender, who is also a child of society and the state, whose improvement can never be despaired of . . . and also considering that a very different kind of legislation would be more suited to the increased gentle-ness and humanity of the present century and especially of the Tuscan people, we have arrived at the decision to abolish for ever the death penalty for any kind of offender.

And yet, just a few years before these words were written, Beccaria himself, in Milan, heard learned arguments in defence of torture coming from the lips of Gabriele Verri, a great person-ality and legal expert. Even in Lombardy there was a long and arduous path to be trodden before the ideas upheld by Beccaria could be put into practice.

Thus from this point of view too, every Italian state had its own history. A century ago Cesare Cantù drew the picture—a mosaic of hopes and illusions and a few important steps forward. It is not the details which are important but the basic fact: Bec-caria succeeded in creating in Italy a humanitarian tradition which could overcome obstacles and interruptions but which had its deepest roots in him and, when necessary, could find itself again and recognise itself in his work. Perhaps the finest praise

that has ever been written of Beccaria alludes precisely to th
fact. It is by his grandson, Alessandro Manzoni, in *Fermo e Luci*
(an earlier version of his great novel *The Betrothed*): 'With th
ever-present splendour of his genius he could make what wa
paradoxical into common sense.'

7 Pietro Verri in Germany and Russia

From Leghorn to the German World

IN 1771 Pietro Verri's *Meditations on political economy* were published in Leghorn 'by the Printers of the Encyclopaedia'. The work was an instant success in Italy. There was a succession of editions in Naples, Genoa, Milan and Leghorn and a particularly animated discussion of it in the reviews. The Florentine *Novelle letterarie* said that it was 'the most suitable code for a minister of finance in any government' and added 'we are convinced that if it were consulted and followed, it would bring happiness to every nation'. In Palermo, Isidoro Bianchi in his *Notizie de' letterati* placed this work on the same level as the works of Genovesi and Hume. Everywhere Pietro Verri's *Meditations* were recognised more or less explicitly for what they were: the most important programme of reforms presented to Italians at the beginning of the 1770s.

Outside Italy the book was just as widely discussed; the effect it produced varied from place to place, as if to reflect the complexity of the situations in different European states during the latter part of the eighteenth century. The first responses came from Switzerland, as had happened less than ten years earlier with Beccaria's famous work. Giuseppe Gorani, who in those years had withdrawn to Noyon and was still wavering between his youthful enthusiasm for Rousseau and his new-found faith in the physiocrats, was among the first mediators between Milan and Switzerland. It was he who introduced the *Meditations* to Georg Schmid d'Avenstein, one of the most important writers on economic and political matters in Argau and one of the most enthusiastic followers of the Marquis de Mirabeau. On 5 June 1772 Schmid wrote to Verri about his 'excellent ouvrage'. 'Vos Meditazioni", he said, 'répondent parfaitement à l'idée avantageuse que je me suis faite d'avance de tout ce qui peut sortir de votre plume.' He encouraged him 'à éclaircir une science aussi importante que l'économie politique, où vous venez de porter déjà tant de lumière'.

Very soon there came from Switzerland the greatest homage which Verri could desire: a translation, with a preface which was not only full of praise but also showed a genuine interest in the progress of enlightenment in Italy. This translation was published at Lausanne in 1773 by Jules Henri Pott and was the work of Gabriel Mingard, 'théologien éclairé et philosophe judicieux', one of the principal editors of the Swiss re-issues of the *Encyclopédie*. His translation opened with an introduction which constituted one of the most important and best informed pictures of Italian intellectual and moral life to be drawn in those years. What struck the Reverend Mingard in particular was the originality of the ideas and writings which were arriving in ever increasing numbers from Italy.

> Il n'y a pas longtemps, Messieurs [he told his readers] que l'Italie nous offre des morceaux de ce prix à traduire . . . Depuis longtemps il ne sortoit de la plume des Italiens que quelques traités de théologie, encore bien scholastique et très dénouée de toute empreinte de philosophie, des dissertations et des recherches sur les antiquités, pour lesquelles ce pays-là fournit plus de sçavans qu'aucun autre, quelques ouvrages de mathématiques.

And it was not the fault of Italians if problems of civil life were so rarely touched on in their country, 'Ce n'est pas, Messieurs, défaut de talens, de goût ou de secours existans pour faire mieux, ce n'est pas même défaut de lumières actuelles si l'Italie semble depuis longtemps rester en arrière et croupir dans une ignorance étonnante sur la partie la plus intéressante de la philosophie et des autres connaissances utiles aux hommes.' What was lacking was the political incentive and freedom to achieve greater and better things. 'Un gouvernement singulier' was in fact crushing all initiative in Italy and for many decades had cancelled out any attempt at improvement, 'un gouvernement dont l'autorité ne s'appuye que sur les préjugés, dont la base n'a pour fondement que l'ignorance de ceux qu'il tient sous le joug'. It was a régime which had only one aim, 'de s'opposer aux progrès des sciences, parce qu'il n'a point d'ennemis plus à craindre que les lumières réfléchies de ses sujets'. Italians were not lacking in either traditions or intellects. But even among them enlightenment would not develop except when 'les Italiens seront libres'.

Ne désespérons donc pas, Messieurs de voir renaître, pour ces belles contrées, des tems plus heureux pour le progrès et la perfection des connoissances utiles et agréables, pour lesquelles leurs habitans semblent nés plus que ceux des autres pays . . . Il n'est pas besoin pour cela d'aucune de ces révolutions qui bouleversent les états; un peu plus de liberté d'esprit, un peu plus de légéreté dans le joug dont on les charge, un peu plus de douceurs dans les mains qui tiennent les rênes et qui manient le sceptre et les siècles de l'Italie reviendront.

The names of Paolo Sarpi, 'cet homme qu'on ne nomme jamais sans respect quand on le connoit', Galileo ('quel philosophe tant qu'il se crut libre et qu'il suivit son génie!'), Muratori, 'dont les lettrés regretteront longtemps la perte de sa patrie' and who had shown 'de quoi il eût été capable s'il eût vécu dans une dépendance moins gênante', constituted a firm guarantee upon which he could place a similar hope. Antonio Genovesi had by that time succeeded in publishing a philosophy course which was clearly superior to any other which had appeared in Italy for some time. 'Vraisemblablement ce bon génie a eu de bons disciples; que n'auroit-on pas à attendre des efforts de leur génie pénétrant et actif, tel que celui des Napolitains, si une liberté raisonnable leur permettoit de se développer sans gêne?' Had not the Swiss publisher of the *Encyclopédie*, Fortunato de Felice, come from Naples, 'homme qui, gêné par mille entraves dans sa patrie, n'y auroit peut-être jamais fait connoître son génie, mais qui, mis en liberté par un séjour parmis nous, s'est montré tel qu'il est, éclairé, philosophe, doué de la plus grande pénétration et digne d'avoir été l'ami de Genovese'?

The part of Italy which promised the best and most rapid results was Lombardy, thanks to an 'administration politique, sage, modérée, amie de l'humanité'. Already forming there was a school which openly professed 'les vérités qui fournissent à l'homme des principes de bonne conduite et lui tracent la route du bonheur', preferring these 'à tous ces objets de recherches purement curieuses et spéculatives qui, flatant l'orgueil par l'appareil de la science et de l'érudition, éloignent l'homme de lui-même'. Beccaria's work had arrived in Switzerland some years previously to announce a new progressive phase in Lombardy. Almost at the same time the *Meditations on happiness* had arrived, the work of 'un autre gentilhomme milanois', in fact Pietro Verri. In 1770 Giuseppe Gorani's *True despotism* had appeared, 'ouvrage plein de bonnes choses, de pensées utiles, de réflexions intéressantes'. And now here were the *Meditations on political economy* to assure everyone that 'l'aurore d'un beau jour' was rising over

Milan. 'Qui sera plus propre que ces Messieurs à occasionner, pa
leurs ouvrages, dans l'esprit de leurs compatriotes une révolutio
avantageuse aux progrès des sciences utiles?'

Le fanatisme n'aveugle point ces auteurs estimables, un espri
sage et prudent les éclaire, les vues les plus louables les dirigen
l'enthousiasme ni l'orgueil ne conduisent pas leur plume, il
tendent au vrai et au bien, leur but est de rapprocher la philo
sophie de l'homme pour le conduire au bonheur par l'observatio
des règles respectables que prescrit la nature.

Discussions of Pietro Verri's ideas in France were certainl
more important and of greater depth. We find Condorcet in tw
letters, one dated 7 November 1771 and the other 1773, discussin
with him all the essential problems of eighteenth-century politic
The judgment which the Milanese writer had formulated on th
governments of his age and their benevolent and humanitaria
intentions was said to be too optimistic. There were in existenc
states and governments in which political and moral slavery wer
far from being abolished. And, in general, how could it be mai
tained that 'dans tous les états, c'est toujours par l'avis du plu
grand nombre que tout est réglé'?

Il me semble [said Condorcet] que cela est tout au plus vra
dans les démocraties. Est-ce que presque partout le plus gran
nombre aurait été d'avis de se sacrifier pour le plus petit, de s
priver du nécessaire pour que quelques hommes regorgeasser
de richesse, de s'excéder de travail pour que leurs oppresseur
fussent rassasiés et encore dégoûtés de plaisirs?

One had to recognise that the great majority of men were crushe
by the will of a small number who were rich and powerful.

Vous avez, à ce que je crois, trop bonne opinion de la natur
humaine, non pas de cette espèce malheureuse qui souffre e
se tait, mais de celle qui jouit et qui opprime. Je crois les homme
naturellement bons, mais je suis toujours tenté de faire un
exception en faveur de ceux qui veulent être les maîtres d
autres. Vous tâchez, sans les révolter, de leur faire entendr
que leur véritable intérêt est de faire le bonheur du peuple . .
Mais ne craignez-vous point d'avilir un peu le peuple aux yeu
de ses maîtres, de leur faire voir comme des bêtes de somm
qui ne valent que ce qu'elles rapportent?

Here is the reply of Baron d'Holbach who, writing to Paol
Frisi on 1 December 1771, confessed to him that many of Verri

ideas would encounter some difficulties in being published in France where the censorship was increasing in strictness in the closing years of Louis XV's reign.

J'ai reçu et lu avec un grand plaisir l'excellent ouvrage économique de M. le comte Verri : je vous prie de lui faire mes très humbles remerciemens pour l'exemplaire qu'il a bien voulu me destiner; tous ceux qui ont été en état de le lire en sont très satisfaits; je ne doute pas qu'une traduction française ne valût à l'auteur des applaudissemens universels, mais depuis quelque tems la presse est si gênée chez nous qu'il est presque impossible de dire les moindres vérités; nous somme réduits à jouïr de celles qui nous viennent des pays étrangers.

Perhaps most important is the reaction of the physiocrats : Abbé Pierre-Joseph Roubaud accused Verri of failing to follow the doctrines of the masters and of passing continually 'de la vérité à l'erreur et de l'erreur à la vérité'. But although he had not followed the doctrine of true science and had placed his faith in a 'théorie souvent fausse', he arrived nevertheless, he said, 'presque toujours à des résultats pratiques conformes aux loix données par la nature : le sentiment du vrai et du bien le redresse, lorsqu'il a perdu les notions, et même lorsqu'il s'est égaré il sème à chaque pas des idées ingénieuses et sérieuses'.

Next the response of Voltaire, who proved to be closer to Verri than either Condorcet or Roubaud : 'On n'a jamais rien écrit de plus vrai, de plus sage et de plus clair. Il n'y a qu'un homme de qualité, appelé aux premières fonctions, qui puisse traiter ainsi ce qui regarde le bien public. C'est ce qu'est arrivé en Espagne au seul Uztariz, en France au duc de Sully, en Angleterre à plusieurs membres du Parlement.' Voltaire went on to praise Verri for his definition of interest rates ('always in direct ratio to the demand and inverse to the offer'). 'Les théologiens, qui ont tant embarassé cette matière, auraient mieux fait de ne point parler de ce qu'ils n'entendaient pas.' And in conclusion he said : 'Je vois par votre livre que le Milanais prend une face nouvelle. Il ne faut qu'un ministre pour changer tout un pays. Vous avez chez vous un grand homme [Firmian], digne d'être secondé par vous. Je gémis que mon grand âge et mes maladies ne me permettent pas de vous admirer de plus près.'

And finally the *Journal encyclopédique*, echoing the translation of the *Meditations* which had appeared in Lausanne :

Il n'est plus ce tems où la patrie des Cicéron, des Virgile, des Césars, des Tacite, des Tite Live etc. n'offroit d'autres productions littéraires que des sonnets, des chansons, des dissertations sur les antiquités, ou des traités de théologie scholastique. La lumière qui, dans ce siècle, a accompagné les progrês de l'esprit humain, a éclairé ces fameuses contrées et l'on a vu paroître les immortels ouvrages des Muratori, des Genovesi, des Beccaria, des Verres [sic] etc.'

After summarising and quoting at length, the writer concluded :

Il y a très peu de neuf dans l'ouvrage que nous venons d'analyser, et si l'original a eu beaucoup de succès, l'auteur en est principalement redevable au choix judicieux, en général, qu'il a fait des meilleures observations publiées sur les différentes branches de l'économie politique, et qu'il a sçu accomoder à sa façon de penser. Quant à la traduction, elle nous a paru assez exacte, mais le style n'en est pas toujours pur et correct.

And yet, in spite of its limits and stylistic defects, it was Mingard's translation, as can be seen in this review in the *Journal encyclopédique*, which was responsible for introducing Verri's work in Europe and causing it to circulate outside Italy. It was this version which very soon evoked a response from the German-speaking world.

In 1774 there appeared in Dresden the *Betrachtungen über die Staatswirthschaft* (*Meditations on political economy*) 'by Count Verri, Imperial Royal Chamberlain, Privy Councillor and President of Commerce in Milan'. It purported to be a translation from the Italian but the translator had certainly kept his eye on the French text. He reproduced in full Mingard's long presentation of the work and thus was instrumental in introducing to the German public one of the sharpest, most interesting visions of Italian intellectual life in those years. We have not succeeded in discovering the identity of the translator. A review of the work was published in the *Litterarische Nachrichten* on 17 May 1775, in which stress was laid on the fact that 'the excellent Genovesi' had 'drawn the attention of the public to Italian works on political economy'. Now Verri's *Meditations* had come to strengthen and deepen this interest.

In 1777 Detune at The Hague published a second edition of Mingard's translation. 'On a cru rendre un service essentiel à tout citoyen qui cherche à s'instruire', said the foreword, 'en lui facilitant l'acquisition d'un ouvrage italien, à peine connu dans ce pays, et dont au moins la traduction faite à Lausanne en 1773 auroit dû pénétrer dès longtemps dans nos provinces, si c'étoit le sort de ce qui excelle d'être toujours le plus répandu.' The writer of the preface not only praised Verri's work but described a strange adventure which it had had on the other side of the Channel.

Un insigne plagiaire, sous le nom de D. Browne Dignan, a publié chez Grant, à Londres, en 1776, un *Essai sur les principes politiques de l'economie publique*, qu'il osa effrontément dédier à Milord Comte de Rochford 'comme connoisseur, dit-il, des objets qu'il traite, et de la langue dans laquelle il écrit, des idées aussi neuves qu'intéressantes. . .' Or cet *Essai*, à la réserve des paragraphes omis et de quelques termes estropiés, est, d'un bout à l'autre, servilement et mot à mot, transcrit de la traduction françoise que M. Mingard avoit publiée à Lausanne l'an 1773 de l'ouvrage italien de M. le comte Verri . . .

A new translation of the *Meditations* appeared in Germany in 1785. The complete title was: *Meditations on political economy. Translated from the Italian of Count Verri, accompanied by observations and an essay on projects* by L. B. M. Schmid, Aulic Councillor, Public Professor in Ordinary of Political Economy, Policy, Finance, Natural and International Law at Heidelberg, Ordinary Member of the Palatinate Society of Natural Philosophy and Economy, Mannheim, at Swann's Bookshop, 1785.

Ludwig Benjamin Martin Schmid (d. 1793) had for years been a great admirer of Verri. In his first courses, held in the Hohe Schule at Lautern, where he had taught before going to Heidelberg, and published under the title *Lessons on political economy* (Mannheim and Lautern 1780), he had attempted to find a point of contact between two works which seemed to him fundamental and upon which he had based all his lessons, Isaak Iselin's *Treatise on legislation* 'and Count Verri's *Meditations on political economy*'. He added in the preface that he always recommended to his listeners Genovesi's *Lessons on commerce*, Stewart's *Political economy* and Montesquieu's *Esprit des lois*, 'together with the rule that they should meditate diligently and read much and a variety of works'. But Iselin and Verri had to be read and they remained at the basis of his teaching in politics and economics. In the first of the two volumes of the *Lessons* the influence of Iselin predominated, but in the second volume Verri's *Meditations* played an important part. On the very first page the author declared that 'I cannot praise enough Count Verri's *Meditations on political economy*'.

The translation published in Mannheim in 1785 was therefore the work of a true admirer of Verri. The book opened with a dedication to the Crown Prince of Norway, Peter Frederick William, who, in his capacity as Duke of Schleswig, Holstein and

Oldenburg, not to mention Coadjutor of Lübeck, was the 'Graci‹
Prince and Master' of L. B. M. Schmid. This was followed by
introduction where the latter explained what had induced him
undertake this work and gave an account of the procedure adop‹
in his translation :

> With this work the author has produced something excelle
> belonging to the best of its kind, whether one considers
> subject itself, the depth and correctness of the thought or
> manner of presentation. This is so intimately connected w
> the subject matter and develops the thought with such sin,
> minded purpose that I have followed the structure of
> sentences in great detail, only departing from it in the m
> difficult sections, and even then I have kept as close to
> original as possible. In other ways this translation could h
> been more fluent, but the purpose of the book and the total eff
> was obscured less than if I had proceeded differently. Whoe
> compares it with the original with that care which is necess
> when one translates, will find that it would have cost me m‹
> less time and trouble had I allowed myself more freedom.

The author had then included a substantial *Contribution t‹
practical concept of projects*. It was the declaration, the confess
almost, of a moderate, well-meaning representative of the ref‹
movement of the Enlightenment on the very eve of the Rev‹
tion. The air resounded with new, adventurous aims and pl‹
'Projects' were certainly not lacking in an age in which rev‹
tionary thought was in seething ferment and in which refo
themselves sometimes took on the appearance of violent sub‹
sions planned and executed from above, in the hands of enlighte
despots. L. B. M. Schmid recognised the quality of vitality in
political discussion and activity which was going on around h
but he was hesitant. He could not decide whether to throw h
self in and be swept along by the tide or to remain on the b‹
to enumerate and explain the dangers and difficulties which wc
be encountered by those who allowed themselves to scheme
make plans for the future. 'This is truly a time of total ferm
This is earth and air for forming projects. Oh happy times w
everything is in ferment! No, not happy but unhappy! Ev
period of ferment, as long as it lasts, is a period of disorder.
happy times follow inevitably. That is the unchangeable co
of nature.' L. B. M. Schmid was convinced in fact that hist‹
like nature, 'always goes forwards and completes its course
ceasingly and without interruption', and he believed that the wl
of the modern world had been born of a grandiose revolut
'eine Revolution, ein Sturz', a profound upheaval which had c

pletely changed the medieval world. But was a similar revolution really necessary at the end of the eighteenth century? 'When one thinks back to previous centuries in Germany and Europe, there were times when revolutionary changes in fundamental and essential things were necessary. The times which preceded these made it necessary. But one or two of the most recent centuries preceding our own were not so and likewise the first half of our own century was not so.' Things had certainly changed in the last few decades. 'However, are these times not thus regarded by the present prevailing atmosphere, almost as though the second half of this century had begun a general revolution of awakening after a long, impotent sleep, as though it were the maturity of the last thousand years?'

L. B. M. Schmid took up the arms of empiricism and conservative historical wisdom against those who sought to accelerate the course of history with their dreams and plans in such a way as to transform it into a revolution: every nation developed in its own way and it was necessary to take into account the circumstances and nature of every people. Any attempt to violate this historical reality could only end in the worst kind of despotism, that of the 'planners' who held the power in their hands. 'Planning in government is despotism and indeed the worst kind of all.' To destroy the existing law was the most dangerous of political acts and worse still if it were carried out by the government. 'Planning by those who wield power possesses the appearance of law, the complexion and features of the best laws. It seduces the powerful planner, especially if he is sincere and believes in what he is doing, into thinking that his project is the essence of law. Then despotism is the role of the powerful, slavery the role of the underlings from birth onwards.'

We can tell that we are in the age of Joseph II and the reactions of the professor from Heidelberg might have been of interest to Pietro Verri—if he had been acquainted with them—since he was engaged, precisely in those years, upon a much more important and original attempt to interpret in terms of freedom his own resistance and that of others in Milan to the Emperor's 'planning' and 'despotism'.

Thus Schmid's words introduced the *Meditations* into the midst of the political debates in Germany in the 1780s, reflecting, we may say in conclusion, both an urge towards reform and a repugnance for violent and revolutionary means, both Verri's idea of a solely economic dictatorship able to create in a short time a new situation and the intuition of a new freedom. From the very way in which he had reasoned them out, the fundamentally conservative conclusions of the professor from Heidelberg did not prevent him from performing what was essential in his task as translator, that is to place the German public in direct contact with the reformist, enlightened nucleus of Verri's work.

The principal periodical of the *Aufklärung*, the *Allgemeine deutsche Bibliothek*, echoed these doubts and problems in an important, comprehensive review, showing once more what a penetrating and lasting effect the *Meditations on political economy* had had in Germany.

At the end of 1772, also in Leghorn, Verri's *Ideas on the nature of pleasure* had appeared. Once more there was extensive, animated discussion in Italy which, among other things, gave the Barnabite Father Marcantonio Vogli a chance to publish a pamphlet against Verri's conception. The effect of the work on Germany came later but was no less considerable. The *Göttingische Anzeigen für gelehrten Sachen* gave a full review of it in the issue of 4 April 1776. 'Despite the fact that we have this work rather late, we compensate for this because it deserves to be better known in Germany than it is at present.' The work was anonymous but the author was evidently 'a man of great discernment with acute powers of observation'. He presented himself in such a paradoxically original way as to appear as a 'Selbstdenker'. But from a more attentive reading it became quite clear that he had started from Descartes, Maupertuis, Wolff and Sulzer. A detailed analysis of the work confirmed the interest which the reviewer had obviously felt on reading it. Two days later, on 6 April, the same periodical also gave an account of Vogli's work. The judgment was not favourable: 'The author of this pamphlet has not adapted himself to his opponent in any way; he has not read more than the latter and has certainly thought less.'

The author of the review and, in all probability, also of the article devoted to Father Vogli, was Christoph Meiners, one of the most fertile and versatile writers of the latter part of the eighteenth century in Germany, 'Professor der Weltweisheit in Göttingen' and author of innumerable books on various branches of knowledge. It was precisely in those years that he published his *Miscellaneous philosophical writings*, which included sections on the Greek philosophers, a 'short history of the Nile', Cicero, the Southern Isles, Socrates and the mysteries, with the accent always upon the value of men's education and moral training. In the following years and decades his indefatigable activity must have led him to put his humanistic ideal into increasingly conscious historical forms. He was one of the creators of the study of popular traditions, he became enthusiastic about the problems of social classes and the relationship between political progress and moral improvement.

Meiners was still young and at the beginning of his career (he was thirty) when he read and became enthusiastic about Verri's work. He was not content with introducing it in the *Göttingische Anzeigen* but shortly afterwards was responsible for a fine, elegant translation of it, preceded by an extensive commentary, both of which he published 'in der Weygandschen Buchhandlung' in Leipzig in 1777, under the title *Gedanken über die Natur des Vergnugen.*

In an introduction dated April 1777 he described his experiences as translator and presenter of the work. An appendix to the book contained his own *Examination of the preceding theory of pleasure and some of the principles extracted therefrom by the author,* which took up as much space as Verri's small book.

'The unknown author of the preceding theory,' he said on the first page, 'belongs unquestionably to the philosophers of the new era, that small company of chosen ones who do not only think for themselves but make others think too'. Meiners admired the quality of Pietro Verri's mind. 'He combines the finest powers of observation with the rare perceptive quality which is required in order to test and order his personal experiences and to raise them to the level of general principles.' His brilliance and insight appeared even more remarkable when one considered the difficulties and the interest of the problem he had chosen to treat.

The author's work is also an example of the fact that it is much easier to dispute all explanations hitherto given of the origin and nature of pleasure than to establish a single new one against which one could not bring forward just as many objections and difficulties as against the old ones.

Not that it was difficult to trace the origins of his thought.

The elements of the present theory are a combination of Locke's meditations and the ideas of Maupertuis . . . The author has not only united the ideas of these two very dissimilar philosophers but defined them as well, carried them as far as they can be carried, anticipated all objections and difficulties and tried to strengthen them as much as possible. He had courage enough to produce these objections himself, in all their strength, which would have discouraged a less bold spirit from his beloved hypothesis, and he not only produced them but could even turn them into apparent proofs for the statements which they were really disputing.

In each of these two philosophers, said Meiners, it was possib
to find contradictions and lacunae. Verri had not lingered ov
these but instead had constructed his logical edifice with gre
coherence—which Meiners promptly and somewhat pedantical
proceeded to repeat and comment on.

We shall not follow him along this path which would bri
us to touch upon some of the most typical problems of t
eighteenth century about the calculation of pain and pleasure an
in general, of the moral and gnoseological ideas which acco
panied the birth of modern political economy. The discussi
between Verri and Meiners would lose some of its significan
if it were not considered in this broader context, too broad
be attempted here. But we cannot pass over in silence one fact
which is well known—that it was Meiner's translation and co
mentary which attracted Kant's attention to Verri's work. Aft
quoting a few sentences of it in his *Anthropologie*, Kant co
cluded: 'I can subscribe to these statements of Count Verri wi
complete conviction.'

When, in 1781, Verri put together the three works to which
attached the most importance in one volume entitled *Discours*
*of Count Pietro Verri of the Scientific Institute of Bologna on t
nature of pleasure and pain, on happiness and on politic
economy, revised and augmented by the author*, which was pu
lished in Milan by Giuseppe Marelli, it did not fail to make
impression in Germany also. The *Göttingische Anzeigen von gele*
ten Sachen, in their fifty-first issue of 21 December 1782, hai
'these miscellaneous writings of one of the brightest and mo
penetrating minds'. The reviewer was probably Christoph Meine
again, who took the opportunity to continue his discussion wi
Verri of the relationship between pleasure and pain, using as
pretext the modifications which the latter had seen fit to ma
in his essays. As for the *Meditations on political economy,*
stressed the fact that one was concerned with a work by a m
who had enjoyed important administrative and political respon
bilities and who therefore based what he said on extensive fir
hand experience of the problems in question.

It is remarkable that in his refutation of the physiocrats he see
to prove that their system which imposes all taxes on land co
not exist without the ruinous ban on importation of forei
corn and produce; because landed property which has to be
the burden of all the taxes cannot compete in prices with i
ported produce and will necessarily be ruined. Where then
this beneficial free trade that the economists preach? Th

system is so inconsistent—a system which many authors have nevertheless admired on the grounds of its very consistency.

Thus, up to the verge of the Revolution, Verri's economic thought was an incitement to criticism, rethinking and testing of the physiocratic system. We have been able to establish this by quoting the reactions of Roubaud and Voltaire and we have noted it while following Verri's work in its various peregrinations throughout the German world. We can still see him in 1782, as we reach the end of our piece of research, which does not claim to be exhaustive but which will at least have proved the richness and variety of the response which Pietro Verri aroused in Europe and particularly in Germany.

In the Russia of Paul I and Alexander I

It is quite possible that a wider and more accurate investigation than the one which we have so far been able to carry out in Russian magazines and books of the eighteenth century may one day reveal a trace of Pietro Verri's thought in Petersburg or Moscow as early as the 'seventies or 'eighties of the century. It is significant, however, that the voice of the Milanese Enlightenment philosopher made its impact upon Russia just at the time when the elimination of Paul I was in preparation and the era of great hopes and plans was just beginning—in the years, that is, which immediately preceded the accession to the throne of the young emperor, Alexander I. A journal was being organised around the brilliant but eccentric writer, Ivan Petrovich Pnin, a journal which lasted just a year, but which even in such a short time was able to formulate a new moral and political programme. The *Sanktpeterburgskoj Žurnal* was a real return to enlightenment after the years of tyranny and mystic fantasies of Tsar Paul. It also represented a return to reason after the terrors and hopes produced by the far-off French Revolution. The writings of Montesquieu, d'Holbach, Filangieri and Volney were featured in the journal along with those of a large number of young Russian poets and essayists and side by side with these is to be found the translation of numerous chapters of Pietro Verri's *Meditations on political economy*. The translation was not by Pnin but by I. I. Martynov and it was not taken directly from the Italian text but from a French translation which must be the one which appeared under the title *Réflexions sur l'économie politique*, published in Lausanne by Jules Henry Pott and Co in 1773 and then republished, this time with the name of the translator, Gabriel Mingard, by the bookseller Detune at The Hague in 1779. I. I. Martynov had read with interest the *Avertissement* and the *Lettre du traducteur à ses amis les membres de la Compagnie littéraire de Lausanne* which accompanied this last edition and which contained the most remarkable eulogy of eighteenth-century Italian culture to appear in the European press in those years. Not only was there the presentation of Verri and his work but there was also mention of his brother Alessandro, and the 'célèbre marquis Beccaria', the *Caffè* and even Gabriele Verri. There followed a discussion of Genovesi, Gorani and the whole of the Italian reform movement. Martynov extracted various elements from it for an article which appeared in the February issue of the journal. He furthermore took the opportunity of speaking about Italian classical culture, the Trecento and the primacy of Italy in the arts and sciences, altogether a thorough illustration and defence of Italian culture. In the March issue there was the translation of paragraphs I and II of the *Meditations*, in April paragraphs III and IV, in June VI, in August VII and in September paragraph IX. The choice of passages was significant: leaving aside the more theoretical chapters, the translator had chosen those which most closely concerned Russia, those which discussed the export of grain, foreign trade and internal economic freedom.

Shortly before the publication of the *Sanktpeterburgskoj Žurnal*, Alexander Radischev, the first Russian *intelligent* and revolutionary, had returned home from exile in Siberia. He could not but be interested in such ideas. He never quoted Verri in his writings, the memoirs which he wrote during the few years which still remained to him to live, but when a new edition of the *Meditations* appeared in Paris under the title *Economie politique du Comte Verri, de l'Institut des Sciences de Boulogne, traduite de l'Italien sur la septième édition*, published in the year VIII (and some copies bear the date 1799), Radischev hastened to obtain a copy for his library, placing it alongside the other things which concerned eighteenth-century Italy and which he had already collected. (One day it will be necessary to list them and assess the importance of these Italian books which had come into his hands.)

This last French translation which we owe to 'citoyen Chardin, professeur au Prytanée français', according to a manuscript note found in a copy preserved in the Bibliothèque Nationale in Paris, served as the basis for a Russian translation, complete this time and entirely different from the one by I. I. Martynov. It appeared in Petersburg in 1810 with the following title: *Politiceskaja ekonomij a ili o gosudarstvennom chozjajstve. Tvorenie grafa de Verri, člena Bulonskago učenago obščestva. Perevedeno s francuzskago, a na francuzskoj s ital'janskago s sed'mago izdanij a,* printed by V. Morskoj. This time the *Meditations* came out in the company of Condorcet, Montesquieu, Beccaria and Adam Smith, all translated by order of Alexander I. 'Pour le moment nous nous occupons de faire traduire en russe plusieurs bons ouvrages', the Tsar had written to La Harpe soon after his accession to the throne. Verri's work had been assigned to Alexei Ivanovich Pomeranchev, who came from a family of orthodox priests and who in 1819 was to organise a 'Praktičeskaja Akademija', in short a typical writer and official of the era of Speranskij and Alexander I. This translation, 356 pages long plus index, was dedicated to Nikolai Petrovich Rumanjanchev and is a real mine of information for those interested not only in the history of thought but also in the history of economic terminology in Russia.

8   The Position of Galiani between the Encyclopaedists and the Physiocrats

THE time at which they were written, the allusive a[nd] sometimes deliberately ambiguous style employed [by] Galiani and the debates they immediately aroused [in] all areas of the Parisian intellectual world, must all ha[ve] helped to render the interpretation of the well-known *Dialogu[es* *sur le commerce des bleds* (1770) somewhat difficult and uncertai[n.] The polemic did not die out with the passing of the years. [In] 1938 Eduard Ganzoni could still call Galiani a 'misundersto[od] economist' and Luigi Einaudi showed his agreement by re-exami[n-] ing the whole problem of the historical significance of the Neapo[li-] tan economist.

After so much discussion it was obvious that the only w[ay] to progress significantly further was to publish a fully critic[al] text, together with a dossier on the genesis and discussion of t[he] *Dialogues,* containing notes and letters written by and to Galia[ni,] articles for and against him, to enable one to trace the origi[n] and development of the thought of the author and his opponen[ts.] This was exactly what was done by the greatest expert on Galian[i's] work, Fausto Nicolini, in the attractive and useful edition whi[ch] he published in 1959.

The text was less easy to establish than appeared at first sig[ht,] both because of the variants—well-known to anyone familiar wi[th] old editions (which are always less uniform than one wou[ld] imagine)—and especially because of the recent discovery [in] America of an autograph manuscript of the *Dialogues* contai[n-] ing an earlier version of the text which sometimes differs co[n-] siderably from the one which was subsequently published

1770. Fausto Nicolini devotes the latter part of his *Introduction* and *Appendix Six* to an explanation of the problems raised by the existence of these two versions and an account of the most important variants.

The dossier on the *Dialogues* fills three hundred pages of the book and is packed with valuable material, mostly very difficult to find or previously unpublished, and always very well annotated. Obviously it does not claim to be complete. Every reader, the present writer included, may be tempted to revise the work in his own mind, adding here and perhaps taking away there. It all depends, of course, upon the angle from which one views the situation. The conflict of ideas revealed in these pages is so stimulating, the economic and political interests involved are so important, as to make one wish to leave aside all the mundane, purely anecdotal elements in order to concentrate on certain essential points. After all, the debate opens with a famine which took the lives of thousands in Naples in 1764 and closes with the greatest political and economic crisis of the *ancien régime* in France before the Revolution, the crisis of the last years of the reign of Louis XV. On the intellectual plane, the dossier on the *Dialogues* begins when the *Encyclopédie* was finished and the movement which had grown up around the great dictionary began to splinter and fall to pieces, giving way to a real struggle for the succession among physiocrats, *encyclopédistes* of various persuasions, groups linked with d'Holbach, Necker or with others. For about ten years, up to the advent of Turgot in 1774, when these forces were once again drawn together in a temporary alliance, we witness the internal struggles of French *encyclopédisme* and the rise of new conflicting forces, for and against the Enlightenment. In order to assess the true political and polemical value of the *Dialogues* it is necessary to look at them in the context of those conflicts and debates of which they form part.

The documents collected by Fausto Nicolini prove just how much Galiani was influenced by the atmosphere around him and how sensitive he was to the problems of those years. Often he appears to us to reflect, in however brilliant a manner, these debates and problems, rather than to state his own personal viewpoint. We can see him changing with the times and adapting to the different circumstances, always perceptive and lucid as he views the drama going on around him. At first he too was in favour of free trade in cereals and supported the ideas of the physiocrats; but he saw the difficulties, protests and objections to the policy established with the edict of 1763 growing up around him and for a long time was torn between the arguments for and against the doctrines of free trade. Eventually he became convinced that they were mistaken, or at least that they should be interpreted and put into practice in entirely different ways from those employed by Trudaine, l'Averdy and others with authority in France.

As Fausto Nicolini explains, Galiani ultimately took up his antiphysiocratic position somewhere between March and November 1768. It is sufficient to look at George Weulersse's history of the *Mouvement physiocratique en France (de 1756 à 1770)* (1910) to realise the significance of that year and of those months in particular. The physiocrats felt, or rather knew, that to make the edicts of 1763 and 1764, which had been persistently and blatantly disregarded by the government and local authorities, really work, they had to aim at much more fundamental changes in the structure of the state and the economy (abolition of the corporations etc.). They sought in all possible ways to spur the government to action but their efforts met with sluggish resistance. The unbridled attacks to which free trade policies were subjected increased in violence. Bachaumont wrote at that period that 'cette intervention dans la police du gouvernement n'est que le prélude de la subversion totale que se proposent ces philosophes patriotes'. The forces which were opposed to the physiocrats grew ever wider. The *parlements* became more and more disorderly and rebellious and revolts broke out in Normandy, Maine and Touraine. L'Averdy was replaced by Maynon d'Invault, but this did not make the economic policy any stronger or more purposeful. In November 1768, Galiani drew these conclusions and declared to Diderot: 'Il faut laisser subsister les mauvaises lois partout où il n'y a pas dans le ministère des hommes d'assez de tête pour faire exécuter les bonnes et pourvoyant aux inconvénients des innovations les plus avantageuses.'

Thus Galiani gave up the idea of reform because he considered the obstacles to be insurmountable. Practical considerations, crude facts, took the upper hand over ideas and programmes. Why? What made him react in this particular way and come to this particular conclusion?

Political and ideological motives were jostling for position in his receptive and lively mind at the moment when the *Dialogues* were born, and it was there that these different, often conflicting elements became arranged in a form of discussion, a *concordia discors*. But one essential political element emerged to become uppermost in his mind. Galiani was a passionate observer of the French political scene, but ultimately he was influenced even more deeply by the recent experience of famine in Naples, an experience shared by all Neapolitans, by Tanucci, the prime minister, and the whole of the southern ruling class. In Naples the lesson had been much more brutal than in France. The terrible famine of 1764—the last great famine of the Italian *ancien régime* and a key date in the eighteenth century in Italy—had revealed the frightening inadequacy of the grain provisioning system in the Bourbon state and the city of Naples. Other Italian regions—Tuscany for example—emerged from a similar and contemporaneous experience with an entirely new attitude towards the corn laws. In 1765 Peter Leopold was to begin the free trade era of his grand duchy. But the obstacles to progress, tradition and sectional interests, were much weightier in the South, and Tanucci's policy had shown that his empirical reformism was by this time completely inadequate. Naples had suffered more than any other part of Italy. The toll of victims had been very high. A succession of complaints and lawsuits were to keep the memory of this bitter experience alive for a long time to come. One day historians will have to study it in detail, comparing it with what happened in the other states of the peninsula and the rest of Europe in order to assess its significance exactly. Galiani had tried to suggest technical and economic measures and remedies (new crops and new laws) and he had done this enthusiastically, with reforming zeal, as his letters to Tanucci testify. But he had had to resign himself to the facts, facts that appear so often in the pages of his *Dialogues*. He had followed the ideas of his friends, the *encyclopédistes*, and had attempted to apply them far away in Naples. But he had not succeeded. His 'realism' was born of defeat.

Thus at the root of Galiani's position at the end of 1768 lay concrete experiences in France and Naples. He undoubtedly elaborated them in a brilliant manner and here and there was able to draw some original conclusions. But the evolution of his thought was not guided by philosophical conceptions. His polemic against the abstractions of the physiocrats cannot be considered a fundamental element, nor even a very important one, in his evolution. Despite what Fausto Nicolini has to say in his introduction, it seems to me that this polemic against the abstractions of the physiocrats is the least original feature of Galiani's writings. French pamphlets, newspapers and books of those years are full of this attitude, which Galiani was merely taking up and reiterating. When Voltaire published *L'Homme aux 40 écus* in 1768 Condorcet merely commented that Voltaire had been driven to write this pamphlet by his hatred for the physiocrats' 'esprit de système'. 'Dans un moment d'humeur contre les systèmes qu'il s'amusa à faire ce roman.' The previous year, 1767, had seen the appearance of Forbonnais's two volumes entitled *Principes et observations oeconomi-*

ques, which was perhaps the most noteworthy attack agair
the physiocrats at that particular time. We read in the fo
word among other things, that:

> Dès qu'il est question d'agir ou de la pratique, on reconnoit l
> bornes de l'utilité qu'on peut tirer des abstractions . . . l
> métaphysiciens, ennivrés de leur sublimité, se pressent trop
> prétendre orgueilleusement que le monde peut être gouver
> avec des sillogismes . . . Il est de la prudence, avant d'engager
> croïance, de bien examiner si quelqu'abus n'est pas le foïer de c
> explosions sistématiques.

In a review of Forbonnais's book, which appeared in its Septemb
1767 issue, the *Journal de l'agriculture, du commerce et d
finances* stressed that 'cette métaphysique [of the physiocra
conduit à voir les choses en abstraction; on croit les simplifier
les généralisant . . . Les économistes . . . laissant de côte les fai
ont enfanté des systèmes qui cadrent mal avec les faits. La mé
physique leur en a tenu lieu, elle les a conduits à voir les chos
en abstractions'.

Undoubtedly this campaign against the 'abstraction' of t
followers of Quesnay was to have profound effects. Here we c
find one of the sources of that attack against the mentality of t
eighteenth century which was ultimately to involve the who
of the Enlightenment in its condemnation and to be handed dov
to its opponents and enemies. But these philosophical—or termin
logical—aspects of the dispute must not close our eyes to t
historical significance of the commonplaces against the 'econ
mists' which were circulating around 1768. The term 'abstractio
meant the general programme, the policy based on principles, t
move towards reform, which, hinged as it was upon agrarian fr
trade, tended to invade all aspects of social life in France. And
was for this reason that the enemies of that policy were so co
cerned to counter 'abstraction' with facts, empiricism and t
practice of judging each case on its own merits. In this too, Galia
only expressed a much wider trend. His polemic was merely t
theoretical formulation of his resignation and admission of defe
in the face of the obstacles which were blocking the way of mo
radical reform and which in Naples as in Paris had proved insupe
able.

The *Ephémérides du citoyen*, organ of the physiocrats, w
quite right to begin its discussion of the *Dialogues* with the obse
vation that 'cet ouvrage n'est pas d'une petite importance puisqu
ne tend à rien moins qu'à établir que ce ne sont point les princip
du droit naturel, ni les règles de la justice qui doivent décider c

l'administration du commerce'. It was not an excess of ideological politics but a lack of principles which caused the failure of the laws of 1763 and 1764 over free trade and free export of cereals. The laws contained dangerous limitations and compromises, while the government had not proved vigorous, systematic or forceful enough to apply them. It was moderation, not excessive daring, which weakened French economic policy. This was repeated over and over again, even in argument with Galiani, by those who upheld the ideas of the physiocrats. And there is no doubt that their observations touch on a fundamental aspect of this situation. Morellet, who was a very different person from the grey figure which Galiani, half jokingly, half polemically, tends to present in his letters, hit the mark when he spoke about the large number of persons 'qu'on appelle gens sages, réservés, modérés, mais dont la sagesse, la réserve, la modération ne sont souvent que l'art d'écarter tous les mouvemens qui pourroient troubler leurs tranquilles jouissances, et, puisqu'il faut le dire, une véritable indifférence pour le bien de leur nation et de l'humanité'. Tracing the history of these discussions, Du Pont, the well-known physiocrat, recalled that 'cet esprit de conciliation, ou plutôt de faiblesse, cet art de chercher en tout un *mezzo termine* est une des causes qui ont le plus contribué à couvrir la terre de mauvaises lois'. The man who finally judged Galiani himself on these grounds was Turgot:

> Je n'aime pas à le voir toujours si prudent, si ennemi de l'enthousiasme, si fort d'accord avec tous les *ne quid nimis*, et avec tous ces gens qui jouissent du présent et qui sont fort aises qu'on laisse aller le monde comme il va, parce qu'il va fort bien pour eux, et qui, comme disait M. de Gournay, ayant leur lit bien fait, ne veulent pas qu'on le remue. Oh! tous ces gens-là ne doivent pas aimer l'enthousiasme, et il doivent appeler enthousiasme tout ce qui attaque l'infallibilité des gens en place, dogme admirable de l'abbé, politique de Pangloss, qu'il étend à tous les lieux et à tous les temps.

It was Turgot who was to set out again on the path of reform after the crisis of the final years of Louis XV's reign, and he was able to do this in 1774 because he had held firm to the principles of free trade, even when opposition had been very strong and the return to a short term policy on empirical lines had seemed to many the only possible solution.

This debate had results which went beyond the sphere of strictly economic problems. At the moment of maximum conservative resistance to the edicts of 1763 and 1764 the physiocrats formulated and publicised their political idea of legal despotism, of a strong absolute power capable of clearing the ground of all the obstacles which stood in the way of the free play of economic forces and hence of a total application of the physiocrats' programme. Quesnay with his myth of China, Le Mercier de la Rivière and the others in their books and pamphlets thus created the political doctrine which best corresponded to their needs: they sought the establishment of an 'enlightened despotism', as it was later called in France where it encountered daily new obstacles and new limitations. Morellet, Turgot and Du Pont were quite right to stress that Galiani's moderate attitude constituted an admission of defeat on the economic plane as well as an inability to conceive of the political instrument equal to the task of carrying out a 'réforme vigoureuse', to use the expression which Linguet launched in these years.

Politics and economics: it was specifically about the relationship between the two that Galiani and his French critics differed so greatly. While Galiani went back to 'reason of state', to arguments about expediency and a considered analysis of the various forms of government, the physiocrats and their friends laid stress upon the increasingly clearcut distinction between power and the laws of economics, between the various forms of government and civil society, affirming and expanding upon their great discovery, the autonomous existence of an economic reality and an economic science.

One has to admit, when reading the *Ephémérides*—especially issue XI of 1769, which is largely dedicated to the controversy with Galiani—that the journal's editors displayed considerable insight into the workings of Galiani's mind. The most sensitive and painful spot for him was the memory of what had happened in Naples during the last few years. Yet a bitter form of humour and cynical irony were used to reveal, and at the same time conceal, this experience. The editors of the *Ephémérides* were shocked but also felt the violence of Galiani's language:

'. . . plaisanterie qui nous a paru *atroce*. Immédiatement après l'horrible description de la famine de Naples, l'auteur peint avec la plus grand gaité des habitants, deux à deux, suivant en procession un pain . . . Une chose nous a serré la poitrine et fait bouilloner le sang. C'est le second tableau, pire que le premier, de la famine de Naples et des horreurs lamentables qui l'accompagnoient . . . Quel détestable séjour seroient nos villes, et quelle compagnie seroit celle qu'on appelle la *bonne* s'il étoit vrai qu'elles puissent désintéresser l'homme de l'homme à ce point.

Fine words of reaction in the face of the extreme consequences to which Galiani seemed to have been driven by the pessimism which had penetrated deep into his heart and the abandonment of all hope in a 'réforme vigoureuse'.

Oh! ce n'est pas ainsi [concluded the *Ephémérides*] que son compatriote, M. le marquis de Beccaria, traite des matières qui peuvent influer sur le bonheur de l'humanité. On voit à chaque page de l'illustre auteur *des Délits et des peines* qu'il cherche de bonne foi la verité, son âme parle à toutes les âmes sensibles, et elle parle leur langage: on reconnoit qu'il est homme et de plus homme de bien. Mais on ne peut deviner ce que cache le masque à ressorts dont M. l'abbé se plaît à se couvrir.

What in fact was hidden behind Galiani's shining mask? Several of his opponents came to the conclusion that all that was there was pure scepticism. At times he himself seemed ready to admit this. He seemed to identify with Chevalier Zanobi, the character in his *Dialogues* who 'ne croit ni ne pense un mot de tout ce qu'il dit, qui est le plus grand sceptique et le plus grand académique du monde, qui ne croit rien en rien, sur rien, de rien'. Morellet ended up by believing that this was the case and he wrote a letter which definitely captured one aspect of Galiani.

Il m'a toujours été impossible d'être sceptique sur les grands questions de la liberté, de la propriété, des droits des citoyens . . . Je ne serai donc pas sceptique comme Bayle ou plutôt comme vous voudriez que je le fusse, car permettez-moi de vous dire que Bayle n'est pas sceptique à votre manière. Les sentiments de Bayle ne sont pas difficiles à démêler. Son scepticisme n'est qu'apparent et le vôtre est réel . . . Bayle n'a jamais douté de l'injustice des intolérants et de l'absurdité des fanatiques.

Yet for Galiani too, scepticism was the result of experience, not experience itself. The *Dialogues*, it is true, did not contain a political and economic programme. He himself admitted that the conclusion which he gave to his work, where he proposed a system of tariff protection for France, was contrived, basically of slight importance, and written solely 'en faveur des badauds de Paris, qui aiment à conclure'. This was not where his inspiration lay.

It was the combination of such different experiences as those of England, Lombardy, Genoa and particularly Naples and France, which sparked off his brilliant gift for analysis. He had seen and perhaps guessed at the existence of different worlds, different men, and had been possessed by a passionate desire to compare them, to test them one against the other. No law, no general principle

had emerged from his work—to the point that he felt able to
deduce that the philosopher and the statesman merited their
names precisely because they possessed 'la clef du mystère', be
cause they knew that 'tout se réduit à zéro'. His analyses and
comparisons, it is true, were halfway between historical intuition
and sociological vision. They were often unfruitful because they
were not supported by a desire for action, they were frequently
hasty, based on hunches rather than facts. Yet they bore and
still bear witness not only to his outstandingly brilliant intelligenc
but to all the richness of his cosmopolitan experience.

The editors of the *Ephémérides* understood this when they said
that the fifth dialogue contained 'les grands principes de la doc
trine de l'abbé G'. This was where that extraordinary comparison
between agricultural and manufacturing countries was to be found
a source of constant astonishment to the reader because of it
wealth of ideas, suggestions and truths. Gianrinaldo Carli lingered
over these pages in particular, commenting upon them in his letter
of September 1770 to Pompeo Neri on 'free trade in cereals'. It wa
in vain that Morellet and others attempted to deny the validity
of the contrast which Galiani had established between the materia
and moral situation of purely agricultural countries and the
superior level of civilisation in countries where manufactures had
developed. This was one of the root causes of Galiani's opposition
to the ideas of the physiocrats and it provides an explanation and
justification of the neomercantilism of backward countries in
eighteenth-century Europe, particularly Spain and some of the
Italian states. Behind Galiani we can hear Uztáriz, Bernardo Ulloa
Genovesi, to give but a few examples. The fifth dialogue, per
haps more than anything else which appeared in those decades
clarified the differences of social and economic structure in the
various countries of Europe and the different degrees of economic
development. The conclusion that an economic science valid for
all did not exist might well be considered sceptical, negative and
sterile, but the different situations were very real and Galiani des
cribed them with extraordinary vividness and clarity. Morellet's
refutation was undoubtedly sound from a political point of view
(let us begin, he said, by making radical changes in the laws of
the poorer countries like Sicily, Sardinia, Apulia and the Roman
Campagna). But this did not invalidate Galiani's intuition about
the destiny of the purely agricultural countries.

It was the comparison between Naples and France which in
duced him to align himself with the supporters of commerce and
manufactures, of the 'citizens' against the 'agricultural' econo
mists, with the consequent polemic against the high prices and

188

high wages supported by the physiocrats, and in favour of some monopolies such as the restriction of grain transport to the national marine. He reacted all the more violently against the policy inspired by the physiocrats in France because it seemed to him impossible or harmful in Naples. An economic vision dominated by the problems of an economically more backward country thus became the weapon and instrument of those social forces in France which were opposed to the reforms. In Italy it was necessary to solicit the creation of manufactures and to pray to God that the rulers of the peninsula would finally change 'sa qualité actuelle de pays agricole' and allow her to 'reprendre son ancien état de pays manufacturier'; it was a question of overcoming once and for all the great crisis which had destroyed Italian industries in the seventeenth century. In France, by contrast, it was sufficient to preserve and administer carefully what had already been achieved by Colbert and Louis XIV. Thus his conclusion was that it was simply a question of defending the interests of French manufactures and France's great ports, Marseilles and Nantes.

Galiani was certainly not alone in his defence of manufacturing and commercial interests. It is enough to examine, for example, one after another, the little volumes of the *Journal de l'agriculture,* a real barometer of public opinion on the changing fortunes of the physiocrats. It began as a periodical of the 'economists', then it slipped out of their grasp. From 1767 onwards Forbonnais's ideas predominated. It became the meeting point of the various opposing factions, though perhaps it mitigated and tempered those rivalries which were too compromising and personal (Linguet, Mably). In 1768 an active campaign opened in defence of commercial and manufacturing interests. The approach was panoramic, international: there was an overall tendency to stress the difficulties and crises faced by countries who made grain exports the keystone of their economic policy. Even the Sicilian example was quoted: 'ces insulaires orgueilleux, jaloux et ennemis de la France, qui, il y a dix ans, transportoient leurs bleds dans l'Europe et l'Asie, sont maintenant dans la disette et appellent dans leurs ports les étrangers dont ils achètent les grains que leurs terres ne produisent plus'. A series of articles demanded explicitly that state benefits should not be reserved exclusively for agriculture. From January 1769 even the title of the review was changed: no longer *Journal de l'agriculture, du commerce et des finances.* but . . . *de l'agriculture, du commerce, des arts et des finances.* Hence it is no surprise that the review should have warmly welcomed Galiani's *Dialogues*. The book seemed to be the synthesis, or at least the meeting point of all the earlier controversies. The element of 'moderation' which formed the basis of the *Dialogues* seemed there expressly to reconcile the most widely differing theses and interests. Even the man who declared that he was 'bien éloigné de la forme d'administration que cet auteur propose pour le commerce des bleds' found something in common with Galiani in that he also was 'éloigné de l'enthousiasme', so that he was able to reach agreement with him 'aisément sur les conséquences'. Once again it was the comparison between agricultural and manufacturing peoples which made the most impact upon the editors of the *Journal de l'agriculture*. They found many new examples, like that of Sardinia, where 'tout ce peuple est agricole, fait un grand commerce de bled et est très pauvre'. This periodical had to return into the hands of the physiocrats before it produced a criticism of the *Dialogues* and before the arguments of the 'economists' began to reappear in it.

The discussion, as can be seen from this example, was not in general tied down by any theoretical principle (abstract versus concrete, organised system versus pure empiricism). These elements had their part to play but they mingled with definite conflicts of economic and political interests. And we cannot say, as Galiani would have us believe, that the physiocrats were all aligned against him and the *encyclopédistes* were all on his side. Agriculture and commerce, manufactures and industry, the intellectual currents of the Enlightenment—all presented a more complicated situation than Galiani made out. It is true that on this occasion the physiocrats once more presented that united front which led their contemporaries to call them a sect. But the *encyclopédistes* were deeply divided. After all, Forbonnais, Turgot and Morellet had also been *encyclopédistes* and had much greater claim to the title than, for example, Grimm, who was the only one who really gave unconditional support to Galiani. In reality each of the men who had taken part in the preparation of the great dictionary held a different position in the debate which Galiani's ideas aroused. The most important case and the one which is least easy to understand and interpret, but which remains of interest, is that of the creator and driving force behind the dictionary, Diderot himself.

Not all the elements needed to trace Diderot's position between physiocrats and antiphysiocrats have been included in the volume edited by Fausto Nicolini. The predominance of the figures of Grimm and d'Epinay means a risk of obscuring the attitude of a man like Diderot, of far greater stature and importance.

When Le Mercier de la Rivière published his *L'Ordre naturel et essentiel des sociétés politiques* in 1767 Diderot was enthusiastic about the book and its author, and praised both to Catherine II. He seemed, in short, to have accepted the ideas of the physiocrats and to approve of the political instrument which they had devised to put their theories into practice. But then, in the following year 1768, he too underwent that change of opinion which gradually became more and more clearly defined. Grimm and Galiani were the two main instruments of this rapid switch to an antiphysiocratic position. Political considerations seemed to have played their part: legal despotism was a doctrine which Diderot could only accept as a temporary, tactical measure. Even the opposition of the *parlements* was not viewed by him with the same hostility which characterised Voltaire and many other Enlightenment writers. Diderot was sensitive to the element of freedom which he seemed to catch sight of even in the defence of such old institutions and ancient privileges. Then, on the economic plane, Galiani's arguments seemed to him increasingly to correspond with the reality. He too, in November 1768, was finally convinced 'ou il n'y a rien de démontré en politique ou il l'est que l'exportation est une folie'. He earnestly besought Galiani to put his ideas on paper, he made sure that they were presented in perfect French and did his utmost to help the *Dialogues* overcome the obstacles created by the censorship and the suspicion of the authorities.

Diderot's attitude must obviously have surprised many of his contemporaries and especially the physiocrats. 'Nous avons presque autant de peine à croire que des gens respectables, et qui font profession de *philosophie* aient part, comme on l'assure, à l'ouvrage dans lequel on doit attaquer' the doctrines of the 'economists', wrote the *Ephémérides* in their fifth issue for 1769. But they hastened to add that not all the *encyclopédistes* were hostile to them. 'Un véritable philosophe des plus célèbres dont l'Europe s'honore', that is Diderot himself, had given them to understand that the fact that he had been so active in publicising and defending Galiani's *Dialogues* did not mean that he gave wholehearted support to the ideas contained in it.

Indeed he had attempted to justify his strange position with two fables, published in the fifth and twelfth issues of 1769. The second one, entitled *Le bal de l'Opéra*, was particularly significant and is worth quoting here because it gives us the key to Diderot's attitude at the end of 1769:

Par hasard, un philosophe se trouvoit au bal de l'Opéra à côté d'un homme du monde.—Si cette assemblée duroit un an,—dit-il

à son voisin,—que pensez-vous qu'il en arrivât?—Il en arriveroi
—répondit l'autre—que malgré la variété de leurs déguisement
tous ceux qui sont ici se connoîtroient réciproquement pour c
qu'ils sont.—Eh bien! ces masques et ces dominos sont le
préjugés et les sophismes qui voilent les erreurs. Priez Dieu qu
le bal dure.

Diderot repeated this concept many times in those month
What mattered to him was the discussion, the debate. Philosoph
was nothing if not the desire to continue the work of unmaskin
prejudices. In his friend Grimm's *Correspondence* he wrote tha
what he admired particularly in the physiocrats was the way i
which they had spoken and continued to speak 'avec une libert
que nous ne connaissons pas'. 'A la longue la police, la cour e
les magistrats s'accoûtumeront à tout entendre et les auteurs
tout dire. La nation se familiarisera peu à peu avec les question
des finances, de commerce, d'agriculture, de législation, de pol
tique.' And he concluded, paraphrasing his own fable: 'Prior
Dieu pour que cette école se soutienne, toute ignorante et tout
bavarde que notre abbé napolitain la suppose.'

It is understandable that the physiocrats were not at all displease
with Diderot's position and they immediately expressed their sati
faction at the second fable with the following comment, whic
is not without significance: 'Elle nous a fait d'autant plus plais
qu'elle nous a fourni le mot d'une énigme assez embarassante
They recalled how the ideas of the physiocrats had grown upo
the trunk of the *Encyclopédie* and said that it was surely th
philosophes themselves who sought general principles and ide
in politics and economics. Galiani 'soutient qu'il n'y a aucun
règle générale applicable au gouvernement de tous les pays . .
Ce seroit là une philosophie très commode pour les visirs qui fon
semblant de gouverner les empires orientaux . . . Cela s'appelle l
formule du despotisme le plus arbitraire . . . le temps est passé o
l'on pouvait prêcher le despotisme avec ingenuité . . .' That is, o
the political plane Diderot would have to be on the side of thos
who believed in the possibility of modifying the situation i
France by establishing general principles of economic policy. O
the practical plane discussions could and should continue. 'O
commençoit à se taire sur la liberté de commerce des bleds, e
cependant elle n'est pas encore entièrement établie . . . Le ba
alloit finir et l'on ne connoissoit point les auteurs. Il faut qu'
dure', concluded the *Ephémérides*, thus accepting and even encou
aging the discussion with the *philosophes*.

During 1770 and 1771, however, the economic situation becam
progressively worse, and tension in the countryside and the tow

led an increasing number of people to consider the continuance of free trade in cereals impossible or harmful. All those difficulties and conflicts which came to the forefront were to turn public opinion away from the programme of the free-traders and then of Turgot, towards Necker and all those who were both more conservative and more sensitive to the sufferings and perhaps also to the prejudices of the people—who showed, in short, that they understood better than the physiocrats the price to be paid for the economic transformation envisaged by the latter. This trend became more pronounced and widespread after the failure of Turgot's experiment, the decisive test of the groups which had developed in the preceding years. Diderot too looked towards Necker and, while holding fast to the principle that the most important thing was that 'the ball should go on', was increasingly tempted to agree with Galiani's observations and opinions on economics. He wrote at that time the *Lettre à M. *** sur l'abbé Galiani*, a witty and daring apologia of the man and his work.

Diderot eventually turned all his impulsive enthusiasm, along with his doubts and hesitations, into a lively fragment called *Apologie de l'Abbé Galiani, ou réponse à la réfutation de Dialogues sur le commerce des bleds par l'abbé Morellet*, which was published only in 1954. It was the conclusion of the long discussion between the *encyclopédiste* Morellet and Galiani. Diderot rewrote his *Apologie* several times, putting his economic ideas to the test over and over again, fervently re-examining his position with regard to both Galiani and the physiocrats.

He first put pen to paper with some *Notes sur un ouvrage intitulé Réfutation de l'ouvrage qui a pour titre Dialogues sur le commerce des bleds*, probably immediately following the publication of Morellet's work and the subsequent ban placed on it by the minister Terray, after April 1770. The aim of these *Notes*, rather than to defend Galiani and enter into a debate with the physiocrats, is to attack Morellet, and with considerable violence and bitterness. These pages by Diderot give us an idea of just how serious were the divisions which by this time had grown up among the *encyclopédistes* and how deep were the internal rifts in what had been the 'parti des philosophes'. In Diderot's eyes, Morellet's principal error had been to uphold, in June and then September of the previous year, the need to wind up and liquidate the Compagnie des Indes, against the opinion of the shareholders and Necker. Diderot adopted Necker's line and fiercely defended the acquired rights of the shareholders. For him Morellet was guilty above all of the crime of supporting the government with his hostile action towards the Company. 'Homme vendu au ministère, celui qui, sans rime ni raison, sans avoir la démonstration de ce qu'il fait, se prête à la ruine de quarante mille de ses concitoyens', 'qui n'a servi que le despotisme'. Even if Morellet may seem to have behaved like a follower of reason, his work was nevertheless treated by Diderot as that of 'un raisonneur, ce qui n'est pas l'ouvrage d'un homme qui a raison'. And finally Diderot addressed him: 'Vous qui par bassesse et par intérêt vous êtes fait le bourreau de quarante mille de vos concitoyens.' And a few pages later: 'L'abbé Morellet n'est rien, ni philosophe, ni homme de bien, ni citoyen, ni ami; il est la machine des grands qui en font tout ce qu'il leur plaît.' In short, Morellet had succeeded in offering a service to his government at the price of ruining a whole sector of French commerce and he was now indulging in a repetition of this grievous fault in a much more important debate, that of freedom of trade in cereals. In order to please Trudaine and annoy Terray, Morellet was trampling on a whole range of interests and dismissing a whole series of problems. All this was the result of a basic insincerity, of a scarcely disguised egoism: 'C'est l'homme le plus personnel que je connaisse; c'est un homme violent et étourdi, qui court après tout et qui manque tout. C'est un homme qui s'aime, qui s'embrasse sans cesse, mais qui s'étouffe à force de s'embrasser.' Diderot could not but recognise Morellet's ability to present clear and lucid arguments and conclusions, but in his eyes this did not justify the lack of generosity and humanity which he felt he could detect in all Morellet's writings and attitudes.

However, this did not mean that Diderot was tempted at the time he wrote these first *Notes* to agree entirely with Morellet's adversary, Abbé Galiani. It is clear that he was attempting to maintain a position somehow *au dessus de la mêlée*, in keeping with the attitude which he had adopted a few months previously in the *Ephémérides du citoyen*. Morellet was an egoist, but this did not make Galiani right.

> L'abbé Galiani pense et vous fait penser; l'autre se fait écouter parce qu'il a raison, mais il ne vous fait penser parce qu'il ne pense pas et qu'il vous fatigue et vous ennuie. Il relève très bien les bévues de son adversaire, mais il en fait de son côté, qui sont grosses et très lourdes. En ne disant que des choses communes, il a plus de morgue que Montesquieu. Il est insolent, il est mauvais plaisant, et après avoir prouvé et bien prouvé en cent endroits que son adversaire a tort, on ne sait s'il a raison, et la question reste plus embrouillée que jamais.

Shortly afterwards, still in 1770, Diderot went back to his *Notes* and had them copied. He removed completely the excessively personal attacks on Morellet and at the same time began to play down considerably his reservations about Galiani. Finally he arrived at the third, definitive version which he quite rightly called *Apologie de l'Abbé Galiani*.

What then were his conclusions? First of all he considered Galiani to be a great writer and profound thinker precisely because he kept to the fundamental laws of the dialogue, laws which do not allow the writer to identify completely with any of the characters, but demand that they should live their own intimate intellectual life. Dialogue and freedom eventually become equated and to create the discussion means to throw away the masks. The entire *Apologie* is permeated with the deep convictions on which his policy was founded.

Diderot's main criticism of Morellet was that he was 'dogmatique, tandis que l'abbé est enquêtant'. Thus not even the justifiable objections which the former could and did bring against the *Dialogues* were convincingly persuasive, as they lacked the desire to investigate, a real acceptance of discussion and dialogue.

Diderot made a similar criticism of Morellet's political position, which was often correct in its desire for reform, but which ignored the need for the assent of those who were to be or had been reformed. Without this, dogma took the place of freedom. Even prejudices needed to be understood. 'Mais pourrais-je vous demander, à propos d'opinions communes, pourquoi vous mépriseriez si fort les notions du peuple? N'est-ce pas son instinct pour ce qui lui est avantageux qui doit être à la base de vos sermons sur la liberté?' It was precisely this sense of respect that Diderot believed he had found in the *Dialogues*. 'Voilà précisement l'idée de l'abbé Galiani.' Dialogue and respect for forms of life different from one's own were certainly in Galiani, although presented in a sceptical manner and with a sceptical conclusion which Diderot tried hard to justify. 'Vous n'aimez pas sa manière sceptique de procéder; tant pis pour vous, car elle est très fine, très agréable, très délicate, très amusante, mais elle demande du génie; rien de plus conforme à la recherche et à la persuasion de la verité: à la recherche parce qu'en doutant on s'assure de tout, à la persuasion parce qu'on donne le change à la passion.'

Politically, this meant keeping one's ears open to a wide range of opinions and not withdrawing into a dogmatic shell. The world around was in ferment and it was wrong to shut oneself off from it. Trading in cereals in time of shortage was not a normal economic operation, it was 'un conflit tumultueux de crainte, d'avidité, de cupidité'. It was not sufficient to oppose these passions with general ideas. The idea of property, for example,

violated a thousand times in civil life, was not an adequate defenc
Social conflicts were showing their dangers. 'L'abbé Galiani crain
le peuple; et quand il s'agit de pain, il n'y a qu'un homme iv
qui n'en ait pas peur. On voit bien que M. l'abbé Morellet vit
Paris et qu'il ne l'a pas vu menacé de la disette de nos province:
Social conflicts were the more serious when property conflicte
with the general interest. Then 'la société tend droit à sa ruin
parce que le droit de propriété de quelques particuliers croisera
sans cesse les vrais moyens de son opulence, de sa force et de s
sûreté'. 'Comment la liberté illimitée remédiera-t-elle au désord
de cet effrayant monopole?'

The poverty of the countryside was not dependent on th
political situation nor on any particular economic measure, b
on the very existence of the big landowners.

> Ce ne sont pas les fermiers aisés qui forment la condition de
> campagnes, c'est la multitude des salariés; et je demanderai
> les premiers devenus plus aisés, leur richesse refluera sur l
> derniers et les tirera de leur misère . . . Pourquoi la culture es
> elle plus belle et plus riche dans les contrées de Maroc, nou
> ricières du midi de l'Europe, et accablées sous le plus cru
> despotisme, qu'en Europe, qu'en Angleterre même, le pays de
> liberté? Pourquoi les provinces de la Pologne, le païs le pli
> pauvre, et sous le plus infâme gouvernement, sont-elles la mèr
> nourricière du Nord? Je le prie de rêver un peu à un monopo
> national et tout formé en Pologne, c'est le monopole du Roi
> des Grands. Eh bien, je demanderai si ce monopole n'est pas e
> grand ce qu'est le monopole de trois ou quatre fermiers aisés e
> nos campagnes. Ce sont, et ce seront à jamais les Palatins de
> Brie, quoi que puisse faire l'auteur avec sa liberté illimitée.
> leur permet d'être riches, je le vois bien, mais ils ne le seron
> pas et je ne verrai jamais dans la Pologne que des esclav
> indigents et quelques tyrans monopoleurs riches, et dans no
> campagnes quelques fermiers aisés, riches même, si l'auter
> l'exige, et une multitude de salariés gueux et malheureux.

One social conflict appeared particularly serious and deep ar
that was the rivalry between town and country, between man
factures and agriculture. On this question Diderot seems to hav
been basically in agreement with Forbonnais, Galiani and Neck
and not with the physiocrats. However, those brilliant pages k
Galiani on agricultural and manufacturing peoples merely i
creased Diderot's awareness of how enormous were the problen
which had to be faced and how far away they were from
solution: 'il faut que l'accroissement de la culture le suive. C'e
qu'il y a un point que l'abbé Galiani et l'abbé Morellet or

méconnu tous les deux. Ils ont à l'envi sauté par-dessus en sens contraire; et le saut fait, ils se sont trouvés l'un et l'autre loin de la vérité.'

These problems and forebodings reached the heart of the crisis of the last years of Louis XV's reign. They were formulated in the strange and fertile encounter between the Neapolitan thinker and economist and the circles of physiocrats and *encyclopédistes* in Paris.

9 The Enlightenment in Southern Italy

HE Neapolitan reformers had no doubt at all about when their movement began. 1734: the end of Austrian rule, the arrival in the South of Charles of Bourbon's troops and the setting up of an independent kingdom were felt to be the starting point of a new, different period of history, the beginning of their own age. The words which they used were often words of praise or even of adulation, but beneath the ornate phraseology lay a firm conviction: 1734 marked the beginning of a period—a period which was to end in tragedy in 1799. Later historians have tended to verify this concept rather than to investigate its origins and assess its significance over the longer term. Michelangelo Schipa has been miserly in his estimate of the value of the work of Charles of Bourbon and the first generation of Enlightenment reformers. To Schipa the reality appeared pale in comparison with the myth of the sovereign who launched a new period of history.

This image, which men of the time had created for themselves, is worth considering for a moment, leaving aside the question of how closely it resembled its model. It marks the birth of a new vision of the South tinged with national feeling, it is the starting point of an urge to renew and reform, an aspiration towards autonomous action, the creation of an awareness of being an independent country. Like any nascent national ideology, this seemed to act as both a stimulant and a source of illusions. But it is not enough to prove, as Schipa has done, that independence from Spain, particularly in the early years, was little more than a formality and that the possibilities of independent action in the

Mediterranean and European world were extremely few. It is more interesting to see how this nascent aspiration and consciousness, steering between the rocks and sandbanks of a very harsh reality, was deflected, on the one hand, towards a form of diplomatic Machiavellianism, the formulation of a theory of weak and crafty states, while, on the other hand, it led the most able men to concentrate entirely upon economic, commercial and agricultural problems, so that eventually they were drawn towards the study and knowledge of the social structure of their country. Eighteenth-century southern Italian Machiavellianism and enlightened reformism had a common root in the initial hope and desire to exist once more as a nation after centuries of being a province.

This root is not completely illusory. In the mid-eighteenth century, at the precise moment when the era of changes, successions and wars was coming to an end in Italy, when political ambitions, both old and new, seemed to be on the wane in the North and Centre—in Turin, Venice and Florence—the Kingdom of Naples came into existence again and laid the foundations of its own foreign policy, on land directed against the Papal States and on sea aimed at keeping a balance between France and Spain and attempting to open up new markets in the Mediterranean. Tanucci's policy was fundamental in this process. In the period which followed, in the time of Acton, the ambition to create new military and naval instruments and the aspiration towards reform inside the country continued to make equal progress, though sometimes coming into conflict and often cancelling each other out.

This situation had lasting effects upon the whole movement. It is sufficient to recall Ferdinando Galiani and his combination of the 'Machiavellian' and the economist. On the other hand, the profound and lasting influence among the reformers of the neo-mercantilist mentality and programme and the continual return to the hope or illusion of an independent economic life for the Kingdom of Naples were closely linked to the idea of a state which would eventually be free and independent. Even when the ideas of the physiocrats were helping to sweep away all aspirations towards a self-sufficient economy in the other Italian states, in Naples such hopes were to resist firmly throughout the century. Seventeen hundred and thirty-four is definitely the starting point of the movement for reform in the South and the awareness which men of the time had of this corresponds to a psychological and political reality.

The convergence of a particularly favourable situation with the action of one man, Antonio Genovesi, transformed these initial aspirations and hopes into a concrete movement. The 'thirties an 'forties had seen the end of the two great currents of thought whic had been dominant in Naples at the beginning of the centur; Cartesianism and Platonism seemed by this time to have nothir more to offer. When Genovesi, as a young priest who had onl just left his seminary in Salerno, arrived in the capital to see his fortune in 1740, the two great figures of southern culture of tl Austrian era, Giambattista Vico and Paolo Mattia Doria, wei old, tired and isolated. Their deaths, which occurred very clo together, in 1744 and 1746, were marked by a painful, en barrassed silence, the silence which accompanies the death (those who have outlived their usefulness. And it was to last twent or thirty years, a whole generation. We have to wait for the di ciples of Genovesi, the second generation of Enlightenment r formers, before Vico and the culture of the early eighteenth ce tury are rediscovered. By 1740 the other great man of the a¿ of solitary philosophers and isolated geniuses was also missing Pietro Giannone was a prisoner in Piedmont in the cells of Charl Emmanuel III. Genovesi spoke about him in his early years at tl university but without mentioning his name. Giannone too w. to be, if not rediscovered like Vico, at least rehabilitated by tl following generation. At the beginning of the Bourbon era the remained in Naples those men who in the 'thirties had attempte to open up new paths, dismissing or leaving aside Descartes, Pla¹ and the great jurisdictionalist tradition. Bartolomeo Intieri an Celestino Galiani had already made an effort to organise a academy completely dedicated to the natural sciences an 'mechanics' and had grafted Newtonian branches onto the o Galilean trunk. In law too, as in science, Tuscan, particular Pisan elements were to make a considerable contribution to tl creation of a new mentality. From the very beginning of Charl of Bourbon's reign Tanucci was the most representative figure (this revival.

Neapolitan culture in the 'forties—so interesting, yet ¿ little studied—clearly reflected this meeting of earlier traditio and new curiosity. Some idea of this meeting is given in tl strange letter which Father Paciaudi, a Piedmontese, wrote fro: Naples to Monseigneur Giacomelli on 1 August 1744. Paciaudi to. him about the controversies which Muratori's *Of the defects (jurisprudence* was arousing in the capital. At the basis of the discussions, one can catch a glimpse of the real question of tl total reform of all legislation. There is a glance back to the vei recent past: 'Yesterday there appeared a new edition of *The Ne Science* by the famous Vico, now dead. The Abbé Conti conside that this work contains pearls of wisdom but I find it a Leibnizian confusion.' And there too are the elements of a culture reflected or derived from abroad: De Gennaro's *Republica jurisconsultum* was reprinted in Leipzig and from Spain came Father Feyjóo's *Universal theatre*. If we read the numerous works of Antonio Genovesi of his first years of teaching at the university, the impression made by this letter is accentuated. Genovesi's works contain continual references to the demands of local culture—even if only because the discussion is about books which originated in the school and for the school. But equally, if not more intense, is the search for something new, beyond the bounds of tradition and the borders of the kingdom. Genovesi rapidly turns to ideas coming from England and France, towards problems of the philosophy of nature, science and logic, characteristic of empiricism after Locke and Newton. Even the deist element—from the 'impious Tolland' to Voltaire—is given a place, apparently with the intention of refuting it. The struggle and conflict between this culture and the theological, philosophical, juridical framework inherited from the past is as vigorous as it is confused, as complex as it is inconclusive. There is manifest evidence of a desire to use these new instruments in order to challenge them, adopt them for didactic ends and for practical purposes. Appiano Buonafede was also in Naples in those years and his culture was not very different from that of Genovesi. Genovesi was inspired to seek a new path and to dedicate himself to studying political economy not by a victory, but by a defeat, by the fact that the religious and civil authorities made it impossible for him ever to obtain the chair of theology which he so ardently desired. He soon realised that this was a fortunate defeat, and felt that this was the chance which fate had granted him to bring out his best qualities. Nevertheless it was symptomatic of that atmosphere of compromise and ambiguity amidst which the new ideas came to prevail both in him and around him.

Genovesi's assumption of the chair of political economy created by Intieri in November 1754 represented, if not a real break, at least a definite move away from the world of tradition, the clergy and the academics. It is to his credit that he made his teaching the centre of a real school which grew into an organisation and a party, originating in the university and spreading, in just over ten years, to every corner of the Kingdom of Naples. It is a pity that research on this subject has been far from exhaustive. We have a complete list of Beccaria's students in Milan but in Naples we have no record at all of those who listened to

Antonio Genovesi. We have no document to indicate where his students came from, and in the case of many of these we are unable to ascertain with any accuracy what later became of them, whether they were able to achieve anything or whether they went back to stagnate in the lethargy and silence of the southern provinces. And yet, between 1754 and 1769, Genovesi's activity in the university acted as the pivot of the reform movement and it is to his group that we must trace those who attempted to create agrarian societies, to improve specific cultures (oil, silk, grain, etc.), to establish a lively contact with the Georgofili Academy in Florence and the Venetian Societies, to create and to criticise the government's economic policy.

What had Genovesi given to all these? There has been much insistence upon his moral qualities—these are unquestionable and bear the stamp of the highest form of enlightened humanism, open to an understanding of the diversity of human nature and instinctively ready to support the wretched and the oppressed. There has been much praise of his excellent gifts as a teacher and as evidence of this we have the enthusiastic reports of his contemporaries. But, above all, Genovesi offered a programme fitted to the needs of the country and at the same time perfectly in tune with the most advanced European thought. The writings of Uztáriz and Ulloa from Spain, Véron de Forbonnais and Plumard de Dangueil from France and of men like Child, Gee and Hume from England had influenced him in formulating a programme which presupposed a state policy aimed at helping the development of manufactures, directly or indirectly, and at the same time at breaking down the excessive obstacles which stood in the way of the free circulation of goods, particularly of cereals. Genovesi's own position often varied considerably as he attempted to establish a relationship between his neomercantilism and his leanings towards free trade. The French model of Machault and Gournay, and the English example and the Spanish vision—which had so many points of contact with the situation in Naples—succeeded one another and became superimposed in his writings. One sometimes has the impression of a confused kind of eclecticism but it is really the example of a search for a programme through various repeated experiences and the rapid broadening of his field of observation.

The decisive experience came in 1764, which was the crucial year for Genovesi's generation. Thousands of deaths, the humiliating spectacle of the inefficiency and useless brutality of the state, the ever-present conflict between intentions and reality, the glaring privileges of the few and the terrible poverty of the masses, led Genovesi and his school to re-examine the basic problems of Neapolitan society and administration. From the time, at the beginning of the 'fifties, when he had withdrawn to the hills of Massa Equana to study economic problems—with Intieri, by then a very old man, Galiani, who was still very young, Rinuccini, Cerati and others—he had seen the gulf which divided the great city of Naples, an enormous head on a slender body, from the countryside which surrounded it. It was not necessary to go very far to see sections of the population living in such poverty and primitive conditions that they could be compared with those Hottentots towards whom he directed the avid curiosity of an armchair traveller in search of effective social comparisons and parallels. The great famine of 1764 had driven thousands of these wretched peasants into the towns to die of hunger. On the immediate economic plane there could be only one remedy: the abolition of all those grain deposit structures inherited from the past which had made the situation worse and had been among the principal causes of the terrible crisis. Genovesi published the French work most explicitly in favour of free trade in cereals—that of Claude-Jacques Herbert—prefaced with an essay of his own which was even more closely enthusiastic in its attempts to persuade and educate in this direction. But this was not enough. He had constantly before his eyes a serious and deteriorating problem. How could reforms be carried out in a land with such a gulf between town and country, rich and poor, educated and ignorant? He sensed the danger of an even more serious crisis, of an actual dissolution of the social structure. This thought was to remain alive in the whole of the reform movement in the South, appearing sometimes as a threat, a fear, sometimes as the dreaded limit to any attempt at civilisation and transformation. From 1764 to 1799 the reformers were to remain conscious of it. The last years of Genovesi's life, which were extraordinarily active and productive, provided a series of answers to those questions which the situation imposed. It seemed obvious to him that there was an absolute and impelling necessity to organise a programme of public education. From his *Logic for young people* to the divulgation of agrarian techniques, from the creation of schools to the reform of the university, from teaching in Italian to publishing manuals on morality, economics, law, etc., he made every possible effort, with the express purpose of creating a common language among the different classes and sectors of the population which were haphazardly thrown together in his country.

Politically, nothing could be more concrete than his desire to educate and instruct the population, since here was the only

possible instrument to create the basis for full-scale reform. The
could be nothing less abstract than the spreading of enlighten
ment in Naples in the 'sixties. Genovesi saw quite clearly whi
were the biggest obstacles the reforms were bound to meet.
made shrewd and penetrating observations on the lawyer cla
They seemed to him the mandarins of the Kingdom of Napl
who used legal formulae and doctrines to conceal and perpetu
abuses and who revealed how 'childish'—backward and at the sa
time cruel—the whole country was. By this time Tanucci's ju
dictionalist policy had demonstrated its own limitations and
longer seemed capable of meeting the country's economic pr
lems with any degree of success. Genovesi's writings contain
seed of that detachment and then of that profoundly critical a
tude towards a legalistic mentality which was to become
creasingly common among the second generation of reform
from Galanti to Delfico. In the very last years of his life Genov
was particularly severe with the clergy. Throughout Italy the
of the 1760s marked the height of the struggle against the pow
of the Church. The expulsion of the Jesuits, the polemic conce
ing the teachings of the Decretals and the discussion with M
achi on church property marked the three stages of this ba
in the South: Genovesi was there in the front line. As for
barons, he condemned them outright, particularly towards the
of his life. But the abolition of feudalism was not yet for h
as it was to become for his immediate followers, the cen
objective. His social programme was both broader and m
general. He was inspired with strong egalitarian feelings wh
sometimes led him towards visions of utopia only to make
return rapidly to a programme of creating freeholdings, divid
the great estates into emphyteuses and so increasing the num
of smallholdings.

Thus, beyond the lawyers, priests and barons, Genovesi m
an appeal to that intermediary class which he saw as the m
active and promising element in modern society. And in parti
lar he turned towards the educated representatives of that c
as to the only ones who seemed in a position to effect a tr
formation of the men and things around them. It was to those v
came to learn from him at the university that he made his app
whether they were of noble or of peasant origin, priests or l
yers. He put before them, in the last analysis, his own ideal
society economically completely active in which bureaucra
administrative activities would be reduced to a minimum
where only the smallest possible proportion of the popula
would not participate directly in production. 'The general

fundamental principle from which follow all the particular rules proper to economics is, as has been said, that the class of men producing income must be as large as possible and, conversely, that those classes which are not immediately productive should be kept as small as possible.' Genovesi's testament was in this vigorous economic mentality and when he died, in 1769, everyone could compare his model of society with the human reality in the Kingdom of Naples. His *Lessons on commerce* had offered precisely such a comparison and the picture which emerged was far from encouraging.

The task of the second generation of Enlightenment reformers was first and foremost to explore and learn about that reality which Genovesi had shown them. He had been responsible for the publication in 1760 of the *Reflections upon commerce ancient and modern in the Kingdom of Naples* by Nicola Fortunato, which was the first successful attempt to explore the economic history of the South. The capital itself was a world still to be discovered. Already in 1750 the Duke of Noja had said that 'people had no clearer idea [of Naples] than they had of the cities of Japan or Tartary', and that while very fine maps existed even of Petersburg and Moscow, there was no decent map of the 'largest city in Italy'. Besides this, the city was 'extremely badly constructed', without any plan or design, unlike Paris, Vienna or Rome. There were no 'broad, straight' streets, no squares and it was totally unsuitable for carriages. There were no places to meet and take refreshments and the dwellings were distributed in a way which, above all, was socially dangerous. 'It is clear how much narrow winding streets contribute to making a people restless and quarrelsome.' It was only then that the historical development of Naples as a city began to be known. From the middle of the century it became clear that certain problems existed and that they were desperately in need of a solution. But the exploration of the country with new eyes was, above all, a provincial trend which very soon became tinged with hostility against the capital, a parallel phenomenon to that which appeared in most of the Italian states of the *ancien régime*, in Venetia, for example, and the Papal States. In the Neapolitan provinces, however, it assumed a particularly economic character, as it appeared in the name of agricultural and commercial progress and not of memories of the past and local political traditions.

From 1770 onwards the voice of Domenico Grimaldi could be heard in Calabria. Starting from an examination of silk, oil, pasturage and cereals, he expanded his subject into a complete

Plan for reform, as he entitled one of his pamphlets written ten years later. After a long, rewarding period in Genoa and a journey to Piedmont and France, he had become convinced that the most important thing was to improve agricultural techniques, making the most of the possibilities which each area had to offer (hence his interest in *sulla*, a fodder crop), introducing new methods of producing silk and oil, taking as a model Swiss stock-raising and northern Italian irrigation. This was a vast programme, to be tried out first of all at home, in his Seminara, in the oil presses, silk-spinning workshops and pastures belonging to his family. In this way the Seminara became a kind of 'pilot village', fired with a new urge to build, produce and trade, a village which Grimaldi showed to foreign visitors with pride and defended energetically in his writings. The experiment was of great interest and proved at least two things: (1) that the initiative could and should be taken by the big landowners—or, as he more aptly put it, 'by the barons and the bishops'; (2) that the obstacles were enormous and capable of discouraging anyone who was not fired with a particularly vigorous reforming zeal. These obstacles did not arise only from the ignorance and narrow-mindedness of the peasants on his own and neighbouring fiefs, even if looking at them did cause him to exclaim that they were part of a nation which was dying on its feet. They derived from objective factors: a legislation which prevented any profit from being made on silk from Calabria and which limited income from olives, and a state which was incapable of supporting local initiative from either an administrative or a financial point of view. There was not even a map of the country in existence. A proper exploration of the province was necessary and Grimaldi hastened to provide the programme for this vast, essential inquiry, making explicit references to the encouragement he had received from his great master, Antonio Genovesi. More serious still was the lack of credit. His family was being ruined by its experiments in land improvement. However, his requests for some concrete aid and his plea for a policy which would at least encourage the adoption of new techniques were all in vain. Domenico Grimaldi eventually became convinced that it would only be possible to work from the centre. He himself became one of the inspectors whose creation he had advocated. He spent most of his time in Naples and wrote perhaps the most important of his pamphlets, in which he declared that an important public work—the construction of a great canal in Apulia by means of forced labour—seemed to him the best starting-point for a state reforming policy. He maintained that there was no point in spending too much time, as was the custom, discussing the merits of freedom or control of the cereal trade. The troubles of the South originated not so much from 'political causes' as from 'physical causes'. Until techniques had been improved there was no point in talking about anything else.

The population continued to increase while productive capacity remained the same. How could the increasing poverty be avoided? New and better cultures were required but to grow these it was essential to have manure which could only be produced by animals. But for stock-rearing to develop, new pastures were necessary and these required intensive irrigation. As examples from northern Italy had indicated, water represented the keystone of plans for transformation. And it was precisely in canal construction that state intervention was necessary. There was too much prejudice in the villages and fiefs for the inhabitants to 'root out the old abuses' on their own. Only the state, by an effective utilisation of forced labour, could destroy the poverty and ignorance which made the situation constantly worse. When writing this pamphlet in 1781, Domenico Grimaldi was increasingly drawn towards the conclusion that the fate of the reform depended in practice on the way in which state power worked and what it would be able to achieve. In the following year he was admitted to the Supreme Financial Council. The twenty years which he still had in front of him were to be spent in an attempt personally to put into practice from above all the things which he had planned and studied in his youth, in the midst of a situation which rapidly became more and more difficult.

If Domenico Grimaldi is the most important voice from Calabria, Palmieri is the most important and also the best-known spokesman for Apulia in the eighteenth century. He also came to Naples in the 'eighties after long, valuable experience in the provinces. The years he spent in military service and meditation on the art of war represent a personal element distinguishing him from the other reformers. But we can still recognise, in the periods which he spent in the countryside, the essential steps on the path trodden by the generation to which he belonged. He attempted to improve his own lands, to promote an agrarian academy at Lecce and to participate in local administration. At the same time he read widely, particularly about French and English economics. From all sides he was induced to consider the problem of credit and capital fundamental. How could agriculture be improved and the desperate poverty which he saw around him be tackled without money? Private citizens, even the largest owners, were in no position to meet this need. Credit had to come from the state but where would the state find the

money? Emphasising what Genovesi had taught, Giuseppe Palm
saw neomercantilism as the necessary instrument for accumu
tion. There would have to be a campaign against luxury, agai
the export of raw materials and the import of manufactu
articles, against anything which absorbed the capital so indispe
able to the landowners who alone could put into practice
necessary land reforms. Palmieri was the first to add to this vis
an element of real resentment against foreigners and to sh
complete intolerance against the great nations to whom
could not be more blindly obedient nor more shamefully
slaved'. He gives the feeling of living in a colony: 'Let us h
that the foreigners may at least stop short of treating us I
Indians.' Thus Palmieri was able to plan a whole program
of credit and financial reforms. He found the physiocrats' p
gramme acceptable as long as it did not harm the interests of
owners and thus he rejected the single land-tax. He fought ope
the stranglehold of usury over the southern countryside. E
'general poverty' seemed to him preferable to this harmful
ploitation. 'General poverty would rouse everyone to emerge,
individual wealth, content with the certain advantage to
gained from assisting the poor, does not aspire to yet gre
wealth; and the poor, content to exist by means of this aid,
not aspire to bettering their own existence.' As we can see,
quiet scholar, Giuseppe Palmieri, knew his Neapolitan coun
side very well. He had put his finger on his country's deep
darkest evils. And they are so dark that even today we do
have a history of usury in the South in the eighteenth cent
which can work its way through the complications of the cha
able institutions, grain deposits, landowners and bankers.

The conclusions which Palmieri reached were moderate
firm. Let the King of Prussia 'boast about instant full-scale
forms'. What could be done was 'to remove the most tang
evils'. The country was sick and needed to be treated as su
It was not Frederick II who was needed, nor Lycurgus, nor
lightened despotism, nor enthusiasm for equality. 'It is necess
then, to adapt the laws to the customs of the nation.' I
Grimaldi and so many others, he too found himself faced w
the fundamental problem of the second generation of reform
in the South. Was the state a suitable instrument for carry
out reforms? By this time the programme to be followed
quite clear to him: what was needed was an intelligent distr
tion of credit in the provinces, initiative on the part of the
landowners, a free pardon for their cruel feudal past on condi
that the barons really turned into entrepreneurs on their c

lands and, following the English example which Arthur Young had impressed upon his mind, a policy of 'maximum employment' (the definition is his own), which would finally eliminate the terrible disparities in the agricultural labour market, where crowds of beggars and numerous bandits, smugglers and assorted down-and-outs did not flow into the fields of the gentry—in spite of the fact that the latter were eager to find a large number of hands very cheaply in order to make them yield as much as possible. Palmieri too arrived at Genovesi's economic approach, not as an ideal, but as the conclusion of a long, detailed inquiry. His attacks on monks, bandits and all loafers and layabouts are among his most effective pieces of writing. When he turned once more to observe the work of the state, he concluded that the blame for a large part of the disproportionate distribution of wealth and for the poverty lay with state authority which had proved incapable of breaking monopolies, removing tolls and destroying privileges and prejudices. The task of the state should be to clear the ground in preparation for necessary freedom. 'For an evil produced by slavery, I cannot see that there is any remedy other than freedom.' For only freedom could shake off the 'inertia', the 'deadly torpor', the atmosphere of 'negligence' and 'indolence' which hung over the whole country. Palmieri, like Grimaldi, was put to the test. He became a member of the Supreme Council in 1787 and was eventually to be entrusted with a considerable share of the responsibility for the government's financial and economic policy. For him too, the task was a heavy one and full of difficulties and contradictions.

Around him in Apulia there were to be many important signs of active participation in the reform movement. Closed up in his ancestral home in Gallipoli, Filippo Briganti ended by losing direct contact with the economic affairs of the land and became completely absorbed in complicated legal and philosophical constructions. His two books—an *Analytical examination of the legal system* and an *Economic examination of the civil system*—have been overrated. Nevertheless he was still a man of his time and his most interesting aspects came from having lived through 1764 and having concerned himself with tunny fisheries and oil and the conflicts between nobles and merchants. Beside him there was his brother, Domenico, together with a few other cultured men from Gallipoli who, looking further afield, followed with admiration the development of a policy of enlightened despotism. Domenico Briganti was the author of a work *In praise of the immortal glory of Joseph II, written on 6th April 1790 in the Oratory of the town of Gallipoli* and published there in the same year. Gallipoli could be taken as the central point of a study aimed at following more closely the parallel development of a new reality and a new economic mentality. As an international oil market, this port reflects the attempt to return to production of refined oil—alongside and instead of massive exports of the crude variety destined for soap-making and wool manufacture. One could say that the clearest and most obvious symptom of the development of a class of noblemen who were both cultured and active in that area is to be seen in the effort to introduce refined oil, in the difficulties it encountered and the obstacles it had to overcome. Giovanni Presta, an agronomist with an insatiable curiosity, expressed these needs better than anyone else and his numerous writings on oil and olives are among the most revealing documents on Apulia in the eighteenth century. There is a strange marriage between classicism and an urge to transform. The age of Magna Graecia appeared in his eyes as the age of the olive. Afterwards, 'agriculture had become a slave forced to produce oil for barbarians who were almost totally unaccustomed to anointing themselves and had a passion for meat and butter'. This period had coincided with the decadence of the South. Now, at last, refined oil was coming back, when 'the light of true philosophy is shining brightly throughout the whole of Europe'.

Proceeding up the Adriatic coast to Bari and Molfetta, one finds various manifestations of a similar state of mind. One feature of this was a more open attitude towards the East, especially the lands of Catherine II, 'the Pallas of the Russias', as Giovanni Presta called her when sending her samples of his oil. There was also direct contact with the experiments which Domenico Grimaldi, 'the Columella of our times'—to quote the same author once again—was carrying out in Calabria. Alongside the voices of Palmieri and Presta in Apulia came numerous other exhortations to transform the landed ruling classes. As late as 1792 G. B. Gagliardo wrote that 'the state of our agriculture will become increasingly wretched and neglected until the clergy, that is the leading members of society, those in whom the people place all their trust, as the illustrious Abbé Genovesi so wisely says, make it into a pleasurable occupation'. During those same years and in the same places began the fundamental debate about the Tavoliere plain of Apulia and its archaic, oppressive judicial, financial and economic structure. Palmieri, Filangieri, De Dominicis and others helped to pose a crucial problem which laid bare the very roots of ideas on ownership, state initiative and technical progress.

Further inland, the area which was most active and in which the seed sown by Genovesi was most productive was the mountainous Molise where Francesco Longano, Giuseppe Maria Galanti, Giuseppe Zurlo and Vincenzo Cuoco were born, to mention but a few of the best known and most important names. We find in their writings the problems of their land, the disorderly expansion of grain production after 1764, with the consequent destruction of pastureland and woods, the deterioration and impoverishment of the soil and, at the same time, the rise in population without any commensurate improvement in its cultural level or degree of technical knowledge. In the same way we see the new roads and communications bringing the hinterland nearer to the great capital city but without producing any flow from there of money, energy or initiative. The reformers made every attempt to understand the situation, to enlighten others and, as far as was possible, to make up for all that was lacking. The *Description of the countryside of Molise* by Giuseppe Maria Galanti is a masterpiece because it tackles both local and general problems and links the wretched reality of Campobasso or Morcone to the whole history of the South. In exploring his land, Galanti first found inspiration in his four volumes of a *New description of the Two Sicilies* which undoubtedly represents one of the most important and lasting results of the whole movement of the Neapolitan Enlightenment reformers.

There is a much simpler, less ambitious work, but one which is full of enthusiasm, by Francesco Longano (Don Ciccio, as he was affectionately called by Genovesi who considered him his best student and in his last years desired that he should succeed him in Intieri's chair). Longano came from a family of poor peasants, wore a priest's habit and was a tutor to those boys whom he managed to gather about him in his little private study. He too dreamed of international trade and egalitarian and cosmopolitan utopias in the wake of Raynal and Mercier. But his most genuine passion was the one which led him to write booklets which could help to improve agriculture in his own area and to study and describe its nature, its defects and their remedies. His journeys in Molise and Capitanata remain the best evidence of the clearness of his vision and of his human identification with these regions.

In the neighbouring Abruzzi, at L'Aquila and Teramo, Dragonetti and Delfico embarked on parallel courses in the 1780s which led them both from more general ideas about morals and philosophy to the economic and political problems of their own countryside. Dragonetti began in 1768 with a little book called *On virtues and rewards*, which is a faint, rather contrived echo of Beccaria's work. Delfico, in 1774 with his *Philosophical essay*

on marriage and in 1775 with his *Signs of morality*, laid th
foundations of a philosophical construction firmly based upo
sensist, empirical ideas, polemically opposed to traditional instit
tions and prejudices. His writings already contain an element o
political ferment. 'Equality and liberty are reciprocal words
politics and morality'—he wrote, for example, in the latter of th
two works—'since you cannot have the one without the othei
His books represent the solitary, provincial, learned response t
the new age which seemed to be beginning in the years in whic
Tanucci's government came to an end. These early writings of h
are inspired and enlivened by 'the sweet allurement of seeii
happiness in perspective'. A few years later, in 1788, we con
across Dragonetti as the author of a large, important volum
entitled *Origin and quality of the fiefs in the Kingdoms of Napl
and Sicily* which, as a contemporary said, 'caused the powerf
feudal lords, of whom there is a large number in these two kin
doms, to cry aloud'. In 1782 Delfico had begun that series o
writings on the various political and social problems of th
Abruzzi which he was to continue for ten years and which mac
him one of the most openminded, intelligent and unprejudice
counsellors of a government which it was hoped or suppose
would carry out reforms. The *Discourse on the establishment of
provincial militia* is a most penetrating attempt at finding a r
lationship, which had been sought in various ways in thes
years, between military reforms and economic and civil ones, an
at the same time at estimating the worth and the influence of th
officers at the centre of Neapolitan society at the end of th
century. The *Memoir on the cultivation of rice in the provinc
of Teramo*, 1783, and the *Memoir on the Tribunal of Meat Pr
visioning* (*Tribunale della grascia*) reveal an exceptional ability t
combine a firmness with regard to defending the principles o
free trade with a remarkable sensitivity towards the plight o
the peasants. Thus Delfico continued in the years which followe
to oscillate like a pendulum between Naples and the Abruzzi, an
between an urge to act and exert influence and a desire to be fre
and independent—to join in the life of the Neapolitan ruling cla
or to live in his mansion at Teramo. In 1786 he wrote to h
brother that he could not wait to escape from Naples, 'from th
tedium and squalor of existence here which infects both body an
soul'. But then, in conclusion, he says that 'the province and th
capital are equally unfortunate places for a gentleman, a ma
with a sensitive soul'. In Delfico's letters and works there is
clearer reflection than anywhere else of the contrast between th
provinces and the capital, between the formation of a culture

and enlightened society in the most varied and distant centres
and the attraction that it could not help but feel for the city from
which everyone hoped and expected that the initiative for reform would come.

If we wished to sum up the situation in the 'eighties, some
twenty years after the death of Genovesi, we should have to
conclude that each of these provincial centres contained a city
mansion which was the meeting place of noblemen and doctors,
scholars and enlightened clergymen who considered the problems
of the society which surrounded them as an immediate object
of study and of their existence. Often they gathered in the
masonic lodges, for example in Delfico's mansion in Teramo or
the house of Grimaldi's friends in Reggio etc. But it is difficult for
us to know exactly how much influence this secret organisation
had. We have no precise, detailed map of masonic activities in the
southern provinces in this period. However, the lodges at least
partly made up for the gaps and omissions left by other comparable attempts at organisation. Even in places where the agrarian
societies advocated by Genovesi had been set up, they had led a
very difficult life and in most cases had disappeared fairly rapidly.
In some cases they picked up again in the following decade but
even then it was only in Teramo and Salerno that these groups
succeeded in producing their own periodical, a magazine concerned with technical and economic problems. All told, we can
say that the agrarian societies had not proved equal to the representative and driving function which Genovesi had assigned them.
Despite mistrust, hostility and criticism, all eyes were turned towards Naples, which was the only place from which the necessary impulse could come.

It would be false to separate the movement in the capital from
that in the provinces, to put Domenico Grimaldi in a different
category from his brother Francescantonio, or Gaetano Filangieri
and Francesco Mario Pagano from Melchiorre Delfico, or again
Francesco Longano from Giuseppe Maria Galanti. Nevertheless,
within the movement these men do fall into two groups. And
there seems to be no doubt that the more philosophical, utopian
trend was to be found in Naples, while the more observant, technical, descriptive trend had its roots in the provinces. Even without
wishing to simplify or crystallise the two groups which sprang
from Genovesi's school, by the beginning of the 'eighties we can
see them becoming more and more clearly outlined and dis-
tinct one from the other.

In 1779 Francescantonio Grimaldi's *Reflections on the inequality
among men* had begun to appear; 1780 saw the publication of the

Science of legislation by Gaetano Filangieri, and in 1783 Francesco
Mario Pagano's *Political essays*. It was the high summer of the
Neapolitan Enlightenment. The environment which produced these
works had been formed gradually, no longer around a university
chair (since for many years after Genovesi's death there was no
one to replace him and the position of the young Pagano, who
held the chair of penal law, cannot really be ranked in importance
with that of the man who had taught him too and had been his
inspiration). A delightful villa belonging to the Di Gennaro
brothers, situated between Mergellina and Posillipo, provided the
environment from which the group of enlightened thinkers was
to emerge. One of the two Di Gennaro brothers, Antonio, Duke of
Belforte, was a poet. The other, Domenico, Duke of Cantalupo,
was an economist and actively supported the need to destroy the
protectionist system which still controlled food supplies for the
city and the whole kingdom, if for no other reason, he said, than
that 'the memory of the terrible disaster of 1764 still remains'.
Literary interests and concern with social problems were combined in that world of writers which gathered around them and
where we find Bertola and Fortis, Fantoni and Domenico Cirillo,
Zacchiroli and Bettinelli, Calzabigi and Pianelli. Raffaele Liberatore
tells how the author of the *Science of legislation*, 'so great and yet
so modest', was sometimes to be found there and how 'a vast flow
of legislation, history and public economics was released by Pietro
Napoli-Signorelli, Mario Pagano, Melchiorre Delfico and the Duke
of Cantalupo, Domenico Di Gennaro'. For two years this group
also had a review, the *Miscellaneous selection* which appeared in
1783 and 1784. Material published here included previously unpublished writings of Vico and Genovesi, reviews of Alfieri's
tragedies, opinions on the Constitution of the United States of
America and examinations of books by Grimaldi, Filangieri and
Pagano. Not that this *Miscellaneous selection* was always in agreement with the ideas of these three—there was certainly no lack
of differences and criticisms. If one looks through this periodical,
it is as if one can see the nucleus of the more daring thinkers,
more openly in sympathy with the ideas of the Enlightenment,
detaching itself from the literary matrix which had housed them
for a time. Certainly in that period, around 1783–84, a group was
forming which in the years immediately following, around 1786,
was to consolidate within freemasonry (and the catalyst was
Friedrich Münter's journey in that year and his determination to
establish a masonic lodge of *Illuminati* in Naples).

The death of Filangieri in 1788 was to mark the breaking up of
the group—its members gradually dispersed and moved further

away from one another towards activities and attitudes which were often totally unrelated and contradictory. Baffi, the Greek scholar, was to shut himself up in a personal world of learning and religious daydreams and return to ardent Catholicism through Swedenborg and masonic esotericism. Tommasi took the first steps towards that successful administrative career which was to make him forget the ideals of his youth. Zurlo too was to prepare for that career as a financier and minister which was to make him the best exponent of reforming ideas in a situation which by that time, at the close of the era of hopes and revolutions, had undergone profound changes. Albanese set out in silence towards the tragic destiny which awaited him in 1799. Mastellone continued to live in that environment of provincial magistracy from which contact with men like Filangieri and Pagano seemed for a time to have rescued him. We could easily continue with this list: this is just a first, exemplary nucleus of a ruling class at the transition between the eighteenth and nineteenth centuries which had found a common starting-point in the age and society in which Pagano, in masonic manner, took the name of Janus Baptista La Porta, Mastellone became Giovanni da Procida and Tommasi, Giano Gioviano Pontano. These men could often be found at the Arenella, Pagano's house, for example on that evening of 29 October 1786, when they had with them at dinner the German historian Heeren and the Danish bishop Münter—and when they had all ascertained that they were 'brothers', 'since they were alone' they held a 'convivial lodge'.

The ideas of Filangieri and Pagano—the two great personalities of this group—grew out of an increasingly intense impatience and bitter discontent at seeing the reforms which they had so earnestly hoped for postponed from year to year, from one occasion to another. Filangieri was still very young. In 1780 he was twenty-seven but he had already had considerable political experience, starting with his presence in Sicily, at the age of twenty, just on the eve of the Palermo revolt of 1773. In the following year he published his *Political reflections* which expressed both a personal undertaking to concern himself throughout his life with the problems of society and a hope with regard to the reforms of the closing period of the Tanucci government. Eventually he had become aware of the reactionary attitude of the magistracy and the legal world towards any substantial transformation in the legal structure of the country. He threw the whole of himself into his work. 'There are few days in my life when I can reckon to have worked less than eleven hours.' Finally the great volumes of the *Science of legislation* appeared to express all that stored-up pas-

sion. Still more violent and tempestuous was the drive with
Mario Pagano. He had not been brought up in one of the famou
ancient families of Naples and had not had an education whic
brought him into contact with the best in European culture of th
time but had come from an obscure, penniless family of nobl
men in Basilicata and had a tremendous struggle, despite Gen
vesi's support, to free himself from the weight of a narrov
minded, provincial culture. Even more, Pagano had to find th
means of earning a living between the law courts and the unive
sity. When, after he had finally been made a professor, he pu
lished his first book on the subject which he taught, *Consideratio*
on criminal trials (1787), he chose as a motto a line fro
Tacitus which could not have more aptly expressed that increa
ingly acute sensation of a deteriorating situation which was uppe
most in his mind and in the minds of his friends: 'Sed, du
veritati consulitur, libertas corrumpebatur.' What use would
the extraordinary culture promoted and nurtured by them if
were not eventually turned into facts? What was the point
planning reforms if the country remained indifferent and th
government did nothing? His mind was obsessed with the fea
of a possible defeat and catastrophe not very far away.

This fear and anguish were not just personal. Others around hi
looked at the same reality and came to the same conclusion
For an example let us open Luigi Targioni's *Physical, political an*
economic essays, published in Naples in 1786. The author had rea
extensively and knew Venetian, French and other reformers an
agronomists. He too looked to the example of Joseph II and oth
enlightened despots. He stressed the need to spread educatic
and broaden knowledge and the use of new techniques. But i
conclusion he observed that a particular danger was lurking in th
South in the course of this work of enlightenment. Only by a
increasingly intense effort to educate could there be any 'resi
tance to the powerful causes driving towards dissolution or eve
any hope of tempering and breaking up the effects in such a wa
as to bring about a reorganisation in the nation without allowin
it to be cast once more by the perils of revolution into a dreadfu
state of barbarity'. The reformers well knew that they wer
walking on the edge of an abyss. The danger of an agrarian lav
—which was something that Pagano was always discussing, fron
the time of his youthful writings to those of the revolutionary er
—was also present in the mind of Luigi Targioni. It was essentia
he said, 'to bring help and enlightenment to the peasants'. It wa
necessary to improve the conditions of the common people an
in this way 'prevent a division of the land' towards which th

'big owners' were heading, 'with the desolation of their estates' unless they proved clever and far-seeing enough to grant to the 'poor peasants' 'numerous, reasonable, long-term contracts'.

Filangieri too had hoped for great things. Perhaps even to become Viceroy of Sicily, when for a moment it had seemed that Domenico Caracciolo might ask him to be his successor. He had had experience of the army, the court and high state administration—and then found that he had a rebel's soul. His *Science of legislation* was both the utopian theorisation of an efficient, fertile, enlightened despotism, always longed for and never put into practice, and the search for other, far-off models and ideals, capable of firing his hopes and helping him to overcome his profound disappointment. He moves from far-away America, shining out over every other utopia, to a grandiose policy which would make use of pedagogy, schools and colleges to modify the whole country, to a profound attack against feudal jurisdictions, and ends with a vision of religious reform in which the masonic bases which inspired it appear. Filangieri thus expressed, with his anxious interpretation of the situation which surrounded him, that atmosphere of expectancy, of incumbent rebellion and tremendous hope which was in him and his closest friends and which simultaneously dominated Europe on the eve of the French Revolution. The response which this book aroused everywhere and the acclaim with which it was met provide a confirmation of this deepseated connection.

In Pagano's *Political essays* and in Francescantonio Grimaldi's *Reflections on the inequality among men* there is an attempt to insert these ideas and aspirations into a vast vision of the development of civilisation. Everywhere in Europe the philosophy of history had become one of the most typical expressions of the culture of the closing decades of the eighteenth century. The Neapolitans wanted to have their say too in this widespread movement. Their original contribution was in following Vico and rediscovering the *New science*. Their adherence to Vico had the effect of disguising with unfamiliar words and suggestive, pregnant symbols a sociological concept which in reality had its points of reference particularly in Boulanger, Chastellux, Condillac and Ferguson and in many other eighteenth-century exponents of the philosophy of history. As early as 1785 this return to Vico had led to the polemic between Napoli-Signorelli and Pagano, the former giving an orthodox, conservative interpretation of the *New science*, the latter an interpretation influenced by the Enlightenment. Grimaldi, Filangieri and Pagano sought above all to find by means of Vico's symbols the answer to their own problems and doubts. The origins of nobility, its function and the reason for its existence and power were very soon to become the crucial question.

Everyone approached it in his own way, beginning from the feudal oath, customs, the very roots of human civilisation. Thus everyone arrived at the core of the antifeudal polemic. Even the oddities confirmed this predominant concern. In 1780 a 'priest of the royal congregation of Chinese' published a large volume on *Biblical-feudal antiquities compared with the barbaric antiquities of the Heruli, Goths, Longobards etc.*, where Moses, Jason, David and Solomon are to be found in the guise of feudatories and vassals. Yet, from the other works of the author, Felice Cappello, it can be seen that he was not far from the world of Filangieri or Niccolò Valletta. Feudalism had become the theme of the day —and the philosophy of history, whatever form it took, was to serve the purpose of explaining its origins and facilitating the polemic against it. In 1781–82 two volumes appeared, edited and annotated by Giuseppe Maria Galanti, which contained the essence of all that had been written in Europe upon this problem: Robertson, Chastellux, Hume. 'Feudal government', said Galanti, 'has occupied an infinite number of writers . . . it is also one of the subjects most worthy of attention in modern history: one can go so far as to say that in our time it is more interesting than any anecdote'. For this reason he had wanted to provide this precious and essential collection of documents.

Simultaneously a whole discussion was being unleashed of the question of the political function of the nobility. For the first time in Naples there could be heard an open defence of the aristocracy on the grounds that it had succeeded in preserving its traditional freedom in the face of the rise of modern despotism. In opposition to these patrician apologias could also be heard the reconfirmation of the superiority of the modern state. And this precisely was the most important discussion which Filangieri's work aroused in Naples. At the same time Pagano's rigidly, physically cyclical conception made feudalism into a form constantly recurring in societies. In general the vision of a return to an age of barbarism, the whole concept of 'courses' and 'recourses' in the history of nations eventually became for him, as for all Neapolitan culture at the end of the century, the symbol of the impossibility of finding a smooth linear path towards progress, gradual improvement and a harmonious sequence of reforms.

A catastrophic element was undoubtedly inherent in Pagano's vision and we see it appearing in all its violence in the introductory pages with which he prefaced the first edition of his

Essays, where the Calabrian earthquake of 1783 is raised to a symbol of the dissolution of society and a return to a primitive equality and liberty. This natural catastrophe revealed to him a parallel catastrophic element which lay deep in the social situation. The structure of his *Essays* is anything but optimistic and even the very fine concluding pages, particularly those of the first edition, though they reveal a deep faith in reforms, are permeated with a growing anxiety in the face of a deadly inertia and an increasingly obvious impotence to transform the already mature reform programme into factual reality. He thought that the great intellectual flowering in Naples in the eighteenth century ran a serious risk of meeting the same fate as sixteenth-century culture, that age in which Italy had been 'the first to revive'. 'Italy was like a garden in which the flowers began to bloom before the fruit trees could grow which were meant to feed the gardener who was to cultivate the flowers.' And it was precisely the Calabrian earthquake of 1783 which had come to prove once more how violent and ineffective, corrupt and discontinuous government action was: it had failed to utilise ecclesiastical funds (the *Cassa Sacra*) in the interests of the stricken areas, it had listened to the enlightened counsels of Domenico Grimaldi and so many others without putting them into practice and altogether had succeeded in doing very little—if it had not made the situation worse by its intervention. It seemed as if a fundamental need was being expressed in Calabria in those years, which was perhaps best expressed by Francesco Saverio Salfi: after so many theories, he wrote in 1787, '*a little practical application . . . is what the interest of the people now cries out for*'.

Between 1782 (the date of the formation of the Supreme Council of Finances) and 1794 (the year which saw the end of all attempt at reform by the Bourbons) lay the period in which this need made itself felt most forcefully and in which most progress was actually made in the direction of practical application. These are the years of Joseph II and Leopold II and the comparison with Lombardy alone should suffice to show where the substantial weakness of the South lay: the instrument for action, the state, was incredibly ineffective, backward and weak. From the summit to the provinces it revealed its anachronistic structure. It would be of some value to follow the course of each of the principal reforms (legal, financial and customs reforms) to see the kind of quicksands on which the reformers were attempting to advance (Galanti's *Legal testament* is the most precise and pathetic witness to this fact). In these years the reformers made a valid attempt to close ranks and move nearer together, no longer in groups or trends, not only in lodges or academies but at the summit, in the controlling organs of the state, in the Supreme Council of Finances, in the magistracy and that ancient post of Visitors of the Realm which was revived for them, in provincial administration. Acton and Medici, albeit in a disorganised manner, supported their attempt to participate. Even Pagano, from his seat in the Admiralty Tribunal, could try to defend the real interests of Neapolitan fishermen, just as Filangieri, Cantalupo, Palmieri and others in the Council of Finances faced the country's greatest problems—from the Tavoliere to the excise, from fiefs to the mortgage of state incomes, from the monetary system to village rights. Domenico Grimaldi and Galanti, together with many others, as Visitors of the Realm, brought to the capital a true picture of the situation in the provinces.

A full assessment of their work has still to be made. It is an assessment of Bourbon reform policy. Any estimate of its effectiveness must take into account the fact that we are concerned with a phenomenon which was already out of date and out of time, forced to operate in a situation of crisis, economic difficulties and growing political unrest. It presents us with the tragic spectacle of an eleventh hour chance thrown away and lost for ever. As Nicola Fiorentino said sorrowfully—in his fine *Reflections on the Kingdom of Naples*, published in 1794, which constitute the last important proposal before the revolution of a comprehensive reform of the state and southern society: '. . . our progress has been far too slow . . . We must now compensate for the time and honour which we have lost with the shrewdness and rapidity of our efforts.' But the obstacles continued to multiply in the face of the most skilful and experienced attempts of the reformers. A typical example is the customs law of 1788, which was passed but never applied on account of local resistance but still more because it represented the long overripe fruit of an economic programme which had been maturing for too many years and was by this time completely out of tune with contemporary reality.

Thus it is also necessary to bear in mind the difference which existed between the law as promulgated in Naples and the way in which it was applied in the provinces. It is sufficient to look at the suppression of the Tribunal of Victual Provisioning (*Tribunal della grascia*)—the archaic provisioning structure which weighed so heavily on the Abruzzi and prevented any development of trade with neighbouring territories. Its suppression was urged and eventually obtained by Melchiorre Delfico, who later, to his sorrow, was forced to realise how little local authorities were prepared to accept reforms introduced by the central government

Finally, it is essential to attempt to calculate the quantity of energy and the useless waste of men and materials which even the measures that were effectively carried out came to cost. The best example of this concerns the fiefs. After the profound, brilliant and exhaustive discussion of the 'eighties, finally, in 1792, one tangible result emerged: the decree which made fiefs which had reverted to the demesne equivalent to non-feudal lands (that is, which equated the feudal lands of nobles who died without descendants and which therefore passed into the hands of the state to freehold estates). This measure was accompanied by a spate of writings, polemics and discussions (and one of the most interesting books among the many which appeared at the time is Angelo Masci's *A Political and legal examination of the rights and prerogatives of barons*). This was the first step on the path which Neapolitan society was to follow in the coming decades, stripping the great estates of the barons of their feudal character and thus, on the request of the most active part of the nobility itself, consolidating the enormous latifundia and the system of extensive culture. But here the programme was being applied on one point only (estates which had reverted to the Crown), while avoiding the more general problems (especially communal village lands and local administration) which Genovesi, Filangieri, Galanti and so many others had pointed to as implicit in their polemic against the fiefs. Besides, in this case too, the extent to which the law was applied was certainly very limited.

The figure of Galanti alone—perhaps the most typical and characteristic of this concluding phase—will suffice to show the kind of force which was still present and alive in the reform movement. His *New description of the Two Sicilies* which began to appear in 1786—and only stopped in 1794 when an explicit ban prevented him from continuing—is undoubtedly the masterpiece of these years and the synthesis of the combined efforts over many years of himself and all his generation. His philosophy of history was no longer cosmic and universal as in Francescantonio Grimaldi, Filangieri and Pagano. Although he criticised it, he is connected with that trend in legal history which stemmed from Giannone and he was able to provide what was by this time an elaborate picture of the South's past. It was a distressing and terrible picture. While, in Milan, Pietro Verri had only to turn back a few centuries to encounter a period of freedom and economic expansion, the civilisation of the communes and the nobility; while the Florentines could rediscover the Florence, Pisa and Siena of the fourteenth century and the Renaissance, in Naples Galanti had gone back hundreds and thousands of years:

but to find a world of freedom he had had to return to the Samnites, the primitive Italic tribes of his native Molise.

From the Roman conquest onwards he had not been able to find one century on which to place a hope or from which any inspiration could be drawn—apart from the brilliant but all too brief parenthesis of Frederick II of Swabia. The history of the South appeared as a succession of upheavals and conquests, ruin and neglect. Galanti's conception was totally dominated by historical pessimism and yet he had not become discouraged. He had derived from this bitter vision an urge to understand and to act promptly and vigorously upon individual problems. His campaigns against feudalism, against legal chicanery and the lazy, inane mentality of the provincial gentry were extraordinarily effective.

Our laws, for the most part belonging to feudal government, have scorned the condition of the farmer and have favoured the classes of idle men . . . All those among us who have talent and a little money devote themselves to the lawcourts or to medicine or to becoming a notary or a priest and in this way scrape a living among the people . . . From here stems the wretched and wasteful kind of existence in which the inhabitants of small provincial towns aimlessly idle away their time.

Even international events, the French revolutionary storm approaching the beaches of the Gulf of Naples, did not deter Galanti from the conviction that only a solid reform programme could remedy such a situation. What is more, he was one of the few who held the view that it was precisely the Revolution which ought finally to induce the state to carry out fundamental changes.

Right to the end he attempted to use the events in France as a spur, almost an instrument of blackmail.

I showed that the French Revolution should be regarded as a kind of volcanic explosion which threatened all nations with its fires. I asserted that a state must entrust its safety more to good laws than to force of arms, that it was necessary to be armed in order to be neutral and that the principal means of defence ought to be sought in the reorganisation of the state.

Galanti too was very soon made to realise that, in time of revolution, reforms inevitably appear in the eyes of the conservatives as forerunners of subversion. It must be admitted that a new enthusiastic wave of discussions and plans did seem to sweep through the Neapolitan kingdom during the first years of the

French Revolution. To be convinced of this it is sufficient to glance at the reviews of the time—the most lively and important to be published in Naples in the eighteenth century—whereas in general the movement of the Enlightenment had found expression in books rather than in periodicals. The *Reasoned analysis of new books* and the *Literary journal of Naples*, which was its continuation, provide some surprising reading: the last years of the reform movement are certainly not the least lively and interesting. And certain books only serve to confirm this first impression. Few works possess such vitality and penetration as Marquis Giuseppe Spirito's *Economic and political reflections of a citizen concerning the two provinces of Calabria*, published in Naples by Vincenzo Flauto in 1793. There had also been increased contact with other parts of Italy, particularly Tuscany and Lombardy but also Giambattista Vasco's Piedmont and the Venice of the last years of the Republic. But, we must hasten to add, this burst of activity was to be shortlived.

By 1794 it was already over. It is true that a new generation had appeared and had begun to conspire and make contact with French Jacobins, to be arrested and die on the scaffold. This was the third generation, following those of Genovesi and Filangieri. It too had been brought up on the ideas of the Enlightenment but its reactions and programmes were by this time very different.

There was a complex reaction on the part of those old enough to be the fathers of these young men. Pagano defended them and ended up by joining them in prison. Delfico left Naples so as not to live on the same soil on which De Deo was executed. Galanti did not understand the young Jacobins. More and more he turned in upon himself and harboured increasingly bitter feelings of distrust towards the new generation.

It was not only disappointment with the failure of the reforms which caused men like Pagano to play a leading role in the Neapolitan Revolution of 1799. There is no doubt that they came to see in revolutionary France, in Championnet and Napoleon, substitutes for what they had sought in vain in the person of Ferdinand IV. It is true that they were able, often in an original way, to adapt to the new revolutionary situation the questions which Genovesi had pointed out to them: the frightening cultural and moral gaps which separated them from the peasants, the need to find or create a common language with them and the duty to break down immediately the major obstacles which stood in the way of the renewal of the country, from the fiefs to privileges and monopolies. They were able thus to find a place in a new situation, but one which was no longer their own. With the advent of the French Revolution a new era had begun. A study of the way in which the experience of the reform movement of the Enlightenment in the eighteenth century flowed into it would be of great importance and interest, but it takes us outside the immediate sphere of Genovesi and his pupils, which is all that we proposed to discuss here and which dominated the history of the second half of the eighteenth century in the South.

10   The Enlightenment in the Papal States

WAS there a local movement, a specifically Roman tradition which preceded and prepared the way for those attempts at reform which we see appearing even in the Papal States during the latter half of the eighteenth century? Certain scholars, especially in more recent times, have maintained that this is so. If we examine closely the local discussions of the economic and social situation in the States of the Church it appears generally to have been somewhat halfhearted and sporadic, lacking in both energy and continuity. But it did, nevertheless, exist and had its own role and importance.

It is usually considered as having begun with F. Nuzzi and his *Discourse on the cultivation and population of the Roman Campagna* (1702), which, if it is read without preconceptions, testifies to the narrowness of its writer's economic horizon, in spite of the fact that he was the most competent man to discuss such problems in Rome at the turn of the century. He had eyes only for the Agro Romano when all the time one of the chief problems of the Papal States was the fact that it was made up of regions of widely differing characteristics, such as the countryside around Rome and the territories in the Appenines, the lands on the Tyrrhenian coast and the Legations. Even within the range of the age-old problems of the Agro Romano Nuzzi continued to express a historical perspective and political vision which displayed a considerable amount of ingenuousness and superficiality. He accepted the ideas of Giovanni Battista Doni and continued to maintain that the reason for the decadence of the agricultural region around Rome was not to be sought in the structure of the Empire, nor even in the barbarian invasions and destruction wrought by the Goths and Lombards but principally in the sack of Astolf and, he added, that in his opinion the ruin was much more the responsibility of the Saracens. 'So that in these times the air began to be heavy through the abandoning of lands left empty of inhabitants and thus, when the fields were not cultivated, Latium became unhealthy.'

As a remedy for this centuries-old process of involution, Nuzzi suggested a return to a vanished world, almost a plea to revive 'the famous agrarian laws recognised to be so effective and necessary in Roman times'. Was this not perhaps the instrument with which the ancients had succeeded in maintaining for centuries 'the equality of citizens'? From the agronomic point of view, Nuzzi proposed an increase in the number of specialised cultures and the abandoning of grain monoculture—with what little probability of seeing either measure passed in Clement XIII's Rome can be easily imagined. Nuzzi dismissed other possible remedies for this programme of complete renewal, such as greater freedom of trade in cereals (who would buy Roman produce, he said?). When he reached the essential problem, how to finance the transformations which he wished to see, he used words which are surprisingly optimistic and uttered observations of high documentary interest but with little possibility of practical application. The Romans, he said, invested only in state banks, 'the most precarious and unfortunate of all investments', able only to 'encourage idleness and sloth in men's spirits, making them averse to effort and industry'. Why had they not instead carried out the agrarian reform and put their money in low-priced land? In addition to the classical utopias, there remained the picture which Nuzzi drew of the economic passivity of the Papal States, without manufactures, importing wine, oil, textiles, everything apart from essential food supplies.

The only man who was able to move forward from these observations to give us a quite frightening picture of the situation in the States of the Church was Lione Pascoli (*Political testament*, 1733). He was stimulated by a lively political interest and he had before his eyes a comparison against which to measure the reality which surrounded him. To find a comparison Pascoli looked to England, Holland and France, in short, to those parts of Europe which were most active and industrious at the beginning of the eighteenth century. Lione Pascoli's adventurous political career has still to be studied. Up to what point did he throw in his lot with the Austrian imperial party? He certainly felt, as did many in Italy in the opening decades of the eighteenth century, a germ of renewal growing and developing on ghibelline ground. And it was definitely his links with the Spanish ambassador, who was a supporter of the Emperor, which forced Pascoli to leave Rome. His knowledge of Europe proved decisive. He travelled in Spain, was a witness in France of the 'cruel and abominable disaster' inflicted on that country's economy by Law's experiment, he admired Holland and went as far as Danzig, where he observed with curiosity the sale of Italian wines 'through various Polish gentlemen'. He travelled through numerous German states and went to Vienna and northern Italy. He saw Turin and observed river traffic on the Po, never failing to make numerous, sorrowful comparisons with the Papal States.

Pascoli had no illusions on this point. 'The State of the Church is perhaps, or almost certainly is, the most wretched of all states.' Agriculture was 'by now reduced to a pitiful condition throughout the whole state'. It was sufficient to travel through it to see 'in every part of the countryside abandoned, ruined houses'. In the very numerous, tiny provincial towns economic and social life was wretched and dominated by usury and in each one a 'tyrant' held sway, 'who engaging daily in illegal business and keeping everyone in chains either through usury or some other means, even dares to corner the meat supply so that he may more easily have it from his debtors and sometimes at below the just price'. At the centre of the state was a city economically wholly passive. Rome, where the nobles and rich men, instead of investing their capital in commercial companies, preferred the state banks and their 'lazy, meagre, miserable returns'. Meanwhile 'Rome slept sweetly and peacefully'. She consumed cloth, silk and leather, produced on the soil of the Papal States but taken outside her borders to be manufactured and then reimported. Foreigners were amazed at this. 'They are amazed furthermore at our stupidity. I, who have had occasion to converse and have dealings with many, by experience can bear witness to this, to my great displeasure and shame.'

Pascoli had drawn from his stay outside Italy both the literary model for his book and the inspiration for his economic and financial programme. As he said in his note *From the publisher to the reader*, he wanted to write 'in the manner of the states of France and England, which have been published with the consent, approval and under the protection of their sovereigns and had been dedicated to them by their authors . . .' There were indeed many *États de la France* and *Present state of Great Britain* which he could have seen in London and Paris, including *Le Détail de la France* by Boisguilbert, which appeared in 1695 but was

shortly afterwards reprinted under the name of Vauban and give
the title *Testament politique*. This was a literary genre whic
was particularly widespread and a direct influence on the idea
on mercantilism and free trade which were being discussed a
the time of the War of the Spanish Succession and in the year
immediately following.

Pascoli derived a programme which was rigidly protectionis
even prohibitionist, aimed at the development of manufacture
in the Papal States, and at the same time a forceful incentiv
towards the abolition of all obstacles which stood in the way o
the internal circulation of goods, especially foodstuffs, an urg
to introduce new cultures and proceed to the division of th
great estates. His programme evoked a wide and lasting respons
Right up to the end of the eighteenth century we shall hear thes
watchwords resounding and witness the re-emergence of th
urge towards the constitution of a homogeneous domestic marke
which at the same time was to be protected vigorously against a
foreign competition.

It was monstrous, he said, 'that people have to pay taxes o
goods passing from place to place within the same state o
account of the many customs barriers'. Especially since the tax
collected on the outskirts of Rome and not on the borders of th
state only encouraged the most disgraceful abuses and mos
obvious examples of speculation by the rich and powerful an
the higher orders of the clergy. Every aspect of economic lif
should find encouragement in the new customs policy he wa
proposing. It was sufficient to consider, for example, the con
sumption of fish, which in Rome, strangely enough, was provide
for, not from the nearby sea, but imported from much furthe
away. Other countries had an abundance of salt and fresh wate
fish 'yet pilchards, herrings, salt fish and caviar are hardly know
since almost all of them find their way to Italy and two third
of them end up in our state, whose inhabitants, having becom
lazy, negligent, idle and demoralised through lack of activity, ar
not able to handle their affairs like people in other countries'.

But was it possible to have a unified market in a state so lack
ing in unity? The mercantilist programme was invoked by Pasco
—as it was to be continually throughout the eighteenth centur
—as a kind of antidote, a panacea for the very complicate
social and economic structure of the country. The more frag
mented and divided the Papal States became, the more its econc
mists and reformers dreamt of and urged a rigid protectionis
organisation able to stimulate and create a thriving home marke
The greater the problem of transporting goods within the countr

—given the lack of roads, navigable rivers and sometimes communications of any kind—the more the planners tended to believe that a vigorous policy of support for local manufactures and a prohibition of foreign products could provide an effective remedy for the situation. The ideas of Pascoli and those who reasoned as he did arrived at the paradoxical proposal of severing, in the name of this national policy, links which went back hundreds, thousands of years, like those existing between the mountains of the Abruzzi and the plains of the Agro Romano, in order that the subjects of the Papal States should finally be obliged to produce their own cheese, wool etc., and not be cheated by the shepherds of the surrounding mountain regions.

Alongside the paradox, the utopia. A strange utopia full of hopes and suggestions which Pascoli expressed in one of the concluding chapters of his book *Capitol Square (Della piazza di Campidoglio)*. Roman tradition and rhetoric were well and truly dead for him, buried by the new mercantilist ideal which was to find its fullest expression right there on the Capitol. 'London, Amsterdam and Antwerp all have very fine stock-exchanges . . . Other cities in Europe also have some very fine ones, nearly all adorned round about with arcades which are used for shelter when it rains, but none of these can be compared with Capitol Square, and I will make this the stock-exchange of Rome . . .'

The extent of Pascoli's influence and what he actually did between 1720 and 1740 remains to be studied. The net result was certainly a failure. Even Benedict XIV, on whom he placed his greatest hopes, did not respond adequately to his plea. Pascoli remained the most visible and solid point of reference of the local reformist tradition in the Papal States but his ideas made very slow, uneven progress amidst endless delays and countless obstacles.

And yet in the first decade of Benedict XIV's pontificate, 1740 to 1750, the new culture of scientific inspiration, which had permeated even Rome and had been discussed and diffused by the group around Celestino Galiani, Bottari and a few other scholars, had begun to concern itself more and more with economic and social problems. Much has been written about the Pope's personal initiative, that he protected Muratori and saved Genovesi from greater troubles than those which he had to bear. But a considerable amount of the praise belongs to his Secretary of State, Cardinal Silvio Valenti Gonzaga. It was he who opened the doors of the *Sapienza* to the new sciences, experimental physics and chemistry. The Frenchmen Jacquier and Le Sueur came to create in Rome a scientific centre in which, at least for a time, men like Boscovich could work. It was from Valenti that the idea came of 'drawing up an exact topographical map indicating the situation of and distance between places, towns, estates and castles existing within the bounds of the Papal Dominions'. It was Valenti who launched the *Giornale dei letterati* which appeared in Rome between 1742 and 1758. 'It was then', wrote Claudio Todeschi in 1779,

> that the most gifted men turned towards the kind of research which was most advantageous to society and in physics the only principles to be admitted were those proved by observation and experiment . . . Who will not admit therefore that it is to Valenti that we owe the felicitous revolution in studies which has taken place among us, the establishment of modern philosophy through which the misfortunes of life have been alleviated and the benefits increased?

His was the inspiration behind Benedict XIV's first attempts at breaking down the system of tolls then in existence in the Papal States and of monopolies and local and professional privileges. He seems to have given systematic support to commerce and to the development of Ancona and Civitavecchia.

> As soon as privileges and exemptions were granted to merchants and Civitavecchia was declared a free port and various commercial measures and laws were passed and treaties made [wrote the same eulogist], Marchese Trionfi's merchant ship from Ancona went out to ride the seas of the North and trade began with England, Norway and Muscovy . . . The cities of Ancona and Civitavecchia now gave visible proof of the beneficial effects wrought by trade in the growth of industry, population and wealth.

As in the rest of Italy around 1750, much of the interest in economic matters in Rome was directed towards monetary, banking and financial problems. For example, it has not been noted that it was in Rome that two of the most important economists of Peter Leopold's Tuscany gained their early formation and discussed their ideas in those years. This is what we read in a letter from Giovanni Antonio Fabrini, written to Bottari on 13 May 1749.

> Abbé Pagnini and Abbé Tavanti, who are both Tuscans and both pursued their legal studies there, who are friends and united in their studies, translated Locke's book from English into Italian, annotated it and expressed their hope of publishing their work.

Fabrini was surprised that the book had still not appeared. There must have been

> some hidden mystery, as for instance that it might not be to the liking of certain important persons.

Locke's work was later published in Florence; Gian Francesco Pagnini discussed the broad range of monetary problems in his *Essay on the just price of things, the correct value of money and on the trade of the Romans* (1751), which was placed as an appendix to this edition of Locke. As is well known, Pagnini was destined to become one of the major economic historians in the eighteenth century with the publication of his *History of the tithe* in 1765–66. Angelo Tavanti, who after attending university in Pisa went into legal practice in Rome under the jurist Gaetano Forti, 'there dedicated himself to profound meditations on the difficult art of governing peoples'. In 1746 he was back in Florence with the post of Secretary to the Council of the Treasury. Under Leopold he became its director, that is Minister of Finance in the Grandy Duchy in the decisive years of the reforms.

Another Tuscan, also in contact with the Roman world, was Giovanni Antonio Fabrini, who described to us the hopes and labours of Pagnini and Tavanti. He was connected with the circle of Casa Corsini, with Bottari and Foggini, and it was these two scholars who supervised the publication of his book *On the natural and civil character and attributes of money and the historical and natural principles of contracts* (1750). This was a book on law rather than economics, but it does reflect the discussions and subjects of interest which were developing in Rome in the first ten years of Benedict XIV's pontificate. Fabrini was a great admirer of Locke's writings on monetary matters. He preferred him to the classic writer Bernardo Davanzati because he was 'more of a philosopher and he had lived in that sea of mercantile affairs which London may be called without exaggeration'. The English writer was of more use precisely because he was better able to shake hardened convictions.

> The point is to uproot the old prejudice of believing that tolls and taxes, on whatever they happen to be charged, always bring economic advantage to the sovereign and this prejudice can only be removed by the Cartesian principle of reducing all those who think in this way to a state of perplexity, so that they are led to doubt whether this is true or false and to examine the arguments for both sides.

To him too, the classical tradition began to seem a burden. I economic matters the ancient Romans had not understood th essential point that fixing a price by decree is just as impossibl as having 'a public decree stating what in physics is cold c hot and what is light or heavy'. It was essential to heed th modern thinkers: in addition to Locke, Dutot, whom Voltai rightly named 'L'Euclide du commerce'. We shall not be surprise to see Fabrini reading *L'Esprit des lois* with great interest, co cerning himself with the problem of usury and rejoicing when finally looked as though Pagnini's translation would be published 'I do not know how he has overcome those obstacles which considered insurmountable.'

Fabrini's book on money which, as we have seen, came out i Rome in 1750, was dedicated to 'his lordship, Marquis Bellon the most important banker in Rome at that period. And it was i the very same year that Belloni's *Dissertation on commerc* appeared, a work which was to enjoy a widespread and lastin success both in Italy and elsewhere. It is certainly difficult no to share Luigi Emaudi's judgment of Belloni when he termed hi 'an empty head filled with scientific baby-food'. Yet his *Dissert tion*, taken as a document of reformist aspirations in the middl of Benedict XIV's reign, is of considerable significance. Belloni political culture is up to date, he quotes Montesquieu and 'h immortal work on the spirit of laws'. His ideas on money and th relationship between gold and silver, though not original, corr spond closely with preoccupations very common to the admini trators of Italian states in the period immediately following th War of the Austrian Succession. The picture of poverty an decadence in the Papal States which Belloni draws is expresse in moderate, rather euphemistic terms yet is always close to th truth. Economic stagnation, he said, was not dependent on an specific law on food provisioning or monetary measure: it w the whole structure of the country which was defective, unde mined as it was by 'passive commerce' and an unfavourable balanc of trade. Belloni had no illusions about the difficulties whic would be encountered by anyone who attempted to change th situation. It meant no less than 'converting a whole people fro idleness to industrious activity'. Like Pascoli, though with slight! less enthusiasm, he looked to foreign, particularly English an Dutch models. Far off, on the horizon, stood the image of Tsar Pete The measures proposed by Belloni were those of traditional me cantilism: freedom and incentives for exports, a ban on all no necessary foreign manufacture, within the country the abolitio of tax farming and the social advancement of big merchants.

All those subjects who have engaged in large-scale commercial enterprise by sea with foreign countries and those who have undertaken to introduce crafts and manufactures and such things into the country should be admitted to high civil and military positions and when these posts belong to the class of the nobility they should not be considered as having lowered their status.

This forms the basis for the *Plan for the setting up of customs barriers on frontiers* which Belloni produced in 1757 and which is rightly considered the starting-point of that long and tortuous bureaucratic trail which led to the fiscal reforms at the end of the 'eighties.

The numerous reprints of Belloni's work and translations into German, French and Spanish between 1752 and 1788 are proof of the curiosity aroused by his *Dissertation*. But neither the prefaces nor the notes of the translators show any special interest in the problems of the Papal States. However, in the discussion which René Louis Le Voyer de Paulmy, Marquis d'Argenson began in the *Journal oeconomique*, alongside the affirmation of free trade principles, we find the origins of a new, different vision of the questions which had prompted Belloni to write. At the very moment when a local mercantilist and protectionist tradition was becoming crystallised, a different position began to emerge, one which would later be fused with that of the physiocrats: in place of state initiative, the recommendation to 'laisser aller les choses d'elles-mêmes' and the advantages of freedom extolled in contrast to strict, watchful control ('Voyez dans les républiques comment le commerce a prospéré . . . c'est que les républiques ont une âme toujours saine, toujours active, qu'est la liberté'), while for the state was proposed the task of destroying obstacles rather than that of direct economic intervention ('Le *retranchement des obstacles* est tout ce qu'il faut au commerce').

But the debate did not stop here. The editor of the *Journal oeconomique* replied to d'Argenson in June 1751, defending Belloni as being closer to the immediate reality of the Papal States ('La *Dissertation* n'est point le fruit d'une spéculation oisive'): there was the need for a commercial doctrine and an organised effort on the part of the state in the economy. It was essential to make use of customs as the instrument of this economic policy. The exalted republican liberty was a myth while the modern urge towards civil liberty was alive in monarchies as well as in republics. The discussion was continued along these lines in the May issue of 1752 where one of the

things which was stressed was the need for the state to have
different attitude towards 'matières premières nationales' a
'foreign' ones. These problems remained fundamental questic
for discussion throughout the latter half of the eighteenth c
tury. The *Journal oeconomique* made a further contribution
the debate with an article in the September issue of 1759 on t
population of Rome, in January, February and then Novem
1762 on the Pontine Marshes, etc.

At the same time as the first signs of the debate betwe
mercantilists and free-traders began to appear, a third positi
also took shape, that of those who proposed above all a tra
formation of the Roman Campagna. In 1750 there was a repr
of Francesco Eschinardi's *Description of Rome and the A*
Romano. It had an appendix for which Ridolfino Venuti was r
ponsible entitled *Observations on the Agro Romano and*
cultivation, full of penetrating observations and stimulating p
posals. Ridolfino Venuti is a curious figure who would merit clo
investigation. His is an exemplary case of the transition fr
historical curiosity to the new images of a mythology of t
Enlightenment and from antiquarian to economic interests.
we were to believe Pompeo Pozzetti, his official biographer,
life was simply that of a learned archeologist. But let us lc
instead at the *Memoirs* published in London in 1780 by Thon
Hollis, the great propagandist of republican ideas in eighteen
century England. Hollis visited Italy in 1750–51 and establish
numerous contacts with Italian scholars, writers and artists.
himself tells us, in a section on the Venuti family, how he
persuaded Ridolfino to write a dissertation entitled *De*
libertate, eiusque cultu apud Romanos and another, *De libert*
orum pileo, on the Phrygian cap. Archeology and a passion
republican freedom thus began to merge to create the new sy
bolism of the Enlightenment. Ridolfino Venuti, active admirer
Piranesi's 'fervid genius' and illustrator of the excavations
Herculaneum, acquires a new, different dimension if we take
trouble to read his *Observations on the Agro Romano*. In ma
cases he adopts solutions already proposed by Nuzzi and Pasc
but he begins to stress the need for greater freedom of trade
cereals—both inside the country and in foreign trade—and
the same time attempts to find economic ways which will le
to the more widespread use in the Roman Campagna of techni
and specialised cultures. He was in touch with the discussi
going on in Naples and an admirer of Bartolomeo Intieri, but
looked particularly towards Tuscany, Milan and Piedmont (for
cultivation of mulberry trees). He appealed to the public auth

ties to compel landowners to adopt a wider variety of more modern agricultural methods. He no longer thought in terms of agrarian laws but of 'share cropping, following the practice of almost all the rest of Italy'. To facilitate this transformation Venuti proposed a whole series of fiscal and legal concessions and exemptions.

The local reformist tradition could now be said to be established. Its programme, formulated by Nuzzi, Pascoli and Venuti, had by this time found clear expression. For several decades watchwords taken from their writings would continue to be repeated. But their practical effectiveness remained very limited. Benedict XIV died without touching any of the key points of the traditional system. His successor, Clement XIII, was to reign for ten years, from 1759 to 1769—the years in which the Italian Enlightenment flourished, the decade of Genovesi the economist, of Beccaria and Verri—in an atmosphere of stubborn, fearful reaction and bitter determination to oppose the anti-Jesuit reform movement in all the Italian states and the whole of Europe. At the crucial moment the Papal States swam against the stream and lost even more prestige and international importance and came to appear more and more as just a miserable little Italian state. The incentive, however modest and limited in scope, which had come from within, dried up. Pressure came from outside and it looked for a moment, when Clement XIII died, as though it might be strong enough to overcome the obstacles.

The real test came in the Papal States as in a large part of Italy, particularly Naples and Tuscany, with the great famine which with varying rhythm and intensity harrowed the peninsula between 1764 and 1766. In Naples Tanucci's policy, his whole way of thinking, suffered defeat as a result of it. In Florence these were the opening years of Peter Leopold's policy of free trade. The South and the Centre of Italy were embarking on divergent economic policies. But what about Rome?

There are numerous accounts of what was happening in Rome. Filippo Campilli gave his version, from the official point of view, of the reactions of the Curia and the state. Many years later Nicolai recalled the social catastrophe of that terrible year 1764.

Everyone was very anxious to lay in supplies for his own family, so that the bread shortage, which lasted only a short time, was felt much more acutely by a people accustomed to an abundance of good bread at very low prices. The shortage was made much worse by the arrival of many people from outside and the hungry hordes that rushed into the city from surrounding provinces . . . and then fear that hunger would increase and that the influx of so many wretched, under-nourished individuals would cause an epidemic, threw the city into great consternation.

But this was still a somewhat optimistic, official picture. Bernardo Frigerio, writing to Giulio Perini on 19 May 1764, was more effective: the fear was so great, he said, 'that the cowards, in which this city abounds, already believed that they themselves would have to serve as food for the hungry *lazzaroni* who, as they thought, were about to destroy Naples and come to Rome to devour us all'. With all the means at their disposal the authorities had attempted to counter these 'vain fears' with optimistic news. 'Some men have been imprisoned here in Rome because they wrote otherwise and there is a strict censorship in force concerning such matters.'

Abbé Coyer, the well-known French polemicist, on a journey through Italy during those months, also noted with curiosity the means employed by the papal government to fight the shortage. The weight of the loaf had secretly been reduced without any reduction being made in the price. 'Le public s'en est bientôt aperçu. Les *birbes*, c'est à dire la populace de Rome, n'est pas aussi patiente qu'en d'autres pays. Il a fallu rétablir le poids. Il n'y a qu'un cri contre la Chambre de l'Annone.' But this did not make Clement XIII change his economic policy. 'Le pape, versant des larmes paternelles sur l'affliction de ses enfants a dit ces paroles édifiantes: "let us pray to God, we shall have processions" . . .' But the final word, ironic and cutting, came from Galiani, in his *Dialogue sur le commerce des blés* (1770). 'Le chevalier', one of the leading characters in these dialogues, said that he had been in Rome at the time of the famine. It was clear to him that the root of the trouble lay in a misguided economic policy and not in natural causes. The provisioning system with its granaries and the regulation of stock piles and bread making were just so many disastrous errors. In Rome they seemed to imagine that they were still in the time of Augustus, when really it was a completely discredited state with no manufactures, no trade and no prestige. 'L'excommunication même (la seule légion fulminante qui reste à ce vieil empire) n'est plus respectée nulle part.' The rulers still feared the people, as if they were those of ancient times. Instead they were dealing with 'un petit peuple bien dévot, bien soumis, qui ne s'assemble que pour faire des processions et pour gagner des indulgences sous les doigts de Sa Sainteté'. Rome had become simply a place of pilgrimage which ruined the surrounding countryside to entertain its guests.

The policy followed in Rome in 1764 was destined to have

lasting and far-reaching consequences. Instead of taking steps towards liberalisation, as happened in Tuscany, or sparking off
that wave of criticism, proposals and impatience typical of the
reform movement which took place in Naples, in Rome purely
financial measures which profoundly undermined the position of
the state and the local administrations were judged adequate. It
was no good thinking that in some isolated part of the Papal
States, like Benevento for example, the authorities had succeeded
in protecting the population from hunger and all the suffering
that goes with it. It was useless to make speeches and lay stones
in honour of Stefano Borgia, who thus gained such a reputation
for being a good administrator that the burden of responsibility
for the Papal States was placed on his shoulders at the time of
the French Revolution. In Rome it was thought sufficient to take
a million and a half scudi from Castel Sant'Angelo. This was soon
followed by other loans. The debts of the Annona (the provisioning administration) mounted steeply every year. Growing deficits
were faced by provincial administrations. Marco Fantuzzi wrote
that in Ravenna :

> The workers were without work, the fields were not planted
> owing to the lack of cattle which had to be sold, and crops
> ruined or not gathered, houses in the country were not re-
> paired and fell into ruin. Failure to carry out the necessary
> work on rivers meant more flooding and more damage. Those
> labourers who had survived hunger and death were crushed
> by debts, unable to work and stripped of everything. Some
> went into the city to live by begging and robbery, some fled
> elsewhere and the few who remained were on the hands of the
> poor landowners.

There were some attempts made in the Papal States to find a
solution for this situation, with the proposal of new ideas and the
search for a new contact with the world. In 1769 Filippo M.
Renazzi began to teach at the Sapienza. His ideas on penal law
were considered by Carmignani, with some exaggeration, as 'a
broader and more methodical development of the principles of
Beccaria's book'. But his influence on penal legislation was slight
and took a long time to penetrate. The most characteristic example
is provided by Emmanuele Duni. Born in Matera, he had come
to Rome with the burning ambition of a philosopher in the
manner of Vico to understand and expound the fundamental laws
governing human society. He had been praised together with 'the
incomparable Giambattista Vico' in the Roman *Giornale dei
letterati* of 1758–60. In 1763 he had two volumes published by

Francesco Bizzarrini Komarek, called *Origin and progress of the citizen and civil government in Rome.* His correspondence with John Strange, the British consul in Venice, indicates in what frame of mind and with what intentions he wrote them.

> The laws and customs of men [he said], and consequently those of all nations, cannot be considered without recourse to the light of philosophy, and we shall never be able to discover whence they come and what they are made of without the help of philosophy, the mother of all human understanding . . . I should like to be encouraged, nay spurred on to continue the great effort of the principal work. This, to tell the truth, has caused me to sweat blood and often made me very downcast because I find myself not only in an Italy which is full of corruption, but in a city where, more than anywhere else in Italy, lies hidden the purity of that doctrine which it is hardly permissible to adore within the walls of one's private dwelling. (Let this be said in complete confidence.)

Neither the economists, the lawyers nor the philosophers really seemed capable of breaking the cultural and political deadlock of Rome in the 'sixties. The movement towards renewal and reform which had managed to find some kind of expression, however weak, during the past half century, seemed to have come to a complete standstill in the midst of indifference on one side and harsh criticism on the other. Now the incentive had to come from outside.

It came from Carlantonio Pilati, in the thirteenth chapter of his work *For a reform of Italy*, published at the beginning of 1767 and entitled *A Humble request on behalf of the people of Rome to the Most High Pontiff for the restoration of agriculture, crafts and trade.* It was widely read. It could be seen in *Italie reformée*, published by Le Brun in Paris in 1769 with the false imprint Rimini. The Venetian *Europa letteraria*, in its issue of 1 May 1769, was horrified at such daring. The *Gazette littéraire et universelle de l'Europe*, on the other hand, appearing on 15 May of the same year, gave it a favourable notice. In 1775 a German translation of Pilati's work appeared in Zurich and it continued to be discussed up to the end of the century.

Pilati began with the parallel between ancient and modern Rome which he was later to use again in his *Voyages*. The descendants of the ancient Romans turned to the Pope (Clement XIII) imploring 'relief from their utter wretchedness'.

> You will see the countryside deserted and barren for the lack of men to cultivate it, you will find the men who work on the

land reduced to the most abject poverty through the oppression of your ministers and powerful lords. You will find that crafts and manufactures have declined because they have not been protected and controlled. You will find people whom desperation has turned into cowards and you will be amazed to see the people of Rome reduced to a few thousand idle wretches ... Everywhere you will discover decay and death.

But this time the Romans who were speaking through Pilati did not mean to dwell on considerations of the religious causes of their decadence. Their point of view had changed. It was no longer religious or ecclesiastical but economic, no longer legal but social. They were even prepared to kiss 'the feet which have trampled us into such dire distress', provided that the necessary remedies were forthcoming. The eighteenth-century reforming spirit was triumphing over all the disputes and rival claims of the past. The important thing was to begin to put right the financial deficit, particularly because the Papal States were receiving less and less assistance from outside sources. 'No source outside the Roman State now seems willing any longer to throw down holy water for you and much less for your successors.' Salvation could only be attained by efforts within the country. It was necessary to have a complete change of policy, to consider the 'humblest farmworker' instead of pursuing international ambitions which had long since ceased to be a possibility and were harmful to the Papacy and to others. It was the example of the Protestant countries which should be followed because they were the most active, diligent and prosperous, 'full of industrious men useful to the state'. In Germany, where there were no ecclesiastical benefices, the people dedicated themselves 'to industry' and became rich. In Rome 'where there was a great abundance of spiritual sinecures, the people lived in poverty and dissoluteness'.

Send the people back to the deserted countryside and the depopulated towns. Restore agriculture which has been so disgracefully neglected for so many centuries. Revive crafts and manufactures and cover the Adriatic and Mediterranean Seas with the merchant ships of your subjects. In a word, aim at having many prosperous and contented subjects, for then the troubles of the Holy See will disappear and she will become rich and peaceful internally and strong and respected outside.

Pilati's economic programme was very generic—a strange and characteristic mixture of elements of mercantilism and free trade with a passion for the countryside and the peasants, but the force of his reforming drive went beyond all programmes to constitute the common platform for all those, of the most diverse leanings, who were to attempt in the following decades to change the state of things in the States of the Church. The chapter closed with a prophecy and a threat. 'For if you do not listen to our prayers', he made the Romans say, 'it is to be feared that our descendants, reduced to desperation, will set about destroying that seat which is the source of all their troubles and will re-establish the Roman Senate and transfer all authority to that body. If you do not act, this will be the only way to restore the health and fortunes of the Roman people.'

Carlantonio Pilati wrote this in 1767. In the following year Voltaire intervened in the debate in a manner which must almost certainly have been inspired by the *Reform of Italy*. *L'Épître aux Romains* was signed 'comte Passeran', in memory of the Piedmontese nobleman who half a century before had fought openly against papal Rome. Voltaire too began by contrasting ancient and modern Rome. 'J'ai pleuré dans mon voyage chez vous quand j'ai vu des zoccolanti occuper ce meme Capitole oú Paul-Émile mena le roi Persée.' The descendants of the conquerors of the world were short of bread. 'Il n'y a pas un citadin parmi vous, excepté quelques habitants du quartier Trastevère qui possède une charrue.' It was not the fault of the climate, which had always been the same. 'D'où vient que la campagne depuis les portes de Rome à Ostie n'est remplie que de reptiles?' Where the forums had once been there was now a 'marché aux vaches', 'et malheureusement aux vaches maigres et sans lait'. It was hopeless for the Romans to expect a solution to come from the Popes. The ruin brought by Christianity had been terrible. The history of the Popes was a fearsome one and seemed ironically to have culminated in a creature incapable of any beneficent action. 'Romains, serait-ce pour le seul Rezzonico que Jésus aurait été envoyé de Dieu sur la terre?' Voltaire is easily led onto the path of anti-religious polemic, but at the end of his pamphlet he goes back to the Romans, their wretchedness and their state of servitude. 'Eveillez-vous, Romains, à la voix de la liberté, de la vérité et de la nature. Cette voix éclate dans l'Europe, il faut que vous l'entendiez; rompez les chaînes qui accablent vos mains généreuses, chaînes forgées par la tyrannie dans l'antre de l'imposture.'

It was not Voltaire's appeal but the programme mapped out by Pilati which was to influence the reformers. They were much more interested in economics than in religious polemics. Gianfrancesco Scottoni, for example, tells us this in his *Of agrarian matters, by a dilettante*, published in Venice in 1770. Poverty in the Papal States was quite frightening and it was caused primarily by their parasitical relationship with other countries. It was to be hoped that the ever-increasing conflict between the Curia and the Italian and European states would be resolved in a slowing down or even complete break in the flow of gold which for centuries had been pouring into Rome. When no more money came in, at least then they would begin to work. Then and only then could Rome hope for her 'revival'. 'It is a sound principle that an overabundance of gold depopulates countries and that by abundance of work alone are they made to flourish.' The continual defeats which the Curia was undergoing, from the expulsion of the Jesuits from Bourbon courts to the coalition of the whole of Europe against Rome on the occasion of the conflict with the Duchy of Parma, were the necessary preconditions for an economic revival in the Papal States. In this way Rome would be again on a level with the other Italian states and be compelled to face and solve its own economic and social problems. Scottoni added that already, even in the cafés, one could hear that the tone of conversation had changed in Rome. It was no longer just a question of 'satire' and talk about 'promotions'. Men talked about trade in cereals and discussed 'whether good companies of merchants are a viable means of increasing credit and trade'. 'It is a pleasure to wander around Rome and be instructed on matters of such importance while drinking coffee and chocolate.'

Clement XIV, faced with the choice, which had emerged in the years immediately preceding his reign, between religion and economics, reforming the Chuch or reforming the state, chose the former path and concentrated all his efforts on the abolition of the Jesuits. He thereby brought to a close an age-old ecclesiastical dispute, but at the same time caused a temporary pause in the closer, more immediate rhythm of development of reformist ideas in the eighteenth century. To convince oneself of this it is sufficient to read the few works on economics which appeared during this short span of years (1769–75). There were, for example, Claudio Todeschi's *Essays on agriculture, manufactures and trade and the application of these to the advantage of the Papal Dominions, with a dedication to His Holiness, Clement XIV* (1770). As the *Efemeridi letterarie* rightly noted, the ideas expressed in this work were not very different from those of the more moderate wing of the Tuscan reformers, Ferdinando Paoletti, for example. Todeschi's political orientation is also quite clear—he looks to the Bourbon courts for inspiration and finds his models in Paris, Madrid and Naples. He was under no illusions about the situation in the Papal States. As he wrote, he was trying to understand 'why the Papal Dominions are in such a state of poverty and decay', why agriculture 'is not at one-twentieth of the strength that it ought to be', why 'crafts and manufactures are in decline', why 'the balance of trade is always unfavourable'. 'What can be the cause of such frightful decadence?' The net result of the work of Benedict XIV and Clement XIII was a failure. 'All the workshops and manufactures begun by them have either fallen into decay or are on the point of doing so . . . We lack the means to stimulate talent and industry . . . We may liken the state to a machine which has all the necessary wheels but lacks a greater driving force to accelerate its motion.' But where was the incentive to be found? Where could one look for this 'driving force'? Thus Claudio Todeschi's writings, too, closed with this awareness and admission of inadequacy.

For over ten years Pius VI (1775–99) personified a similar state of weakness and uncertainty. He had been preparing for some time, from the days of Clement XIII, the bases of what was his economic policy. With him the old, deeprooted, local reform tradition seems finally to come into its own. Pius VI followed the programme of Nuzzi, Pascoli and Venuti, setting aside the religious controversies and the conflicts of his predecessor. He seemed to be more modern and more political, more open to the concrete, immediate problems of his state. But the drive and incentive were still not there. The struggle against the Jesuits had set great moral forces in motion. Pius VI's financial reforms were spread out over too many years, thus dampening all effort and enthusiasm and dissipating that fund of programmes and hopes which had accumulated in the preceding years.

By this time there was no lack of awareness of the tremendous task which faced the reformers. The ideas, indeed, were often extremely wide-ranging and all-embracing. Strangely enough, it was a talented French adventurer named Ange Goudar who presented them in their entirety right at the beginning of the new pontificate. In 1776 the *Essay on the means of restoring the States of the Church, in which the author gives a plan for agriculture, commerce, industry and finance* was published at Leghorn. It was not difficult for contemporaries to guess who the author was. The *Novelle letterarie* on 2 August of that year said that the book 'seems to us very like one which came out several years ago in French entitled *Naples*, and which, with a different frontispiece, would do for any country'. It was true: Ange Goudar had a reform programme broadly sketched out right from 1756, when he published *Les Intérets de la France mal entendus dans les branches de l'agriculture, de la population, des finances et de l'industrie, par un citoyen*. His adventurous life had later taken him to London and from there to Italy. In England and in Naples his own conduct and that of his wife were such as to relegate him, even for scholars and historians, to the ranks of confidence men and tricksters—the world of the Casanovas. Yet when we read what he wrote, we find ourselves face to face with a man of rare intelligence and an outstanding journalistic gift for putting his finger on the problems of many, very different European countries, including the Papal States in the first years of Pius VI's reign.

Above all Goudar was able to place Italian problems in a European context. The 'revolution produced by crafts', the great transformation which was taking place everywhere and which was substituting prosperity for military valour and luxury for frugality, had had the effect of concentrating the population in the cities, depopulating the countryside and, what was even more serious, had made certain countries of Europe increasingly poor and deserted, while others became more and more rich and populous. 'If you survey Europe you will find moral virtues in great abundance among the better-off nations whose wealth is derived from industry. When you arrive at the poor and unemployed you will think that you have reached the seat of corruption . . . Poverty dampens the spirit and weakens the mind.' Just as every nation was composed of rich and poor, so Europe was made up of poor countries and prosperous ones. 'If we think of Europe as a great family of which the single countries are members, it will become apparent that the inequality of wealth was bound to produce in general society the kind of revolution which it produces in individual societies every day.' Four countries in particular had been left behind or, as Goudar said, had not 'followed the relative progress of the arts'. These were Spain, Portugal, Italy and the Papal States. They, more than any others, needed to concern themselves with the 'revival' and 'restoration' of all economic activities.

The problem, said Goudar, was not political and much less religious. The reasons so often cited for the 'great decadence' of the Papal States (elected ruler, usually an old man, an excessive number of clergy and a complicated, corrupt system of government, ecclesiastical celibacy etc.) were mistaken. These were not the chief causes of Rome's 'depressed state'. The root of the trouble lay in a mistaken economic policy. 'Writing as I am for Roman farmers, labourers, merchants and artisans, it would be wrong for me to confuse them with long quotations, analogies and historical lessons.' It was his intention to 'produce a work of pure economics'.

His programme made some useful points: still looking at things from a mercantilist point of view (population and power of the

state), he sought a solution in a new agrarian policy. He cou
thus appeal to the local mentality and tradition and at the san
time direct attention where reforms were really most urgent
needed. He said that the 'revival of agriculture' was the fundament
task facing the new Pope. 'Agricultural societies' should be pr
tected, an agricultural tribunal set up and maps and registers ma
of the provinces. It was necessary to devote serious effort to 't
education of farm-workers and other country dwellers in t
Papal States'. The whole of the tenth chapter was devoted to th
problem. In the following chapter he proposed that 'poor farme
should be provided with the necessary implements'. Roads shou
be built ('the poor condition of the roads in the Papal States mea
that grain and other provisions are rotting in certain districts wh
in others there is a shortage'). Every possible means should l
employed to diminish the population of Rome and increase th
of the countryside, the number of servants should be limited,
measure that much more necessary in a country 'where there a
only two classes of persons, masters and servants'. Above all
was essential to 'turn all the poor and the beggars into worker
Goudar described the mendicancy which grew around monasteri
and traced the cause of so many evils back to the way in whi
property was distributed in the Papal States.

> The unequal distribution of land in the majority of Europe
> states is a serious hindrance to agriculture . . . This fault is mo
> apparent in the Papal States than anywhere else. There a
> gentlemen in Rome who own whole provinces and many citize
> without even a square inch of land to call their own. Mo
> Romans are foreigners in their own country and the land the
> walk over belongs to masters who have divided it all up amo
> themselves.

However, he did not wish to propose agrarian laws:

> These are no longer compatible with the present state of thin
> . . . Therefore I say that it would be better to prevent the b
> landowners from making any new acquisitions and urge tho
> with very small holdings to expand a little.

Policy on finance and customs barriers would have to be adapt
to fit this programme, lifting restrictions on trade and the expo
of cereals. Goudar ended his book with a long section on the vario
types of cultivation in the Papal States and proposed that effor
be directed towards a development of cattle rearing based on 'goo
artificial meadows'.

The *Diario economico di agricoltura, manifatture e commerc* which Luigi Riccomanni published in Rome in those years showed great interest in the book but the reviewer found it too theoretical and too generic.

> We should have liked to see a more extensive and exact applica-
> tion of the theories and maxims to the setting. This cannot be
> done without prolonged and detailed examination of the physical
> characteristics of the land, the situation of provinces, an exact
> topographical knowledge of all the towns, estates and castles,
> the forces of the state, the system of government, laws, the
> nature of practices and customs and the present state of manu-
> factures and trade.

Here was a deliberate setting aside of the most serious problems of economic policy ('we do not wish to dwell at length on matters pertaining to the public economy because this concerns the ruler alone'), but at the same time an appeal for an enormous task of exploration, study and spread of knowledge which did in fact take place in the Papal States in the 'seventies.

In 1772 the first issue of the *Efemeridi letterarie* appeared in Rome. Despite a certain interest in economic and political matters, it was very soon able to satisfy only a small section of the public. July 1774 saw the publication of the first issue of the *Antologia romana* where the problem of reforms began to take a more important place. Tuscan influence was apparent. A large number of the articles concerned Peter Leopold's territory. Felice Fontana was thanked for his contributions in the July issue of 1775. Despite the cautious attitude of the editors, the periodical began to take a quite clearly 'agricultural', anti-Colbert line. Let us look, for example, at the column 'Politics and legislation' in the issue for August 1774. The writer took the opportunity provided by a dis-cussion of Raynal's *Histoire philosophique* to stress the depressed state of agriculture in Colbert's time and the poverty and famine which had resulted from his policy.

> The worst of it is that the problem seems to be without solution.
> It is easy enough for a ruler and his government at any time to
> make an agricultural nation into a people of shopkeepers and
> workers. The weary peasant can quite happily make the transi-
> tion from ploughing and digging to easier, less tiring work in
> the town. But what can we do to entice back to the fields those
> countless individuals who have been corrupted, weakened and
> emasculated by the easy life in towns?

If we look through the *Antologia romana* of those years we fre-quently come across the problems and dilemmas which Goudar was writing about at the same time. It was in this atmosphere that the plans and ideas of Abbé Anton Maria Curiazio also flourished. In January 1775 the *Antologia romana* published his 'Plan for a school of agriculture and manufactures in order to increase the population in a state rich in fertile countryside but lacking in men to cultivate it', taken from the *Reflections of a philanthropist on the sovereign law of states* (1775).

These were the years which saw a stepping up of specifically agronomic propaganda, in the manner of Giovanni Salvini's *Instructions to his land agent* (1775). Here too we can detect a Tuscan and also a Venetian influence and it is apparent that the proposed agrarian changes (introduction of Tarelli's method, etc.) would necessitate modifications in economic relationships and mentality (peasants who 'will not obey you', the role of parish priests 'skilled in agriculture'). Above all, one great hope: 'We are ever on the point of achieving the impossible . . . so that the structure of property will be transformed and the workers will no longer be poor.' In 1777 Luigi Doria's *Principles of cereal growing for the use of the Agro Romano* was published. 'A time of enlightenment like the eighteenth century', said the preface, 'and a most cultured capital city like my own would take it amiss if I thought it necessary to convince them of the importance of that art which is the subject of the present instructions.' But perhaps the most representative example of this propaganda was Giovanni Battarra's *Agrarian dialogues*, which first appeared in Riccomanni's *Diario* in 1776, then a first edition in 1778, reprinted in 1782, and was, as the author himself said, 'to my surprise, very well received throughout Italy'. To begin with, there was the remarkable definition which one of the peasants taking part in these dialogues gave of agriculture: 'I think it must go back a long way because eating is an old habit. As for what it's worth, I think that it's the worst job of all because those who do it mostly live a life of toil and hardship and die of hunger.' Battarra mitigated the harshness of this judgment by referring to Adam, the ancient Romans and Joseph II, all great lovers of agriculture. Nevertheless the difficulties and hardships of country life can still be perceived in those *Dialogues* in which we are given a vivid picture of the hopes, amazement and reluctance of the peasants in the face of new cultures and techniques, particularly growing potatoes ('Here are some tuberiferous roots which the master has given me to plant . . . How happy we shall be if we can make them grow successfully because then we shall never go hungry again! . . . They taste so good cooked among the ashes that they seem like chestnuts . . .').

For two years, 1776 to 1777, Luigi Riccomanni made Rome the chief centre of this agronomic campaign which was inspired by a clear vision of a policy based on the development of the country-side, the provinces and agriculture as an essential starting-point to achieve a general development of the whole economy, including manufactures and trade. We have already quoted several times from his *Diario economico di agricoltura, manifatture e commercio* and we must now pause for a moment to take a closer look at the author and to assess the significance of this periodical.

Riccomanni was born in Scandriglia in Sabina and came to Rome to be a lawyer towards the end of 1766. If he bore the title of Abbé, it must have been in order to conform with the circles in which he moved, for there does not seem to have been any-thing ecclesiastical about him and he did in fact have a wife and family. From 1775 onwards we find him engaged in spreading knowledge of agricultural techniques. He was in touch with Bat-tarra and very soon made contact with G. Salvini in Osimo, Giovanni Francesco Cigna in Turin and Saverio Manetti in Florence. He already had in mind the creation in Rome of the periodical which was to be his *Diario*. Manetti told him to look at the French agrarian gazettes. Battarra put him into contact with Baretti and he even looked as far as Poland in search of inspiration and examples to follow, echoing the Commission for Education and projects of the French physiocrat, Gautier de Salgues. He wrote directly to the Marshal of the Realm, Francis Rzewuski and read Hume, together with a large number of books of 'political arithmetic', and just about everything that came out in Italy on techniques and economic policy.

In presenting his periodical Riccomanni attempted to place the history of Italian agriculture in the context of the general history of the country. The 'renaissance in literature and the arts' had been accompanied by a corresponding revival of agriculture and trade. Now the example came from outside, from Austria, Poland, Muscovy, Sweden. 'It was therefore essential that in Rome too there should be someone responsible for the encouragement of skills which were not only useful but necessary.' Improvement in tech-niques would lead to improvement in the economy. Potatoes, silk, vines, peat, land reclamation: in issue after issue he presented his readers with news of experiments and discoveries of academies all over Europe, with reports from the leading journals in every country with first place given, of course, to those taken from the 'excellent *Giornale d'Italia*', Francesco Griselini's review. But Ric-comanni's originality lay in the emphasis he always gave to the links between these problems and the more general economic and

political ones. Already in the sixth issue, of 10 February 1776, w
find 'Information about manufactures in England and France', whe
in a comparison made between the structure of the two state
following Hume, stress was laid upon the development of man
factures in France and Colbert's great gifts received recognitio
But what a price France had had to pay! Colbert's policy h
'encouraged farm workers to desert the countryside and becom
producers of luxury and the mainstay of a precarious trade, th
causing the decline of agriculture, by means of which Sul
accumulated for France a store of riches much more reliable th
the riches of Mexico or Peru'. Who was it to be then, Colbert
Sully? As in Paris, where a similar debate was taking place,
Rome as well the two ministers were becoming symbolic of tw
different kinds of policy. Riccomanni knew how difficult it w
to choose, but eventually, if somewhat cautiously, he cast his vo
in the direction of an agrarian policy, considered the necessa
condition of a general improvement.

So first Sully, and afterwards Colbert. But how was this to
accomplished? Riccomanni was very well disposed towards t
'true principles of economic science' of a man like Le Trosne,
typical physiocrat, but he also followed closely attempts to i
troduce new industries, particularly wool manufacture, into t
Papal States. In reading Verri, Hume and Condillac he was seekir
a way out of these contradictions and complexities. He was pro
ably the first Italian to place particular faith in a work which I
discussed at length in his *Diario*, Adam Smith's *Wealth of nation*
He had found there the confirmation of his deep conviction th
it was not gold but 'improved cultivation of the land, active ar
enlightened industry and regular work, wisely distributed amor
the members of the body politic' which constituted the true weal
of nations. It was a maxim which he would have liked to s
'stamped on the hearts of our statesmen (and they are many!) wh
pass their time in idleness and inertia'. Everything Smith said c
value convinced him and likewise all that he wrote on the divisic
of labour and the number of operations necessary to manufactu
a pin. But what had struck him most was a problem much close
to home. Was it a good thing for merchants' capital to be investe
in land? Would merchants really be capable of becoming goc
landowners? Riccomanni had his doubts. 'A landowner born in t
midst of agriculture will be able to carry out twice as many in
provements with the same expenditure.' Yet he agreed with Smit
on one point: 'The merchant who gives up trading usually has
much greater capital than the average country landowner.' In pa
centuries the improvement of the countryside had begun in th

towns. The English economist was right in asserting that this was proved by the example of the Italian communes. In conclusion he said that:

It becomes apparent that neither cultivation of the land nor trade should be neglected: this would certainly be a wise course, which in France could reconcile the supporters of Sully and Colbert, especially if we consider that since Sully found France completely uncultivated and in a state of total devastation, he would have been mad if he had attempted to enrich her by means of trade before providing her with the bread which she lacked. How can you trade if you have nothing to sell? Under Colbert France had an abundance of the necessary materials and it would not have been wise of him to think of increasing their quantity without providing a means of circulation and an outlet for them.

As he himself declared some time later, Abbé Riccomanni 'courageously' continued to bring out his journal for two years. 'But then publication ceased . . . We will not go into the reason for this: it is sufficient to say that the editors were not responsible.' Apparently the papal government would not tolerate the presence of a journal which rendered clearly and explicitly the doubts and uncertainties of its economic policy in those years, at the very moment when it had entered a more active phase. On 16 April 1777 all taxes and tolls were abolished on the transit of goods from place to place within the state; 10 December saw the publication of the edict concerning the creation of a land register. It seemed that the priority of the problems of the countryside was gaining the upper hand and being translated into facts. But when it came to implementing these provisions the deepseated inefficiency of the Papal States could be seen. The obstacles in the way of the abolition of tolls were still very great and provide an edifying example of the hard battle against local privileges. This can be deduced, for example, from Monsignor Giuseppe Giovenardi Bufferli's *Allegations*, which were quoted and discussed at length in the *Efemeridi letterarie di Roma*. As for the land register, 'the probable fear of the harm' which it 'would certainly have caused to the privileged classes if put into operation with adequate means of ensuring accuracy, counselled the adoption of a more moderate but at the same time less efficient measure'.

The rise, development and coordination of the activities of the agrarian societies, and the stepping up of the propaganda for economic improvement in the provinces and smallest towns, were all part of an attempt to remedy this state of weakness and uncertainty. The first move came from an out of the way province, from Montecchio, a town with a population of about seve thousand, not far from Macerata. Here a small group of enligh ened and cultured noblemen was attempting to do alone what the government had proved incapable of accomplishing. Fortunat Benigni, along with his brothers, Callisto and Telesforo, was the spirit behind this enterprise. And beside them was the indefatigab Luigi Riccomanni, the factotum of the group in Rome. On 2 July 1778 the half-dead Accademia dei Sollevati assumed the tit *georgic* and the plough, rake and spade became its symbols. I aims were to carry out experiments, spread the use of new culture explore and chart the surrounding territory and set up a worl house and a reformatory. Choosing new members was rather lik carrying out a voyage of exploration in the scientific, technic and economic life of the Europe of the time. On 19 June 177 Riccomanni sent from Rome a list of 'worthy men alive toda' who ought to be made members, and this included La Grang Prisley, Franklin, Toaldo, Buffon, Felice Fontana. In a postscrip he added: 'Make sure that you do yourselves justice. A hast farewell.' Those who were eventually persuaded to join provide good sample of the world of the most moderate, but also the mo active reformers from every corner of Italy at the end of th 'seventies: Manetti, Griselini, d'Asquino, Luigi Doria, Francesc Gemelli, Francesco Milizia, Spallanzani, Agostino Paradisi, Ferd nando Paoletti, etc. The circle was widening rapidly. Bertola wrot from Naples promising his support. Domenico Grimaldi, also fro Naples, wrote on 12 January 1782: 'I am very pleased to hear th news about the new Georgic Academy in Montecchio . . . I als derive a secret pleasure from the fact that my little work has ha some beneficial effect in the Papal States.' From Palermo Vincenz Emanuele Sergio established useful links which were to last fc some time. Sestini became a regular correspondent.

The prospects seemed good: had not a coal seam been di covered not far from Montecchio? Was there not hope of findin oil and perhaps even iron ore? The letters exchanged betwee Benigni in Montecchio and Riccomanni in Rome around 1779 an 1780 were full of enthusiastic plans and schemes. In 1780 th *Giornale delle arti e del commercio* began to appear in Macerat Here Battarra resumed with particular vehemence his criticisms c the agrarian situation in the Papal States and, alongside review of the works of Frisi, Todeschi etc., we find reproduced wit commentaries some of the most representative works of Italia agronomy of the time, as for example the essay *On the cultivatio of the chestnut to be introduced in Dalmatia* by Abbé Forti Riccomanni in Rome did his best to circulate the periodical. In letter to his brother Pietro, written on 18 November 1781, Alessandro Verri described how this lawyer and scholar had enthusiastically acquired the reprint of the *Meditations on political economy* in a Rome bookshop and how, a year later, when he was again meditating upon this work, 'He stopped suddenly at the paragraph concerning trade in cereals and exclaimed with the book open in his hands: "here is the truth, but they refuse to understand, here is the real treasure of the state".'

Neither Riccomanni nor his friends in Montecchio and Macerata had any illusions. They knew very well how many obstacles were placed in their way by the 'way of thinking of the priests in Rome'. They were not unaware, as their friend Romolo Grimaldi said in a letter to Riccomanni, on the last day of 1784, that they were living 'in the Papal States, home of sluggishness and irresolution'. Yet they did witness a great increase in new initiatives. In Corneto an agrarian academy was founded which allied itself with the one at Montecchio. Romolo Grimaldi expressed 'our happiness at the fortunate union of the two societies which have the same aim in view, the improvement of agriculture'. Ambitions were growing in Montecchio. Everyone wanted a more autonomous administration. Why should they continue to be subject to the Bishop of Camerino and not have better, more efficient local authorities? Riccomanni was officially charged with obtaining all this in Rome by drawing up and publishing memoirs and petitions, recalling Montecchio's past and giving vigorous expression to its present needs. And why not resume the ancient name of Treja? Why not demand more substantial funds and greater support for local initiative? Something of the spirit of the communes seemed to have revived and when the first breath of the French Revolution arrived on the hills of the Marche, this earned for Benigni the accusation of being a political agitator and a Jacobin. Meanwhile the other members of the Academy had not been wasting their time. Even the monument which the town erected to Pius VI came to be one of the more curious manifestations of the reforming spirit in the Papal States: the Pope was honoured there as the man who had successfully fought against vagrancy and unemployment and who had allowed the introduction into Treja of a more modern, stricter discipline of work in fields and workshops. Right up to the end of his life (1788) Riccomanni attempted to personify this reforming ideal. Together with Benigni he discussed elementary and professional schools, never ceasing at the same time to look beyond the confines of the Papal States, for example to Savoy, Tuscany, England and France.

After Montecchio an agrarian academy was founded in Urbania, and in addition to those in Corneto and Macerata, one also came into being in Foligno. In 1786 the *Efemeridi letterarie* said that the 'increasing number of georgic societies' were 'so many points of light which, in a short space of time, must certainly bring great benefit to our agriculture and cause it to be greatly improved'. At the same time, through local initiative, often backed by Cardinals Pallotta and Casali, there was a great increase in the number of pamphlets of agronomic propaganda, recommending the introduction of turnips, potatoes and maize and discussing arboriculture or the breeding of silkworms. The style in which these pamphlets were written, often deliberately coarse, and their insistence upon the social aspects of these technical problems (famine, the fight against ignorance, prejudices etc.) gave a clear indication of the state of mind which caused them to be produced.

The other most interesting centre for these ideas, doing similar work to that of the Montecchio group, was based on an intelligent little publication called *L'Agricoltore*. This too was a creation of the provinces and was directly influenced by and subordinate to Tuscan ideas. It was published in Perugia and Assisi from 1784 by Angelo Fabbroni. If it is true that 'an important contribution' to this periodical was made by 'the well-known Signor Giovanni', brother of Adamo Fabbroni, it is easier to understand how these reforming ideas from the world of Peter Leopold came to be asserted in papal territory. The most direct and immediate appeal was aimed at the parish priests in the hope that they would take the lead in the process of transformation of agriculture.

> Would to God that the clerics could be convinced of this truth and that with their honoured position as leaders of the people they had refrained or might still refrain from engaging in pointless disputes, from writing about minutiae and from fulminating against those who disagree with them on some detail. In this way they would waste less time and cause less trouble.

'The long-awaited reform is the province of the young priests . . .' was the conclusion of this article, signed 'A member of the Florentine Academy of Georgofili' and, in fact, written by Pelli. The reform was to include the abolition of common lands and the definition and assertion of private ownership. It would put an end to cereal monoculture, spread new techniques, introduce land reclamation and, above all, instil a new mentality into both owners and peasants. Instead of concerning itself with disputes over the doctrine of grace, with its Jansenist or Molinist overtones, the clergy ought to turn its attention to a positive improvement of the economic life and social activity of the countryside.

L'Agricoltore hence showed great interest in the pastoral letter of Monsignor Paolantonio Agostini Zamperoli, who, not content with establishing the agrarian academy in Urbania (the second chronologically to be set up in the Papal States), now addressed himself to his parish priests, exhorting them to become the instruments of a technical improvement throughout the diocese. The editors of *L'Agricoltore* were well aware of what the 'dreadful scourge of hunger' was. If they wished to see the widespread introduction of potatoes ('a root by now well known in Italy but unfortunately too little cultivated'), it was precisely because they hoped that they would become 'the staple diet of the people, as they are especially in England and France' and thus in Italy too provide protection against famine. They provide some delightful details about the way in which even the upper classes in Perugia had finally made their acquaintance with the potato : 'a noble lady of this city, among those who, by their dedication to philosophy, rise above the throng', had finally decided, together with a 'learned canon', to taste and enjoy 'a pudding made from potatoes'. Discussions of technical questions in the periodical were always placed within a wider framework. We have only to think of the persistent quotation of passages from Gibbon on the history of the agriculture of ancient Rome. The agronomic information spread by the journal was utilised by A. Fabbroni in his *Elementary instructions in agriculture*, published in Perugia in 1786, which was meant to be a book 'capable of being understood by ignorant peasants and at the same time appreciated by theoreticians and learned men'.

We shall not stop to consider the polemics aroused in Bologna in those same years by the reforming work of Cardinal Boncompagni, but instead shall return to the centre, to Rome. There too, the beginning of the 'eighties saw a much greater discussion of the most difficult problem of all. The Agro Romano was completely static with its malaria, its latifundia, its privileges and its poverty. A measure was passed in 1783 which attempted to extend the area of land used for growing corn. It had little practical effect but started up more fierce debates. In that same year there appeared Filippo Campilli's previously unpublished work, *An Historical account of the corn shortage which occurred in Italy in 1764*. At the same time the publisher Pagliarini reprinted two *Pamphlets on the cultivation of the Roman Campagna* by Ferdinando Nuzzi and Angelo Gabrielli, thus harking back to the debates of the beginning of the century and involuntarily giving further proof of how little anything had really changed in the Papal States. In those same years enthusiastic expressions of approval arrived from all sides for the work undertaken by Pius VI in the Pontine Marshes. This was a clear indication of the importance that 'agrarian' policy had assumed and, at the same time, proof of Rome's inability to face up to the fundamental problems which the reformers had outlined and to which they had been trying to draw attention for decades. The draining of the Pontine Marshes avoided the grave implications of conflict with the nobles and great ecclesiastical holdings which would have been the inevitable outcome of any attempt to touch the Agro Romano.

One of the most important and lucid works to appear in the 'eighties was devoted to the subject of the Agro Romano: *On the means of introducing and maintaining cultivation and the level of population in the Agro Romano* (1785) by Francesco Maria Cacherano di Bricherasio, a Piedmontese, member of a family of soldiers and administrators, who arrived in Rome in 1756. He had had first hand knowledge of papal Italy in his capacity as governor at Todi, Civitavecchia, Fano, Jesi and Montalto. In 1783 he published in Macerata a short work *On the storing of grain and the construction and form of storehouses and granaries*. Should grain be exported at the highest possible prices, in order to serve the interests of the big producers, or should it be sold at low prices to defend the 'purely consumer class, which is also useful to society on so many scores, if it is active and benefits the producers themselves by consuming their products'? He had been a frequent witness of the tragic consequences of this conflict. 'There will be a poor year, the price of grain doubles, trebles and the people become demoralised and suffer great hardship'. It was really 'a very difficult problem to solve', that of 'finding a means of ensuring that the price of grain is not so low that agriculture becomes depressed and comes to a standstill, or so steep that it threatens the subsistence of the consumer class, which has to obtain it by means of its labours and industry, and is thereby subjected to greater hardships . . . and causes the decline of crafts and manufactures'.

Faced with the choice between a physiocratic and neomercantilist policy, Cacherano felt that the solution lay, in the final analysis, in a vigorous increase in production to be achieved by means of land reclamation and transformation, particularly in the Agro Romano. Unless this was carried out Rome's situation would always be precarious, a city without manufactures, where the cost of living was too high to permit any development of artisan activity. Rome was also too large (one only had to compare it with Turin), and it lived on luxury and in luxury while exploiting and impoverishing the provinces. Only by a change in the relationship between the capital and the surrounding territories could a healthy economic life be created in the Papal States. But why had little or nothing been done up to that moment? The causes were not natural ones, malaria etc., but political and social. The big landowners were opposed to any change, preferring stock-breeding to agriculture. 'Fierce opposition on the part of the wealthy landowners' had arisen continually and caused every attempt to fail. As Mably said, it was always those who made a profit out of abuses who turned the people away from agrarian laws. Going back to Roman times, it was from these people that the condemnations and curses which poisoned the memory of the Gracchi had come. The whole history of the Agro Romano, from republican times onwards, appeared in Cacherano's eyes as a struggle between the powerful and the consumers. This was largely responsible for the abandonment of the countryside around Rome, the malaria and the desolation. For centuries the provisioning laws had been, and were still, equally harmful. And besides, if these were the obstacles, one had to admit that the urge to overcome them had always been extremely weak and feeble. Tactfully but firmly, he criticised all the measures taken by Popes from the sixteenth century onwards. Even when the laws had been less bad, it had been easy enough for those who wished to ignore them completely. The state should now take possession of at least part of the Agro Romano and divide it up after taking upon itself the expense of land reclamation, housing, roads, churches and agrarian improvement.

If we compare Cacherano's precise, well-defined, technically detailed plan with Cardinal Nuzzi's words, we can measure the ground covered in almost a century of discussions. When Compagnoni in Bologna read this book, he wrote enthusiastically in the *Memorie enciclopediche*: 'Our self-respect had been preserved until now by making us desire *sovereignty* or *ministry*. This seed of ambition has suddenly flowered in our hearts as we read this book full of sound and reliable ideas'. It really seemed as though the moment had arrived when the ideas would be translated into facts.

But even at this eleventh hour, the practical result of all these proposals was negligible. Cacherano ruined his administrative career with this project which, despite the fact that it favoured a moderate, gradual process of reform, was accused of being utopian. Above all, the great financial effort which would be required seemed out of all proportion to the actual possibilities. And many other similar projects which hinged on the transformation of the countryside met no better fate. *L'Agricoltore* was

forced to 'abandon its undertaking after three years'. 'It was un
able to continue a venture where the public derived all the benefit
and the editor all the blame.' Even the many interesting proposal
arriving from abroad in those years, from all over Europe, had n
power to change the situation. In Neuchâtel in 1783 the publicis
Brissot de Warville published a review which was a kind of bulleti
of European reforms. At almost the same time in Venice ther
appeared an Italian translation of *Universal correspondence abou
every kind of literature,* the first volume of which containe
'Reflections on the depopulation and infertility of the Roma
countryside'. This was one of the most violent attacks to be mad
in these years against the vast Roman estates.

> It is true that the territory around Rome is depopulated an
> badly cultivated, but the reason for this is that it is so badl
> distributed. The trouble is that Rome, unlike other Europea
> states, has no middle class. The whole countryside is divide
> among princes, abbeys and mortmains . . . The properties i
> the hands of parish priests, cathedrals and convent chapters ar
> for the most part deteriorating . . . Vast estates are very harm
> ful to society . . . They are inhabited only by the slaves of th
> owners and the day-labourers they employ to cultivate them

Instead they should become 'the heritage of an enormous numbe
of families and provide a living for those driven out of the countr
by the acquisitions of the rich'. Those lands should be divided int
emphyteuses 'in plots of 300 perches with the ground ren
calculated on the basis of the present yield'. Likewise 'some chec
should also be applied on entails'. There were, of course, numerou
classical reminiscences. 'These laws against the inequality o
fortune were the cause of the prosperity and abundant populatio
of the Greeks and early Romans. All were citizens because a
were owners.' In conclusion he said: 'Let the ownership of th
nation's land be divided among the citizens in equal or at leas
not too disproportionate parts . . . The only way to restore peac
to Italy is by crushing the pride of some feudatories and impover
ishing various rich lords.'

As we can see, the projects which from time to time made thei
appearance in Rome in the course of the eighteenth century ha
by this time begun to assume the tones and accents of the imminen
Revolution. More moderate but no less interesting is the con
temporary judgment of a young Frenchman of physiocrati
formation, Count Claude Camille François d'Albon. The secon
volume of his *Discours sur l'histoire, le gouvernement, les usages
la littérature et les arts de plusieurs nations de l'Europe,* publishe

in 1782, was devoted to Italy which he had visited shortly before. He said that the wellbeing and happiness of the Pope's subjects were illusory. It was true that prices and taxes were low but this meant that the state was so weak financially that it did not have the possibility of carrying out any economic reforms. Beside this, the remaining taxes, although low, weighed 'presque en entier sur la misère'. The machinery needed to exact the taxes was extremely costly and attempts at improvement were generally halfhearted and completely inadequate. The result was that

> les treize provinces soumises en Italie à la domination du pape ne forment qu'un état qui paroît désolé par les fléaux and dévasté par des guerres tant il est pauvre et languissant . . . Entrez dans les villes, vous les trouverez presque dépourvues d'habitants, si vous en sortez pour aller jouir du spectacle de la campagne, vous ne voyez que des champs sans culture ou mal cultivés : vous croyriez le pays abandonné et entièrement désert si des mendiants couverts de haillons ne venoient vous importuner et si de loin en loin vous ne rencontriez quelques paysans dont l'air, l'habillement, le triste maintien annoncent la misère.

In Rome they had not understood even the most elementary principles of political economy. Even the critics had often been mistaken in their diagnoses. The trouble lay not in the 'forme du gouvernement' but in the 'manière de gouverner'. For centuries the attempt to maintain a state of plenty had meant the death of all competition; as a means of controlling the economy a network of monopolies had been created. They wanted charity and they got indolence. By this time it was very difficult to carry out reforms. The people had one fear : that there would be a bread shortage. 'Cette idée l'inquiète et l'effarouche. Il faut ménager sa faiblesse.' Only gradually and very cautiously had a few steps been taken in the direction of free trading in cereals. 'Cependant l'ouvrage n'est encore que commencé. Si l'on s'arrêtoit et qu'on le laissait dans cet état d'imperfection on n'opéreroit jamais la révolution qu'il annonce.' Similar though less explicit conclusions were reached in Germany by Johann Friedrich Le Bret, who knew eighteenth-century Italy well. He devoted a whole volume of his *Vorlesungen über die Statistik* (1785) to a detailed discussion of the situation, giving us an excellent picture, perhaps the best still extant, of the Papal States in the 1780s. In 1788, in London, there appeared Thomas Denham's work on *The Temporal government of the Pope's State*, the product of a thorough enquiry carried out in Rome by the author, together with one of the most colourful figures in England in those years, Frederick Hervey, Earl of Bristol,

Baron of Ickworth and Bishop of Derry, to whom the book w
dedicated.

> Your Lordship . . . with infinite spirit and perseverance h
> visited almost every part of the Pope's State, informing you
> self minutely of every particular respecting agriculture, man
> factures and polity. You have formed your opinion, not fro
> the parade and ostentation of the great in Rome, but from tl
> plaintive, yet faithfull accounts of the bulk of the people. Yc
> judged from your own observation, and your heart sympathise
> with the unhappy. You could not avoid perceiving a similari
> of situation between them and the common people of Irelan
> the sentiment invigorated your patriotism, a holy zeal inflame
> your affections.

Vast estates, wretched peasants, public debt, ignorance: ever
thing recalled far-away Ireland. Denham gave a detailed descriptic
of the corruption, incompetence and unwieldiness of the machine
of the Pope's economic administration. The Roman provisionii
organ (*Annona*) was an 'abominable institution'. 'The state
agriculture in general is languishing to the verge of ruin.' Tl
comparison with Tuscany was disastrous for the Papal States.
seemed to him that, all things considered, the prelates who co
trolled the various branches of the Apostolic Chamber were mo
ignorant than corrupt, although he cited numerous cases where tl
opposite was true. It was certain that 'all ideas of improvement a
treated as visionary and scoffed at by these self-sufficient men'.

Why, after so many analyses and exhortations, so much agr
nomic propaganda and so many projects for land reclamatio
did the papal government, at the end of the 'eighties, take up Lio
Pascoli's antiquated programme and launch into an anachronist
attempt at a mercantilist policy? Why, after spending so mu
time discussing the respective merits of Sully and Colbert a
repeatedly asserting that it was first of all necessary to look to tl
fields and the provinces and to follow a policy which resembl
the Tuscan one, did they decide in the final analysis, through tl
work of Fabrizio Ruffo, to adopt a policy modelled more
Neapolitan lines, protectionism and prohibitionism aimed at d
veloping national manufactures? It is not easy to answer this que
tion. Undoubtedly financial reasons carried great weight. Agrari
reforms cost more than tariff reforms. Social reasons were also
considerable importance: we have seen how the men of the tir
knew very well that to touch the Agro Romano, abolish tl
Annona or change the relationship between the capital and tl
provinces would have meant first of all a clash with the aristocrac

both lay and ecclesiastical. We must also not discount the influence of those who had an immediate interest in the development of manufactures, who preferred to keep the Agro Romano as pasture-land so that they could use the wool of its flocks and those who were counting upon the privileges, monopolies and subsidies which went with a mercantilist policy. In spite of all the difficulties and obstacles, there had been a certain development of manufacturing activity. Denham noted it too: 'Upon the whole, though the efforts for introducing manufactures have been hitherto feeble and wrongly directed, yet they are certainly increased within these years.' These manufactures exerted their influence in the capital itself. The position of the Papal States in Italy, on the other hand, led to a clash, or at least a conflict with the two states who stood to gain most from the development of a free trade policy, Tuscany and Venice. In any case, throughout Italy the influence of anti-physiocratic and anti-free-trade ideas could once more be felt, in combination with the newer, more modern arguments in favour of manufactures and a growing awareness that the exclusively agricultural countries were also the poorest and most unfortunate. Galiani and Carli were read and their words heeded. The French model was gradually being eclipsed by the English one. All these trends influenced Cardinal Ruffo's policy, although it was basically inspired by the old mercantilist model, the tradition of Uztáriz, Ulloa and Pascoli and the old local tradition of the Papal States. The very limited success which the more advanced reforming ideas had had in penetrating the Roman ruling class now made its effects felt. 'Étoit-ce dans le Sacré Collège, même à la fin du dix-huitième siècle, que la philosophie pouvoit trouver son asyle?', wrote François de Bourgoing in 1800.

On 26 April 1786 customs barriers were set up on the borders and, after much talking and a great deal of uncertainty, a tariff was fixed. The process of applying it was slow, painful and incomplete. There was strong opposition, particularly from the Legations, which had been exempted only provisionally and feared that they would soon be included in the common tariff area. Ferrara, included in 1790, was immediately exempted again. Bologna put up particularly strong resistance. This opposition to a reform which should have led to the economic unification of the Papal States was a major factor in its disintegration.

Under the influence of Fabrizio Ruffo's policy, there was a rapid crystallisation of the two trends which had come to the surface, with varying degrees of coherence according to the time and the men concerned, during the course of the preceding decades. Paolo Vergani was the fairly intelligent spokesman for the mercantilist policy and Nicola Corona was able to give effective expressic to the ideas of those who, after starting from a physiocrat position, by this time were leaning towards a more egalitaria distribution of land and a fight against luxury and the privileges the aristocracy and the clergy.

Vergani, educated in the Milan of Firmian, Carli, Verri ar Beccaria, had hoped for a time to find a place for himself in t world of Maria Theresa's reforms and then to go to Spain to wo alongside Campomanes in revising the laws of Charles III's kin dom. He brought to the narrow, closed world of the Papal Stat a wider experience which enabled him to provide a quite remar able diagnosis of Rome's troubles—even if it was not matched a forceful application of remedies. According to Vergani, it w not just the discoveries nor the change of the trade routes whic brought about the decline of the great age of trade in Rome ar throughout Italy in the sixteenth century. The policy of t *signorie* was equally to blame for this phenomenon. Instead protecting the economy of their own countries, the Italian prince including the Popes, had indulged in spending on luxuries, t building of great palaces and magnificent towns. This course h rapidly resulted in impoverishment. Other nations had followed very different path from that trodden by Italy—England, f example, which Vergani once again suggested as a model, Colbert France and the Spain of Uztáriz, Ulloa and Campomanes. In h attempt to define his own economic programme Vergani pai particular consideration, among his contemporaries, to the worl of Galiani, Genovesi, Carli and also Pietro Verri. He was always violent conflict with the physiocrats and eventually became ca tivated by Adam Smith.

The result was a programme which aimed at using custon barriers to stimulate local production not only or particularly luxury goods, but remembering that these too were essential in modern economy (unlike De Miller, Vergani does not distinguis in his policy between different types of products). The limitatio of his programme and his mentality become more apparent as o reads on in his work: the lack of capital to inject into his pr posals for revival, the obstacles which would be encountered b his plan for customs barriers on account of the widely differin economic factors to be taken into consideration in the variou territories which comprised the Papal States. It is also clear th there was a danger of discouraging existing trade (the fairs Sinigallia were a typical example) without managing to crea new manufactures. What is missing, above all, is the driving forc which had accompanied similar programmes and projects in Spa and in the Naples of Genovesi and his pupils, a determination to forge an insoluble link between mercantilism and protectionism and the fight against privileges, against legal, political and moral obstacles and the traditional barriers which stood in the way of economic development in the country, from tax exemptions to mortmains, from special jurisdictions to municipal provisioning systems, from the lack of roads to inadequate schools. The reasons for these gaps are easy to see. Reforms like these would, of necessity, have encroached upon the privileges of the clergy. And these privileges could only be fought effectively by embracing the spirit and enthusiasm of the enlightened reformer. This Vergani did not possess and, though his programme was lucid and significant, it remained lifeless, lacking any inward capacity to develop and assert itself.

His violent polemic against the physiocrats is extremely revealing for it derived directly from his own unwillingness and that of his government to be drawn onto a wider terrain which would unite in a single vision both commerce and agriculture, manufactures and the transformation of landed property. His hostility to physiocracy is the most conservative element in his policy, even if by this time he could support his polemic against the 'economists' with arguments taken from authors from countries which were developing industrially, particularly the English. Thus Adam Smith could teach him that 'manufactures have been the cause of the present improvement of the land in England itself'. But meanwhile in the Papal States, while waiting for some future development of manufactures, agricultural relationships remained unaltered, Rome continued to be a zone privileged in its provisions and no one dared lay a finger on ecclesiastical property. It is true that Vergani had before him the example of Bologna to strengthen his adherence to this line: 'Since there are in this city many more manufactures than in any other part of the Papal States and its territory is also the best cultivated in the land and perhaps in the whole of Italy.' But he did not examine the economic and political elements and the contradictions which arose precisely out of this state of development of the towns of Emilia and which would lead them to oppose his tariff laws and those of Cardinal Ruffo and make Emilia the main centre of revolt against their tardy attempts at mercantilist concentration in the Papal States.

If we follow the complicated fortunes of the Corona family who moved to Rome from Sora, we can witness the formation of a violent opposition among the educated classes to what the physician Camillo Corona called 'the Pope's meretricious financial system, from which the state derives no benefit and honest men much inconvenience'. In 1795 Nicola, under the pseudonym Stefan Laonice, published his *Economic, political and moral reflection on agriculture, population, manufactures and commerce in th Papal States*, the most substantial attack to be made in those year against 'the reawakened mania for the teachings of Colbert Amazed by the quantity of hardships and sacrifices that the pr tectionist policy of Cardinal Ruffo and Vergani was imposing o the subjects of Pius VI, shocked by all the privileges which th Pope's economic policy aimed to maintain intact or increase, an horrified by the overwhelming luxury which he saw, Nicol Corona was persuaded to take a step backwards and join up wit the agricultural tradition of the free-traders and physiocrats, onc more proclaiming the cultivation of the fields as the sole basis c all wellbeing and seeing all progress in terms of an improvement i the lives of the peasants and in agrarian techniques. First the field then manufactures. First the fight against luxury and privilege an then the development of industries. It was a step backward wit regard to neomercantilism, but at the same time it was a mov toward the egalitarian, popular mentality of the Jacobins. It wa precisely the slowness with which reforms were carried out in th Papal States, their incomplete, defective character and the fact tha they failed to reach the roots of the problems (from the estate belonging to the Church and the nobility to the reorganisation c finances) which led Laonice to adopt the most radical themes c the reformers and economists of twenty or thirty years previousl and to embrace a more optimistic and utopian vision.

The *Giornale letterario di Napoli* was impressed by Corona' views on luxury and his defence and description of agriculture. N one objected any longer, said the review, 'to the encouragement c manufactures in an agricultural state'. 'But Signor Laonice has The whole of the second part of his first volume was dedicated t proving that 'agriculture is the essential basis of the wealth of an state and must be promoted before manufactures and commerce It would be absurd for the Papal States to try to imitate the Eng lish or the Dutch or to be dazzled by the example of Colbert. I was necessary to take a firm stand against all those who ha allowed themselves to be 'deceived along with Colbert', particu larly Uztáriz and Ulloa, in whose works Ruffo and Vergani ha sought inspiration and support for their opinions. In order t oppose them, it was necessary to follow Boisguilbert and th physiocrats and in particular the example of land reclamation an colonisation provided by Frederick II in Prussia, both for the forc fulness with which he had carried out the operation and for th way in which he had distributed land to the peasants. Not tha

Corona was in favour of an 'agrarian law', but he saw the need to divide up the lands belonging to the *latifondisti* (like Prince Borghese for example). 'The farmer needs to be enticed by the promise of owning his own land.' At the very centre of his programme was the 'system for allocation of land based on the size of the farmer's family'.

The second volume was concerned with the results of following such a policy. The population would increase only if there was development of agriculture. Ancient Italy and modern France provided proof of the fact that the population could only increase where there were abundant provisions and food prices were low. 'The disproportion of population in the Papal States', as he had already noted, was basically the result of the 'decline of agriculture'. A detailed comparison with the situation of the other Italian states furnished further proof of this thesis. When agriculture had begun to flourish, then and only then should manufactures be encouraged and developed. In Rome the opposite had been done, with grave consequences. 'And thus the whole working class languishes in idleness and poverty when there is a lack of people to demand their products. Therefore it is necessary to work on the premise that it is not manufactures which must go out looking for buyers but the buyers who must come to the manufactures.' It would be better to follow the example of Ireland which was in a position not unlike that of the Papal States and where an effort was made first of all to improve the conditions of agriculture and the peasants. However, one need only consider the whole of Italy. What was the reason for its inferiority compared to foreign countries if not precisely the fact that 'the order of progression necessary for the development of industry and the increase of manufactures had always been disregarded'? 'All the benefits and rewards, enticements and favours have always been offered to the artisans while the farmers have remained despised and oppressed.' Thus Italians had gone against a natural law. 'If it ever happens that this order of progression is disturbed and an attempt is made to introduce crafts before the nation has reached a stage of sufficient maturity to support manufactures, they neither grow nor develop but on the contrary wither and perish.' And much the same could be said about commerce, to which Corona devoted the last part of his work. His conclusion was tinged with economic liberalism, though of a very moderate and cautious kind. The last of his numerous quotations was taken from Adam Smith—a statement concerning the importance of culture in the general development of a country. In order to combat Vergani and the late mercantilism of the Papal States, he had mobilised both the old egalitarian, physiocratic polemics and the most modern conceptions of economic freedom. His desire was, as he said in his *Conclusion*, that 'in the future there should be born more Catos than Luculluses'.

We can sense that we are already in the age of the French Revolution. Vergani and Corona had brought into what was now a different era the voice, and to some extent the contradictory conclusions, of a century of discussions and attempts at reform in the Papal States.

11 Spanish and Italian Economists and Reformers in the Eighteenth Century

A N investigation into the connections between Italian economists and reformers and their Spanish counterparts during the eighteenth century means a journey from southern to northern Italy, from Sicily to Lombardy by way of the Papal States and Tuscany; at the same time it means tracing the whole evolution of thought in the two countries from Uztáriz's mercantilism to Valentín de Foronda's free trade policy and liberalism. This is a curious, winding path but one which, if it sometimes risks skating over rather than exploring in depth the problems of the two countries in the eighteenth century, will nevertheless, we feel, eventually lead us to a renewed and not inaccurate vision of Italy and Spain in the Age of Enlightenment.

When the Marquis of Bedmar, Viceroy of Sicily, arrived in Palermo in 1705 he had at his side the man who was destined to become the most influential Spanish economist in the early part of the eighteenth century, Gerónimo de Uztáriz. He was to remain on the island for two years as Secretary of State and War, subsequently returning to Spain in 1707. These were troubled years. Spanish rule in Italy was in the process of collapsing and the future of the Iberian peninsula was likewise uncertain. This is the situation which forms the background to Uztáriz's great book *Theory and practice of commerce and shipping*, of which the author published a very small number of copies, reserved for high officials in Madrid in 1724.

Italy was far from absent from this mature programme of Spanish mercantilism. On the contrary, Italy seems to offer the proof of his ideas, precisely on a point of particular importance.

He stressed the need to re-establish a favourable balance of trade in Spain. To do this it was necessary to encourage manufactures. But was there a large enough population? Would there be enough hands for agriculture and for workshops? The example provided by Italy suggested to Uztáriz that the answer was yes. 'It has a much smaller population than Spain yet nevertheless possesses an abundance of workers for the great quantity of excellent cloth which is produced in Turin, Milan, Genoa, Lucca, Venice, Florence, Naples, Messina, Palermo and other cities, without there being on this account any lack of men to cultivate the land and carry out other necessary functions.' In general, compared with the desolation of Spain, even the situation in Italy at the beginning of the eighteenth century seemed relatively rich and prosperous. Uztáriz's optimistic evaluation was not just a question of memories from the past and historical reminiscences. The major centres were manufacturing towns and their products were often quite exceptional ('most of the paper that is used in the dominions of His Majesty is made in Genoa and elsewhere with rags from Spain'). The commercial policy of some of these cities was very daring. Witness for example the relationship between Genoa and Sicily:

> Between Sicily and Genoa there is frequent and reciprocal trade: Sicily abounds in silk and grain which are scarce in Genoa . . .; and since Sicily does not need Genoese merchandise to the equivalent value of that which she sells to Genoa, the Genoese find themselves obliged to make it up in money, thus depriving themselves (even with great violence) of what they most seek to gain; and thus it is clear that when they send their ships to Sicily for silk and grain, they usually take as part of their ballast chests crammed with Genoese doubloons, coins of high quality silver, held in great account throughout Italy; and this offers proof of how strong the secret force of commerce is and how active and efficacious are its natural trends and movements, that a nation as economical and sagacious as Genoa can be stripped and despoiled of its best coin.

As is natural, France and Holland remained for Uztáriz the fundamental models upon which he continued to base his economic policy. A few decades later his disciple and standard-bearer, Bernardo Ulloa, would continue on the path opened by the master. In his *Re-establishment of factories and commerce in Spain*, published in 1740, he did not fail to cite examples from Venice and Genoa regarding the development of trade and shipping, without forgetting that great slave-trader, the Genoese Grillo.

The works of Uztáriz and Ulloa were both made known to a

much wider European public in the middle of the century, in 1753, during the fiscal and monetary crisis which followed the War of the Austrian Succession. Their translators, Forbonnais and Plumard de Danguel, both had an excellent knowledge of the various countries of Europe, including the Italian states. Forbonnais had devoted particular attention to them. He added to his translation of Uztáriz a long introduction and a series of penetrating notes where Italy's problems recur constantly. A survey of the history of commerce from the Middle Ages down to his day made him see proof in the cities of Italy of the primordial importance of manufactures. When these declined, he said: 'le commerce et le rang de l'Italie se trouva réduit à ce qu'elle avait conservé d'industrie'. When he came to the modern era, he proved to be better informed than Uztáriz on Italy's demographic situation and with great insight underlined the considerable differences which could be observed, even from this point of view, between the various parts of the peninsula:

> L'Italie paroît presqu'aussi peuplée que la Catalogne, excepté dans l'Ombrie et le reste de l'Etat Ecclésiastique, jusqu'aux frontières de Naples le long des côtes, dans quelques marèmes de Toscane et dans les montagnes de l'Apennin. En revanche le Piémont, le Plaisantin, le Milanois, l'état de Venise, la Toscane, le Boulonnois, Naples, la Calabre renferment plusieurs villes très peuplées et les campagnes sont bien cultivées.

He too was convinced that Italy could show that, as Uztáriz had written, 'the advancement of manufactures owes half its effectiveness to the way in which agriculture is encouraged and made to flourish'. Fourbonnais too looked to the past history of Italian cities for confirmation of this fact.

However, neither the Spanish author of the work, nor his French translator and not even Bernardo Ulloa or Plumard de Danguel, the man who translated his work into French, seemed to think that the neomercantilism which they were planning would be applicable to Italy, nor that there existed a set of immediate problems which were common to both Italy and Spain. Perhaps the first man to realise this, who, valuing greatly the experience of these writers, attempted to apply it to the situation in Italy, was Antonio Genovesi. He was acquainted with Uztáriz and Ulloa through the French translations and they were decisive texts in his intellectual formation. This was not a mere fashion or a passing enthusiasm. The reason for the success of these Spanish writers in Naples in the 1750s was deeprooted. In Naples, as in Madrid, the urge to re-establish the balance of trade met with all the count-

less obstacles which in both countries were the legacy of the pas
from tolls to mortmains, from technical backwardness to lac
of roads. And there was one circumstance in particular whic
linked them in a common destiny. Though in different ways ar
to a varying extent, they were both countries which were i
capable, but desirous, of achieving an independent economic polic
They were envious of French mercantilism and of the spirit whic
the English and the Dutch showed in trading, but they were powe
less to free themselves from the numerous heavy burdens whic
the Treaty of Utrecht had imposed on both Spain and Naple
Countries at the same time backward and ambitious, they we
both dominated by a political situation which was slipping fro
their grasp and by economic circumstances which required e
ceptional effort and energy to bring them under control. Only
dynamic reform policy, as Uztáriz and Ulloa had predicted, cou
extricate them from the situation into which they had been forc
by centuries of decline.

All his life Genovesi retained his well-founded enthusiasm f
the works of the two Spanish writers. When he had only just beg
to teach his course on political economy, he was already calli
Uztáriz's work 'most scholarly'. He quoted constantly from it
length with accompanying praise, together with Ulloa's wor
and termed the latter's book 'the finest work to be written abo
trade in our time'. When he was revising the second edition
his *Lessons on commerce*, towards the end of his life, he conclud
that 'the two learned, wise, far-sighted Spaniards, Uztáriz and Ullo
were worthy of the greatest praise'. He had in fact learned muc
from their writings. To them he owed in no small degree h
introduction to the wider range of European discussions and d
putes, which a man like Broggia, for example, lacked. Broggia w
not devoid of talent and character but was nevertheless incapab
of exerting an influence on his country and generation comparab
to that of Genovesi. The latter owed to Uztáriz and Ulloa son
of his fundamental ideas on active and passive trade and t
relationship between size of population and economic develo
ment, between the need to form a national market and the e
pansion of foreign trade.

When the ideas of Uztáriz finally began to be put into practi
in Spain and became, as Campomanes stressed from then on, t
very basis of Charles III's economic policy, Genovesi's ideas t
were given a warm reception in Spain. He was often quoted ar
eventually, in 1784, his *Lessons* were translated by Victorian
Villava, professor at Huesca. There were two editions of the boc
which aroused considerable interest and was talked about for son

time. The translator added a number of notes which helped to place Genovesi's work in a Spanish context by continually referring the reader back to the local situation, to the popular superstitions in Aragon, the difficulties which reform of the university or the introduction of vaccination against smallpox were encountering in Spain, to the discussions aroused by Campomanes and Lardizábal or again to the 'mournful spectacle' of a prolonged passive balance of trade. The world around Victorian de Villava was already very different from the world of Genovesi and he was well acquainted with Raynal's ideas and those of the physiocrats, besides the books of Galiani, Carli and Filangieri. But he constantly returns to Uztáriz as to the source of all economic thought in Spain in the eighteenth century. It remains his basic point of reference. He persists in his campaign against élites and privileges inside the country and intervenes energetically, for example, against corporations. But at the heart of his conception remained the idea of state intervention to stimulate manufactures and improve Spain's relations with other countries.

In 1775 the Spanish translation of Ferdinando Galiani's *Dialogues* was also grafted onto this traditional trunk of eighteenth-century economic thought. We have not succeeded in establishing the identity of the translator, but he signed the dedication to the *Dialogues on the wheat trade, attributed to Abbé Galiani, translated from the French* with the initials F.A.D.L.C. In just over half a page at the beginning he offered a justification of his work, saying that

> although there are many these days who could read the original, since the French language is so well known, there are also many who do not understand, especially in the interior of the provinces, where the doctrine it contains would perhaps be of most relevance; besides, the original might have much more difficulty in finding acceptance than the translation, purged of certain slips which, however amusing, are not compatible with the dignity and gravity of our censors, nor with the serious character of our nation.

The translator also recalled how the *Dialogues* had been mentioned and praised by Campomanes in those 'patriotic writings' with which he was 'continually instructing the nation in order to place it in that flourishing state of which it is capable'. And we may formulate the hypothesis that it was the reforming minister Campomanes himself, to whom the *Dialogues* had been sent as early as 1770, who promoted and encouraged this translation. Thus Galiani too found his way into the world of the Spanish reformers.

It is particularly interesting to note how the nucleus of this policy, Uztáriz's conception, turns up again in Italy, in its most original and genuine form, in the very place where the decades of the age of reform had passed without leaving any appreciable results, where the neomercantilism of the Spanish economist could still appear, at the end of the eighteenth century, as a valid, desirable starting-point: by this time, in reality, a utopia for a static, backward country. The great German publicist, August Ludwig Schlözer, had already noted this in 1782 when he included in his periodical *Staats-Anzeigen*, published in Göttingen, a very interesting article entitled 'Political report on poverty in the Papal States'. Was not Rome's fate similar to that of Spain? The decadence of the latter was the result of the importation from America of gold and silver into a country where industry was in a constant process of decline. Had not perhaps the same thing happened to Rome? 'In just the same way the fall of Rome began when Hildebrand's empire was at its height and the whole of Christendom was paying enormous sums in taxes every year for nothing.' Hence the idleness and sloth of the Romans. Then the Reformation had come to limit the flow of riches into Rome. 'But this was not so serious that the Romans who had been idle for centuries had to work again.' Finally Voltaire and Joseph II had arrived, along with the regalism of absolute monarchs (and of Spain itself); people went less and less on pilgrimages to Loreto and paid less and less money to the Datary. The situation in Rome was fast approaching that of Madrid almost a century before in its period of maximum decline. And it was even worse. 'At the beginning of our century Rome had really sunk lower than Spain, according to the accounts of Uztáriz and Ulloa.'

These very things—Schlözer went on—had been stated very frankly and forcefully by Cristoforo Moltò, a writer of Spanish origin and a Jesuit, driven out of his country after spending a long time in Mexico, who had much experience of travelling. His book, which no one had been willing to publish in Rome and which had eventually appeared in Naples (with the false imprint Venice), 'is for the Papal States what the *Theory and practice of commerce* by Don Geronymo de Uztáriz, Madrid 1724, is for Spain.'

It is curious to note how it was under the banner of the Spanish economist that the last attempt to launch a reform programme in Rome was made by Cardinal Fabrizio Ruffo. The translation of the *Theory and practice of commerce and shipping* which we owe to the Abbé Consalvo Adorno Hynojosa, published in two volumes in Rome in 1793, was dedicated to the Cardinal. As the translator tells us, it was Cardinal Ruffo himself who urged him to undertake the translation. 'You searched in vain in Rome and the other capitals of Italy for the work of Uztáriz and you gave me the task, not only of obtaining a copy in Madrid, but also of translating it into Italian for the benefit of this fair land and especially the Papal States.' Hinojosa (as his name is more often written) was struck by the similarity between Cardinal Ruffo's economic policy and that which in the past had been favoured in Spain. 'You who, being an expert in these matters, are more than anyone else imbued with the spirit of Uztáriz.' According to him Ruffo's greatest accomplishment was 'to have struck the first blow against the old harmful system in Rome as our own Uztáriz did in Spain'.

Hinojosa too had not confined himself to translating but had added numerous notes to the text. He was convinced that the Spanish economists were the first and the best of all, that 'economic science was born in Spain and we owe to the Spaniards the fact that it is known and treated according to its true principles'. His notes often constituted a defence of Roman institutions and traditions (the Datary etc.), but there were others which provided useful statistics and extensive information about the economy of the Papal States and some which dealt more generally with the economic problems of Italy. He said, for example, that trade in Genoese paper in Spain had ceased almost entirely after the Madrid decree in 1756 which forbade the export of rags and thus deprived 'the Genoese paper-mills of an enormous quantity of essential materials, while at the same time giving considerable encouragement to those of the Spanish kingdom'. Similar steps ought to be taken by the Papal States. Hinojosa was constantly reiterating the mercantilist theses of Uztáriz and placing increasing stress upon the merely protectionist aspects of them.

As if to confirm what constituted one of the major obstacles to reform in the Papal States—the great diversity and differentiation of its territories—the echo of the Spanish economists sounded differently outside Rome, in the towns and the countryside of Emilia. Here it is not Uztáriz who is discussed but Campomanes, no longer a throwback from the early eighteenth century but a live, active contact with the Spain of Charles III.

There had gathered around the University of Ferrara a thriving group of ex-Jesuits, some of whom had come from the neighbouring republic of St Mark (like Alessandro Zorzi who even went on to plan an Italian Encyclopaedia) but most from Spanish territory. This had led to the formation of a highly varied and lively environment. These men brought news and ideas from the most farflung lands. Poor and uprooted as they were, they were open to a wide variety of cultural experiences. When Giambattista Biffi, a friend of Beccaria and Verri, in the course of his travels through Italy arrived in Ferrara in 1777, he described in a letter to Isidoro Bianchi the evenings spent with 'my friend Ximenes at the home of the Marquis C. Bevilacqua, with the Abbé Zorzi and Dr Malfatti: the D'Alemberts and Diderots of Ferrara, the men who have undertaken to produce the Italian Encyclopaedia; we talked about travelling and literature'. With Raimondo Ximenes, at least, Biffi shared a common bond in freemasonry. This Spanish ex-Jesuit was undoubtedly one of the most curious figures in that circle and an active element in the lodges at Cremona and Pisa.

It is in this world, some years after Biffi's journey, that we find Antonio Conca, another Spanish ex-Jesuit. He was, of his contemporaries, the man who did most to introduce eighteenth-century Spain to Italian scholars and reformers. He was born at Onteniente (Valencia) in 1746, joined the Society in 1760 and, like the others, was expelled from Spain in 1767. We know little or nothing of his early years in Italy. But, starting from 1781, we have an impressive collection of letters, packed with detail and good humour, which allows us to follow this Spanish priest both in the little day to day incidents of his life and in his intellectual activity. For years he never let a post go without writing to his friend Giulio Perini in Florence, who was a famous scientist and organiser of the Academy of Georgofili. Their correspondence, not so regular at the beginning, became more frequent between 1784 and 1789, only to tail off in the following years, more difficult and troubled times, ceasing altogether on 5 March 1798, when Antonio Conca left Ferrara in the hope of being able to return to his own country.

This is not the correspondence of an ex-Jesuit: he was far away in body and mind from the life he had known in the Order in his youth, by this time very receptive to a totally different range of experiences and firmly convinced that the Society was dead and buried. 'That *parce sepulto* of the noble Virgil' seemed to him the only thing that there was left to hope for. He went as far as to ask Giulio Perini for a copy of one of Scipione de' Ricci's pastoral letters, referring to the latter as a holy bishop and, what was equally surprising, took to defending and publicising the ideas of Charles III and his ministers, and even their regalist policy which had caused him to be driven out of his native land. If he no longer had the mentality of a Jesuit, he continued to feel and think like an exile, for he desired and asked for only one thing: to be able to return home, to be among his own people again, in Valencia, in the midst of the problems and the struggle for reform which was being carried out in his country. He had taken some time to

adapt to Italian customs and language. In 1781 he was still having
to ask his friend in Florence to excuse his 'Hispanic-Italic expressions. I have made no study of the language, as you well know, and
then I live in a place where it is spoken very badly.' As soon as
he had the opportunity, he hastened to introduce his 'patriots',
putting them in the best possible light and praising their 'zeal for
the nation'. The environment in which he lived often made him
angry. 'The other day', he told a friend on 9 May 1785, 'a Ferrarese
made so bold as to say in my presence that Spanish noblemen were
all proud and fanciful. You can imagine what Conca, who is all
on fire with love for his country, might have said to him.' Every
year, on the anniversary of his departure from Spain, he felt sad.
'I am writing to you', he said on 3 April 1786, 'on the day which
marks the nineteenth anniversary of our expulsion from Spain . . .
Imagine my spirit plunged in this abyss of melancholy, without
catching sight of the merest glimpse of hope.' He was moved by
sincere sentiment which embraced the desire to make known to
the Spanish authorities how much he was suffering and how ready
he was to sing the praises of all the good that was being done in
Spain and tell the world about it in the hope that this would
finally win him permission to return home. He became more and
more disillusioned as the years went by and he remained in exile.
In the summer of 1789 he would have liked to go to Leghorn 'to
see the Spanish squadron and my compatriots. If I could have
brought about such a meeting I would even have pawned my
trousers.' At the same time, together with other ex-Jesuits, he was
asking the new King of Spain, Charles IV, for permission finally to
leave Italy. His letters show a crescendo of 'love of country' which
is in line with the development of patriotic sentiments all over
Europe at the end of the eighteenth century, yet which, in him,
has something typically and characteristically Spanish. In spite of
the fact that the desire and the need for amnesties and pensions are
mixed up with this 'love of country', it still remains passionate
and sincere. It would be difficult to find among the thousands of
Italians scattered throughout the world and in Spain, for example,
anything comparable to this.

It was therefore a combination of the urge to make his country
known and the desire to distinguish himself which encouraged
Antonio Conca to offer a series of 'summaries', reviews of Spanish
books and pamphlets, to what was one of the liveliest and most
widely read Italian periodicals of the time, the Florentine *Novelle
letterarie*. At that moment the editor was the provost Marco Lastri
and an increasing amount of space was given to news of works on
economics, administration, law and technical matters. Antonio

Conca often wrote about books on these problems which we
coming out in Spain. Through a series of correspondents, of who
the most frequently named in letters to Perini is Carlo And?
brother of the famous Jesuit historian and writer, he received wh?
cases of works which he sent to Florentine booksellers and schol?
and often reviewed himself in the *Novelle letterarie*. He then s?
his articles to authors and politicians in Spain. He had gradua?
become the centre of a lively intellectual exchange between ?
two countries and in this way he introduced to the Italian read?
to mention a few examples, the Spanish version, revised by ?
Duke of Almodóvar, of the famous *Histoire philosophique*
politique des établissements et du commerce des Européens d?
les deux Indes by Abbé Raynal, Cavanilles's writings on natu?
history, *The idea of Spanish agrarian law* by Manuel Sisternes?
Feliu, the works of Sempere y Guarinos, etc.

In these years he had a growing urge to do something more,
produce a translation of a Spanish work which was really rep?
sentative and which at the same time was capable of attract?
upon himself and his exiled 'patriots' a benevolent glance fr?
his government in Madrid. At the end of 1784 he announced
intention to his friend Perini. 'Perhaps I shall translate Señor Cor?
de Campomanes's work on popular industry and education. W?
talk about it.' He could not have chosen better. The *Discourse*
the encouragement of popular industry, published in 1774, ?
one of the fundamental books of the Spanish Enlightenment. ?
the first time an official document, read in provincial towns, fr?
the pulpits, in convents, proposed the model of a society direc?
towards work and production, inviting everyone to banish id?
ness and mendicancy and at the same time urging all those w?
had a social responsibility to create there and then independe?
patriotic and agricultural societies with a view to putting i?
practice such a political and economic programme. As Sempere?
Guarinos was to say: 'Scarcely will one find a work which ?
such short space comprehends so many of the most import?
principles and maxims for the advancement of national indus?
and of the commonweal.'

Conca translated this work in the course of 1785. At the e?
of that year he sent the translation to his friend Perini to be c?
rected. On 30 January 1786 he wrote that he was 'relieved, beca?
I thought that it was much worse'. In May he was still engaged
revising it. At the same time he was establishing contact w?
Campomanes himself and obtaining from him 'some informat?
that I required'. The Spanish minister also accepted the dedicat?
of the book. 'What do you think of that? Keep it quiet', he wr?

to Perini. On 4 September he was able to tell his friend how he had managed to be so successful. It was Carlo Andrès who took the manuscript to Campomanes. The minister 'was very busy . . . he just flicked through it, reading a page here and there and said it was fine and that he had no doubts about it'. In October Conca wrote the preface and sent the dedication to Madrid for it to be officially approved. He could not decide whether to have it published in Parma (but Bodoni was too slow), in Florence or in Venice. Eventually he chose Venice. 'I don't expect to make a profit but I don't want to be out of pocket either.' At the end of March 1787 he left for Venice, to remain there until May of that year, supervising the work that the printer, Carlo Palese, was carrying out to his satisfaction, 'on the best paper that I could find in Venice and with the best possible type'. He paid for the edition himself 'so as not to have to go running after printers, who want to be assured of making a profit. I am relying upon friends to help me dispose of some of the copies.' In Venice he had lived a solitary, withdrawn life. Nevertheless he met the Abbé Luigi Mari, translator of Necker, whom after a certain initial distrust, he eventually came to like and respect. In the summer the book began to circulate and very soon it was mentioned in periodicals like the *Novelle letterarie*, the *Giornale fiorentino di arti, commercio ed economia politica* and the Roman *Efemeridi letterarie*. At the same time the book arrived in Madrid and was presented to Campomanes after being 'given a magnificent binding'. In spite of the tortured doubts of the translator, who by this time was accustomed to misfortune, it was well received. The minister said that the 'preface and what he had read of the translation were to his liking'. Conca did, however, have to wait until May of the following year before he was granted a pension to supplement the one he already had.

The *Discourse on the encouragement of popular industry, by Count Campomanes, translated from the Spanish by Don Antonio Conca, member of the Florentine Academy of Georgofili* aimed above all at providing, as can be read in the preface, a comprehensive account of 'the different revolutions which have occurred in Spain in the last three centuries, her period of great prosperity, followed by decline and then her amazing recovery'. All of this, said Conca, could have considerable significance for Italy.

It is undeniable that industry and manufactures have also declined in Italy, whose fertile soil produces in abundance all the raw materials necessary for those crafts, in the practice of which Italians are by nature disposed almost to rival the Greeks in delicacy and good taste. This is a subject which would deserve the attention of a citizen who was in equal measure enlightened and enthusiastic, so that Italy might be able to regain a balance and obtain some relief from the ills which she has suffered through passive trade in many manufactures and many kinds of work which could easily be carried out within the country.

Spain was in a position to provide an example and a stimulus precisely because it had a single centre as focal point.

This need for uniformity is the main difficulty to be overcome by Italian writers, and there are many, in a system which has to be adapted to a province divided into a number of states all independent of one another. This impulse is given to Spain by Señor Campomanes.

Not that stimuli were lacking in the various parts of Italy. In Naples and Milan chairs of economics were already in existence. As Campomanes himself wrote: 'Abbé Galiani showed France that agriculture alone is not sufficient and is incapable of sustaining a country.' But what was important was a comprehensive programme which, as Conca stressed in his notes, should cover both industry and agriculture. Above all it should mobilise all available forces in the country, reducing the number of holidays, spreading the practice of 'small-scale silk manufacture' among parish priests and among lords and ladies, introducing 'popular industry' even 'inside convent walls', spreading new cultures, new methods of rearing animals and new manufactures, improving sanitary conditions and popularising the use of inoculation and everywhere establishing those agricultural academies which should become the fulcra of all economic initiative and which had been described in great detail in Campomanes's work.

It was a programme which aimed at the creation of a network of artisans, at internal colonisation by means of the creation of a large number of small centres of production. It is interesting to note how Campomanes, even if with some hesitation, was convinced that the class of independent artisans could and should assert itself all over Spain. 'Popular factories', he wrote, 'cannot prosper through the usual channel of companies, nor through merchants. These, reducing the producers to the class of day-labourers, would be left with all the profit, while the condition of the populace would not be improved.' What we have here then is a consciously individualistic, artisan and popular programme brought to the attention of Italians in the closing years of the eighteenth century.

This implicit comparison and parallel between the situations in Italy and Spain was far from being an isolated phenomenon. Conca himself a few years later was to present his *Traveller's description of Spain, in which information is given especially concerning those things appertaining to the arts worthy of the attention of the curious traveller* (1793–97), which Bodoni published for him in Parma in four fine volumes. This provides a comprehensive picture of the Iberian peninsula for the benefit of the Italian reader interested not only in the history of Spanish art and antiquities but also in the living, present reality of the country. A friend of Antonio Conca, Don Miguel Generes, who was also living in Italy in those years, had reflected upon the economic situation in Spain and at the same time had made a detailed study of the problems of economics and commerce in the region of Bologna. He sent home from Bologna a series of observations and proposals which were later published in book form in 1793. The *Political and economic reflections on population, agriculture, crafts, factories and commerce in the Kingdom of Aragon* by Don Miguel Damaso Generes provides in fact a striking comparison between the economic and social situation in Aragon and that in Emilia. He too aspired towards a 'complete restoration' of his country of origin and sought his example and stimulus among the English and French economists. He too spoke about 'our great Uztáriz' and had obviously been profoundly affected by the situation in Italy. The medieval communes of Italy remained a proof of what economic diligence could achieve. Thinking again of Pisa and of Amsterdam, Generes could not help exclaiming: 'How extraordinary are the different effects produced by the diligence and idleness of men!' Even examples from modern Italy were valuable: that of Tuscany 'for its new wise legislation', that of the city of Bologna itself, where, as for example silk production showed, there was an intense and flourishing artisan and manufacturing life, in spite of restrictions, corporations and controls. Generes was also struck by the density of the population when he looked at the situation around him in Italy. 'This city of Bologna has 70,000 souls which, added to those of the surrounding district, make 265,637, and of these it would not be rash to say that half belong to families engaged in agricultural work. How much greater is the population than that of this kingdom [Aragon] which, compared with the province of Bologna, is at least four times the size.' Finally Generes gave an enthusiastic description of Bolognese agriculture, the variety of produce, the great quantity of supplies which it provided for the city and the abundance of fruit, vegetables and wood. 'Why cannot the same be done in this kingdom . . .?' And Generes too concluded by stressing the importance of the work of Campomanes and the widespread creation of agrarian societies.

Perhaps the main contribution towards establishing a contact and comparison between the Spanish and Italian economists was made by Antonio Conca when he succeeded in arousing in Georgofili circles in Florence a lengthy and detailed discussion of Manuel Sisternes y Feliu's *Idea of Spanish agrarian law*. Sisternes too was from Valencia, in fact he was Conca's brother-in-law. He had a brilliant career and very rapidly rose to the heights of 'the illustrious post of Procurator of the King's Council and Chamber'. His book, which he wrote in 1785 and published the following year, was one of the numerous plans for an agrarian code to appear in those decades. The initial incentive to write it had come from Campomanes. A debate had been going on for thirty years and was to reach its climax in 1795 with the *Report on the agrarian law* by Jovellanos. Sisternes is a follower of late mercantilism and a continuator of Campomanes and Olavide. The interventionist, colonising spirit of the great administrators and statesmen in Spain in the eighteenth century finds expression in his work. Even in Madrid there was no lack of opposition to his *Idea*, opposition inspired by the urge to ensure a greater degree of freedom for landowners or the prevalence of large holdings over small, thus creating the prerequisites for an agrarian free trade system of typically physiocratic inspiration.

Thanks to Conca, this debate—which was fundamental in Charles III's Spain—had repercussions in Italy too. In February 1787 he sent Perini a 'summary' of Sisternes's book, explaining to his friend how important it was to him to make this work known: 'The work is surprising and the subject is treated in a masterful way . . . Please see that the summary is published soon.' A few days later he announced his intention of writing another summary for the *Giornale fiorentino di agricoltura, arti, commercio ed economia politica*, to which from time to time he sent news from Spain. He was completely caught up with enthusiasm for making this and other Spanish works known in Italy. 'What I am doing is sowing; if the seed falls on *terram bonam, fructum afferet*, but if *inter spinas*, you know very well what will happen.'

His review appeared on 23 March 1787 in issue number twelve of the *Novelle letterarie*. It mentioned the enquiry launched by Charles III and the replies given by the provincial intendants and other authorities. Sisternes, 'in whom knowledge and patriotism go hand in hand', had also wanted to give his opinion:

> The condition of those who possess nothing should be improved by sharing among them plots of uncultivated or vacant land, whether they belong to the Crown or to the community . . .

those restrictive and oppressive elements which are prejudicial to progress in agriculture must be removed . . . no land should be left uncultivated but all of it should be used to procure some benefit for the population, crafts and commerce.

A hierarchy of juntas in village, town and province with a central junta in the capital were to put this 'agrarian plan' into action. 'In conclusion we may say that a good law for the benefit of agriculture is worth more than a hundred works by distinguished writers but these are the forerunners of such a law and it is in this way that philosophers and legislators are able to contribute more than anyone else to the public good.'

For a while a translation of the book was under consideration. Sisternes wrote to Conca that he would prefer it to be discussed in Florence first. If it were not possible to do that publicly, he himself would see to translating it and making known the objections brought against him. Andrès, who was going to Florence, was also commissioned to convey to the Academy of Georgofili Sisternes's desire to have his work examined by them. That summer three views appeared in writing. The first was by Luigi Tramontani, the second by Giovanni Bencivenni, formerly Pelli, and the third by Andrea Zucchini. Beneath all the generous compliments lies the reaction of the Tuscan physiocratic, free trade mentality. No land at all should be left in common, said the first. And then 'to deprive a man of ownership of a piece of land because he has not cultivated it for four years is a violation of cultural practice which offends the freedom of the owner and, in any case, when a man is not moved by interest, violence is often of no avail'. 'A man who will not or cannot cultivate his land shall sell it to one who will.' But how would the state decide who was and who was not in a position to cultivate a piece of land? How would the land be redistributed? 'To apportion a small plot of land to the poor and artisans is an excellent idea if they have the necessary funds to cultivate the land properly . . . Cultivation requires strength and a certain degree of wealth; where this is lacking, the land soon comes into the possession of those who are rich and in a position to cultivate it.' Furthermore it was necessary to irrigate the lands before distributing them.

Pelli too, in his report dated 13 July 1787, had some objections to make, but had to recognise that Sisternes's book revealed a particularly interesting and promising situation. 'One must admit that Spain is daily becoming more enlightened and that societies and writers of the calibre of this excellent Procurator are capable of restoring the kingdom to its former prosperity before too many years have passed.' But it was necessary to abandon the remaining prejudices. Not a single wood or meadow should be left without a private owner. 'I shall not take upon myself the task of proving how badly common land is cultivated.' The idea of demanding a portion of taxes in kind was mistaken. Experience had shown that a situation must be reached where the whole amount could be paid in money. There were also several objections on the technical plane: oxen and not mules or horses were needed for ploughing, as Giovanni Fabbroni had written in his *Réflexions sur l'état actuel de l'agriculture*. As for horticulture, the example of Liguria had indicated the path to follow.

The third man to offer his opinion, Canon Andrea Zucchini, showed that he too was cultured and well-informed but also somewhat pedantic in his advice to Sisternes to read Jean Bertrand, Vittorio Gera, G. B. Corniani and Montesquieu. He too was against payments in kind. 'In Tuscany they have been completely abolished.' And this was not the only example which Florence had to offer to Spain. From reading

> certain laws and decrees passed by our Royal Sovereign Peter Leopold, Archduke of Austria, about the sale or apportionment of communal property or farms and about regulations for local magistracies . . . one can derive many excellent proposals concerning these matters. And since these very wise laws have brought enormous benefit to the Tuscan countryside they will also perhaps do some good in Spain.

Finally a *Vote of deputies* was compiled, a collective opinion which officially represented the attitude of the Georgofili as a body towards Sisternes's *Idea of agrarian law*. It was signed by Andrea Zucchini, Luigi Tramontani, Giovanni Bencivenni, Jacopo Ambrogio Tartini and Bernardo Lessi. 'The subject', it began, 'as everyone can see is imposing in itself and of paramount importance for the whole of Europe . . .' The author had followed the right path and had given his preference to agriculture, following the example of 'other enlightened governments who have staked the happiness of the nation on this one point'. His bases were sound:

> Security of tenure, a man's right to cultivate what he wished and to trade freely in the produce, equal division of public dues among landowners of every class, abolition of demesne lands which, being common, belong to no one and the assignment of these and the lands of the Crown to private individuals, public works in the interest of the health of the population no less than to improve communications between provinces and, as far as possible, destruction of ties on property.

'The patriotic zeal' and 'Georgic enlightenment' of the author were therefore beyond question. Nevertheless Sisternes appeared too cautious and timid in their eyes. 'Certain local circumstances in some provinces, about which we know nothing, are perhaps responsible for determining those maxims of his with which we cannot agree . . . To leave any lands common for the benefit of the respective members of communities conflicts with the public economy.' The same observation must be made with regard to the proposal to 'share out land among shepherds, poor artisans and workers, to substitute land for money in the case of those entitled to a pension, to give preference to local people over those from other districts and, finally, to set public contributions as a quota of produce.' Common lands were the object of 'continual plundering by the needy'. Likewise it was a 'prejudice' 'to give preference to the poor and to artisans in the apportionment of land'.

Anyone can see that as neither group could provide the necessary outlay for the initial and then the annual cultivation of the land, the plots will be left in that sterile state in which they were handed over to them. This will all be to the detriment of the nation and, finally, through the lack of produce over a number of years, the land will fall into the hands of the rich. But these are precisely the ones able to make the land yield.

It was equally absurd to hinder the influx of foreign capital and initiative. The inefficiency of contributions in kind had been proved. 'Indeed such contributions have been completely abolished in Tuscany.' The *Vote of deputies* went on to sum up the observations made by the commissioners on agrarian contracts and the conclusion was expressed in a particularly forceful manner : 'Freedom must reign, even though the idle may benefit, because only thus may the active members of the population predominate.' The other observations are of more limited interest : why prevent the rich from having large gardens? Genoa surely constituted an example of the advantages of this type of culture. On the question of the choice of horses or oxen for ploughing, much certainly depended upon the quality of the land, but, on the whole, one should always prefer the latter and Giovanni Fabbroni had given conclusive proof of this in his *Réflexions sur l'état actuel de l'agriculture*, published in Paris in 1780. The Georgofili said in conclusion that, in spite of these individual criticisms, the ideas of Sisternes were extremely useful for a nation which had to awaken out of lethargy and foster enthusiasm for cultivating the land.

When Conca had these opinions in his hands, he could not hide an impulse of disappointment: '. . . to tell you the truth I thought that they were too severe.' The praises and honours had not been lacking and Sisternes had been made a member of the Academy of Georgofili but Conca thought that his critics had not taken sufficient account of the circumstances in which he was writing. Sisternes himself later intimated that 'on many points' his views coincided with those of his critics, but that 'certain considerations' had prevented him from 'adhering to such views'. And this was precisely on the key point of the discussion of the 'observations which aimed at greater freedom for the farmer'. Conca considered that with more flexibility and less pedantry Sisternes could have been helped in a concrete way to carry out his measures for reform. If they had been set out in a more acceptable manner, the objections could have been of use to Sisternes 'in the new edition where his pronouncements on greater freedom could be supported by the judgment of the Academy; since we know that on many matters his views are the same but he did not want to risk making this public for certain political motives without first hearing what the scholars had to say'. It is indeed a pity that the objections could not be published. 'Although Sisternes wishes to be answered with philosophical frankness, nevertheless he loves his country and hates pedantry.' So ended this typical and rather curious discussion which had brought out the clear (though at times somewhat doctrinaire) economic vision of the Tuscans and its encounter with the Spanish agrarian tradition and heritage.

A few months later Conca introduced to the readers of the *Novelle letterarie* another Spanish publicist who was also actively concerned in making the comparison with the Italian reality and ideas. Sempere y Guarinos had begun his career as a writer by translating and commenting on Italian works. In 1782 he published in Madrid the *Reflections on good taste in the sciences and the arts. Free translation of what Antonio Muratori wrote in Italian, with a discourse on the present-day taste of Spaniards in literature*. Thus he had turned his eyes towards his own country after reliving what Muratori had written. And in Spain too he continued to see the traces left by Italians alongside the deeper and more obvious ones left by the English and French. In the field of law, beside Fleury and Von Espen there was Berardi. Besides Robertson and Campomanes there was 'the well-known Abbé Genovesi, professor of commerce at Naples, having been appointed by our August Sovereign when he was in that kingdom', the same Genovesi who, in his *Lessons*, had warmly praised the Societies of Friends of the Country which had sprung up all over Spain. Sempere y Guarinos had then dedicated himself to economic and social problems; 1785 saw the publication of the first volume of his *Essay from a Spanish library on the best writers of the reign of Charles III* : a precious book and a real encyclopaedia of Spanish reformers in the eighteenth century. The second volume, which came out in the same year, contained an excellent article on Campomanes. The *Novelle letterarie* discussed it at great length. Antonio Conca went into even greater detail about the *History of luxury* which Sempere published in 1788. There was the announcement that the volumes of the *Library* which had already appeared were to be translated by Giuseppe Bianchi, a Mantuan gentleman, and that another work by Sempere, on almsgiving, would be translated by Count Crispi. Only this last work ever saw the light and Conca was certainly closely connected with it. He was well acquainted with Count Benedetto Crispi : he used to obtain books for him and information about writers, Mably for example, and circulated his translations outside Ferrara.

From Campomanes to Sempere : thus Conca had traced for his friends in Florence the curve which led from mercantilism to liberalism in Spain. He well knew that, among the many friends whom he had made in Italy, these were the men who were in the best position to respond to the message of modern Spain. He had no difficulty in choosing between Florence and Venice. As for the situation in the Papal States, there was no point in wasting words on it. It was a country 'chock full of gossip and prejudices'. If he needed books, for example the eulogy which Condorcet had written for d'Alembert of a reprint of Catherine II's *Instructions*, it was obviously to Florence that he had to turn. The censorship, or as he put it, 'the strictness surrounding Florentine writings here' did not prevent him from having printed matter of all kinds sent from Tuscany. It was just a question of entrusting parcels to the carrier rather than using the post. Florence remained at the centre of his desires and aspirations. After spending some time in Venice he concluded : 'Although this place is original in everything and wonderful in so many ways, I shouldn't like to stay here for a long time. I wouldn't have to say the same about Florence.'

By the end of the century the lands of Peter Leopold had evidently become the favourite meeting ground for reformers from Italy and Spain. It is there too that we find the most substantial evidence of the presence of the man who was undoubtedly the most interesting of the Spanish personalities whom we have encountered in the course of this research. Valentín de Foronda completed the last decisive stage of this journey from the physiocrats' freetrade policy to a political, rebellious liberalism. An active and influential member of the Basque Society of Friends of the Country and a teacher in the Basque Royal Seminary, Foronda was initially interested in problems of mendicancy, unemployment and poor relief. In 1779 he produced a *Comparison between the Société de St Sulpice in Paris and the House of Mercy in the city of Vitoria*. This marked the beginnings of his untiring activities, when he translated Condillac and Marmontel's *Bélisaire* and conceived of numerous economic and pedagogic plans. He went on long journeys in Europe and in 1781 was in Bordeaux, where he published an annotated translation of that part of Baron Bielfield's work which concerned Spain and Portugal. We have not succeeded in establishing when he was in Italy. He certainly saw Venice, as he tells us in an impassioned letter maintaining the need for public accusations, *On certain criminal laws*, from Vergara, 10 July 1788. 'When I was in Venice and went up to the Doge's Palace, I saw two, four, eight, twelve lions' mouths appearing everywhere to invite accusations.' It is likely that he also went to Florence. In any case, he must have come into contact, either personally or through his works, with Giovanni Fabbroni, who was the youngest and most determined defender in Tuscan circles of what he was wont to call 'social freedom'. When he read the letters on economic, legal and political matters which Valentín de Foronda had been publishing in the 'eighties in Madrid reviews like the *Espiritu de los mejores diarios*, *El Censor*, *El Memorial librario*—and which he later collected in two volumes in 1789 and 1794—Fabbroni could see that their ideas coincided and that the Spanish author had succeeded in expressing them in a particularly lucid and effective manner. He very soon decided to translate some of these letters. He explained in a short preface to the first pamphlet which he drew from them that they contained 'a quantity of notions which are certainly not new to us but which here are contained in a very small space and dressed in Spanish attire. Who knows whether the style of dress might not prove a source of attraction and the slimness of the volume encourage men to read it and so to meditate upon it'. What he must have liked particularly in these letters, besides the warmth and the persuasive quality of the arguments, was the broad cosmopolitan scope of the writing, the vision of a single world market. Even the authors whom Foronda followed could not have been more typical of the atmosphere of late, mature physiocratic thought which both the Italian and the Spanish economist breathed.

As Fabbroni himself tells us, the public gave the pamphlet a warm reception. 'And to prove that I cannot be disappointed at the result, I shall now produce three more by the same author and translator', he wrote three years later. 'A slim volume, costing very little, can easily reach a wide audience . . . It is useful . . . to attract the attention of tradesmen and artisans (who do not have time to study the writers of treatises) and make them reflect upon the true interest of the society of which they are part.' Fabbroni adapted Foronda's text more than he had done the first time, adding elements here and there which had direct bearing upon the difficult situation in which Tuscany found herself in 1791.

The battle between the free-traders and the supporters of state intervention and restrictions was becoming more intense. Still in 1791, Fabbroni brought out a *Letter on the effects of free trading in crude or raw materials, free translation from the Spanish, prefaced by another letter on the same subject by a landowner from the Valdarno*. The landowner from the Valdarno was Giuseppe Pelli. The second letter had come in manuscript form, according to Fabbroni, from the 'famous and practical Basque Society, pride of Biscay'. He also added a note in which he sang the praises of the group in Vergara, 'the centre of good taste, the theatre of literature and the sanctuary of patriotism' and described how studies and schools had developed there. 'Besides this, there is no branch of industry, science or art, together with agriculture, fishing, manufactures and trade that this excellent society, which has earned the protection of the Sovereign and the esteem of the whole nation, has not attempted to make prosper.'

He had obtained the information about all these activities, he said, from the 'excellent notes accompanying Count Campomanes's great work on popular industry', meaning, of course, the book by Antonio Conca, whom we see continuing in this way, even after so many years, to transmit his message of praise for Spanish reformism. It is not certain who was the author of the *Letter on the effects of free trading in crude or raw materials*, but this is a case where the discussion is centred so directly upon Tuscany, on the relationship between agriculture and industry, free trade and protectionism, on the way in which it was being discussed at that time in Florence, in fact the whole pamphlet is so immediately linked with the local situation as to make us think that this time, in all probability, the anonymous Spaniard hid the work of Giovanni Fabbroni himself. The references to Spain stem from famous works by economists and travellers: Bowles, Swinburne, Cavanilles, Ponz and particularly Campomanes. Fabbroni's work was certainly well documented. The contact with Spain had been so important for him and would continue to be so in the years

which followed, but by this time it was a question of a distant outline filled in by an entirely Tuscan reality.

Nevertheless the polemic was still being continued in Spanish
guise. An imaginary character, Don Diego Lopez, was created and
naturally imagined to be an ex-Jesuit. Fabbroni continued to
identify himself with Valentín de Foronda. In December 1791 there
appeared a *Letter from Don Diego Lopez, ex-Jesuit, to the author
of the Spanish letters, or an exact idea of the book recently published under the title Impartial Judgment on the Production and
Manufacture of Silk and Wool in Tuscany.* After a long interval
full of many turbulent events, the discussion was revived in 1803
with another pamphlet: *The Gold-mine. A letter from Diego Lopez
to Valentín Foronda.* The works of Campomanes and other Spanish
writers continued to be quoted freely. What had happened in the
Iberian peninsula was, in fact, taking on a paradigmatic value.
'The whole of Europe has in Spain a shining example of the difference between freedom and chains.' Even the problem of unemployment and beggars still appeared clothed in Spanish dress. In 1804
there was the *Letter concerning poor beggars, written by Diego
Lopez in Florence to Valentín Foronda in Madrid on 1st February
1804.* And Filippo Mazzei answered this with *The Reply of Valentín
Foronda in Madrid to Diego Lopez in Florence on the subject of
poor beggars.* The book entitled *On the measures to be taken
concerning grain provisions* (1802), in which Fabbroni took up
again all the themes of his free trade policy, was interlaced with
frequent quotations from Spanish writers and repeated references
to Spain. We constantly find mention of 'the most praiseworthy'
Campomanes and his *Popular industry and popular education,*
together with J. Ulloa, 'the learned Cavanilles' etc. But, if we are
not mistaken, there is no further mention of Valentín de Foronda.
Was Fabbroni aware of what had happened to the Spanish economist? It would certainly have been of great interest to one who,
like himself, had observed with particular attention what was
happening on the other side of the Atlantic, who had entered into
correspondence with Jefferson and had often discussed America
with his friend Filippo Mazzei. Foronda had, in fact, become Consul
General in Philadelphia in 1801, only to be made shortly afterwards the Spanish *chargé d'affaires* in the United States. He had
published a pamphlet there in 1803 in which he was the first
Spaniard to urge the South American colonies to follow the example
of North America. Foronda had become more and more deeply
involved with the world of American freedom and had returned
to Spain early in 1809 (and so, let us add, was not in Madrid in
1804 as the imaginary Don Lopez wrote in his pamphlet on the

Poor beggars, which would lead us to suppose that Fabbroni and Foronda were no longer in contact). Back in Spain he began to write again and became directly involved with the war and with the fortunes of nascent Spanish liberalism. Some letters of his on Jean Jacques Rousseau were particularly noticed and it seems that, when absolutism was restored in 1814, these were one of the main causes of his being thrown into prison in Pamplona. He remained there until 1820 and died shortly after his release. The point of departure had been the same for him as for Fabbroni, but life had made of one a liberal revolutionary and of the other an encyclopaedic scientist, a great administrator of the Napoleonic era and the Restoration in Tuscany and Italy and an energetic and dogmatic defender of economic liberalism.

When Campomanes's *Discourse on the encouragement of popular industry* came out in Venice in 1789, the *Giornale enciclopedico* in Naples published an extensive review of it with the conclusion that: 'What the illustrious President Verri is for us, Count Campomanes is for Spain.' The juxtaposition of these two names sums up the parallel between Italy and Spain as it developed in the eighteenth century and it is sufficient to remember the different relationship which these two men had seen between agriculture and artisan activity and between freedom of trade within their countries and outside them, to understand how significant this comparison is. Campomanes was not unknown in Milan. Ever since the translation of his *Treatise on the royal tax on amortization* (1767) the Spanish statesman's realism and down-to-earth attitude had been much admired. 'There is no ranting and raving, no fanaticism, no partisan spirit, but reasons, facts and the examination of history', was the comment of the *Estratto della letteratura europea*. His work had been quickly reprinted in Venice and had been very widely read. Rather then Campomanes the economist, it was the administrator and financier who had made such an impact in the North.

And among the northern Italians too, it was on the whole the reformers, and particularly Beccaria, who were well received and talked about in Spain. There is a lively set of letters from Pietro Giusti, a Lombard resident in Spain, to Beccaria, giving him an account of the fortunes of his book and of his own attempts to make it known. In a letter to his friend Paolo Frisi in the autumn of 1775, Pietro Giusti gave a picture of the situation in Spain, where

the darkness of centuries is gradually beginning to fade and it seems that the dawn of a beautiful day is about to break, thanks to the efforts of three new Bacchuses, or rather Orpheuses, who have begun the revolution: Marquis Grimaldi with his open protection of the arts and sciences, Count d'Aranda with his improvements in the public economy and the police, and the Procurator Campomanes by destroying the ingrained prejudices of ecclesiastical jurisprudence. They seem to me like so many Caesars, swimming against a torrent with a code in their hands. The steps now being taken have come very late: the inborn national indolence, the attachment to deeprooted prejudices, religious superstition which can only be maintained in the dark and the consequent shunning of the light of philosophy, all these contest every inch of ground. If, by some misfortune, the courageous enthusiasm of those who fight them should ever wane, then Spain's destiny is decided: *Sedet, aeternumque sedebit infelix*. There is no shortage of universities, libraries, academies of literature and art: but these seeds planted by an enlightened legislation have not grown roots and are not bringing forth fruit. Perhaps the revolution is to be reserved for a more fortunate century, or it might be even closer than we realise, since it is so difficult to perceive and to recognise the intermediary links in the great chain of events.

Beccaria, as was customary for him, had not replied to an earlier letter of his admirer and the latter complained about this to Paolo Frisi in the following year, stressing once more how much he had done to introduce Beccaria's work in Spain:

He cannot fail to be aware of the fact that he owes it to someone very closely associated with me if this book [*Of crimes and punishments*] was not crushed the moment it appeared by the crowd of fanatics at court who swooped down upon it. However indifferent the author might be, the translator, who does not lack support, either among Spaniards or ministers from abroad, will emerge triumphant from his task, despite the renewed ascendancy of the Inquisition.

Despite all the obstacles, Beccaria's book did, in fact, continue to circulate in Spain, but it bore all the marks of the difficulties which it had encountered in being published there at all. A preliminary note stated that 'the Council, in accordance with the advice of the Procurator, has permitted the printing and publication of this work, solely for the instruction of the public and without detriment to the laws of the Kingdom and their strict observance, commanding, so that all may understand, that this notice be placed at the beginning.' But, as the translator's prologue stated, 'Truth, although it moves with slow steps at first, thereafter makes rapid progress'. He quoted as an example the issue

of 15 February 1774 of the *Gazeta de Madrid*, which discussed the
desire for reform of the law which had become apparent in Russia
and concluded that, even if the problems which had by this time
been raised all over Europe 'had not been made clear enough in the
excellent treatise by Marquis Beccaria, at least the principles can
be found there which will lead to their being decided'.

There would be many indications to prove that in Spain too,
Beccaria's proposals had not fallen on deaf ears. The *Discourse on
the penalties incurred within the criminal laws of Spain in order
to facilitate their reform* by Don Manuel de Lardizábal y Úribe
(Madrid 1783), even if it did not accept all Beccaria's conclusions,
was also proof of this. But perhaps the most enthusiastic words
on the reforms being carried out in Italy in the field of penal law
were written by Valentín de Foronda, in his letter *On the criminal
laws*, dated 2nd October 1789: 'Turn your eyes, Sire, towards
Tuscany and reflect upon the mildness of the penalties inflicted
in that Duchy and the small number of crimes which occur there,
read over and over again the penal code of that Prince.' And this
image of eighteenth-century Tuscany, exemplary even in Vergara,
seems a suitable conclusion for our Italian and Spanish itinerary.

What kind of conclusions can be drawn from this research? Here
at least are the points which are probably worth further discussion and should become the subject of more detailed investigations.

1. In general, Spaniards in the eighteenth century considered Italy
to be a relatively rich and prosperous country where the economic
life was more active and the population density greater than in
their own country. They also often considered that examples or
suggestions could be drawn not only from Italy's past but from
her present situation. Certainly this attitude may derive, at least
in part, from the fact that trade between the two countries in
the eighteenth century gave a clear advantage to Italy. As Don
Policarpo Saenz de Tejada Hermoso said, in his *Memoir on Commerce*, published by the Economic Society of Madrid in 1780: 'In
Italy we make money only on tobacco, while we take from them
all kinds of linens, printed cloths, ribbons and silks.' But what we
have here is not merely a reflection of the existing economic relationship between the two countries. The truth is that Italy
maintained a remarkable function of intellectual and social stimulus
for Spain.
2. The discussions and debates of the Italian Enlightenment and
their outcome had been widely publicised in Spain. The works of

the Italian reformers from Genovesi to Carli, from Galiani and Filangieri to Beccaria, had been translated and commented upon. For the most part their influence was not spontaneous or confined to isolated instances. Campomanes and the Economic Societies promoted by him played a leading part in the diffusion of these works. In a remarkably systematic way, the Italians were incorporated into the work of bringing enlightenment to Spain.

3. Conversely, Spanish writers on economic and social questions exerted a much deeper influence upon eighteenth-century Italy than is commonly thought. We have seen how Uztáriz, Ulloa, Campomanes and Foronda were very much alive and present in Naples, Rome, Milan etc. But it is precisely the Spanish influence in Italy, in contrast to the current flowing the other way, which reveals the internal differentiation and lack of unity in Italy. If one wanted to generalise, one could say that Spanish neomercantilism made a deep impact on the South in particular, while it evoked no response from the North. Naples (and in a paradoxically backward, almost caricatural way, the Papal States in the last decade of Pius VI) could consider and hope to imitate the programme of the era of Philip V and Charles III. Neither Tuscany nor Lombardy could follow a similar path. In central and northern Italy, on the other hand (through the strange and fertile mediation of the Spanish ex-Jesuits who had emigrated to Italy), it was the voice of Campomanes and the Spanish economists of the end of the century which made itself heard.

4. Campomanes's programme, though it had so much to say to Italians, remained on the edge of the great reforming current of the Italian Enlightenment. It had a 'patriotic' and 'popular' character which was specifically Spanish, together with an artisan, individualist, anticapitalist bias which was intriguing to Italians in the eighteenth century but did not arouse any enthusiasm in them. Pietro Verri, described by a review of the time as the Italian Campomanes, was much more deeply influenced than his Spanish colleague by the ideas of the physiocrats, by the vision of a capitalistic agriculture, backed by an intelligent credit policy on the part of the citizen classes and the state. The 'encouragement of popular industry' stands in contrast to the intelligent administration of Austrian Lombardy.

5. Similar reasons made Tuscany lack enthusiasm for Campomanes and led her to consider Sisternes y Feliu's programme relatively backward. She set an orthodox free trade policy against the preoccupations of Sisternes and so many of his contemporaries in Spain with the prejudices, interests and aspirations of the peasant and artisan classes and the people of their nation. Nevertheless the

Tuscans did find a point of convergence with Spain, in the person of Giovanni Fabbroni and thus with the younger, more enthusiastic generation and in particular with the man who was most representative and best able to express the liberal, rebel element. Valentín de Foronda was able to become a symbol in Florence in the closing years of the eighteenth century and the opening years of the nineteenth.

6. It is not so much in their economic programmes that Italy and Spain seem to coincide at the end of the eighteenth century as in their reforming *animus* or even *pathos*. The effect which Beccaria had in Spain is symptomatic in this respect. The amazed admiration with which Italians regarded Spain's progress is proof of it.

7. Nevertheless the two groups were destined to go in very different directions. Foronda became a liberal and Fabbroni became the great administrator in a small country. That 'patriotic' and 'popular' element which was already in Campomanes had grown into a passion for freedom and revolt, into the exaltation of Rousseau, the revolution of the colonies and finally the *sentido liberal* of Spain during the Napoleonic Wars. In Tuscany and Lombardy the success of the reforms, the technical and doctrinaire defence of economic liberalism, effective and efficient technical and social progress had led towards an intelligent moderatism. The experience of the Revolution and the new century were to open up a new cycle of contacts between Spain and Italy.

Index

293

Index

Index

Index

Index